COVID-19'S ECONOMIC IMPACT AND COUNTERMEASURES IN CHINA

COVID-19'S ECONOMIC IMPACT AND COUNTERMEASURES IN CHINA

Edited by

SHIYI CHEN
Fudan University, China

ZHIQING LI
Fudan University, China

Translated by

BIYU WU
East China University of Science and Technology, China

KARL STEFAN | DEBRA ANTHONY

World Scientific

NEW JERSEY • LONDON • SINGAPORE • BEIJING • SHANGHAI • HONG KONG • TAIPEI • CHENNAI • TOKYO

Published by

World Scientific Publishing Co. Pte. Ltd.
5 Toh Tuck Link, Singapore 596224
USA office: 27 Warren Street, Suite 401-402, Hackensack, NJ 07601
UK office: 57 Shelton Street, Covent Garden, London WC2H 9HE

Library of Congress Cataloging-in-Publication Data
Names: Chen, Shiyi (Economist), editor. | Li, Zhiqing (Researcher on environmental economics), editor. | Wu, Biyu, translator. | Stefan, Karl (Translator), translator. | Anthony, Debra (Translator), translator.
Title: COVID-19's economic impact and countermeasures in China / edited by Shiyi Chen, Fudan University, China, Zhiqing Li, Fudan University, China ; translated by Biyu Wu, East China University of Science and Technology, China, Karl Stefa, Debra Anthony.
Other titles: Jing ji zhan"yi". English
Description: New Jersey : World Scientific, 2022. | "经济战"疫" - 新冠肺炎疫情对经济的影响与对策 originally published in Chinese by Fudan University Press Co., Ltd. Copyright © Fudan University Press Co., Ltd., 2020" | Includes bibliographical references and index.
Identifiers: LCCN 2022010502 | ISBN 9789811252914 (hardcover) | ISBN 9789811252921 (ebook) | ISBN 9789811252938 (ebook other)
Subjects: LCSH: China--Economic conditions--2000- | COVID-19 Pandemic, 2020--Economic aspects--China.
Classification: LCC HC427.95 .C6913 2022 | DDC 330.951--dc23/eng/20220304
LC record available at https://lccn.loc.gov/2022010502

British Library Cataloguing-in-Publication Data
A catalogue record for this book is available from the British Library.

经济战"疫" - 新冠肺炎疫情对经济的影响与对策
Originally published in Chinese by Fudan University Press Co., Ltd.

For any available supplementary material, please visit
https://www.worldscientific.com/worldscibooks/10.1142/12742#t=suppl

Desk Editors: Aanand Jayaraman/Lixi Dong

Typeset by Stallion Press
Email: enquiries@stallionpress.com

https://doi.org/10.1142/9789811252921_fmatter

Foreword

The fight against the unforeseeable COVID-19 pandemic is a people's war, a total war, a war of resistance worthy of song and tears, unfolding on a magnificent scale and magnitude. This war is affecting both domestic and foreign affairs and even the course of changes that have been a century in the making.

In the fight against the pandemic, people at Fudan University answered the call and stepped up to the challenge; tens of thousands of party members and students took the lead in the assault against the pandemic, flying the party flag high in the front line. A total of 497 outstanding students at Fudan University of Shanghai Medical College rushed to the aid of Wuhan with thousands of white-clothed medical staff to protect the health of the people and the safety of the city. Dozens of teams delved into scientific research working day and night, and a number of experts provided official information that provided the public with a great deal of confidence. Tens of thousands of faculties and students attended to their duties with utmost dedication, and hundreds of thousands of alumni from Fudan University, at home and abroad, showed unity in their effort to overcome the devastating pandemic.

In the fight against the pandemic, philosophers and social science scholars from Fudan took the initiative and moved swiftly to do their part. The university's think tank platform organized those of different academic disciplines and brought them together to produce collaborative research, provided timely analysis and judgment, strengthened follow-up research, and actively made comprehensive suggestions and proposals based on the development of the pandemic with regards to prevention and control measures, news and public opinion, crisis management, psychological guidance, economic response, emergency response systems, application of big data and intelligent technology, and international cooperation. The professional strengths of a large number of teachers and students was on full display as they provided professional services in emergency management, public health, psychological assistance, social work, and public relations, demonstrating the principle of applying what one has learned as well as the integration of knowledge with practice. In just over two months, Fudan scholars have submitted more than 200 research reports to their superiors, and many of their insights and suggestions have been adopted by policy-making departments, strongly reflecting the responsibility that university think tanks share in serving the country's governance and promoting the modernization of the national governance system and its capabilities. While swift and precise countermeasures for the pandemic-related work is in progress, many experts and scholars are also focusing on the long term with early planning and research on the "post-pandemic era" economic and social recovery. They aim to provide suggestions for resuming work, resuming production, and reopening cities, actively advising for strengthening public management and constructing emergency response systems to improve the governance of China's mega-cities.

The book, *Waging Economic War on the Pandemic: Policy Measures Against the Economic Impact of the COVID-19 Pandemic*, is one of the collective achievements of a team of scholars, mainly hailing from Fudan, documenting their time serving the country and fulfilling their duty to the people. The economy is the foundation of the country's functioning, and the global pandemic has put tremendous downward pressure on China's economy in the short term. In the face of the outbreak of a major pandemic, economic performance, social governance, and public administration are being tested to the limit. More than 40 scholars in the fields of economics and public administration from Fudan University and other well-known universities in China collaborated and worked tirelessly to provide advice and suggestions to make significantly effective policies and turn crises into opportunities to improve the national economy and public governance.

How exactly should we deal with the economic and financial impact of the pandemic? Under what conditions could we safely return to work? The book follows a problem-oriented approach. Starting from these major practical issues, it examines various aspects of national macroeconomic operations, industrial shocks, changes in financial markets, regional economic order, public governance challenges, and changes in the world economy while also integrating economic, financial, industrial, and environmental disciplines to provide well-calculated answers. The book adheres to systemic thinking, respecting objective economic laws and pandemic development laws, while also attaching importance to scientific analysis and precise assessment and putting forward response strategies on these bases.

At the macro level, the book emphasizes countercyclical responses, with an emphasis on comprehensive measures and precise efforts; at the meso level, it emphasizes differentiated development strategies for industries, and promotes structural adjustment and supply-side reform; at the micro level, it emphasizes enterprises' resumption of work and production as well as supply chain management. The book promotes the concept of integration, emphasizing that China's economy was and is sufficiently resilient and the importance of maintaining and improving public confidence. At the same time, it attaches importance to prescribing the correct remedies for shortcomings, strengthening weaknesses, confronting the obstacles and difficulties in economic development, and restoring social order. It is also commendable that the examination of every issue is not limited to the facts, but also focuses on the long term, on transformation and upgrading, on the construction of a modernized socialist economic system and governance system. New development concepts are put forward, putting great value in the realization of breakthroughs and the improvement of quality through solving problems in order to fulfill people's need for a better life.

At the current stage, the prevention and control of the pandemic has achieved stage-by-stage results, with an acceleration in the life order of the economy, society, and production. It is believed that this book will enlighten the management and operation of enterprises at all levels and provide much inspiration for the working life of its readers.

From a practical standpoint, it is the mission and responsibility of contemporary philosophers and social scientists in China to explore strategies and innovative methods to meet our society's challenges, to respond to the demands of the times, and to uphold the "four services". Throughout this book, by following the enthusiasm, thoughts, and efforts of the scholars that participated in the discussion, we can see the determination and action of this generation of Fudan scholars in their written theses on the motherland and the research they have performed in the service throughout such dire circumstances. The efforts of the scholars and the concerted efforts of the whole university are but small snapshots of this important moment in history; they constitute trickling streams that merge into a much greater current that is the bigger picture.

Never let a crisis go to waste. Since the founding of New China, this major public health emergency has been the fastest spreading, most widespread, and most difficult to prevent and control. This classic idiom captures it all — "It is great trials that enlighten the sage, and times of tribulation that cause a nation to rise". President Xi Jinping pointed out that though the Chinese nation has experienced many hardships in its history, it has never been crushed, instead becoming more and more courageous, always rising up and growing stronger from its trials and tribulations. We Chinese believe the perseverance of the Chinese people, the outstanding tradition of Chinese culture, and the advantages of the theories, system, and culture of socialism with Chinese characteristics are the source of our strength, which allows us to tackle two battles at once — pandemic relief and economic development. With social responsibility on their shoulders, firm self-confidence, and respect for the nation's mission, Fudan scholars, teachers, and students have striven to respond to the tests of the times through their hard work and diligence.

We hope that our teachers and students continue to carry forward the fine traditions of Fudan, make even greater achievements in serving the country and society, and make greater contributions to defeating the pandemic and building a moderately prosperous society in time to come.

Fudan University Party Secretary
March 30, 2020

https://doi.org/10.1142/9789811252921_fmatter

About the Editors

Dr. Chen Shiyi is a distinguished professor, Cheung Kong Scholar of Ministry of Education P.R.C, winner of the National Science Fund for distinguished young scholars, and a leading talent in Shanghai. He is currently the secretary of CPC of School of Economics and Fanhai International School of Finance, Fudan University. He is the researcher of Fudan Development Institute and the doctoral supervisor. Dr. Chen's main research fields are economic growth and development, risk identification and management, green finance and sustainable development, etc. He has won many important awards in economics field.

Dr. Li Zhiqing is a Doctor of Economics, Associate Professor, Master Supervisor, Executive Director of Environmental Economic Research Center of Fudan University. Dr. Li's main research fields are environmental economics, energy and climate change economics, green finance and green development. Dr. Li has published five monographs and two textbooks, and more than 100 papers and articles have been published in various journals. He won the honorary title of Shanghai Pujiang Talent and many other important awards.

https://doi.org/10.1142/9789811252921_fmatter

Contents

https://doi.org/10.1142/9789811252921_fmatter

Introduction: What are the Implications of the COVID-19 Pandemic for Sustainable Economic Development in the Medium and Long Term?

Shiyi Chen

Fudan University School of Economics, Fanhai International School of Finance, Shanghai, China

After nationwide prevention, control, and centralized treatment, the novel coronavirus, or "COVID-19", pandemic has now been effectively contained in China. On February 23, 2020, President Xi Jinping delivered an important speech at the deployment meeting for the overall promotion of the prevention and control of the COVID-19 pandemic as well as economic and social development, calling for the orderly restoration of production and normal life on the premise of ensuring that the prevention and control of the pandemic is in place, intensifying policy regulation, and striving to achieve this year's economic and social development goals and tasks. From an objective point of view, the COVID-19 pandemic has had a great impact on China's short-term economic growth. The Chinese New Year season service economy experienced significant shrinkage due to people staying at home to prevent further transmission; after the holiday season, resumption of work was postponed repeatedly due to distancing measures, affecting manufacturing production and supply chain operation. For the first quarter of 2020, a significant decline in economic growth was inevitable. At present, China is the world's second largest economy, accounting for more than 30% of the world's economic growth. China's pivotal position in the global supply chain, especially in the Asia supply chain, means that the slowdown in China's economic growth will also greatly affect the global economy.

The impact of SARS on China's economy was completely different from that of COVID-19, and the means of stimulating growth, such as real estate and heavy chemicals as well as the large volume of import and export that followed China's entry into the WTO, are no longer applicable. Therefore, new stimulus policies are in order; from start to finish they must focus on economic transformation, the positioning of high-quality development, and improving our system of governance. We shall then turn the "pandemic crisis" into an opportunity to remedy shortcomings through effective policies. Short-term policies should not lose sight of their long-term objectives, and it is only by planning ahead that short-term policies can be assured to not deviate from our long-term goals. The key to long-term sustainable economic development lies in increased productivity, the rational and adequate allocation of resources, and the continuous improvement of the market economy system. The market economy system consists of the commodity market, the factor market, and market participants, and of them, the factor market is a necessary condition for the market's role in the allocation of resources and is an important basis for the sustainable long-term development of China's economy. China's commodity market mechanisms are already well developed, but the development of the factor market has been lagging behind, severely restricting the ability of China's market allocation of resources to play a decisive role, and in the extraordinary times of the pandemic, inappropriate policies may further aggravate the distortion of factors' allocation. Therefore, the pandemic should be viewed as an opportunity to break through the long-term lag in the development of China's factor markets, strengthen efficiency standards and productivity standards, and intensify efforts in supply-side structural reform, in order to restore the economy while at the same time upgrading it and building momentum.

1 Implications of the Impact of the Pandemic for the Development of Our Labor Market: How Do We Get People Moving? What Should Be Done?

The emergence of the COVID-19 pandemic coincided with the Chinese New Year season and holiday. To combat the pandemic, holiday travel was slowed greatly, leaving a sizeable impact on China's consumption in the short term, especially in the transportation, tourism, food and beverage, movie, and retail industries.

As a result of the pandemic, spring 2020 passenger traffic decreased by 50.5% from the year before. Among the passenger traffic types, air passenger transport decreased by 47.3%, rail passenger transport decreased by 48.8%, road passenger transport decreased by 50.8%, and water passenger transport decreased by 58.8%. This indicates a tremendous decrease in labor mobility. As for the movie industry, the national box office revenue for the Spring Festival in 2019 was 5.905 billion yuan, while the total box office revenue for the Spring Festival in 2020 was reported at 23.57 million yuan, down 99.6%, according to data released by the Office of the National Film Industry Development Special Fund Management Committee.

Unlike the SARS pandemic which occurred in May and June, this pandemic emerged during the Spring Festival, and the disruption of personnel flow caused by the closure of cities and villages further hindered the resumption of production after the festival. This was especially due to a large number of migrant workers' inability to return to work, causing a substantial negative impact on China's manufacturing industry and industrial chain and employment scarcity. Moreover, prior to COVID-19, Chinese businesses had already been struggling over the past two years due to increasing unemployment. The urban unemployment rate gradually rose from 4.9% in early 2018 to 5.2% in December 2019, and the pandemic has exacerbated the issue. Also, some enterprises with thin profit margins, especially small and medium-sized enterprises (SMEs), may have to cut costs by laying off workers and cutting wages, and may even go out of business outright if they can't resume operations in a timely fashion. There are a large number of small, medium, and micro enterprises in China, and according to the latest statistics of the Fourth National

Economic Census Series Report released by the National Bureau of Statistics, as of the end of 2018, there were 18.07 million small, medium, and micro enterprises, accounting for 99.8% of all legal entities among scaled enterprises, keeping 233.004 million people in employment, and accounting for 79.4% of all people employed by enterprises. However, MSMEs are also the most vulnerable in a pandemic such as this one. As a result, the COVID-19 pandemic has reduced demand in the labor market and increased unemployment.

The movement of people is the most crucial factor in the rapid recovery of the economy post-pandemic and in lowering unemployment. Therefore, after the initial control of the pandemic and the gradual relaxation of restrictions on the movement of people, it has become a priority to resume work and production as soon as possible, which is the most important step in stabilizing enterprises and employment. President Xi Jinping put forward an eight-point requirement for the orderly resumption of work and production at the deployment meeting for the overall prevention and control of the COVID-19 pandemic and economic and social development. Premier Li Keqiang, at an executive meeting of the State Council, deployed a coordination mechanism for the "six stabilization measures", of which stabilizing employment is the first of the six. In fact, in mid-February, people began going back to work, especially in the coastal regions of Jiangsu, Zhejiang, Shanghai, Guangdong, and Fujian; these areas received employees from the labor export provinces/regions of Henan, Sichuan, Guizhou, Guangxi, and other places through shuttle buses, shuttle trains, and chartered aircraft. Some large enterprises such as Foxconn and Midea also used chartered buses and aircraft to pick up workers to return to work. Some areas have introduced free, subsidized, and rewarded "rush" measures and stable job return policies. According to information on the website of the Ministry of Human Resources and Social Security, as of March 5, the country has issued 11.2 billion yuan to 470,000 enterprises, benefiting 24.26 million workers. In fact, coastal areas such as Jiangsu, Zhejiang, Shanghai, and Guangdong are China's economic boom areas and the locomotive of economic growth; these areas resumed work early and are playing a pivotal role in China's post-pandemic economic recovery. According to information from a series of press conferences on the prevention and control of the COVID-19 pandemic in Shanghai, the city asked all types of enterprises within city limits to resume work no earlier than 24:00 on February 9. After the resumption of work on February 10, industrial enterprises above a designated size reached 40.2%. With the orderly progress of the resumption of work, in just nine days, the industrial enterprises above the designated size reached a "resumed work" rate of 72.6%. As of March 8, the resumption rate of industrial enterprises above the designated size in Shanghai had reached 97%. In addition, the resumption rate of cultural enterprises above the designated size also exceeded 95%, while the resumption rate of the entirety of foreign-funded industries reached 99.9%. Judging from the official public data of the localities, as of March 10, more than 90% of industrial enterprises above the designated size in 19 provinces, autonomous regions, and municipalities have resumed work. In Shandong, Jiangsu, Zhejiang, Guangxi, and Guizhou, the work resumption rate exceeds 99 per cent, of which Guizhou is in first place with 100%.

However, many problems remain in the resumption of work and production. In many places, quarantine measures marked by "caution at all costs" are being added one after another, and some areas less severely affected by the pandemic are nevertheless enforcing strict control, and prevention measures are taken across the board, making it impossible for people from large labor-exporting provinces such as Henan and Sichuan to return to work. As of February 24, 4.052 million migrant workers had returned to work in Henan province, but that was only half of the total number of migrant workers who returned before the Spring Festival, according to a report by Southern Weekend. Personnel couldn't commute, which seriously affected the work resumption rate of enterprises, especially SMEs, which are not counted in the work resumption rate of the above-mentioned scaled enterprises. Vice Minister of Industry and Information Technology Zhang Kejian remarked at the State Council's joint prevention and control mechanism news conference that according to cloud platform monitoring data from the Ministry of Industry and Information Technology on 2.2 million SMEs, the overall rate of SMEs going back to work is still not high; as of February 26, the work resumption rate was only 32.8%. For those that did resume work, productivity still took a major hit as they were also dependent on the resumption of work by upstream and downstream enterprises in the industry chain. According to the National Bureau of Statistics, China's composite purchasing managers' index (PMI) stood at 28.9% in February, down 23.5 percentage points from a year earlier. There may also be regional discrimination in the hiring process as workers from areas hit by the pandemic gradually begin returning to work. For example, workers in some areas heavily affected by the pandemic face a wide range of restrictions, including quarantine measures, or even direct discouragement to return to work, making it difficult for them to resume work or find employment in the short term. When employing people from these areas, enterprises are forced to pay part of the additional costs of controlling the pandemic, including the corresponding quarantine and testing costs. This puts workers in the pandemic-stricken areas at a yet another disadvantage in the labor market, increasing the probability of job loss for those already employed and making it more difficult for new entrants to find employment. The pandemic may therefore have an impact on the structure of labor supply and demand, resulting in an imbalance in the allocation of labor resources and loss of efficiency.

In the short term, the problems roughly outlined above regarding the resumption of work and production should be addressed by taking categorical and graded measures in order to resume economic activities as soon as possible and in an orderly manner. On the regional level, areas severely hit by the pandemic should continue to focus on taking stringent precautions against the spread of the pandemic; areas at moderate risk can partially resume work, while lightly-affected areas should be encouraged to resume work and fully resume production. At the industry level, the first step is to ensure the resumption of work in the logistics industry, such as in the production of medical supplies, daily necessities, transportation, and express delivery. The second step is to resume production in related enterprises along the industrial chain as soon as possible, so as to minimize the risk of supply chain disruption and out-migration. During the pandemic, the State should also continue to roll out relevant fiscal policies, reduce or waive the cost of "five insurances and one housing fund" for employees of enterprises, especially small and medium-sized enterprises, waive health testing costs for those returning to work, and reduce any other economic costs for enterprises to employ personnel from areas affected by the pandemic. This is to ensure a basic level of livelihood for the people, protect wages, maintain operations, and expeditiously repair the imbalance in the allocation of labor resources and the distortion of the supply and demand structure of the labor market. The COVID-19 pandemic will lead to an increase in the number of labor disputes in enterprises affected by the pandemic, especially in the case of pandemic patients and employees of enterprises that are unable to work normally because of the quarantine measures imposed by the government; the labor rights and interests of such workers are particularly vulnerable. Therefore, the government needs to establish a special pandemic service platform to provide "green channels" for legal protection for workers affected by the pandemic, so as to effectively safeguard their legitimate rights and interests. Media campaigns are needed to eliminate the discriminatory mentality toward workers in areas affected by the pandemic.

The reason the pandemic has had such an immediate impact on the labor market is fundamentally because a large percentage of the labor market's employment structure consists of workers in labor-intensive industries, many of whom are rural workers. Since the reform and opening-up, a large number of rural laborers have participated in China's industrialization and urbanization process, which has contributed greatly to China's economic growth. However, China's long-standing dual economic structure of the labor market has not been fundamentally altered, and rural laborers are subject to a series of restrictions, such as regional household registration, that prevent them from competing on an equal footing with urban laborers and enjoying equal access to public services. As a result, they are not fully integrated into the city, their children are still "left behind" in the countryside, and their parents are not in a position to live with them in the city. Although it is cultural tradition to return to one's hometown for the Spring Festival, if we can provide equal public services to the rural workforce so that their children and parents can live with them in the same city, we can greatly reduce the number of people returning to their hometowns for the Spring Festival, which in turn will make it easier for them to return to work and for production to resume. Although the State has put forward the guideline of "industry feeding agriculture, cities supporting the countryside, and realizing the coordinated development of industry and agriculture along with cities and the countryside", the imbalance between urban and rural development has not yet been fundamentally changed, and there is still a significant urban–rural income gap, which is why rural laborers continue to move to the cities in search of work even though they cannot enjoy the same treatment that the local urban residents enjoy. If one day we can achieve balanced development in both urban and rural areas and if both areas offer similar income, then the number of rural laborers going to the cities in search of work will be greatly reduced.

Adequate labor mobility is an essential condition for the development of a market economy. The importance of mobility can also be seen in the impact of the pandemic on the labor market. The next question is: how can we break down the barriers to labor mobility? How does the workforce gain mobility? It's not feasible for the labor force to move into our cities in their current state — densely populated, congested with traffic, lacking adequate public services, heavily polluted with smog, and without the capacity to further absorb outside labor. The biggest difference between China and other countries is its large population. China has built many high-speed rails and highways, but it is still difficult to get a ticket on the Beijing–Shanghai "Renaissance" line before they sell out, and holiday travel congestion and the crowding of scenic spots occur often enough to convince someone to abandon their holiday travel plans. Even the daily commute to work is hassled with congested traffic; the usual 10 minutes of travel can be as long as an hour at peak times. Unfortunately, this situation will only continue to worsen in the larger cities. Such overcrowding and clustering make it easier for the pandemic to spread over a wide area and worsen the problem, and the self-dispersed isolation measures adopted by sparsely populated countries may not be feasible or even effective in China. Although China has effectively controlled the COVID-19 pandemic, if the global community fails to effectively prevent and control the pandemic, and if the number of imported cases increases significantly in the future, or even if it becomes an annual pandemic in winter and spring, the impact on the health of the Chinese people and the economic shocks will be greater than in other countries. Therefore, the question of how to plan and re-plan the development of the country's labor market in order to respond effectively to future public emergencies such as the COVID-19 pandemic is an issue that demands our attention at the present moment. For this reason, in addition to the current grading and classification of the orderly resumption of work as soon as possible to restore economic production, I believe that the impact of the COVID-19 pandemic on the labor market will carry with it, at the least, the following three implications for the future development of the labor market in the medium and long term.

1.1 Urban household registration and equalization of services for rural–urban migrant workers

We will continue to reform the household registration system and the land system, eliminate the drawbacks of the dual economy, expand the employment absorption capacity and related service facilities in large and medium-sized cities, and provide equal public services for the rural labor force in urban employment, so that the rural labor force can work in cities with peace of mind and provide stable labor resources for labor-intensive manufacturing and service-oriented industries.

1.2 Facilitating conditions for rural entrepreneurs

We will continue to break down urban and rural barriers, actively promote the strategy of rural revitalization, continuously improve the construction of rural infrastructure such as roads, sanitation and information technology, develop rural leisure tourism, catering and entertainment, cultural tourism, and other rural specialties. We will promote the integrated development of these rural industries through information technology, so that the countryside can absorb more "homecoming" entrepreneurs and city-to-country entrepreneurs, making it easier for larger numbers of talented people to bring their innovation and entrepreneurship to the vast rural areas.

1.3 Regularization of telecommuting and paid leave

Industries that are able to should adopt telecommuting and online services, encourage employees to work at home, have off-site offices, offer regular debriefings and staggered work, and develop appropriate performance assessment indicators, look at work performance rather than attendance records, require only essential personnel to remain on site, and further develop telecommuting hardware and software facilities. At the same time, paid annual leave models and staggered leave to avoid the congestion of small long holidays and Spring Festival should also be promoted.

The above implications are all based on China's large population and crowded cities, so it is necessary to develop a labor market development strategy with Chinese characteristics; the key terms for such a strategy are decentralized employment, multi-directional employment, and work-from-home. These are all preferred over having crowds of workers flocking to large cities and downtown areas to go to work along with crowded movement on holidays and after-work hours. This way, the mobility of labor can be promoted, the needs of talent can be better met and they can enjoy greater vitality, while overcrowding and its harmful effects can be avoided. I could not imagine a more desirable pattern for future work and employment. With stable employment and no major fluctuations due to unexpected events, the population will have a stable income, and with our country having become the world's largest domestic consumer market and consumption having become the number one driver of economic growth, we will have the basic conditions to further expand domestic demand and promote sustained and healthy economic growth.

2 Implications of the Impact of the Pandemic for the Development of China's Capital Markets: How Do We Get the Currency Flowing? Where Should it Flow to?

The impact from the outbreak and spread of the COVID-19 pandemic on the global and Chinese capital markets cannot be overstated. As of the writing of this book, the three major stock indices in the United States have experienced a number of consecutive meltdowns (historically, only one such meltdown has occurred before); the Dow hit the largest one-day drop in more than 30 years, and over a period of only three weeks the United States stock market evaporated nearly 30% of its value, equal to more than 10 trillion U.S. dollars. International oil prices collapsed more than 30%, creating the largest one-day drop since the 1991 Gulf War; the U.S. WTI crude oil price dropped to a low point of nearly $20 a barrel. U.S. debt, gold, the yen, and the Swiss franc and other safe-haven assets have also uncharacteristically plunged and suffered turbulence. The global panic index hit a new high since the 2008 global financial crisis. A-shares in China's stock market plummeted across the board during the first day of trading after the Spring Festival; the Shanghai and Shenzhen stock indices fell 7.7% and 8.4%, respectively, creating the largest one-day decline since August 2015. The indices quickly rebounded with some subsequent shocks and declines, and although the magnitude was far less dramatic than the turbulence of U.S. stocks, there was still a tendency for the hedging of funds from the stock market to the bond market, resulting in a fall in Chinese 10-year Treasury yields.

Nonetheless, the US–China interest rate differential continues to widen and Chinese assets remain attractive to foreign investors. However, the impact of the pandemic has led to a dampening of enterprises' willingness and ability to raise finance, with many choosing to suspend financing. Credit debt issuance and net financing have experienced a steep decline since peaking in mid-January 2020, and both are now down to three-year lows and have continued to hover at low levels of late. Credit bonds planned for issuance that have been postponed or cancelled in the last month reached $21.51 billion.

Suspension of financing can lead to financial stress, with many companies facing repayment pressures as their bonds mature during the pandemic, making them prone to credit risk, while price volatility can increase the burden for future financing. The public health emergency caused by the COVID-19 outbreak posed inevitable financial and economic risks, and the turmoil and drops in capital markets have fueled expectations of a global recession.

According to a recent report by the United Nations Division on International Trade in Goods and Services, and Commodities, China's share of global trade in intermediate goods has increased from 4% in 2002 to about 20% at present, and China has become an important player in the global industrial chain. Under such circumstances, the delay in the resumption of work and production brought about by the COVID-19 pandemic as well as ineffective global prevention and control of the outbreak will inevitably affect the operation of the industrial chain. As downstream enterprises resume production, it will be necessary for upstream enterprises to resume operations, and as China restores production capacity, world production must not be brought to a standstill; any break in the industrial chain will put further stress on the capital chain. There is a "long whip effect" inherent in the supply chain, and with the continuous transmission of demand signals to the upstream of the supply chain, its fluctuations tend to be amplified; therefore, a break in the industrial chain may heavily impact China's economic fundamentals, and this is the most worrying aspect of the negative economic effects of the pandemic (Liu Zhibiao, 2020).

In fact, the COVID-19 pandemic has had a significant impact on the demand for capital in Chinese capital markets. Over the past three years, the cumulative year-on-year growth rate of the operating income of China's industrial enterprises has been declining, while the cumulative year-on-year growth rate of total profits fell to negative figures in 2019; the overall profit level of enterprises is already low.

The pandemic-related delay in the resumption of work means that enterprises cannot operate normally to earn income while they wait for employees to return to work, but at the same time they will still need to pay fixed costs such as rent, loan principals and interest, employee wages, and the "five insurances and one housing fund" for employees. There is also the possibility that commercial banks, out of consideration for their own risk management and control, may draw or cut off loans, which objectively increases the stress on enterprises' funds and the risk of a break in the financial chain. As a result, the short-term capital requirements of firms will increase accordingly, creating an impact on the demand for capital in the capital markets.

According to information provided by the National Bureau of Statistics on the losses of industrial enterprises, the peak period of annual losses for industrial enterprises is the first three months of the year, after which losses decline month by month throughout the year; this is true for both the loss-making portion of enterprises and the total number of enterprises as a whole. This means that the first quarter of the year is the most difficult for industrial enterprises to operate. The peak of the pandemic occurred in January–February 2020, which will further exacerbate the first-quarter operational difficulties of enterprises, especially small, medium, and micro enterprises, and will increase their working capital requirements.

Small and medium enterprises play a very important role in China's economy, not only absorbing nearly 80% of employment, but also contributing more than 50% of tax revenue and more than 60% of the GDP. According to the latest data released by the General Administration of Customs, more than 50% of China's export trade was accounted for by mainly small and medium-sized private enterprises.

However, in terms of financing, the loan coverage rate of commercial banks for small and micro enterprises is less than 10%, SME loans account for only 24.7% of total bank loans, more than 40% of SMEs face financing difficulties, and the cost of financing is 1.5–2 times higher than that of large enterprises. A recent survey conducted by Tsinghua University on approximately 700 SMEs during the pandemic found that more than half of the surveyed companies' business revenues fell by greater than one-third, and even more considering only a little over 10% were able to sustain their operations with their own funds for more than three months (Chen, Haiqiang *et al.*, 2020). As SMEs are the least able to withstand risks, this pandemic will further exacerbate their financing difficulties, and in severe cases, they may even go bankrupt and close down.

As early as February 1, the People's Bank of China and the Ministry of Finance led the implementation of 30 measures for short-term financial support for pandemic prevention and control. On March 3, Premier Li

Keqiang presided over an executive meeting of the State Council, emphasizing the integrated promotion of pandemic prevention and control with economic and social development, and the deployment of working mechanisms to stabilize employment, finance, foreign trade, foreign investment, general investment, and expectations. The People's Bank of China has prioritized support for the recovery and development of the real economy, implemented prudent monetary policies, strengthened countercyclical adjustment, maintained reasonable growth in money and credit, promoted continuous optimization of the credit structure, unblocked the transmission of monetary policy by means of reform, and has made every effort to reduce enterprise financing costs.

Main elements of the measures include: increasing open-market reverse repurchase operations, guiding open market reverse repurchasing, medium-term lending facility bid interest rates, dropping loan market quotation rates (LPR) by 10 basis points each to drive down overall market interest rates; the establishment of 300 billion yuan of special low-cost refinancing, precision support for enterprises directly involved in the fight against the pandemic, setting the actual cost of financing for these enterprises after the financial discount at 1.30%, below the State Council's requirement of no greater than 1.60%; strengthening financial inclusion for small, medium, and micro-enterprises by adding 500 billion yuan in special credit lines for agriculture, small-enterprise refinancing, and rediscounting, and 350 billion yuan in special credit lines for policy-oriented banks, while also lowering interest rates for agriculture and small enterprise refinancing by 0.25 percentage points and providing extension services for existing loans.

On March 13, the People's Bank of China (PBOC) decided to implement a targeted reduction in financial inclusion on March 16, 2020, with a targeted reduction of 0.5–1 percentage point for banks that meet the assessment criteria, and an additional targeted reduction of 1 percentage point for qualified joint-stock commercial banks to support the issuance of loans in the field of financial inclusion, releasing a total of 550 billion yuan of long-term funds. This targeted reduction and release of long-term funds can effectively increase the banks' stable source of funds to support the real economy; the flow of funds through the banks will be conducive to the reduction of real loan interest rates for small and micro private enterprises.

Since the outbreak of the pandemic, a series of financial policies have also been introduced in each region to support the recovery of the real economy. For example, the city of Chengdu made full use of the direct financing policy dividends to help the city's enterprises actively use the "green channel" opened up by the inter-bank market and the Shanghai and Shenzhen stock exchanges to promote the issuance of corporate bonds to raise funds to fight the pandemic and resume production. As of March 11, Chengdu enterprises realized direct bond financing of 39.714 billion yuan, out of which 13 pandemic prevention and control bonds were issued, raising a total of 11.31 billion yuan and ranking fourth in the country. Of course, in order to counteract the pandemic and restore the economy, financial services still have a great deal of work to do; in addition to targeted refinancing, they can also appropriately reduce the regulatory tolerance of non-performing assets to give more efficacy to policy-based financing, strengthen policy guarantees, and employ other means of targeted support for loans to industries and regions affected by the pandemic. Such measures will help protect the continuity of credit and new investment and support the smooth progress of the resumption of production and work. In particular, it is recommended that local governments take the lead in strengthening collaboration among banks, enterprises, and local credit enhancement agencies to provide appropriate credit enhancement and credit support to help enterprises and self-employed persons resume normal operations on the basis of a prudent assessment of their liquidity risk and business fundamentals.

Nonetheless, it is important to emphasize that we should consider not just the short-term effects but also the long-term objectives of the various financial policies used to support the post-pandemic economic recovery. As a country dominated by indirect financing, China's banking sector has played an important role in the country's economic development. China's capital market has also grown rapidly since the 1990s and is now the second largest capital market in the world. It is the reliance on diversified financing from fiscal, banking, and capital markets that has led to China's investment-driven rapid growth model and China's economic miracle.

After the SARS pandemic in 2003, land finance and real estate investment sharply lifted the economy's growth rate, and after the 2008 global financial crisis, the $4 trillion stimulus package featuring infrastructure investment allowed us to overcome the risk of recession. However, the marginal returns from such extensive investment have diminished sharply, the economic growth model characterized by factor quantity expansion is unsustainable, and China has embarked on a stage of high-quality development characterized by total-factor productivity improvement. The

Fourth Plenary Session of the 19th Central Committee of the Communist Party of China (CPC) also called for strengthening the construction of basic capital market institutions, upgrading to a modern financial system that is highly adaptive, competitive, and inclusive, which will effectively prevent and resolve financial risks.

In recent years, more than 20 Chinese provinces, autonomous regions, and municipalities have announced future infrastructure investment plans totaling more than 30 trillion yuan. The economy needs confidence, the market needs expectations, and the "post-pandemic era" naturally requires a sufficient amount of investment. At the same time, the downsides of past investments and their shortcomings that were made apparent during the pandemic can shed a lot of light on this capital investment. A basic principle is that we can no longer engage in "flooding investment"; that is to say, we can no longer invest in the high pollution, high energy consumption of heavy industry and the real estate industry in large cities, but rather we need to pivot to long-term positioning, precision investment, and targeted support. In my opinion, there are at least four important areas of investment.

2.1 Take advantage of the pandemic to fundamentally solve the problem of difficult and expensive financing for small and medium enterprises

The difficulty and high cost of financing for small and medium-sized enterprises is the primary manifestation of the imbalance in the allocation of resources in China's capital and credit markets, which has not been effectively resolved for a long time. Small and medium-sized enterprises (SMEs) are also the most heavily affected by the pandemic, especially those in the traditional labor-intensive service and manufacturing industries. Therefore, solving the financing problems of SMEs is not just a short-term emergency; it must be based on finding a fundamental solution. On the one hand, banks should continue to make good use of special refinancing policies for SMEs and give play to the supportive role of structural monetary policy tools, such as generalized small-scale refinancing and rediscounting as well as targeted downgrading. LPR reform should be utilized in guiding the decline in real interest rates on loans. On the other hand, the implementation of capital market reform measures should be stepped up to provide reasonable access to long-term financial support for SMEs. Recently, a series of capital market reforms, such as the revision of the securities law, the full implementation of the registration system, and the introduction of new regulations on refinancing, transfer listing, venture capital holdings, etc., will make it more convenient for enterprises, especially small and medium-sized enterprises, to list, delist, transfer, and raise capital. This will have the effect of minimizing the space for arbitrage and speculation, which is conducive to investing capital in the real economy, especially in science and technology enterprises.

2.2 Continue to increase the construction of online payment, mobile payment, and third-party payment platforms to further enhance the convenience of online payment, settlement, and financing

I think a lot of people have had bad experiences in the bank office. The advent of online banking and mobile payment systems have greatly enhanced the efficiency of the process and reduced the cost of doing business. The characteristics of online payment also make it preferable for pandemic prevention and control, having the dual effects of reducing physical gatherings and outings while also reducing the use of banknotes and coins, thus slowing the spread of the pandemic. In the future, the amount of business conducted at the counter should be reduced to the greatest extent possible and a revolution in the efficiency of business offices should be implemented. Third-party payment platforms can also perform this function along with the functions of online settlement, which can reduce payment costs, stimulate consumer impulses, and provide consumer credit to boost consumption and economic growth. It can be said that third-party payment platforms have contributed to the rapid development of China's e-commerce and made an important contribution to the prevention and control of this pandemic. Another important reason to continue to develop third-party payment platforms in the future is that they can leverage their information and technology advantages to provide financing services to micro and small businesses and individual merchants. Third-party payment companies have a closer proximity to users, and through big data, they can obtain more comprehensive information on micro and small enterprises, thus allowing a more accurate assessment of the credit of enterprises, and can provide micro and small enterprises with more flexible options as well as lower thresholds and costs for financing services. In the future, commercial and foreign banks will also enter the field of third-party payment. Regardless of the type of third-party payment platform, the viability of future development will depend on the convenience of online payment, settlement, and financing.

2.3 Improve traditional infrastructure construction and increase investment in the construction of new intelligent green infrastructure

As early as the 1940s, Paul Rosenstein-Rodan, one of the pioneers of development economics, argued that infrastructure was the first capital for social development and should take precedence in economic development policies, a theory that became known as "The Big Push Theory". Over the past 10 years, China has achieved leaps and bounds in the construction of high-speed railways, highways, and airports, and the country has built a well-connected transportation network, laying a solid material foundation for sustained economic development. The current transport network is mainly based on arterial roads, and future infrastructure construction should be extended to more cities as well as to the west and rural areas with greater breadth and depth, supplemented by the construction of rural roads, so as to form national modern transport "arteries" and "capillary blood vessels" with full coverage. This will create better hardware conditions for the two-way flow of labor between urban and rural areas and for urban-rural integration. At the same time, it is necessary to accelerate the transition of infrastructure investment to new intelligent infrastructure and green infrastructure, such as driverless vehicles, car-sharing, and other intelligent low-carbon transportation systems, intelligent energy storage, electric charging, and hydrogenation, distributed energy, and other intelligent micro-grid systems. These should be coupled with new energy sources, new materials, and energy-saving and emission-reducing urban infrastructure. The new infrastructure should have positive externalities, advanced technology, sustainable debt, and other advantages, and should feature both short-term stimulus and long-term sustainable investment. It should be regarded as a new category of infrastructure investment and should serve as the focus of the next phase of investment.

2.4 Fixing the shortcomings of the construction of medical hardware and software and public health infrastructure in accordance with high standards to ensure capability to respond to major public health emergencies

The pandemic has shown that the country's current medical and public health infrastructure falls far short of what is needed to deal with outbreaks. In the aftermath of the pandemic, greater investment in medical and public health infrastructure must be made to ensure that future public health emergencies can be met with a resilient response. According to the International Monetary Fund, China's healthcare expenditure accounted for 7.07% of total general government expenditure in 2018, compared to 24.44%, 19.80%, and 13.47% in the US, Japan, and Singapore, respectively. The shortage of healthcare resources and the imbalance in the distribution of resources between large, medium, and small cities and between urban and rural areas are two major deficiencies that are in urgent need of being addressed. Therefore, more hospitals should be built in China in the future, and there is an urgent need to fix and strengthen the hardware and software shortcomings of hospitals at all levels and medical institutions in both big cities and small and medium-sized cities. Additionally, small hospitals should be equipped with the same medical equipment as large hospitals. Of course, this will require an increase in the number of highly qualified physicians and healthcare workers. Cities also need to improve the public health prevention system and the emergency response system for infectious diseases outside of conventional hospitals and medical institutions, which serve as a strong safeguard in the event of a public health emergency. This kind of investment cannot be left entirely to the market, but rather requires investment input from the central and local governments, which in itself can lead to GDP growth, thus precipitating a win–win scenario.

3 The Impact of the Pandemic on the Development of China's Logistics Services: How Can We Ensure Smooth Logistics? What Should be Done About it?

The response of the logistics industry to the COVID-19 pandemic reflects the industry's outstanding role as it made a huge contribution to the fight against the pandemic. In January 2020, retail sales for the express delivery support network are expected to exceed 600 billion yuan. During the five days of January 24–29, the national postal industry received 81.25 million parcels, and the Spring Festival (February 4–9) saw a growth of 76.6% compared to the same period the previous year. To ensure that people's material life is not affected during the pandemic, a total of 78.17 million pieces of parcels were delivered, representing an increase of 110.34%. However, we should also observe that the logistics industry is under tremendous pressure due to the impact of pandemic prevention and control measures such as village road closures and home quarantines. According to a report on the logistics industry resumption index in Henan province, after the Spring Festival in 2020, the duration of logistics vehicle operation and journey distances were essentially similar to the Spring Festival in 2019, but the logistics vehicle resumption index was less than 30% of the level from the same period last year, meaning that during resumption of operations, the vehicles had to run with a high load. According to the G7 logistics monitoring data, before the logistics industry fully resumed work on February 10, the national truckload logistics flow only resumed slightly over 10% of the normal amount of operations, and zero-load freight was basically at a standstill. After the resumption of work on February 10, the national truckload logistics flow continued to rise, but up to early March only returned to slightly over 60% normal operation levels, while the national zero-load freight logistics flow was still less than half of the typical amount.

During the pandemic, the logistics industry was most directly affected because many logistics employees returned to their hometowns for the Spring Festival, resulting in a severe shortage of on-the-job personnel and an inability to resume work on time and on demand after the holiday. This is also a result of the nature of the logistics industry at present. The logistics industry is still a labor-intensive industry, with most of its workers coming from rural areas. The National Post Office's 2019 Survey Report on the Existence Status of Delivery Personnel shows that 76.31% of personnel come from rural areas, 15.89% from small county towns, and only 7.8% from cities. In many parts of the countryside, the entire village workforce is engaged in the industry, and the closure of villages and road networks has prevented workers from returning to their workplaces normally. Like many other businesses, the overall fundamentals of the logistics industry declined in 2019, with more than 90% of companies experiencing some level of operational difficulties. Under the effects of the COVID-19 pandemic, the logistics industry itself is not the only one experiencing difficulties resuming work; there are also delays in resuming work in the manufacturing industry and other service industries, resulting in a decline in the volume of commercial express mail, and further resulting in a lengthened payment cycle for small and medium-sized logistics enterprises, exacerbating operational difficulties. Small and medium-sized logistics enterprises as well as operating outlets for large logistics companies are thus under considerable survival stress.

On March 3, Premier Li Keqiang presided over an executive meeting of the State Council to further clarify the guidelines for supporting the transport, express delivery, and other logistics industries to alleviate their difficulties and accelerate their recovery. Accelerating the resumption of work and production in the logistics industry can not only provide strong support for pandemic prevention and control, but also help smooth out economic cycles and better meet the needs of people's livelihoods. Specific requirements put out in the meeting include: zoning classification with precise and orderly guidance of logistics enterprises for resumption of work, the abolition of unreasonable approval processes for resumption of work, requiring localities to give non-discriminatory access to both postage and express delivery companies, facilitating easy access to villages; increasing reductions for taxes and fees, continuing to implement, within a certain time frame, a policy to halve the urban tax on the use of land for storing bulk commodities, which had originally expired at the end of last year; exempting import and export goods from port construction fees; reducing by 20% government-priced fees and charges such as cargo port fees; abolishing mandatory emergency response services and fees for non-tankers and cargo ships; halving fees for railroad insurance, extended use of containers and stranded trucks, and reducing fees for some government-run airport services and security links. Furthermore, insurance companies are encouraged to provide appropriate reductions or waivers of insurance premiums for operating land vehicles, ships, and aircraft that were suspended during the pandemic through such means as extending the insurance period and offsetting renewal costs, and localities are encouraged to adopt measures such as the phased reduction or waiver of "share fees" to help taxi drivers tide over the difficult times. The function of the logistics industry in economic development of providing resource flow as well as its role in securing emergency materials in the pandemic prevention and control bring two points of inspiration to our attention.

3.1 Continue to vigorously develop the modern logistics industry

First of all, we need to improve the wages, benefits, vacation time, and other benefits of logistics employees, and conduct regular training for business skills, personnel quality, and traffic safety. We must continue to increase our construction capacity for rail and waterway transport capacity in order to take full advantage of their use as main transport lines, thereby reducing the proportion of usage allocated to China's road transport. The flexibility and regional advantages of road transport can help solve logistical and transport issues for villages (Tian Xin *et al.*, 2020). During the pandemic, due to the lack of unified deployment and effective communication, cross-district delivery has been greatly restricted. Many community control regulations did not allow entry for delivery personnel; delivery workers had to notify each resident by phone to pick up their parcels and then wait outside the community indefinitely for the resident to collect their parcels, resulting in inefficient distribution. In the future, it will therefore be necessary to increase the construction of intelligent delivery infrastructure, improve terminal distribution capacity, and digitalize the entire logistics network of the whole chain. Construction of digital networks would not only be conducive to improving the logistics industry business model by enhancing operational efficiency, but would also serve to strengthen industry oversight. During the Chinese phase of the pandemic, global supplies rushed to the aid of Wuhan. The global spread of the pandemic and the role of Chinese emergency supplies and medical personnel in international assistance also require the logistics industry to continue to enhance internationalization, continue to strengthen China's global distribution network, and further promote customs integration and facilitation reform. At the same time, logistics companies are not merely transporting goods, but also need to be extended forward and backward, facilitate in-depth integration of upstream and downstream supply chain enterprises, strengthen logistical connections with large foreign manufacturing enterprises, and provide a platform for upstream and downstream enterprises to seek cooperation. The modern logistics industry is not only an artery of economic operation, but also a life-saving channel for responding to unexpected public incidents, and therefore needs to be vigorously developed in the future.

3.2 Promote the development of a green logistics industry

The whole process of logistics services exists under the mutual restraints of the human–environment–material relationship. The occurrence of this pandemic can also be said to be a consequence of the imbalance between the constraints of mankind and the natural ecological environment. China's logistics industry is currently operating in a relatively crude manner, with all links in the industry causing serious pollution; transport trucks are the main source of transport carbon emissions, storage and transport consume large quantities of fossil fuels, packaging contributes to deforestation and garbage pollution, leading to loss of wildlife habitat, while in the human world the logistics industry increases the possibility of the spread of viral infections.

4 Implications of the Impact of the Pandemic for the Development of China's Data Element Market: How Can We Facilitate the Flow of Data? What Else Needs to be Done?

The digital economy refers to the activity of producing goods and services with computer technology, internet technology, and data as the necessary and key means of production. In contrast to the traditional economy, it usually takes the form of or is dependent on new inter-organizational relationships, forms, and boundaries, and can be said to be an economic form of its own (Mao Kiye, 2019). In recent years, China's digital economy has developed rapidly, and as of 2018, the total volume of China's digital economy has reached 31.2 trillion yuan, accounting for as much as 34.8% of the GDP (1). With the rise of the digital economy, "data" have also been newly included in the category of production factors as decided by the Fourth Plenary Session of the 19th CPC Central Committee. The COVID-19 pandemic has had a huge impact on the country's consumer services and manufacturing industries, but during the pandemic, the country's digital economy grew tremendously and became an important force in maintaining consumption and fueling the online office.

During the pandemic prevention and control period, there was a surge in demand for digital economy consumption of online content such as games, online reading, and videos. Online shopping, offices, healthcare, and education all underwent large-scale popularization. According to official data from WeChat applets, from New Year's Eve to the seventh day of the first month of the lunar calendar in 2020, the number of applet transactions in the fresh fruit and vegetable category increased by 149%, while the number of transactions in the community e-commerce increased by 322%. The daily activity of independent apps for online medical consultations on the Internet was significantly higher during the Spring Festival of 2020 than in 2019, reaching 6,712,000 on January 30 (the sixth day of the first month of the Lunar New Year), up 33.2% from the same period in 2019, according to data monitored by Analysys. It is understood that the implementation of hybrid online and offline education and flipped classrooms in colleges has been limited by the shortcomings of online teaching and learning, but this time it has received sudden popularity and promotion due to the advent of online learning during the pandemic. Students have participated in a hybrid of offline and online learning, where students send questions to teachers online and teachers give lectures and answer student questions. This new experience has yielded promising results. At the same time, various kinds of online conferences, video lectures, and cross-campus transnational video and audio seminars have been held, and although most students have not yet returned to school, online teaching and research work have already started in normal fashion. I believe that after this pandemic, some business models, office models, teaching and research models will be completely new, and the older inefficient models may never return. In my opinion, the main lessons that this pandemic has brought to us include the following two.

The first is to work hard to turn the digital economy into an industry of the future. The core driving force of the digital economy is digital technology innovation, and the core factor of production is data, including 5G technology, artificial intelligence, cloud computing, the Internet, the Internet of Things, block chain, and big data centers, all of which are the most innovative and dynamic elements of the economy. These elements all belong to the category of new infrastructure, which is the optimal combination of stimulating short-term economic growth and promoting long-term high-quality development. China's overall direct investment in 5G technology, for example, is expected to reach $1.2 trillion, with an investment cycle likely to exceed eight years. The 5G industry chain and its enabling industries, including smart transportation, smart cities, smart factories, smart healthcare, smart education, smart agriculture, etc., will generate billions of dollars of investment. In addition to increasing investment in the digital economy, the government should also support digital economy entrepreneurship, nurture digital economy talents, promote digital economy employment, and fully develop the data elements market. The government can increase its support for digital economy entrepreneurship by establishing a special digital economy innovation support fund in addition to financial support and financial policy support, and can also direct venture capital funds to invest in the digital economy to enhance capital market support for innovation and entrepreneurship in the digital economy.

The second is a big push for jobs in the digital economy. According to the White Paper on China's Digital Economy Development and Employment (2019) released by the China Institute of Information and Communications Technology, the scale of China's digital economy grew by 20.9% in 2018, while the number of jobs was 191 million, up 11.5% year-on-year and significantly higher than the overall employment scale growth rate in the country; the digital economy's ability to absorb jobs is constantly growing. Therefore, we can vigorously develop the digital economy with employment as the main focus, and simultaneously promote the digital transformation of the industrial structure and the upgrading of workers' digital skills in order to cultivate more "digital talents". The pandemic has promoted the rapid development of the digital economy, and also highlighted the urgent need for the marketization of data elements. It is necessary not only to continuously improve data market trading mechanisms, but also to strengthen the protection and management of data, clarify data supervision rules, and continuously improve data trading laws and regulations.

The above is a preliminary summary of ten major implications, or ten general directions, for the long-term sustainable development of China's economy under the coronavirus pandemic from the perspectives of the labor market, the capital market, logistics services, and the data market, respectively (of course, in reality there are more than just the ten mentioned here). Some people will echo the tired platitude that even if no pandemic had occurred this year, these implications must still be heeded, while others will say such measures are too little too late for saving the economy, like trying to quench a raging forest fire with a bucket of water. Regardless, after the experience of this pandemic, I believe that these ten implications do in fact constitute our future response to major emergencies and the maintenance of the long-term healthy development of the economy. Many of them are effective in stimulating the economy in the short term, and with long-term considerations in mind, they are valuable references for us in formulating short-term policies to prevent and control pandemics and restore the economy. The key is that these ten implications are all closely tied to the lagging development of China's factor market. The development of China's factor market has been a subject of discussion for many years, with little progress, and if we can take advantage of this "battle against the pandemic" to successfully promote the development of China's factor market, it could be regarded as turning a crisis into an opportunity. Without a fully developed factor market, any ideas about building the capacity to respond to future crises and cultivating the essential momentum for sustainable, high-quality economic development are just empty talk. If the people, money, and things necessary for economic activity are able to both flow in physical space as well as interface without contact in the digital space, then the decisive role of the factor market in allocating resources can be fully realized, and the driving force for long-term economic growth — an increase in total factor productivity — is a certainty. At that level, the basic conditions for the integrated development of areas such as the Yangtze River Delta will naturally reach maturity. Factor market reform is the essence of supply-side structural reform, and also the key building block for enhancing the resilience of our entire economic system and governance system for coping with future emergencies. Therefore, the government should target the above key directions with precise policies and targeted support.

https://doi.org/10.1142/9789811252921_0001

Chapter 1

Five Basic Facts About the Economic Impact of the COVID-19 Pandemic

Jun Zhang

School of Economics, Fudan University, Shanghai, China

Since the beginning of the current COVID-19 outbreak, there has been much discussion about the pandemic, especially in regards to how it will impact China's economy and various aspects of our society. Such questions have become a focal point in the media and the general public. In mid-February, the central government realized that China's massive economy could not be shut down indefinitely, and eventually proposed a "two-handed approach", with one hand set on prevention and control of the pandemic, and the other on the recovery of the economy and resumption of production. In some ways, we have already entered the second phase in prevention and control.

Since the end of January 2020, I have published a number of articles and participated in discussions about some of the changes that have occurred in the Chinese economy as a result of the pandemic. Rather than repeat these discussions, in this chapter I want to provide a few common-sense facts about the macroeconomic impact of the pandemic. "Common-sense facts" refer to basic knowledge that we should already be fully cognizant of and armed with. It is sometimes said that when discussing complex issues, what we often lack is not sophisticated theories, but rather common sense, which is easily forgotten. Sometimes, common sense can provide the simplest solution to the most complex of problems facing us. I think we should have an understanding of some basic knowledge when we think about and discuss the impact of the pandemic on the Chinese economy. To this end, this chapter will share and discuss five basic common-sense facts related to the impact of the pandemic on the Chinese economy.

1.1 The Impact of the Pandemic on China's Economy is Short-term

The first fact is that any single economy is an organic system that exhibits trend growth, whether it be single-digit growth (such as the level of growth seen in developed countries under normal conditions) or double-digit growth (such as the extraordinarily long spurt of growth China has maintained over the past few decades).

In either case, the economy will maintain trend growth under normal circumstances, rebounding and going through a recovery whenever external shocks are encountered. This is why we often say that external shocks will only divert the economy from its growth trend temporarily; as soon as the shock has passed, the economy will have a strong rebound and return to its original growth track.

We all know that wars and natural disasters (e.g., earthquakes, tsunamis) hit economies particularly hard, and that such shocks often destroy the productive capacity of the economy. After a war or natural disaster, an economy will undergo a massive reconstruction process to restore productive capacity through a large number of investment projects. However, for an especially large shock, the rebound will be stronger because it comes back from a lower starting point.

In the midst of this pandemic, strict national pandemic prevention policies have been adopted that restrict the movement of people, which may affect not only consumption but also production. Since workers who cannot return to their jobs on regular schedules and logistics are unable to distribute goods in a timely manner, the production of both the supply chain and downstream companies will be affected, and the longer the outbreak lasts, the greater the impact will be. However, growth will still rebound after the shock, and the larger the shock, the stronger the rebound.

Here, it may be instructive to review the impact of the SARS outbreak on the Chinese economy in 2003. In terms of magnitude, the outbreak occurred only during the second quarter of 2003; in terms of economics, real GDP growth fell by roughly 20% in the same period. The trend growth rate at the time was 10%, and afterwards the economy as a whole still maintained a real growth rate of 10%. In the long term, despite the SARS outbreak in 2003, the overall economic growth trend underwent little change. That the economy is able to rebound and recover from external shocks, almost like a living organism, should therefore be a basic common-sense fact.

Of course, economists tend to say that the economy will automatically rebound and return to its original trend growth trajectory after an external shock, but this actually hides a basic assumption: after an external shock, any government will enact appropriate countermeasures; inaction is never an option. This is similar to what has been said about the Kuznets curve in the past; Kuznets studied data from many countries over a long period of time and found that the gap between per capita income levels and income distribution shows an inverted U-shaped relationship. Later, many economists generalized this relationship to the environmental field, saying, for example, that the same inverted U-shaped relationship exists between improvements in environmental quality and per capita income. In the view of economists, this relationship can be seen as a regularity, but behind it is actually government policy, without which perhaps we would not be able to observe this relationship. The government needs to promptly adjust some of the policies already in place and introduce new ones to help the impacted enterprises and work units tide over difficult times when the economy encounters external shocks. Such measures will result in the relationship between an economic shock and the subsequent rebound and recovery of the economy as described above.

This is the first common-sense fact introduced in this chapter. That is, when the economy experiences a shock, it rebounds and there is a return to growth.

1.2 Shortening the Duration of the Pandemic is Conducive to Rapid Economic Recovery

The second common-sense fact relates to the duration of the pandemic, i.e., there is a relationship between the impact on the economy and the duration of the pandemic; the shorter the duration, the better, and for this reason it is necessary to adopt a very robust pandemic prevention policy.

There are three factors involved in this relationship: the duration of the pandemic, the severity of the pandemic prevention and control measures (e.g., they may lead to a temporary economic and social shutdown), and the extent of the pandemic's impact on the economy. There may be contradictions and tensions between these three, and ultimately it is up to us to carefully weigh the trade-offs in order to decide what to do.

Recently, many people have been discussing and reflecting on the question: Are the current measures taken in response to the outbreak at least somewhat excessive? Could there be a more scientific prevention policy that would reduce the negative impact on the economy? I have also published an article discussing whether what we are doing now is optimal from a global perspective.

I personally don't think the current measures are optimal. The reason is simple: we want to find a generalized solution for the whole country that is the most scientific and carries the least economic impact. However, we cannot satisfy such conditions because we have incomplete knowledge of the new coronavirus, and we have not yet found an effective treatment. Therefore, in this case an optimal approach can only be implemented on the local level, at each individual locality (which can be as small as a street or a village). The overall result for the country will be suboptimal, but it is better to suffer in the short term than in the long term, and if the optimal solution is beyond reach, then we should implement the next-best solution. Adopting rigorous preventive and control measures will admittedly have a large impact on the economy in the short term, but it will also shorten the duration of the pandemic and be extremely beneficial to the subsequent economic rebound and recovery. In other words, although stringent prevention and control is a suboptimal solution, it is well worth the price.

The point to emphasize here is that when economists say the economy will rebound on the basis of growth rate, they are not saying that this rebound will come completely naturally, without any need for policy adjustments. In this way it is similar to environmental protection; when we say that the quality of the environment will improve after the economy reaches a relatively high stage of development, we are not saying it will happen naturally or automatically, but that when the economy reaches a certain stage, people will start paying attention to the environment and consciously exert themselves in this direction, and only then will the environment improve. Therefore, when the pandemic is over, policy adjustments will be necessary for an economic rebound. In fact, policy adjustments are being made as of this writing, including the introduction of supportive policies in all regions for industries that are more affected by the pandemic, especially in the service sector, where there are more small, medium, and micro enterprises.

Let's take a simple example. A restaurant that closes its doors for several months has no revenue, but the owner still has to pay his employees' salaries and pay the rent. Under this kind of "stress test", a restaurant may be well able to last for one month, but after two months, the percentage of restaurants that can survive such conditions will decrease, and after three months only a tiny fraction of restaurants will still be in business. In such a situation, local governments should be encouraged to introduce many relief policies. Fiscally speaking, it will be necessary to bear more deficits during extraordinary times, as tax cuts and fee reductions for enterprises will cause short-term fiscal spending to increase and revenue to decrease. This means the government's fiscal deficit may widen a bit, but this is unavoidable given the special circumstances, just like times of war, the country will also increase financial spending.

In fact, similar response initiatives are now being implemented in every region. The pandemic is not over yet, and taking into account the "stress test", if the government does not launch a timely relief policy, many businesses may not be able to survive. In order to reduce some of the uncertainty that the economy may encounter later in the rebound, policies need to be put in place now. Moreover, policies can later be flexibly adjusted, including on the financial level, such as through loans, treasury bonds, local special bonds, etc. Such measures can also help the real economy to both survive and preserve strength. As the pandemic gets under control, demand will start to rebound. Once demand rebounds, many enterprises, including service sector enterprises, will accelerate the start of operations and quickly restore production capacity, thus further boosting the economic rebound.

Of course, local governments are more concerned about economic recovery and unemployment due to the impact of the pandemic on the local level. In the past, we often proposed measures to reduce taxes and fees, optimize the business environment, and support small and medium-sized enterprises, but this is a process of learning, because when the economy is not experiencing a shock, there is no real feeling of a crisis, and many local governments will be relatively idle. It is therefore entirely possible that the measures mentioned above will be implemented ineffectively. However, when it comes to emergencies, one doesn't even need to look at the statistics, just read the news and you will know that many industries are facing difficulties; in this case, the resolve of local governments must be greater than before.

Furthermore, it is a matter of horizontal comparison as to how well the economy of each region will rebound and recover after the pandemic is over. Horizontal competition is still a very important mechanism in China's governance model that local governments will pay attention to, hoping that their local economies will recover faster than others, that employment issues will be more secure, and that they will smoothly survive this special period. Unlike before, it may now be easier to reach a consensus, as it may be easier for local governments to make up their minds under the pain of the circumstances.

At the same time, some of the policies introduced during the current special period should be continued, because they were already in line with the general direction or goals of policy reform, and should not be withdrawn after the pandemic ends. For example, the 28 measures recently released in Shanghai also mention an option to extend the measures for an average of three months after the end of the pandemic. Of course, some of these supportive policies do not need to be retracted at all, such as the government's reduction of corporate taxes and fees, which were already a previous reform goal that hadn't been achieved; now that they have had the chance to be implemented, they should be kept in effect for the long term. In addition, there are some temporary policies that can be retracted later, such as enterprises in Yiwu City, Zhejiang Province, chartering buses to pick up employees for work, etc. This is what I call the second common-sense fact.

1.3 Putting the Impact of the Pandemic on GDP in Perspective

The third common-sense fact I want to discuss has to do with how the pandemic affects revenue and output. Here I would first like to clarify a question regarding the concept of GDP. Obviously, GDP is not statistically as large as revenue or output, which people don't always realize. When we say that the pandemic or pandemic prevention policies have caused some industries, especially in the consumer sector, to lose a certain amount of revenue, we are not actually talking about GDP. How big is the impact of the pandemic on GDP? This requires us to do a very good job of estimation.

When discussing the impact of the pandemic on China's GDP growth for the first quarter or for the year as a whole, many people forget what the concept of GDP actually is. Sometimes, common-sense knowledge is easily forgotten in the midst of these complex discussions. The third common-sense fact I want to discuss with everyone here is actually related to GDP. When we're talking about the economic impact of the pandemic and all this lost revenue and output that we're seeing, is that GDP? In reality, GDP is a total sum of value added; although the so-called "value added" for each industry is related to the revenue and output of each industry, the two concepts are not exactly the same. How much turnover and revenue did various industries lose in the first quarter of this year under the impact of the pandemic, and is this the same thing as lost GDP? In fact, it's not the same thing. What is counted in GDP is not the revenue or output of each industry, but only the value-added portion of it.

According to a report released recently by Ren Zeping's team at Evergrande Research Institute, the revenue lost by the tourism industry due to the pandemic during the Spring Festival in 2020 is expected to exceed 500 billion yuan when compared to tourism revenue in 2019. This loss is equivalent to about 2% of GDP in the first quarter of 2019. In addition, they also expect that due to the impact of the pandemic, this year's Spring Festival movie box office woes may lead to "zero growth" or even negative growth in movie box office revenue for the year. "Based on the current impact on the 2020 Chinese New Year, when considering only the three most impacted sectors –$7 billion in movie box office (market forecast) +$500 billion in restaurant retail (assuming a cutback) +$500 billion in the tourism market (complete freeze) — in just 7 days, the direct economic loss of over $1 trillion will be incurred, accounting for 4.6% of the $21.8 trillion GDP for Q1 2019." However, behind these figures lies a common-sense fact. Is the seven-day $1 trillion loss for these industries equivalent to a loss in GDP? In fact, this is not the case.

Let's start with what it means to have zero or negative GDP growth in the first quarter. Most ordinary people do not realize that GDP is the sum of the value added from each industry, not the sum of business revenue or output. As for how the value added is measured, it is actually very complicated.

As far as I know, the method of measuring value added varies for each industry and each subsector. Take tourism for example. The value added is measured according to the *Value Added Accounting Method for Tourism and Related Industries* developed by the National Bureau of Statistics, and the data required for the accounting are obtained from national economic accounting data and consumption structure survey data of tourism and related industries. The data is organized into a two-level classification method involving 85 industry subcategories. As one can see, the accounting for value added is quite complex, especially in the service sector. The average reader certainly does not need to know how the value added of each industry is measured, but we do need to know that what is actually included in GDP is value added, which is much smaller than an industry's revenue or output. Taking the tourism and restaurant industries as an example, data from the National Bureau of Statistics show that the total revenue of China's tourism industry in 2018 was about 5.97 trillion yuan, with an added value of 3.7 trillion yuan and a value-added rate of about 60%, while the total output value of the restaurant industry was about 3.9 trillion yuan, with an added value of 1459.41 billion yuan and a value-added rate of only about 35%.

Many people have commented online that GDP growth is likely to be negative in the first quarter of this year. I also see that some people are even more pessimistic, arguing that the concern is not whether there could be negative GDP growth in the first quarter of this year, but how much negative growth there will be, whether –5% or –10%. Therefore, it is necessary to briefly discuss how likely this is to happen.

In fact, nationally, the average value-added rate for all our industries combined would not exceed 30%, as most manufacturing industries have a value-added rate of less than 20% (although a few energy industries may have a value-added rate as high as 70%). Let's assume that the value added of each industry in the country accounts for 30% of its revenue or output, then we can deduce that a GDP of $21.8 trillion in the first quarter of 2019 would be equivalent to almost $65 trillion in revenue or output for all industries combined.

Based on the growth trends we have had over recent years, the Chinese economy has maintained an average nominal growth rate of about 8% per quarter, if not subject to external shocks (this is nominal at current prices, real growth at constant prices is in the range of 6–6.5%). Thus, our nominal GDP in the first quarter of this year should be at least 23.55 trillion yuan (GDP in the first quarter of last year was 21.8 trillion yuan, and according to the nominal growth rate of 8%, the total GDP by the first quarter of this year is 23.55 trillion yuan, which is a gain of 1.75 trillion yuan), which, if converted into revenue or output and multiplied by 3, is equivalent to about 71 trillion yuan. Compared to the first quarter of last year, GDP increased by 1.75 trillion yuan, which, multiplied by three, equals 6 trillion yuan. In order for the first quarter GDP to fall into zero growth or negative growth due to the impact of the pandemic, the decline in nominal GDP growth rate would first have to offset the original growth trend; that is, the nominal growth rate would need to fall by more than 8 percentage points. For such a steep fall to occur, the revenue or output of all industries in the first quarter would have to be reduced by about 6 trillion yuan or more. This gives us some room to objectively speculate on whether the pandemic is likely to be "fatal" in terms of lost revenue.

Many industries are reporting the revenue losses they have suffered. We should be aware, however, that there is significant crossover and double counting of these losses. Each industry accounts for its own revenue or output in terms of all sectors covered by the industry, but the results will be different when losses are viewed from the perspective of consumer spending. For example, when we travel, we spend on dining, shopping, hotel accommodation, entertainment, sightseeing, transportation, etc. The consumer data on these expenditures will be more realistic. When the income from tourism is calculated, the categories of restaurant, shopping, hotel accommodation, entertainment, sightseeing, and transportation are all included in the calculation. Generally speaking, the travel agency industry, the passenger transport industry, and the hospitality industry represented by hotels are the three pillars of tourism. The total revenue of China's tourism industry in 2018 was 5.97 trillion yuan, with an added value of 3.7 trillion yuan, a figure that has long since partially included revenue from the categories of restaurant, shopping, hospitality, entertainment, excursions, and transportation; likewise, the total output value of the restaurant industry of more than $4 trillion includes part of the revenue from the tourism industry. Therefore, we cannot simply add up the loss of revenue or income from, say, the restaurant, retail, and tourism industries, because there is too much double counting involved. The same applies to income and loss statistics for other industries in the service sector; simply adding up the loss of revenue across industries would overestimate the impact on the service sector as a whole. The consumption expenditure of households is part of the expenditure method of calculating GDP, but instead of simply adding up the income of various sectors of retail and service industries, the expenditure data of households are used for the calculation, which avoids the problem of double counting. This is the third common-sense fact I want to point out, which is about the relationship between revenue, output, and GDP — namely, that GDP is the value added, not the sum of revenue or output.

So just how much of an economic impact will the pandemic have? Based on the situation as described above, I predict a worst-case scenario of a substantially large decline in GDP for the first quarter of the year. If the pandemic is contained in the first quarter and economic activity recovers quickly in the second quarter, the economic downturn will be (at least partially) hedged out by the rebound growth in the second quarter. With macro policy adjustments in place that are conducive to growth recovery, economic growth will tend to accelerate from the second half of the year onwards. When considering the full year, as long as there are no new imported outbreaks or other shocks from outside, the ongoing policy adjustments and policies that kick-start domestic demand should be sufficient to ensure that the decline in GDP growth stays at about two percentage points.

Of course, there are prerequisites for such an estimate: first, the pandemic lasts for a relatively short period of time; second, there is no subsequent rebound of the pandemic or imported outbreaks; and third, economic activity recovers relatively quickly after the pandemic. Therefore, it is important that the government make huge adjustments to fiscal and monetary policies at the appropriate time, especially in favor of small and medium-sized enterprises and the service sector, which were greatly affected during the prevention and control of the pandemic, and make more use of credit policies, fiscal subsidies, and tax breaks to support them and ensure the maximum recovery of economic activity and employment.

1.4 Resolving the Supply Chain Crisis is the Key to Hedging against the Impact of the Pandemic

The fourth common-sense fact is about the supply chain. If the negative impact on consumption is the "flesh wound" inflicted by the pandemic on the economy, then we must understand that the biggest point of impact on the economy will be the supply chain crisis; it is like "breaking the bones" that allow the economy to move.

How serious will the supply chain crisis be? Previously, we may not have realized the importance of the supply chain and its place in the Chinese and global supply chains. Now, in light of the pandemic, we can see that the supply chain is the "blood system" of our economy. If the economy shuts down, then it must be the result of a supply chain crisis.

The existence of the supply chain allows the whole division of production labor, which in the past was horizontal, to be longitudinal or vertical. In fact, this has become the new mode of division of labor and specialization in the era of globalization, and because of this, traditional trade has given way to the trading of added value. The same applies to both international and domestic industries. Therefore, the global chain refers to a supply chain system that transcends national boundaries. The supply chain involves every country and couples the economies between different countries, so that the global economy is interdependent and no one country can be isolated from the others. This pandemic has shown us the importance of the supply chain and the real presence of globalization. Wuhan's "city closure" has had a major impact on the international auto market. Some believe that the outbreak in China is the best time to decouple the U.S. and Chinese economies. The implication is that the U.S. wants to use the pandemic as an opportunity to move the industry chain out of China and back to the U.S. I think it's just a pipe dream.

It is because of the supply chain that every downstream company has inventory. Inventories play a large role in macroeconomic fluctuations. For the enterprise itself, inventory is also very important for responding to uncertainty and unexpected events. Of course, inventory can also cushion the impact of the pandemic on manufacturing enterprises. However, inventory takes up capital and resources, so inventory volume cannot be too large. In this pandemic, we have seen real-world cases where companies are less affected by the pandemic because they have kept their inventory in stock for a longer period of time.

For example, the automotive industry has a large presence in Wuhan, Huanggang, Yichang, Shiyan, and other cities in Hubei. Data from the Hubei Automobile Industry Association shows that in Hubei Province there are more than 1,300 auto parts enterprises that make more than 20 million yuan annually (via their main business operations), and according to statistics from the China Automobile Association, there are more than 13,000 auto parts enterprises that make more than 20 million yuan annually (via their main business operations) in China, which means that about one-tenth of the country's auto parts enterprises that make more than 20 million yuan annually (via their main business operations) are in Hubei Province.

"Car companies will not have very many simple parts in reserve, and the inventory cycle of core parts is relatively long. Generally speaking, the inventory period of auto parts is about 1 month on average. If we cannot resume work for a long time, it will affect the production in other domestic provinces as well as overseas factories," Xue Jiang, who has worked in an auto parts company in Hubei for many years, told reporters.

In addition, there is a large amount of foreign investment in Hubei, and Japanese and Korean auto companies are also greatly affected. Taking Korean car companies as an example, statistically speaking, 87% of their wiring harness parts come from China. Currently, South Korea's Hyundai and Kia Motors are suffering from supply chain disruptions, with their three wiring harness suppliers — Yura, Kyungshin, and TNH — all having factories in China. A few days ago, South Korea's Hyundai Motor announced that the company will suspend production in South Korea due to the disruption of parts supply. This makes Hyundai the first multinational automaker in the world to suspend production outside of China due to supply chain disruptions caused by the pandemic.

Therefore, to prevent further serious economic impacts from the pandemic, we must start by getting a strong handle on the recovery and stability of the supply chain. The shutdown must not be too long, and we must resume work and production as soon as possible. If we begin with the leading and core companies in the supply chain, it will have extraordinary significance not only for our own manufacturing industry, but also for the global supply chain and the global economy.

1.5 Small, Medium and Micro Enterprises Should Be the Main Targets of Post-pandemic Relief and Assistance

The fifth common-sense fact we should know is that the weakest and most vulnerable economic agents will be hit the hardest, as is true for any country. So in economic terms, who is the weakest and most vulnerable group? It is the micro, small, and medium enterprises. This common-sense fact tells us that the most seriously threatened by the pandemic are the micro, small, and medium enterprises (MSMEs). In order to ensure the future recovery and rebound of the economy, MSMEs should be the target of government bailouts to help them tide over these extraordinary times.

The number of MSMEs is huge, tens of thousands are born and tens of thousands die every day. There are about 80 million in total, of which more than 20 million are small and medium-sized enterprise legal persons and more than 60 million are individual businesspersons. MSMEs account for 95% of the total number of enterprises in the country and can be said to be the living cells of the whole economy. They are distributed across the manufacturing and service sectors, with the service sector accounting for the majority. In previous years, the state introduced tax incentives to support the development of small and medium-sized enterprises. The starting point for tax benefits has been raised from $500,000 to $1 million. Of course, the size of MSMEs varies from industry to industry, with some industries having a workforce of 10–20 and some over 100. Although MSMEs have different sizes across different industries, in general they account for the majority of any given industry, yet they are also vulnerable and have no advantages in financing, technology, human capital, etc. Although they make up the majority, they are the least resilient to risk.

A few years ago, in order to meet the needs of macroeconomic management and national economic accounting, the National Bureau of Statistics established the *Sample Survey on Small and Micro Enterprises*, which covered main economic indicators, questionnaires, and basic information on the survey sample. A system was set up to conduct a sample survey for mapping the basic situation of MSMEs and making estimates on the contribution of MSMEs in GDP. Because MSMEs are too small to be included in the online direct reporting system, estimates can only be based on basic data obtained through sample surveys. The current estimates are that MSMEs contribute about 60% of the overall GDP, create about 70% of the employment, and pay about 50% of the taxes. This is the significance of MSMEs in the Chinese economy. For this reason, the state attaches great importance to small and medium-sized enterprises, and regularly introduces supportive policies. In any country, MSMEs are not very resilient, although they are the majority enterprise type in the economy. Any pandemic, any disaster, will hit them the hardest.

Under the pandemic, the impacted MSMEs are especially vulnerable, so national policy should first implement bailouts or fiscal and monetary policy relief for MSMEs. Such measures would include rent reductions, tax reductions, and requests for local banks to grant loan extensions without withdrawing or cutting off loans or reducing interest rates.

The above-mentioned five basic common-sense facts will give us a more objective understanding and a more scientific judgment of the economic impact of the pandemic, especially on GDP growth in the first quarter of this year and throughout the year, and will give us a better grasp of what kinds of policies the country should introduce and readjust during the pandemic, where to start from, and where to aim.

It is hoped that the contents of this chapter will be a useful reference for the wider community to observe and understand the impact of the pandemic on our economy.

https://doi.org/10.1142/9789811252921_0002

Chapter 2

Industry Dynamics Under the Impact of the COVID-19 Pandemic

Kou Zonglai

School of Economics, Fudan University, Shanghai, China

This chapter will first provide a general analysis of the impact of the COVID-19 pandemic in terms of division of labor and specialization. We will then analyze the economic impact of the COVID-19 pandemic and the policy responses from several different dimensions, giving particular attention to the measures and costs of targeted relief for MSMEs and how to understand the transmutation of business models in "crises" and "opportunities".

2.1 How Can We Know the Overall Impact of the COVID-19 Pandemic?

In contrast to the traditional economy of "self-sufficiency", the essence of the modern economy is the high degree of division of labor and specialization, as well as the resulting trade and interconnectedness between people, enterprises, and even countries. If the shock from the pandemic can be seen as pressing the "pause button" on the functioning of the economic system, then in a theoretical sense, however important the division of labor, specialization, and trade are to the modern economy, the economic impact from the pandemic will be equally as large, at least in the short term.

Given the complexity of the economic system and the lag in available statistics, one would still like to quantitatively estimate roughly how large the negative impact of this pandemic actually is. A natural reference point is SARS in 2003, as it similarly was a coronavirus outbreak that caused a national panic. According to historical data, although SARS caused substantial economic downturn in the short term, the effect of its negative impact was barely observable on the time scale of the entire year of 2003. Some analysts therefore believe that if the COVID-19 pandemic can be effectively controlled in the near future, its negative impact on the Chinese economy will be almost negligible.

We believe that such an estimate may be overly optimistic and may seriously underestimate the negative effects of the shock from the pandemic. The main reason is that, compared to 2003, the Chinese economy is now significantly different in several ways: first, the Chinese economy now has a much greater degree of internal integration. Second, the industrial structure of China's economy has undergone a fundamental change, with the service sector dominating, which is "person-to-person contact intensive". Third, since its accession to the WTO in 2001, China's integration into international trade and division of labor has increased significantly, and manufacturing in China has become a vital link for the division of labor in the international industrial chain. Fourth, due to its dependence on real estate over the past twelve years or so, China's economy is at risk of "devolving into a fictitious economy". This puts a very big question mark over the effectiveness of relying on real estate stimuli to maintain growth. Fifth, judging by the most recent developments, the COVID-19 pandemic has evolved into a global pandemic. As a result, the entirety of international trade will be hit hard, and this will certainly be a huge negative impact on China's economy, which is already highly integrated into the world economy. Taking the above points together, we believe it is implausible to simply use the impact of SARS as a frame of reference and make an overly optimistic conclusion about the limitations of the negative impact of the COVID-19 pandemic.

In sharp contrast to the underestimation of the negative impact mentioned above, some argue that the COVID-19 pandemic will hit the Chinese economy hard and set it back many years, particularly by exposing the Chinese economy to the huge challenge of accelerating the relocation of the international industrial chain. First, as China's labor costs have risen sharply in recent years, the country's competitive advantage in labor-intensive industries has declined, and there are already many companies considering moving from China to other developing countries such as Vietnam and India. Second, the pandemic has temporarily halted China's economy, severely disrupted cross-regional transportation, and made it difficult for companies to effectively resume work and production, all of which have caused huge losses for multinational companies investing in China. This in turn will inevitably increase their incentive and determination to move their industries out of China.

As mentioned above, while the negative impact of the pandemic cannot be underestimated, and while it cannot be denied that there has indeed been a relocation of industries from China to other developing countries in recent years, we do not believe that this should be used to draw the overall conclusion that the pandemic will accelerate the relocation of the industrial chain to regions outside of China. First of all, multinational companies enter China for a wide variety of motives; some want to take advantage of China's cheap labor, some are attracted by China's good infrastructure, some are trying to take advantage of China's capacity to support the entire industrial chain, and some are taking aim at China's enormous consumer market. Of course, more often than not, these factors are working together simultaneously. Taking these motives into account collectively, the only multinational companies that have a strong incentive to move their operations out of China are those whose production is particularly dependent on cheap labor, do not require much industrial chain support, do not need good infrastructure, and do not have China as a major sales market. Second, the effect of rising labor wages must also be viewed in two ways. On the one hand, on the production side, rising labor wages do raise the cost of labor for enterprises, which can increase their incentive to move out of China. On the other hand, on the demand side, rising labor wages imply an increase in the purchasing power of the population and in the attractiveness of the Chinese market, which in turn reduces the incentive for enterprises to move out of China.

Further, specific to the topic of this chapter, those who conclude that the COVID-19 pandemic will accelerate the industrial flight of multinational companies do so on the implicit premise that the pandemic is only occurring in China and not in other countries. However, it is clear that the reality has largely falsified this presupposition. In short, for MNCs, there are costs associated with industrial relocation, and while they can make the decision to relocate simply because of a COVID-19 outbreak in China, they have absolutely no way to ensure that an outbreak will not occur in the destination country to which they are relocating. It is in fact possible that the opposite is actually the case. Based on the evolving dynamics of the pandemic, we can even infer that China may become the country with the lowest level of "pandemic uncertainty" for some time to come, precisely because of the strong precautionary measures taken. It is important to emphasize that the most difficult issue to deal with in both personal and business decisions is uncertainty, i.e., the "unknown unknowns". Although the Chinese economy has been hit hard by the pandemic, once that hit has materialized and become a "sunk cost", staying in China is the safest investment decision because there is very little uncertainty about the pandemic going forward. The importance of the "home market effect" should also be further emphasized. With the emergence of a global COIVD-19 pandemic, international trade will be hit hard, and the whole world will temporarily enter a "lonely country" state, and in this case, companies staying in China will have a greater chance of survival thanks to China's enormous consumer market. In the light of the above analysis, we believe that while the negative impact of the pandemic should not be underestimated, the risk of industry chain relocation catalyzed by the pandemic should not be exaggerated either.

2.2 Using Differentiated Measures[1] in Order to Respond Effectively to the Negative Impact of the Pandemic

Following the previous discussion of the overall impact of the COVID-19 pandemic, it is important to emphasize the discussion around "differentiated measures", as the same pandemic can have different effects on different market players, and different policy measures will yield different heterogeneous effects. This is the reality we are faced with, and we should do well to accept it. Confronted with the impact from the pandemic, the most pressing matter is to enact differentiated measures in order to respond effectively to the various serious negative effects of the pandemic. The pandemic had a huge impact on the whole of society, not only because of the direct loss of life and assets among the general population, but also because of the social panic it generated and the extensive quarantine measures enacted afterwards by the state and individuals to stave off the pandemic, which led to a temporary standstill of the whole Chinese

[1] http://www.xinhuanet.com/english/2020-02/14/c_138782385.htm.

economy. Therefore, on the one hand, it is obviously necessary to "put the fire out at its source" in order to reduce the damage incurred, that is, to truly bring the pandemic under control and eradicate it. This can be done by finding and improving medical treatment options. On the other hand, on the basis of scientific assessment of the risk of outbreaks, we should resume work, resume production, open up the cities, and open the schools in a differentiated and step-by-step manner (for the sake of convenience, unless otherwise specified, we will collectively refer to these as "resumption of work" and "return to work"), so as to gradually restore all economic and social operations back to the normal track.

Given the regional nature of the spread of the pandemic, the country has adopted the principle of regionalization in its response to the pandemic. The first key point in implementing differentiated measures is therefore to scientifically assess the risk of the pandemic in different regions. Given the variation in risk for different regions, areas that are at low risk from the pandemic should be the first to resume work, at least in principle. But things are clearly not that simple. Modern economies have a high level of specialization and division of labor, and the scope of many economic activities will inevitably transcend artificially drawn administrative boundaries. In particular, if there is an upstream and downstream relationship between enterprises in a low-risk area and those in a high-risk area, it is difficult for enterprises in the low-risk area to resume work until an effective alternative is found.

Combining the above analysis as shown in Figure 2.1, there are four basic scenarios for differentiated measures based on the risks and benefits of resumption of work. In the first scenario, the resumption of work is highly beneficial, but the associated risk is also high. Whether it is because an entire industrial chain is located in areas with severe outbreaks, or because some important parts of the chain are located in areas with severe outbreaks, the country will, at least in the short term, have to

Policy Measures		Benefit from resuming work	
		Large	Small
Risk level of resuming work	High	Seek industry chain alternatives	Continue tough control measures
	Low	Resume work immediately	Continue waiting, resume work on an opportunistic basis

Figure 2.1: Differentiated measures for resumption of work.

look elsewhere for domestic alternatives to the entire chain or parts of the chain. In this scenario, the state must also follow-up with precise support measures to offset the long-term negative impact of these inter-regional industry chain shifts on areas with severe outbreaks. In the second scenario, there is a high benefit to resuming work and low risk. In this case, the immediate resumption of work is obviously the best choice, but actual implementation is likely to be difficult due to the hesitancy of local governments to take responsibility for such measures. Officials who prefer the "lazy governance" of "non-action" are enthusiastic about keeping strict pandemic prevention measures in place; this is because strict measures allow officials to minimize the political risk created by new COVID cases in their districts while simultaneously allowing them to use the excuse of "thorough pandemic prevention measures" to cover up any deficiencies that arise during the resumption of work and production.

In the third scenario, resuming work carries a large risk and little benefit. The best option for this scenario would be to continue stringent control measures to prevent the spread of the pandemic and its serious impact on society. However, in the specific implementation process, the state must provide strong external assistance to the enterprises, individuals, and various units involved. Such external assistance not only has a basis in the spirit of humaneness, but is also in line with the basic principles of economics. Because the pandemic is a contagious disease, restricting the freedom of movement of people in these areas is essentially providing a public good to society. In the fourth scenario, resuming work involves both little risk and little benefit. In this case, considering the huge harm that may be caused by the spread of the pandemic, a policy of continued waiting and opportunistic resumption of work is recommended as a safe option.

2.3 Providing Relief for Small, Micro, and Medium Enterprises

In the face of impact from the pandemic, the question of how to precisely and effectively provide relief for MSMEs is a major one worthy of special discussion. There are at least three main reasons why special emphasis should be placed on relief for MSMEs.

First, MSMEs not only suffer the most severe negative effects of the pandemic, but also have very low risk tolerance and transferability compared to large enterprises, and many will go bankrupt if they do not receive timely and strong relief. In terms of industrial classification, the vast majority of MSMEs are in the service sector. Considering that service industries such as restaurants, travel, and entertainment are "people-intensive," the most immediate and powerful impact of the COVID-19 pandemic is the disruption of offline human interaction, whether caused voluntarily by people fearing infection or by government mandates to prevent the spread of the virus. In the restaurant industry, for example, during the Chinese New Year, when the pandemic control measures were at their most stringent, almost all restaurants were closed, whereas under normal circumstances the holiday is a peak season for many restaurants to bring in revenue from New Year's Eve dinners. To add insult to injury, even if restaurants are now allowed to reopen, the majority of consumers will try to avoid eating out because of the panic generated by the pandemic. This means that the impact of the COVID-19 outbreak on the restaurant industry will be more long-lasting than the outbreak itself, and it may take at least a few months after the end of the outbreak before the restaurant industry can truly return to pre-pandemic levels.

Due to the highly interconnected nature of the modern economy and roundabout production, each enterprise has upstream and downstream relationships with other enterprises and even with the final consumer in the chain. Therefore, no matter which link is hit by a negative external shock, the negative effects of the shock will in principle not be fully borne by the link directly hit, but will be more or less transferred to other links of the chain. The less substitutable a player is in the industrial chain, or the greater the player's market power, the greater its ability to transfer an external shock. Considering that the vast majority of MSMEs are nearly "in full competition" and highly substitutable in the chain, it is difficult for them to transfer the negative impact from the pandemic on to other parts of the chain. Although previous media reports pointed out that during the pandemic, stronger restaurant chains such as Xibei Restaurants achieved good results by vigorously developing their take-out business, it is very difficult for the majority of small and medium-sized enterprises to make effective adjustments to their business models in the short term, whether because of business characteristics or because of the limitations of their own capabilities, and they cannot be expected to do so. In short, without external relief measures, they are essentially left alone to bear the economic losses of the pandemic.

As such, can MSMEs bear and withstand the negative impact of the pandemic on their own? The basic conclusion should be clear: without strong external relief measures, the majority of MSMEs will find it difficult to bear the negative impact. First, as mentioned earlier, the majority of MSMEs belong to the service industry, and the impact on their business is very large and difficult to pass on. At least for two to three months from the beginning of the pandemic, year-over-year revenue will drop sharply, and many enterprises may even have no income at all. Second, for MSMEs, existence itself carries many rigid costs such as rent, wages, social security, and taxes, and according to the "small profit" characteristics of most MSMEs, these costs are roughly equal to their operating income during normal operation. Again, based on the micro-profit characteristics of MSMEs, they will have very limited cash flow and profit retention. Finally, from the point of view of the banks, compared with large enterprises, MSMEs are variable and risky, thus making it difficult to obtain bank loans. Even if they can obtain financing through formal or informal channels, their capital costs are relatively higher, which is the case in all countries around the world.

However, the Chinese financial system also has a unique factor that is even more detrimental to MSMEs, namely the existence of so-called ownership differences: Considering that the majority of MSMEs are private enterprises, it is more difficult for them to obtain financing support from formal channels than state-owned enterprises, even without considering the factor of size. Putting the above points together it is not difficult to draw the inference that given the sharp decline in MSMEs' operating income due to the impact of the pandemic, the rigidity of their costs means that they will inevitably suffer severe losses. Furthermore, if the impact of the pandemic is difficult to overcome in the short term, the very limited cash flow, profit retention, and equally limited external financial resources they hold will not only be unsustainable, but will also provide a strong incentive to pursue a "stop-loss", i.e., a move to declare bankruptcy, due to the bleak prospects for profitability.

Second, due to their large numbers, active MSMEs are extremely important for maintaining the operational efficiency of the economic system. Both economic theory and empirical evidence suggest that innovation and technological progress are the most important drivers of long-term economic growth, and major technological innovations are as likely to be accomplished by large firms as they are by small ones. As China's economy enters a new normal, the original crude growth model characterized by large-scale factor mobilization has become unsustainable. For this reason, the Chinese government has proposed an innovation-driven development strategy with the aim of making the great transition from "Made in China" to "Created in China". To achieve this strategic goal, we cannot rely on large enterprises or small enterprises alone, but rather we should create an industrial ecology that allows large and small enterprises to compete in an orderly, symbiotic, and win–win manner, allowing both to employ their respective innovative advantages.

Once new technologies are introduced, old technologies will be replaced and technological innovation will be "self-replacing" in nature. As Nobel laureate Kenneth Arrow pointed out, larger enterprises will be more reluctant to innovate because of greater "incumbency advantage". On the other hand, as Schumpeter emphasized, innovation is also a process of "creative destruction". Many small enterprises enter the market through technological innovation and eventually replace the original incumbents to become large enterprises, which must also innovate in order to retain their huge "incumbency profits" in the face of strong entry threats. In this sense, the threat of entry from innovative small enterprises is a necessary condition for "spurring" large enterprises to continue to innovate.

Not only is there a competitive relationship between large and small enterprises, but in many cases, especially in the field of innovation, the two may also present a symbiotic and win–win relationship. This primarily involves the acquisition and integration of small enterprises and their technologies by large ones. Specifically, technological innovation not only presents many possibilities, but also carries a great deal of uncertainty. Even big companies such as Apple, Tencent, and Alibaba cannot afford to explore all possible innovative solutions on their own. In fact, they do not need to do so, because with the exception of core innovation projects that require large investments, large companies can "outsource" other innovation activities to smaller companies and then select and acquire the most suitable small companies or their technologies according to their actual needs. From the perspective of large companies, despite the potentially high cost of acquisition "after the fact", the cost still outweighs the risks involved in technology development. Moreover, because the acquired companies have often already passed the initial tests of the market, the commercialization risk of the integrated products is relatively low. The vast majority of the technology in Apple's phones, for example, was not developed by Apple itself, but was acquired and integrated in the marketplace. For innovative small businesses, being acquired by a large corporation has been an important way for venture capital to exit and innovators to benefit, in addition to public offerings (IPOs) and management buyouts (MBOs). Since large enterprises have a high market share and strong marketing capabilities, the social value created by the acquisition and integration of the same technology by large enterprises is also greater, and thus the benefits to the innovator after the acquisition are likely to be much higher than the benefits obtained by promoting the products or technologies themselves. In this case, large enterprises and MSMEs form a beneficial symbiotic relationship in which both sides win.

Thirdly, and most importantly, MSMEs play a vital role in solving the issue of employment. According to the Fourth National Economic Census, at the end of 2018, there were 18.07 million small and medium-sized enterprises in China, accounting for 99.8% of all enterprises; small and medium-sized enterprises collectively employed 233.04 million people, accounting for 79.4% of the total number of employed people in all enterprises. Since the Fourth National Economic Census has not yet published the number of MSMEs and employed persons for each province and municipality, the number of MSMEs and their employees in each province and municipality can be roughly estimated by combining the total number of enterprises and the total number of employed persons in each province and municipality, as shown in Table 2.1.

Table 2.1 Number of MSMEs and employed persons by province, autonomous region, and municipality in China at the end of 2018.

	Number of enterprises (10,000)	Number of employed persons (10,000)
Beijing	86.1	839.1
Tianjin	25.3	301.1
Hebei	100.3	883.5
Shanxi	36.1	471.5
Inner Mongolia	22.5	290.3
Liaoning	52.3	548.5
Jilin	14.6	253.9
Heilongjiang	20.0	290.7
Shanghai	38.4	732.3

(*Continued*)

Table 2.1 (*Continued*)

	Number of enterprises (10,000)	Number of employed persons (10,000)
Jiangsu	178.9	2,388.9
Zhejiang	134.6	1794.7
Anhui	63.5	830.6
Fujian	61.2	1049.4
Jiangxi	35.5	599.6
Shandong	156.9	1708.4
Henan	99.9	1449.9
Hubei	66.6	942.7
Hunan	48.7	820.8
Guangdong	272.4	2803.4
Guangxi	37.1	456.5
Hainan	8.7	96.0
Chongqing	38.8	595.3
Sichuan	57.7	1066.7
Guizhou	26.4	357.1
Yunnan	34.3	438.4
Tibet	3.6	48.9
Shaanxi	40.3	564.2
Gansu	17.4	240.2
Qinghai	5.5	71.9
Ningxia	5.2	82.7
Xinjiang	18.4	283.0
Total	1,807	23,300.4

In all things, success lies in preparation. Although we hope that the pandemic will soon be over, we must prepare for the worst in the "protracted war" of pandemic prevention and control, and take precise and strong policy measures to rescue small, medium, and micro enterprises and protect the employment of the low-income class at a manageable cost, so as to prevent the COVID-19 pandemic from becoming a serious economic pandemic as well. Our recommended policy measures include the following four specific elements.

(1) Issue an administrative order from the central bank prohibiting commercial banks from drawing loans to MSMEs during the pandemic and within six months of the end of the pandemic and automatically extending credit that has expired by six months. Faced with the negative impact of the pandemic, the prospect of profitability suddenly becomes very bleak for many MSMEs. Without strong administrative intervention from the central bank, every commercial bank will compete to withdraw loans from these MSMEs for "risk control" reasons, leading to and accelerating the bankruptcy and liquidation of MSMEs, thus plunging the economy into a "self-fulfilling" economic pandemic.
(2) Define the COVID-19 pandemic as a "force majeure" and require real estate lessors to reduce the rent collected from MSMEs by half until the end of the pandemic so that all may survive the ordeal together. While there are certainly market negotiations between landlords and tenants, and it is true that some large companies have already offered rent reductions to their tenants, we suspect that a larger number of MSMEs may not be receiving rent reductions from their landlords and thus must fully absorb the negative impact of the pandemic. A "force majeure" approach not only provides a "reference point" for negotiations between the landlord and the tenant, but can also significantly reduce the costs of such negotiations.
(3) To effectively and efficiently reduce the burden on MSMEs, waive the social security contribution they are required to make during the pandemic, and reduce it by half for the three-month period following the declaration of the end of the pandemic. According to our understanding, there are already some places that have introduced relief measures to defer the payment of social security as well as temporary partial refund of social security. These measures are all well and good, but they do not essentially solve the huge dilemma of "continued expenses but no revenue" that these enterprises face. Since the deferred social security will still need to be paid in the future, its effect is equivalent to providing a loan to MSMEs, which can supplement their liquidity but cannot improve their profitability prospects, and also increases their gearing or "leverage". In other words, such measures must work on the basic premise that MSMEs will not close down, but the problem that needs to be solved is to prevent a large number of MSMEs from opting for bankruptcy and liquidation in face of the "continued expenses but no income" dilemma. Based on the

above analysis, we believe that adequate social security-related policies should be put in place all at once in order to increase the likelihood of MSMEs' persistence and survival by effectively reducing their burden.

(4) Using the past year's social security contributions as a benchmark, the state should set up a special relief fund for (MSMEs) and those employed in MSMEs whose wages are less than 60% of the average local wage. The relief fund should directly pay these employees the equivalent of the "minimum wage" through their social security accounts until the end of the pandemic. In addition, a "Five Insurance and One Pension" should be provided, using the lowest level of social security contributions as a benchmark.

It is more logical for this measure to be implemented at the central level. For one, most local governments, with the exception of a few developed provinces and cities, do not have the financial resources to do so. Second, given the existence of cross-regional mobility in employment, local governments are not sufficiently motivated to adopt such a measure. This measure would have the following three benefits:

First, by effectively reducing the labor costs of MSMEs, it can serve to stabilize the confidence of entrepreneurs and thus increase the survival rate of MSMEs and reduce the risk of unemployment.

Second, it can provide basic livelihood security for low-income employed people, which in turn can play a role in calming the populace and eliminating social instability. At the same time, this measure can also stimulate consumption due to the high Engel coefficient seen in the low-income class. A large number of randomized controlled experiments (RCTs) conducted by Professor Gan Li's team at Southwest University of Finance and Economics showed that income subsidies for low-income workers already engaged in the workforce provide a very substantial economic boost.

Third, and crucially important, although this is an extraordinary measure, its cost is very manageable. According to our highest estimate, the number of employed people affected by government subsidies to MSMEs would be about 39.983 million, and the amount spent each month would be 125.59 billion yuan, of which 78.57 billion yuan would account for wage subsidies and 47.02 billion yuan for social security cost subsidies (the details are shown in Table 2.2). If the pandemic lasts for three months, the government would spend 376.77 billion yuan on subsidies;

even if the pandemic lasts for six months, the total expenditure of about 753.54 billion yuan is still affordable.

In addition, it should be emphasized that the above amount actually overestimates the social cost of rescuing MSMEs once the economic "opportunity cost" is taken into account. A classic illustration of this principle is as follows: if a country invests more in education up front, it can save money on prison costs later. By the same reasoning, in the event of a massive bankruptcy of MSMEs and the resulting mass unemployment, the state will have to spend even more to cover the costs of maintaining stability. This means that in order to calculate the true cost of bailing out MSMEs, we must also account for the future cost of maintaining stability in the absence of bailout measures.

China's current social security payment policy stipulates that for employees whose wages are lower than 60% of the local average from the previous year, the social security payment base will be 60% of the local average wage from the previous year. Accordingly, in order to estimate the amount of subsidies and the required funds, we designated employees of enterprises with annual wages lower than 60% of the average wage of the previous year in the same province (or region or municipality) as the low-income labor force, and then calculated the percentage of low-income labor force within MSMEs in each province (or region or municipality) using 2019 employment data from Chinese enterprises and the average wage of each province (or region or municipality) from 2018[1]. We then used the number of MSMEs employed in each province (or region or municipality) multiplied by the percentage of low-income labor force to get a rough estimate of the number of low-income laborers within MSMEs in each province (or region or municipality). Taking into account the highest minimum wage in each province (or region or municipality), the wage subsidy for a given area will be equal to the number of MSMEs' employees to be subsidized multiplied by the corresponding minimum wage. In this case, the social security subsidy will be equal to the number of MSMEs in each province (or region or municipality) that need to be subsidized multiplied by 60% of the average local wage from the previous year, and then multiplied by the social security rate that the enterprise should pay. Finally, the total amount of government subsidies should be equal to the sum of the wage subsidies and the social security subsidies. The distribution of the total amount of estimated subsidies for each locality is shown in Table 2.2.

Table 2.2 Impact of the pandemic and amount of subsidies the government can introduce.

	Number of affected enterprises (10,000)	Number of subsidized employees (10,000)	Total monthly subsidy (hundred million yuan)	Monthly subsidized salary (hundred million yuan)	Monthly subsidized social security (hundred million yuan)
Beijing	86.1	385.7	158.6	84.9	73.7
Tianjin	25.3	132.7	44.8	27.2	17.6
Hebei	100.3	147.9	41.6	28.1	13.5
Shanxi	36.1	97.1	24.9	16.5	8.4
Inner Mongolia	22.5	62.5	17.0	11.0	6.0
Liaoning	52.3	91.5	24.6	16.6	8.1
Jilin	14.6	48.2	12.9	8.6	4.3
Heilongjiang	20.0	54.4	13.7	9.1	4.5
Shanghai	38.4	328.7	141.4	81.5	59.9
Jiangsu	178.9	376.9	117.8	76.1	41.6
Zhejiang	134.6	270.4	85.7	54.3	31.3
Anhui	63.5	116.2	29.5	18.0	11.4
Fujian	61.2	122.0	33.8	22.0	11.9
Jiangxi	35.5	66.4	17.1	11.2	6.0
Shandong	156.9	252.2	72.3	48.2	24.2
Henan	99.9	160.9	43.7	30.6	13.2
Hubei	66.6	136.2	37.0	23.8	13.2
Hunan	48.7	60.5	15.9	10.3	5.7
Guangdong	272.4	381.1	127.5	83.8	43.6
Guangxi	37.1	60.5	16.6	11.0	5.7
Hainan	8.7	17.1	4.6	2.9	1.7
Chongqing	38.8	108.9	31.0	19.6	11.4
Sichuan	57.7	171.9	48.2	30.6	17.6
Guizhou	26.4	62.2	17.7	11.1	6.5
Yunnan	34.3	106.0	28.6	17.7	10.9
Tibet	3.6	12.1	3.9	2.0	1.9
Shaanxi	40.3	62.5	17.2	11.2	6.0
Gansu	17.4	41.5	10.6	6.7	3.9
Qinghai	5.5	14.3	4.0	2.4	1.6
Ningxia	5.2	20.8	5.6	3.5	2.2
Xinjiang	18.4	28.9	8.1	5.3	2.8
Total	1807	3998.3	1255.9	785.7	470.2

There must be many who find the suggestion of a direct income supplement absolutely inconceivable, but it is not. The biggest challenge in human decision-making is uncertainty, i.e., "not knowing what you don't know", and the greatest advantage of our solution is that it uses a controllable cost to prevent the social costs of unpredictable outcomes. On a similar note, many have suggested that in order to "preserve growth", the country should carry out a large-scale stimulus program for the "railways and public transport". We believe that such a program may indeed play a role in "preserving growth" in the short term, but without considering the various negative effects it may have in the long term, it is very doubtful whether a "flood" of stimulus can provide precise, targeted relief to MSMEs.

2.4 Analysis of the Dynamic Effects of the Impact of the COVID-19 Pandemic

According to Le Chatelier's principle, any system subjected to an external shock must produce a countervailing power to offset the effect of that external shock. It is in this sense that a crisis is not just a crisis, but "an opportunity". When looking at the COVID-19 pandemic, it is important to take a dynamic, holistic view rather than a static, isolated view. This section will use several examples to illustrate the dynamic impact of the pandemic on existing industries and the business model transformations that it may catalyze.

First, the shock of the pandemic will have a dynamic impact on the mobile travel industry marked by an initial depression and then a resurgence.

Analyzing the short-term effects is relatively simple; the pandemic will certainly have a large impact on the mobile travel industry. Reaching this conclusion does not require any knowledge of economics, just take a look at the streets: The streets and alleys are all empty. Everyone is afraid of infection, opting to stay at home reading books, catching up on TV dramas, and scrolling social media, so naturally it can't be an easy time for the mobile travel industry.

Long-term effects are both the easiest and hardest to analyze. They are easy to analyze in the sense that "in the long run, we are all dead"; people in the distant future are unlikely to care what conclusions we have come to in our analysis today. Even so, we believe that from a long-term perspective, the current mobile travel model will be severely challenged by new technologies and business models such as artificial intelligence and driverless transportation, because once technological advances allow driverless transportation to become safer and cheaper, the market will inevitably move in the direction of not needing drivers. However, just as the replacement of manual labor by machines at the beginning of the industrial revolution led to a strong "Luddite backlash", driverless transportation is bound to face resistance from driver groups worldwide; governments around the world will intervene, to a greater or lesser extent, in the creation and industrial application of driverless technology for reasons of social stability and distributive justice. If we must link the pandemic to mobile travel, it seems safe to say that fear of the pandemic will marginally promote driverless transportation, as having a driver does increase the risk of infection by a small amount compared to having no driver at all. In practice, however, this is not necessarily the case: While having a driver certainly increases the risk of passenger infection, it is also possible that drivers may increase the disinfection and ventilation of their mobile travel vehicles due to their own sense of caution in the pandemic. Thus, the long-term effects of the pandemic on mobile travel are extremely difficult to analyze.

Perhaps the most controversial — and important — effects to discuss are the medium-term impact of the pandemic on mobile travel. One popular view is that the shock from the pandemic will increase people's incentive to purchase private cars, which in turn will reduce their demand for mobile travel as a public transport mode. From an intuitive point of view, a private car can be regarded as a mobile private home: Because it is not shared with others, it naturally reduces the risk of being infected by others by a significant degree. We believe that this analysis should hold true for some time after the end of the pandemic; that is, private car sales are likely to experience a "small spring" after the "cold winter". However, we also believe it may only be a "small spring" and nothing more. There are three reasons for this: First, the history of pandemics shows that the greatest characteristic of human beings is their forgetfulness. Although the SARS outbreak 17 years ago gave people a warning not to use wild animals to satisfy their appetites, reality has shown the world that there will always be some people who, unless forced otherwise, will disregard lessons from the past, saying that "it doesn't matter", "it tastes good", "it's okay". Second, if one assumes that people are rational, they will eventually find that the risk of infection from mobile travel does not constitute a strong motivating factor for them to buy a private car. Why? Just as the amount of water a barrel can hold depends not on its longest side but on its shortest side, the most important risk people need to avoid to prevent viral infections is clearly not cabs or mobile travel. Compared to cramming into the subway or attending a crowded concert, what is the risk in taking a cab? So in the short term, people may buy and use private cars for fear of infection, but in the medium term, though they may certainly use private cars for other reasons, the reason will not be to protect against infection. Third, immediately following the previous point, we must distinguish between the purchase of a private car and the use of a private car. The use of private cars involves more than just learning to drive and buying gasoline; it also involves the issue of finding a place to park. Considering that after the pandemic is over, most places, especially big cities, will not have had much improvement in available parking space, it will still be a strong constraint on using private cars when people can afford to buy a car but have no place to park it.

Second, the impact of the pandemic will promote the integration of the online and offline restaurant industries.

Similar to the mobile travel industry, the short-term effects for the restaurant industry are already determined to be negative, while analyzing the long-term effects is akin to "looking into a crystal ball". We will therefore focus here on the medium-term effects of the pandemic on the restaurant industry. Specifically, by medium-term, we refer to the time when the pandemic itself has ended, but its impact on social perceptions and preferences is still ongoing. According to economics textbooks, the medium-term impact of a pandemic corresponds to a so-called "change in demand", i.e., people will eat out less often due to a non-price factor such as "fear of catching the virus". In contrast, there is a very interesting issue we need to analyze, namely the integration of the online and offline restaurant industries. To be clear, eating out less and cooking at home are two different things. Although people are less inclined to "dine out" in restaurants due to having cognitive memory of the shock from pandemic, they still loathe the hassle of cooking their own meals. The combination of these two factors will lead to a natural inference: as Xibei and others have demonstrated during the pandemic, the share of "take-out" business in the restaurant industry will increase compared to "dine-in" business; that is to say, more restaurants will adopt an online–offline dual business model. Following this logic, the following four inferences can be drawn: First, delivery will become an important channel of growth for absorbing low-skilled workers in the future. Secondly, Internet companies such as Meituan and HungryMall, which are engaged in online and offline transactions in the restaurant industry, will benefit from this trend. Third, the role of "social learning" in restaurant consumption will be reduced. In terms of product information, restaurants are a typical "experience-based product"; that is, consumers cannot be certain about its quality before consumption, but will generally know its quality after consumption. Because of this information asymmetry, people tend to refer to other people's choices when choosing restaurants, i.e., they will "follow the trend" and "pile up" because they believe that some of the other diners must be "repeat customers" with symmetric information. The more "crowded" a restaurant, the more likely it is to have a higher number of repeat customers, and therefore also have high quality food. Obviously, the competitive advantage of "overcrowding" for high quality restaurants will diminish once people become concerned about the risk of infection from a pandemic. Fourth, as a response to the weakening of the "social learning" signal, high-quality restaurants will be motivated to use a variety of methods to encourage their "dine-in" customers to review their dishes online, thus allowing high-quality information from their offline "dine-in" business to spill over into their online "take-out" business.

Finally, the impact of the pandemic will push emerging industries such as online meetings and online learning onto a new track of rapid development.

Although history does not repeat itself in a simplistic sense, the way the pandemic has catalyzed a new landscape of online business echoes the past. If we can say that 17 years ago, in 2003, the SARS outbreak helped revive the struggling e-commerce companies such as Alibaba and Jingdong, then the COVID-19 pandemic in 2020 will also put newer business formats such as online meetings and online learning on a new track of rapid development.

To understand this phenomenon, it is first necessary to explain a key characteristic of Internet products and services, namely "network externality". This means that the utility of a product or service to consumers is positively correlated with the number of people already using the product or service. For example, the utility people enjoy from owning a cell phone can be divided into two parts: The first is the independent utility, such as alarm clock service, playing single-player games, etc. The second is the network utility, such as being able to call or chat with friends on messaging apps, and the greater the number of friends that join the same network, the greater the utility to the consumer (here, we do not consider subtle issues such as "harassment" messages that require more in-depth discussion).

Network externalities are of great importance to the development and competition of Internet companies. All other factors being equal, the more people use a certain Internet product or service, the greater its competitive advantage over the alternatives, and the greater its competitive advantage, the more new customers it will attract. This cycle will form a self-reinforcing positive feedback loop, which will eventually result in a "winner-takes-all" market pattern.

For this reason, it is crucial for any new Internet business to attract more customers to its product or service network as fast as possible. However, this is easier said than done. A large number of economic studies have shown that the acceptance and diffusion of new technologies over time usually show a typical S-shaped process due to various "switching costs": The customer base (installed base) grows very slowly at first, and once the base exceeds a critical mass, the above-mentioned "positive feedback mechanism" will be triggered in totality, leading to an explosive growth in the number of customers. It is therefore crucial for each Internet company to reach a critical customer base as quickly as possible. This requires overcoming the previously mentioned switching costs, which include not only the monetary costs of new technologies, but more importantly, the learning and cognitive costs involved in getting people to embrace new technologies and business formats.

For new business formats like web conferencing and online learning, the biggest effect of the pandemic was providing them with an enormous customer base in a very short time through extreme circumstances. It is easy to understand that for any team to hold a web meeting there is the basic prerequisite that all the attending members already have the web meeting app installed, but under normal circumstances, this is actually very difficult to achieve. Some people may be reluctant to try new things like web conferencing because they "can't learn it" or "can't understand it". But in the extreme conditions of the COVID-19 pandemic, if people need to hold a meeting but cannot meet in person, web conferencing becomes a "second best choice" as a "last resort". In such a situation, no matter how much resistance someone personally has to using conferencing apps, the pressure he or she feels from the"peer effect" will lead them to download, install, and learn to use a common web conferencing app, whether it be Tencent Meeting, DingTalk, or ZOOM.

Just as there were many consumers who initially distrusted and disliked e-commerce but were attracted to e-commerce after the SARS pandemic, we expect that many users who originally rejected, disliked, and were not used to web conferencing will slowly discover through the "learning by doing" effect that many meetings can actually be conducted online, sometimes to even greater effect than offline meetings. For example, compared with offline meetings, online meetings are highly flexible, do not require any physical space, allow participants to communicate with others at any time regardless of their location as long as they have Internet access, and offer simultaneous recording and archiving of meetings.

Another point worthy of attention is online education, represented by "Mootools", which is an acronym for "Massive Online Open Course" (MOOC). Because of its "massive", "online", and "open" nature, MOOCs are bound to have a huge impact on the way people learn in the future and on the education system as a whole. Although the Chinese stock market has often been criticized for its lack of price discovery, on closer examination it behaves like the stock market of any country, accurately reflecting the nature of the Chinese capital market and giving forward-looking signals. After the first day of heavy losses in the Chinese stock market in the face of the raging pandemic, aside from the expected rise in pharmaceutical stocks related to the fight against the novel coronavirus, some stocks related to online education also performed very well as colleges and universities began expecting educators to teach online. In order to give students a "break from school" until the end of the pandemic, online learning was made available both in the form of livestreaming and online course platforms such as SuperStar and WisdomTree, which offer a variety of publicly released online courses to choose from.

In the traditional classroom model, the teacher provides a "club good"; due to the limitations of physical space and auditory transmission, each class can only accommodate a very limited audience, at most probably not more than a thousand people. In fact, even if there is empty space in the classroom and the teacher uses the loudspeaker to teach the class, the content of the class will not be open to the whole community, because only those who have obtained "membership" in the club are eligible to listen to the class. In addition, the traditional classroom model provides a "consumable" product that is "read and then burned". For this reason, a teacher can teach the same content year after year, but because the cohort of students is different each year, even if the course content remains the same, the combination of courses and students is constantly being refreshed. MOOCs will fundamentally change this state of affairs. On the one hand, MOOCs transform courses from "consumable" products into "durable" products, i.e., once course content is stored in recorded audio or video, it can exist independently of the teacher's body for an extended period of time. In this way, in order to avoid lessons becoming "clichés", teachers will enter a state of "innovation for survival", i.e., they will enrich their lessons by constantly updating their knowledge. On the other hand, because they have become a digital product, MOOCs can be disseminated not only at a very low cost but also on a large scale through the Internet, turning "club goods" into "global public goods". This means that students at Fudan University are no longer limited to, and will not be satisfied with, the courses offered by Fudan faculty, but can also take online courses offered by faculty at Peking University and even Harvard University. In summary, we believe that just as shocks from the pandemic influence the use of online meetings, they can also have an unexpected positive effect on human capital by changing people's habits, both in terms of "teaching" and "learning".

2.5 Conclusion

We believe that this COVID-19 pandemic will be overcome. However, historical experience tells us that the wellbeing and calm order of life and work after the pandemic will probably be very different.

The shocks from the pandemic serve as a mirror through which to see problems and draw lessons. In the aftermath of the pandemic, individuals, businesses, and governments alike should be wary of the danger of the pandemic and embrace a reasonable trade-off between capturing the benefits of the trend and avoiding the risks of volatility. The country should allow for a greater degree of trial and error as well as innovation, which is the only way to make the entire economy and society resilient.

https://doi.org/10.1142/9789811252921_0003

Chapter 3

The Economic Impact of the NOVEL CORONAVIRUS Pandemic on Micro Enterprises and Fiscal Countermeasures

Fang Hongsheng, Wu Qi and Zhao Lexin

School of Economics, Zhejiang University, Hangzhou, China

Since the outbreak of the NOVEL CORONAVIRUS pandemic, a number of scholars have studied its impact on China's economic growth. Zhang Jun (2020) believes that the impact of the pandemic on GDP growth for the first quarter of 2020 is in the range of 2 to 3 percentage points and the impact on annual GDP growth is in the range of 0.5 to 0.75 percentage points; Wei (2020) believes that the impact on first quarter growth is in the range of 1 percentage point, while the impact on annual GDP growth will only be 0.1 percentage point. However, relatively little analysis has been done on the impact of the pandemic on micro enterprises. To this end, this chapter focuses on the mask manufacturers that play an important role in the prevention and control of the pandemic and the small, medium, and micro enterprises that are more markedly affected by the pandemic.

In the present situation, proactive fiscal policies are essential for success in the battle of prevention and control of the pandemic and in achievement of economic development goals. Since the outbreak, governments at all levels have implemented proactive macro- and micro-fiscal policies on four fronts: shortening the duration of the pandemic, reducing enterprise costs, resuming work and production in an orderly manner, and increasing effective demand. Such measures have effectively alleviated the hardships of micro enterprises. This chapter interprets and analyzes the important fiscal countermeasures introduced by the central and local governments at all levels and makes policy recommendations.

3.1 The Economic Impact of the Pandemic on Micro Enterprises

3.1.1 The impact of the pandemic on mask manufacturers

3.1.1.1 *The number and geographical distribution of Chinese mask manufacturers*

Data from Qixinbao show that as of March 5, 2020, China's 31 provinces, autonomous regions, and municipalities (data for Hong Kong, Macao, and Taiwan are temporarily unavailable) have a total of 4963 mask manufacturers, but when listed by province (region, municipality), the data from Qixinbao are found to be missing information for Guangxi, Ningxia, Hainan, Xinjiang, and four other provinces (regions). Therefore, we used data from the "Impact of the Pandemic on the Mask Industry" report released by the CIC Industrial Research Institute on February 16, 2020, to complete the missing data, but since the report is current only as of February 11, the number of mask manufacturers in 31 provinces and municipalities does not add up to 4963 after the missing data are filled in. The distribution of mask manufacturers is mainly concentrated in the eastern region (as shown in Figure 3.1), with Shandong Province having the highest number, accounting for 21.74% of the total.

Among nearly 5,000 mask manufacturers, only 353 have medical mask production licenses, which are distributed in 26 provinces, autonomous regions and municipalities across the country. The top five are Henan, Jiangxi, Jiangsu, Hubei and Guangdong, as shown in Figure 3.2.

3.1.1.2 *Production of masks in China and their geographical distribution*

After the outbreak of the pandemic, China's mask market supply could not keep up with demand. The Party Central Committee and the State Council made it a top priority to, and proceeded with emergency deployment, allowing mask production enterprises to resume work in advance,

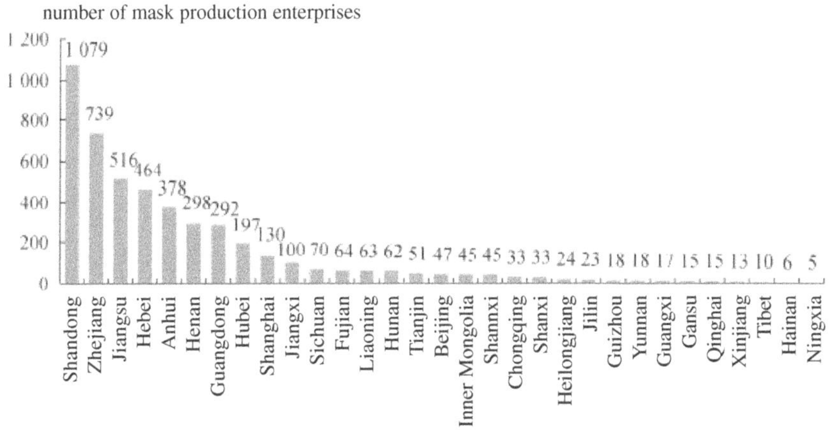

Figure 3.1: Number of mask production enterprises by province, region, and city.

Source: Qixinbao; China Investment Industry Research Institute, "Impact of the pandemic on the Mask Industry," Feb. 16, 2020.

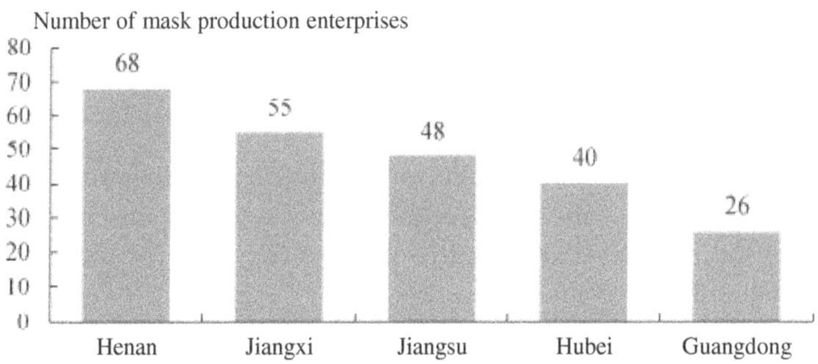

Figure 3.2: Distribution of medical mask manufacturers in the top five provinces, autonomous regions and municipalities.

Source: China Investment Industry Research Institute: "Impact of the Pandemic on the Mask Industry," February 16, 2020.

increase production, and expand production to ensure the supply of masks. Figure 3.3 shows that daily mask production in China increased rapidly from 8 million on January 25 to 116 million at the end of February, a testament to the country's capabilities in mask production and manufacturing.

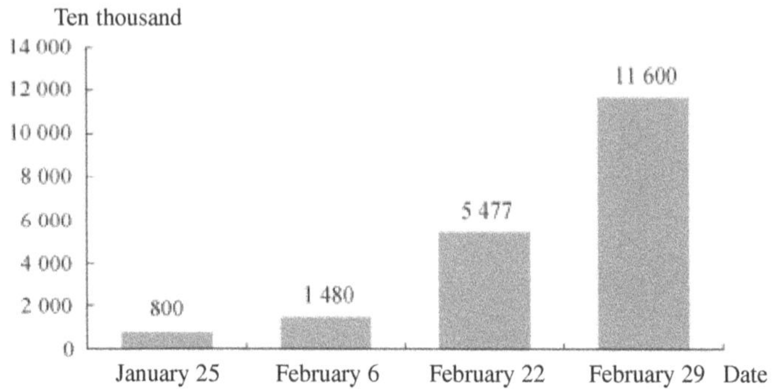

Figure 3.3: Daily mask production in China.

Source: Compiled from relevant news media reports.

In fact, China is the world's largest producer of masks with an annual production of nearly 5 billion in 2019 accounting for about 50% of global production. In 2020, this figure is expected to exceed 6 billion.[1] The main production areas for masks are located in East China and Central China.

3.1.1.3 *The practical dilemma faced by mask manufacturers*

The sudden increase in demand for masks during the pandemic presented mask manufacturers with an opportunity for development. However, the impact of the pandemic also created many difficulties for these firms in production and operations.

(1) Shortage of returning employees and rising wage costs. Due to the need to control the pandemic and prevent its spread, the State Council has implemented stringent traffic control and personnel management measures around the country, which have to some extent hindered employees of mask manufacturers from returning to work. The inability of employees to return to work in a timely manner will lead to labor shortage and shrinkage of production, thus jeopardizing the

[1] Development and Reform Commission: further expand the production of masks in 2020, how much mask production capacity in China? *China Business Intelligence Network*, February 20, 2020.

normal supply of masks. In order to encourage employees to return to work sooner to meet the needs of pandemic prevention and control, many manufacturers have increased their wages by three times the original,[2] or even five times,[3] thus greatly increasing the wage costs for manufacturers.

(2) Shortage of raw materials and increase in raw material costs. With the increase in demand for masks, manufacturers are expanding their production as much as possible, but as the demand for raw materials is also increasing, some manufacturers have been forced to shut down their production because of the shortage in supply of raw materials.[4] For example, the price of meltblown fabric, a key raw material, has surged from about 20,000 yuan per ton to 300,000 yuan per ton.[5]

(3) The price of masks is controlled and the profit margin of manufacturers is narrowed. On February 1, 2020, the State Administration of Market Supervision and Administration issued the *Guidance on Investigation and Handling of Illegal Acts of Price Gouging during the Prevention and Control Period of COVID-19* (State Administration of Market Supervision Competition, 2020, No. 21) to ensure market price stability for protective materials and basic livelihood commodities during the prevention and control of the pandemic. Local market regulatory bodies have also strengthened price supervision and enforcement. For example, Hubei Province mandated that during the first level of response to public health emergencies, medical commodities related to the prevention and control of the pandemic, such as protective and disinfection goods, shall not increase in price. Without reference to the original price of the goods sold, the difference between the purchase and sale price

---

[2] 90-year-old Chengdu mask producer gives 3 times the salary to ask workers to return to work: This is what I should do, *Chengdu All Search News*, January 23, 2020.

[3] Mask enterprises inspected by provincial party secretary. Boss receives more than 1,000 calls a day, 5 times the salary to ask employees to work overtime, *Daily Economic News*, February 1, 2020.

[4] Suddenly, at the critical moment, this factory stopped production of masks, *Cyberland*, March 2, 2020.

[5] Crazy meltblown fabric: Unit price per ton rises from 20,000 to 300,000, *Xinhua Shandong Channel*, March 4, 2020.

was not allowed to exceed 15%.[6] Sales price control will act on factory prices through the industrial chain, but at the same time, mask manufacturers' labor costs and raw material costs have increased significantly, which will greatly compress their profit margins.

3.1.2 The impact of the pandemic on micro, small, and medium enterprises (MSMEs)

The weakest and most vulnerable economic agents in China are the small, medium, and micro enterprises, of which there are about 80 million, accounting for 95% of all enterprises. MSMEs contribute 60% of GDP, 70% of employment, and 50% of tax revenue[7] (Zhang Jun, 2020). In order to stay abreast of the real-life challenges faced by MSMEs during the pandemic, a number of research institutions have conducted research on MSMEs. A summary of existing MSME research can be seen in Table 3.1.

Analysis indicates that the main problems faced by MSMEs during the pandemic include the following three issues.

Table 3.1: Research report authors, samples data, statistics, and deadlines.

Research	Author	Time	Sample
Research on 995 SMEs[a]	Zhu Wuxiang, Liu Jun, Wei Wei	Before February 6, 2020	The sample included 995 SMEs, of which: high-tech enterprises accounted for 18.51%, retail and service enterprises accounted for 17.1%, catering, accommodation, entertainment, culture and tourism enterprises accounted for 15.69%, processing and manufacturing enterprises accounted for 14.19%, logistics, transportation, wholesale trade enterprises accounted for 8.35%, and construction enterprises accounted for 8.15%

(Continued)

[6]How High Do Mask Prices Need to Be to File a Report/Complaint? How Much Higher Than the Market Price is Considered to Be Illegal? *Xianji.com*, February 24, 2020.

[7]On the economic impact of the new crown epidemic — a few common sense things you need to know, March 3, 2020.

Table 3.1: (*Continued*)

Research	Author	Time	Sample
Survival of Small, Medium, and Micro Enterprises under the Novel Coronavirus Pandemic — Enterprise Survey for Innovation and Entrepreneurship in China (ESIEC)	Xiaobo Zhang, Ruochen Dai, Junpeng Hu	February 10, 2020	Sample includes 2701 surveys, of which 2334 are representative samples of ESIEC and 357 are ordinary samples obtained from active surveying
Research Report on the Impact of the COVID-19 Pandemic on SMEs and Suggestions for Countermeasure	China Association of Small and Medium Enterprises	February 14, 2020	A total of 6,422 enterprises were sampled, including: 2,715 in the eastern and southern regions, accounting for 42%; 1,863 in the central region, accounting for 29%; 1,172 in the northeastern region, accounting for 18%; and 672 in the western region, accounting for 11%
China Merchants Bank Small and Micro Enterprises Research Report	China Merchants Bank Enterprise Research Joint Group	February 18, 2020	Includes 20,735 valid feedback questionnaires. In terms of enterprise size, surveyed enterprises mainly consist of small and micro enterprises, accounting for 90.4% of those surveyed; in terms of industry, the majority were in the service industry, accounting for 87.1%; in terms of region, the majority were in Beijing, Shanghai, Guangzhou, Suzhou, and Zhejiang, accounting for more than 67.7%

Note: [a]The contents of which were reprinted on Xueqiu.com on February 6, 2020, with no official research report title.
Source: Obtained from relevant internet sources.

3.1.2.1 *Market demand is low and business revenue has plummeted*

Zhu Wuxiang *et al.* (2020) found that 58.05% of companies believe that operating income will decline by more than 20% in 2020. Zhang *et al.* (2020) found that a decline in annual revenue of more than 8% is expected in the residential service industry, while members of the business services industry were relatively optimistic about the long-term impact of the pandemic, generally believing that annual revenue would decline by less than 6%. A report by the China Association of Small and Medium Enterprises (2020) showed that 30.5% of companies reported a decrease in market orders and 27.09% reported a loss of customers. The China Merchants Bank Corporate Research Joint Group (2020) found that surveyed companies were generally pessimistic about their first-half revenue, with more than 60% believing that their first-half revenue would decrease by more than 20% year-over-year.

3.1.2.2 *Acute financing problems and unsustainable corporate cash flow*

Small and medium-sized enterprises inherently face the problem of difficult financing. With the added burden of decreased revenue during the pandemic, the "blood-making" ability of enterprises is compromised, leading many enterprises to face cash flow difficulties and acute financing problems. Zhu Wuxiang *et al.* (2020) found that only about 15% of companies believe that the cash balance on their books can sustain the business for more than 3 months. Zhang *et al.* (2020) found that 64% of enterprises could not support themselves for longer than 3 months with their current cash flow. The China Association of Small and Medium Enterprises (2020) found that 86.22% of enterprises believe that the funds on their books cannot sustain them for longer than 3 months.

3.1.2.3 *Disruptions in the industry chain and raw materials shortages*

MSMEs are often positioned downstream of the industrial chain, where they not only directly face consumers, but are also highly dependent on the raw materials provided by upstream enterprises in the industrial chain. Under the effects of the pandemic, the movement of personnel is restricted, and many upstream enterprises face problems of insufficient labor force resuming work and reduced production, which will affect downstream MSMEs through the industrial chain and cause them to suffer raw material shortages. According to Zhang *et al.* (2020), nearly 70% of light industry enterprises indicated that they are experiencing a raw materials shortage.

3.2 Analysis of Financial and Tax Policy Response

To alleviate the negative impact of the pandemic on micro businesses, authorities at all levels have focused on shortening the pandemic's duration. Zhang Jun believes that shortening the duration of the pandemic will be beneficial to the rapid recovery of the economy (see Zhang Jun, On the economic impact of the novel coronavirus pandemic — a few common sense things you need to know, March 3, 2020). Proactive macro-fiscal policy and micro-fiscal policy have been implemented on two fronts to help mitigate economic shocks. On the one hand, effective demand is being increased by increasing public health spending and accelerating the construction of major key projects represented by new infrastructure; on the other hand, the burden on enterprises and individuals is being reduced through tax and fee reductions and financial subsidies to aid in pandemic prevention and control and to promote production.

3.2.1 Macro-fiscal policy

3.2.1.1 *Massive increase in public health spending*

The pandemic has exposed the deficiencies in public health spending in China. To control the pandemic and shorten its duration, the government has introduced a series of public health expenditure-related policies (see Table 3.2). As of March 5, the central government has issued 6.28 trillion yuan in transfers to localities, an increase of 1.26 trillion yuan over the same period in 2019. These include 60.3 billion yuan of subsidies for basic public health services, 26 billion yuan of subsidies for medical

Table 3.2: Examples of policies related to increasing public health spending.

Time	Region	Policy documents
January 27, 2020	China	National *Ministry of Finance Notice on Advance Allocation of Subsidy Funds for Prevention and Control of the Novel Coronavirus in 2020* (Ministry of Finance, (2020) No. 3).
January 27, 2020	China	National *Circular of the Ministry of Finance and National Health and Wellness Commission on the Budget of Subsidy Funds for Basic Public Health Services in 2020* (Ministry of Finance, (2020), No. 5).

(*Continued*)

Table 3.2: (*Continued*)

Time	Region	Policy documents
February 14, 2020	China	National *Ministry of Finance Notice on Advance Allocation of Subsidy Funds for Prevention and Control of the Novel Coronavirus pandemic in 2020 (Second Batch)* (Ministry of Finance, (2020), No. 6).
January 23, 2020	China	Hubei *Notice of the Ministry of Finance on the Subsidy Funds for the Prevention and Control of the Novel Coronavirus Pandemic in 2020* (Ministry of Finance, (2020), No. 1).

assistance, and 17.3 billion yuan of subsidies for improving medical services and guaranteeing capacity.[8]

In addition to increasing public health spending, the aforementioned document also points out the need for better performance operation monitoring and performance evaluation. According to Yang, Liang-song (2020), the issue most in need of attention is the improvement of performance, followed by structural optimization, and finally the increase of expenditure.[9] However, given that the first two will be relatively time-consuming, we believe that the most immediate and effective method in the short term would be a massive increase in public health spending. An early end to the war against the pandemic will accelerate the rebound and recovery of the economy. Once the pandemic eases, we should then pay great attention to the deficiencies in public health spending, optimize the structure of public health spending, and strengthen budget performance management.

3.2.1.2 *Accelerate the construction of major key projects characterized by new infrastructure*

In the face of the pandemic and its effects, accelerating the construction of major key projects is an important means of implementing expansionary fiscal spending policies. In order to prevent such policies

[8]Thorough pandemic prevention and control and "three guarantees" funding (State Council joint prevention and control mechanism launch), *People's Daily*, March 6, 2020.

[9]Yang Liang song, Gross, Structure and Performance: The Confusion of China's Health Care Financial Expenditure, THE PAPER, March 3, 2020.

from causing overcapacity, it is imperative that major key projects launched by governments at all levels adhere to a philosophy of new development that is based on innovation, coordination, "greenness", openness, and sharing. The "new infrastructure" includes seven segments, namely 5G infrastructure, ultra-high voltage, intercity high-speed rail and intercity rail transportation, charging stations, big data centers, artificial intelligence, and industrial Internet. These goals are all highly desirable, and have already become the main focus of current government investment. Many jurisdictions have announced their 5G development goals for 2020 (see Table 3.3). For example, Shanghai and Henan Province have proposed 5G base station construction targets, while Fujian Province, Shanxi Province plan to invest in the construction of big data industrial parks. In the medium to long term, digitalization is irreversible. As 5G, industrial Internet, and cloud computing form the main infrastructure of

Table 3.3: Examples of policies related to accelerating the construction of major key projects

Time	Region	Policy documents
February 12, 2020	China	*Circular on Strengthening the Management of Government Investment Funds to Improve the Effectiveness of Financial Contributions* (Budget Division, (2020), No. 7).
February 7, 2020	Shanxi province	*Notice of the General Office of Shanxi Provincial People's Government on the Issuance of the List of Provincial Key Projects in 2020* (Shanxi Govt. Issuance, (2020), No. 9).
February 13, 2020	Henan province	*List of Key Construction Projects in Henan Province.*
February 14, 2020	Fujian province	*Fujian Provincial Development and Reform Commission on the Issuance of the 2020 Annual Provincial Key Projects List*, (Fujian Reform Summary Issuance, (2020), No. 89).
February 24, 2020	Jiangxi province	*Notice from Jiangxi Provincial Development and Reform Commission on the Issuance of the First Batch of 2020 Provincial Key Construction Projects Plans* (Jiangxi Issuance on Key Reform Point, (2020), No. 107).
March 2, 2020	Chongqing	*Notice from the General Office of Chongqing Municipal People's Government on Work Related to the Implementation of Major Projects at the Municipal Level in 2020* (Chongqing Govt. Issuance, (2020), No. 21).

the digital economy, it is both feasible and necessary to be moderately ahead of the curve when technology and funding allow.[10]

3.2.1.3 *Universal tax cuts and fee reductions*

In terms of the statutory tax rate, China's corporate income tax rate is 25%, which is higher than the average of the statutory corporate income tax rate of 208 independent tax jurisdiction economies worldwide (23%) (Zhang, 2019). Meanwhile, the corporate income tax share of GDP in China was about 3.8% in 2018, 1.2 percentage points higher than that of the EU (Liang Ji *et al*., 2020). Given the current domestic economic situation and the rapid global spread of the pandemic, we believe that we can consider reducing the statutory rate of our corporate income tax by 2 percentage points, in line with the world average statutory tax rate of 23%. In addition to the corporate income tax, there should be an increased effort to better organize and regulate administrative fees and government funds (Yang, 2017). In order to alleviate the financial pressure on governments at all levels caused by universal tax cuts and fee reductions, we can consider promoting the expansion of resource taxes, consumption tax reform, and personal tax reform related to invisible income. In this way we can gradually transition to a tax system with direct taxes as the mainstay.

3.2.2 Micro-fiscal policy

3.2.2.1 *Ensuring pandemic prevention and control*

(1) Ease the burden of medical care.
Prevention and control of the pandemic is a top priority, and only when it is effectively controlled can the problems faced by various enterprises be alleviated. To this end, the government has introduced a series of financial subsidies and tax incentives (see Table 3.4), including financial underwriting of the costs borne by coronavirus patients and exemption from personal income tax for provisional subsidies given to pandemic prevention workers.

Policies supporting the prevention and control of the pandemic have been introduced not only at the national level but also by local

[10] China News Network, March 6, 2020.

Table 3.4: Examples of policies related to alleviating health care burdens.

Time	Region	Policy documents
January 25, 2020	China	*Circular of the Ministry of Finance and the National Health and Wellness Commission on the Policy on Financial Security Related to the Prevention and Control of the Novel Coronavirus Pandemic* (Ministry of Finance, (2020), No. 2).
February 6, 2020	China	*Announcement on Individual Income Tax Policies Related to Supporting the Prevention and Control of the Novel Coronavirus Pandemic* (Announcement of the General Administration of Taxation of the Ministry of Finance, (2020), No. 10).
February 6, 2020	China	*Announcement on the Exemption of Some Administrative Fees and Governmental Funds during the Prevention and Control of the Novel Coronavirus Pandemic* (Announcement of the National Development and Reform Commission of the Ministry of Finance, (2020), No. 11).
February 11, 2020	China	*Notice of the Ministry of Human Resources and Social Security, Ministry of Finance on Issues Relating to Salaries and Treatment of Personnel in Institutions during the Prevention and Control of the Novel Coronavirus Pandemic* (Ministry of Human Resources and Social Security Issuance, (2020), No. 9).
February 2, 2020	Hubei province	*Hubei Province Financial and Taxation Support Policies for Prevention and Control of the Novel Coronavirus Pandemic* (Hubei Govt. Issuance, (2020), No. 4).
February 2, 2020	Shandong province	*Notice on Thorough Implementation of Tax and Fee Policies Related to Prevention and Control of the Novel Coronavirus Pandemic* (Administration of Taxation, Shandong Ministry of Finance, (2020), No. 3).

governments. For example, Hubei Province and Shandong Province have waived property taxes and urban land use taxes for properties that are used in pandemic prevention and control, and have waived the deed tax for purchases of houses and land used for pandemic prevention and control. This series of policies not only eases the burden of medical costs for patients, but also reduces the burden on medical institutions and related companies.

(2) Enhance the security of the supply of pandemic prevention materials. In response to the shortage of medical protection materials at the beginning of the pandemic, governments at all levels implemented countermeasures to fully guarantee the supply of necessary materials (see Table 3.5). Measures include government underwriting of the

Table 3.5: Examples of policies related to enhancing the security of pandemic prevention material supply.

Time	Region	Policy documents
February 1, 2020	China	*Announcement on Duty Free Policy on Imported Materials for Prevention and Control of Pneumonia Epidemic with Novel Coronavirus Infection* (General Administration of Customs and Excise, Ministry of Finance Announcement, (2020), No. 6).
February 1, 2020	China	*Notice from the Tariff Commission of the State Council on Measures Barring the Increase of Tariffs for materials imported from the United States for the Prevention and Control of the Novel Coronavirus Pandemic* (Tax Commission, (2020), No. 6).
February 6, 2020	China	*Announcement of the General Administration of Taxation of the Ministry of Finance on Taxation Policies Related to Supporting the Prevention and Control of the Novel Coronavirus Pandemic* (Announcement of the General Administration of Taxation of the Ministry of Finance, (2020), No. 8).
February 7, 2020	China	*Notice from the National Development and Reform Commission, Ministry of Finance, Ministry of Industry and Information Technology on the Role of Government Reserves in Supporting the Response to the Shortage of Pandemic-related Materials by Increasing Production and Supply* (Development and Reform Operation, (2020), No. 184).
February 6, 2020	Hubei province	*Hubei Province Financial and Tax Support Policies for Prevention and Control of the Novel Coronavirus Pandemic* (Hubei Govt. Issuance, (2020), No. 4).
February 10, 2020	Zhejiang province	*Perspectives from the Zhejiang Provincial People's Government of the CPC Zhejiang Provincial Committee on Resolutely Winning the Battle Against the Novel Coronavirus Pandemic through Prevention and Control and Comprehensively Stabilizing Enterprises and Economic Development.*

procurement of key medical prevention and control materials, allowing manufacturers of key materials to deduct the cost of new equipment purchases for a set period, exempting the value-added tax on revenues corresponding to the transportation of key pandemic prevention and control materials, and exempting customs duties for the import of materials directly used for pandemic prevention and control by health organizations and health authorities. The government has also exempted the import of materials directly used for the prevention and control of epidemics from customs duties.

This series of policies eased the current financial difficulties of enterprises and ensured their normal operation so as to increase the output of pandemic prevention materials. At the same time, the exemption of VAT and toll reduction have reduced costs for pandemic-related material transportation enterprises, removed barriers in the transportation channels for pandemic prevention materials, and effectively promoted the timely supply of these materials.

(3) Encourage charitable donations. To further unite all sectors of society to support the prevention and control of the pandemic, the Ministry of Finance and other departments jointly issued a document indicating that the scope of duty-free imports should be appropriately expanded and imported materials donated for the prevention and control of the pandemic should be exempted from import duties and import-related VAT and consumption taxes (see Table 3.6). For domestic donations, enterprises and individuals are permitted to deduct the full amount from taxable income of donated cash and goods for pandemic prevention through public welfare organizations or state organs such as local governments and their departments at or above the county level, and the same applies to enterprises and individuals that donate pandemic

Table 3.6: Examples of policies encouraging public welfare donations.

Time	**Region**	**Policy documents**
February 6, 2020	China	National *Announcement on Duty Free Policy for Imported Materials for Prevention and Control of the Novel Coronavirus Pandemic* (General Administration of Customs and Excise, Ministry of Finance Announcement, (2020), No. 6).
February 6, 2020	China	National *Announcement on Tax Policy for Donations Related to Support for Prevention and Control of the Novel Coronavirus Pandemic* (Announcement of the General Administration of Taxation of the Ministry of Finance, (2020), No. 9).

prevention goods directly to hospitals that undertake prevention and control tasks. Furthermore, the goods donated by units and individual entrepreneurs for pandemic prevention and control without compensation are exempt from value-added tax, consumption tax, urban maintenance and construction tax, education surcharges, and local education surcharges.

Compared to the policies originally in place, these new tax-related policies for corporate and individual donations represent a breakthrough in terms of both proportion and channels utilized. This adjustment incentivizes corporations and individuals to donate directly to the relevant hospitals, thus improving the efficiency of donations.

State-owned enterprises, private enterprises, and foreign-funded enterprises have all provided strong support for winning the battle against the pandemic. As of Feb. 20, 88 central enterprises donated a total of 3.679 billion yuan.[11] As an important part of China's economy, SOEs should be encouraged to give donations according to their capacity, and their participation in pandemic prevention and control should be included in performance appraisals to examine whether they have effectively fulfilled their political and social responsibilities.

3.2.2.2 *Enabling business development*

(1) Reducing the tax burden. To reduce the burden of operations for businesses, the central and local governments have granted various policy concessions to enterprises (see Table 3.7). In terms of universal policies, the Ministry of Human Resources and Social Security has phased out the basic pension insurance, unemployment insurance, and work injury insurance payable by enterprises. In terms of targeted policies, to alleviate the hardships encountered by small and medium-sized enterprises, the Ministry of Finance, together with the State Administration of Taxation, issued a document to exempt or reduce by half the value-added tax for small-scale taxpayers from March to May 2020, while Hubei and other regions reduced or exempted urban land use tax and property tax for enterprises that suffered significant losses due to the pandemic. To support industries severely hit by the

[11] Central Enterprises' Research Report on Fighting the Pandemic, *Responsibility Cloud Public*, February 24, 2020.

Table 3.7: Examples of policies related to reducing tax and fee burdens.

Time	Region	Policy documents
February 6, 2020	China	*Announcement on the Exemption of Some Administrative Fees and Governmental Funds during Prevention and Control of the Novel Coronavirus Pandemic* (Announcement of the National Development and Reform Commission of the Ministry of Finance, (2020), No. 11).
February 20, 2020	China	National *Announcement on the VAT Policy for Supporting Individual Businesses to Resume Work and Operations* (Announcement of the General Administration of Taxation of the Ministry of Finance, (2020), No. 13).
February 28, 2020	China	*Circular on Phased Reduction and Exemption of Enterprise Social Insurance Premiums* (Ministry of Human Resources and Social Security, (2020), No. 1).
March 4, 2020	China	*Circular on Funding Support Policies for Civil Aviation Transport Enterprises during the Prevention and Control of the Novel Coronavirus Pandemic* (Finance and Construction, [2020] No. 30).
February 8, 2020	Hubei province	*Notice of the General Office of the People's Government of Hubei Province on the Issuance of Relevant Policy Measures to Support Small, Medium and Micro Enterprises to Tide Over Difficulties in Response to the Novel Coronavirus Pandemic* (Hubei Govt. Issuance, (2020), No. 5).
March 4, 2020	Beijing	*Notice from Beijing Municipal Medical Security Bureau, Beijing Municipal Bureau of Finance, State Administration of Taxation, and Beijing Municipal Taxation Bureau on the Phased Reduction of Unit Contributions for Basic Employee Medical Insurance* (Beijing Medical Security, (2020), No. 11).

pandemic (such as transportation, catering, hospitality & tourism), the loss carry-forward period for 2020 was extended to 8 years, and the fees for railroad guarantee, container deferment, and freight demurrage before the end of June were reduced by half.[12]

[12] State Council Determines Measures to Support Transportation, Express Delivery and Other Logistics Industries to Relieve Difficulties and Accelerate Recovery, *Xinhua News Agency*, March 4, 2020.

This series of policies combined a variety of measures, such as tax and fee reductions and extension of the loss carry-forward period, to mitigate the potential impact of the pandemic on the ongoing operation of enterprises. At this stage, further research can be conducted to introduce phased and targeted tax reduction and fee reduction policies, such as reductions for enterprises producing important livelihood products, so as to ensure the basic stability of the supply of daily living materials.

(2) Reducing operating costs. In order to help SMEs resume production in an orderly manner, relevant departments of the State Council and localities throughout the country have introduced a diverse array of cost reduction initiatives (see Table 3.8). The Ministry of Industry and Information Technology (MIIT) emphasized that SMEs could implement a phased moratorium on the payment of water, electricity, and gas required for their production and operation during the pandemic, and that "unpaid bills will not be suspended" during the moratorium. On February 22, the National Development and Reform Commission

Table 3.8: Examples of policies related to reducing operating costs.

Time	**Region**	**Policy documents**
February 9, 2020	China	*Notice from the Ministry of Industry and Information Technology on Work Related to Helping Small and Medium-sized Enterprises Resume Work and Production to Tide Over the Difficulties in Response to the Novel Coronavirus Pandemic* (Plain Code Telegram from the IIT, (2020), No. 14).
February 22, 2020	China	*National Development and Reform Commission on the Phased Reduction of the Cost of Electricity for Enterprises to Support the Resumption of Production* (Development and Reform Price, (2020), No. 258).
February 3, 2020	Shenzhen, Guangdong province	*Shenzhen Futian District to Prevent and Control the Pandemic together with Futian Enterprises — Eleven Articles.*
February 9, 2020	Shanghai	*Pudong New District on the Implementation of Measures to Support the Smooth and Healthy Development of Service Enterprises for Comprehensive Prevention and Control of the Pandemic* (Pudong Govt. Regulations, (2020), No. 1).

(*Continued*)

Table 3.8: (*Continued*)

Time	Region	Policy documents
February 10, 2020	Zhejiang province	*Perspectives from the Zhejiang Provincial People's Government of the CPC Zhejiang Provincial Committee on Resolutely Winning the Battle Against the Novel Coronavirus Pandemic through Prevention and Control and Comprehensively Stabilizing Enterprises and Economic Development* (Zhejiang Provincial Committee Issuance, (2020), No. 4).
February 11, 2020	Zhejiang province	*Notice from Zhejiang Province on the Temporary Reduction of the Price of Gas, Water, and Electricity for Enterprises During the Prevention and Control of the Novel Coronavirus Pandemic* (Zhejiang Development and Reform Price, (2020), No. 22).

issued a notice to reduce electricity prices by 5% from February to June for business users other than those in high energy-consuming industries, which is expected to reduce the cost of electricity and gas for enterprises by more than 63 billion yuan. Zhejiang and other regions have reduced the price of industrial water and natural gas by 10% for enterprises that produce materials related to pandemic prevention and control, for at least 3 months.

Local governments are also providing relief to enterprises in terms of housing rent. For example, Zhejiang Province waived two months' rent for enterprises that lease operating properties of state-owned assets. Local governments can introduce such cost relief policies according to local financial resources and conditions, and can encourage different types of lessors to respond positively to the call for rent relief in order to effectively reduce operating costs for enterprises and help them tide over these difficult times.

(3) Ensure the resumption of work and production.

In response to the lack of employees returning to work in small and medium-sized enterprises after the pandemic, the Ministry of Industry and Information Technology proposed to utilize special funds for the development of small and medium-sized enterprises at all levels, and encouraged localities in a position to do so to set up special relief funds. All regions have taken corresponding measures (see Table 3.9). For example, Hangzhou City, Zhejiang Province, arranged subsidies

Table 3.9: Examples of policies related to ensuring the resumption of production and work.

Time	Region	Policy documents
February 9, 2020	China	*Notice from the Ministry of Industry and Information Technology on Work Related to Helping Small and Medium-sized Enterprises Resume Work and Production and Tide Over the Difficulties in Response to the Novel Coronavirus Pandemic* (Plain Code Telegram from the Ministry of Industry and Information, (2020), No. 14)
February 10, 2020	Hangzhou, Zhejiang Province	*Policies from the Hangzhou Municipal People's Government of the Communist Party of China on Stringent Prevention and Control of the Pandemic and Helping Enterprises to Resume Work and Production*
February 15, 2020	Wenzhou, Zhejiang province	*Notice from the Wenzhou Municipal People's Government on the Issuance of Several Measures to Support Small and Medium-sized Enterprises to Tide over the Difficulties in Response to the Novel Coronavirus Pandemic* (Wenzhou Govt. Issuance, (2020), No. 3)
February 15, 2020	Nanjing, Jiangsu province	*Notice on Support for Enterprises to Organize the Orderly Return of Workers to Nanjing to Resume Work,* (No. 12)

to provide transitional accommodation for returning workers, granted subsidies to low-income employees for renting rooms, and gave a subsidy of 500 yuan per person for the "difficult caregiving" situation of dual-employee families in non-public enterprises.

It is equally important to promote the resumption of work and production in a prudent manner.[13] The above-mentioned series of safeguard policies not only provide strong support for the smooth recovery of the economy, but also play an important role in effectively protecting people's livelihood and maintaining social stability. However, it is worth noting that

[13]Policies Related to Resumption of Work and Production Need to be "Precise as Chess", *Xinhua*, February 9, 2020.

the economy and society are organic systems, and enterprises rely on the industrial chain to form close ties. Therefore, the resumption of work and production should be based on the overall situation, and collaboration among the whole industrial chain should be promoted[14] (*People's Daily Online*, March 10, 2020). In addition, although the pandemic has had a major impact on traditional industries, it has also provided development opportunities for new industries such as smart manufacturing, unmanned distribution, and online consumption. Therefore, ensuring the resumption of work and production will not only help enterprises resume their current business as soon as possible, but will also actively promote the transformation and upgrading of enterprises to expand into new types of businesses.

3.3 Conclusion

This chapter analyzed the impact of the pandemic on mask manufacturers and MSMEs from the perspective of micro enterprises. In the face of the surge in demand, the shortage of raw materials and labor supply in the short term has caused the market to experience a serious shortage of pandemic prevention materials, while MSMEs face capital constraints and setbacks in demand due to the pandemic. Although financial and tax subsidies can alleviate the pressure on enterprises to a certain extent, only by strengthening pandemic prevention and control and winning the battle against the pandemic can we fundamentally solve the problems facing these enterprises.

In order to achieve economic and social development goals and accelerate economic recovery, the government has made simultaneous efforts to shorten the duration of the pandemic and mitigate its economic impact by introducing proactive macro- and micro-fiscal policies. Governments at all levels ensured the prevention and control of the pandemic and pushed forward the "anti-pandemic battle line" by increasing public health spending, covering medical expenses, subsidizing pandemic prevention workers and pandemic prevention material manufacturers, and offering special tax incentives. Accelerating the construction of major key projects represented by new infrastructure helped hedge against the negative impact of the pandemic and promoted economic growth. While

[14]Create Favorable Conditions for Resumption of Work and Production (commentator observation).

interpreting and analyzing existing policies, we believe that we should also implement inclusive tax cuts and fee reductions, implement a gradual shift to a tax system dominated by direct taxes and strengthen fiscal performance management, and encourage state-owned enterprises to play an active role. These steps will allow us to better achieve stable economic growth and high-quality development.

https://doi.org/10.1142/9789811252921_0004

Chapter 4

Impact of the Novel Coronavirus Pandemic on Structural Unemployment and Employment Patterns, and the Corresponding Countermeasures

Chen Zhao and Song Hong

School of Economics, Fudan University, Shanghai, China

At the end of 2019, the job market had already been under pressure from economic downturn, trade frictions and deleveraging, and the growth of market demand was slowing down. All of these issues have been compounded by the COVID-19 pandemic. Against this background, how will the new pandemic affect the labor market? Which are the key groups that will be affected? What should be done in the short and medium term to deal with the possible crisis and challenges? The answers to these questions are crucial to stabilizing employment and promoting growth, and are the focus of this chapter.

This chapter analyzes and interprets the economic and social impact of the COVID-19 pandemic from the perspectives of employment and the labor market, and proposes countermeasures and recommendations. The first part provides an analysis of the impact of the pandemic on the labor force and job market. The second part summarizes the recent countermeasures introduced by various domestic sectors for key groups. The third part presents a summary and future outlook. It is hoped that the research summaries, factual discussions, data descriptions and realistic observations in this chapter will provide detailed evidence for a more comprehensive and in-depth understanding of the impact of the COVID-19 pandemic on the labor market structure and offer insights for the formulation of relevant policies.

4.1 Analysis of the Impact of the Pandemic on the Labor Force Job Market

This section includes the following: first, an overview of labor market and employment in 2019; second, a focused discussion and analysis of key populations affected by the pandemic; third, a discussion and summary based on the findings of the employment situation in domestic companies; and fourth, a review and comparison of the impact on the labor market during the SARS period. It is hoped that through data description, factual analysis and historical review, we can understand the impact of the COVID-19 pandemic on the labor market from multiple dimensions.

4.1.1 Overview of the labor market in 2019

The overall employment situation in 2019 was relatively bleak: 13.52 million new jobs were created in urban areas nationwide, down 90,000 compared with the previous year, with the target completion rate dropping by 0.8 percentage points; by the end of the third quarter of 2019, the number of people receiving unemployment insurance benefits increased by 6.42 million compared with the end of 2018, and the number of people with employment difficulties who found employment decreased by 2.2% year-on-year. The manufacturing PMI employment index was 47.3% in December 2019, down 7 percentage points year-on-year, while the non-manufacturing sector was down 2 percentage points year-on-year.

In particular, there are two specific groups whose employment situation was even less optimistic: small and medium-sized enterprises (SMEs) and college graduates. At the end of 2018, SMEs accounted for a total of 18.07 million legal entities in China, absorbing 79.4% of the total number of employed persons, and collectively serve as the primary conduit for employment in China. The number of college graduates has been increasing year by year; however, they face relatively high employment pressure. The employment rate for graduates with 4-year degrees has decreased for four consecutive years, and the ratio of "employed jobs" for this group has decreased for five consecutive years, resulting in them facing greater employment pressure.

4.1.2 The impact of the pandemic on employment in the service industry

In the short term, the rate of resumption of work in SMEs is low. Data from the Ministry of Industry and Information Technology show that the return-to-work rate of SMEs nationwide is only about 30%. This may be due to two reasons: first, transportation has not been fully restored, making it difficult for workers to reach their workplaces; second, some private enterprises have been affected by the pandemic, and the demand for employment has dropped.

More specifically, the pandemic has had the most pronounced impact on service industries such as hospitality, restaurants, transportation, sports and entertainment, and has had a strong negative impact on employment in the short term. In the restaurant industry, for example, in order to avoid cross-infection and the occurrence of cluster outbreaks, large and small restaurants have been "closed" for the past two months, while some restaurants that have resumed operations still need to strictly control the number of personnel in the building. Long-term closures and irregular operations have resulted in huge losses and forced service staff to go on standby. In addition to the restaurant industry, the tourism industry has also been severely affected. Statistics show that as of the seventh day of the first month of the lunar calendar, the number of passengers traveling by national railroad dropped 81.9% compared to the same period last year, while the number of passengers traveling by civil aviation fell 74.5%. Based on the scale of tourism revenue during the 2019 Spring Festival, the loss of revenue in 2020 is expected to exceed 500 billion yuan. Due to the COVID-19 pandemic, many workers in tourism industry have lost their income recently and even risked being laid off.

4.1.3 The impact of the pandemic on the workforce of MSMEs

Due to their small size and weak risk resilience, many MSMEs are facing bankruptcy and closure due to the impact of the pandemic. Pandemic control and prevention efforts have created a multitude of difficulties for the resumption of work and production, such as cumbersome procedures for the resumption of work approval, obstruction of personnel flow and delayed logistics in industrial chains that MSMEs rely on. These conditions all cause operating difficulties for MSMEs, and if they close down, a large number of employees will face the risk of unemployment.

The weekly report of Wisdom Tree Recruitment shows that the unemployment rate for workers in micro enterprises (enterprises employing fewer than 20 people) reached 30% in addition to another 32.8% of workers being at risk of unemployment. Considering the fluctuating income and weak risk resilience of employees in micro and small enterprises, there is an urgent need for relevant employment policies and support in the pandemic. Of course, policy support can directly target the unemployed individuals as well as micro and small enterprises, which will also benefit the employees indirectly.

4.1.4 The impact of the pandemic on college graduates

The number of college graduates will reach 8.74 million this year, an increase of 400,000 year-on-year. This number grows to enormous proportions when added to the previous year's number of unemployed persons. Over the past two years, the economic situation has shown an overall downward trend with fewer job opportunities, with the employment situation this year becoming even worse in the wake of the COVID-19 pandemic. On the one hand, the pandemic has led to a decline in recruitment demand in the whole market; on the other hand, offline recruitment activities have ceased, putting a large number of graduates at loss in their search for employment. Although the Ministry of Education has organized several online job fairs and promoted online employment services, they are eclipsed by the above-mentioned negative effects, thus having a marked impact on the employment of fresh graduates.

4.1.5 The impact of the pandemic on the migrant worker population

Migrant workers represent the main body of industrial workers in China, reaching 290 million in 2019, of whom 170 million are working away from their hometown. In addition, under the export-oriented economic development model, China's "world factory"-style export expansion has made the employment of migrant workers less stable (Shao Min and Wu Peng, 2019), so they are more directly affected by the pandemic. At present, although many large labor-exporting provinces have launched measures to promote the resumption of work for migrant workers, the return of migrant workers to employment in secondary and tertiary industries will still have a large impact in the short term, with the current return rate of migrant workers in many areas reaching less than 50%.

4.1.6 Historical review: Evidence from the SARS era

Based on similarities between the impact of the COVID-19 pandemic and the SARS epidemic in 2003, in this section, we provide a historical perspective for judging the impact of the COVID-19 pandemic on the labor market through data analysis and historical review. In general, the impact of SARS on overall employment in the labor market was not significant; however, the impact on laid-off unemployed workers, migrant workers and college graduates was more significant and sustained. The impact of SARS on the labor market is as follows.

First, the SARS epidemic did not have a significant impact on the national economy as a whole, with output and revenue growth remaining relatively stable throughout the year. The negative impact was relatively short-lived, mainly confined to the second quarter of 2003. As the epidemic was brought under control, the economy gradually stabilized and rebounded.

Second, as far as the affected industries are concerned, those directly affected by SARS were labor-intensive. The control of cross-regional movement of the population and the suppression of consumer demand led to a severe impact on tertiary industries, especially tourism, restaurants, and passenger and freight transportation, which have high mobility and high elasticity of demand. However, for the year as a whole, the production and employment of the tertiary sector did not show a significant contraction. In the retail trade sector, for example, which accounts for the largest share of tertiary industries, the growth rate of total retail sales of consumer goods declined significantly in April and May and then quickly began to show a sustained rebound from June onwards. The number of people employed in retail trade still maintained year-on-year growth, but the growth rate dropped to 1.5%, before rebounding significantly in 2004 (see Figure 4.1).

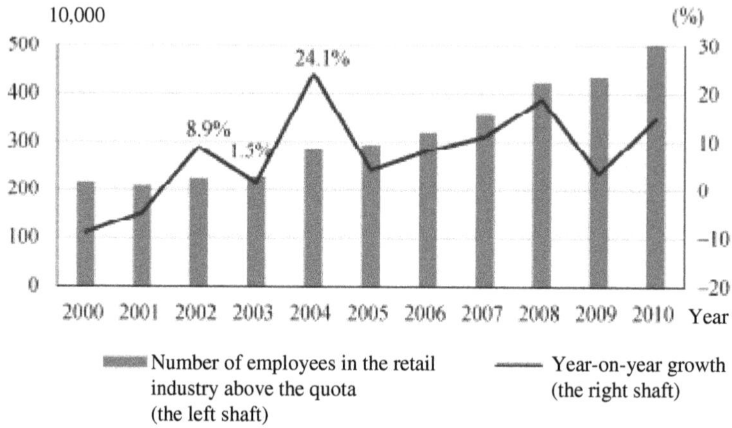

Figure 4.1: Number of employees in the retail industry above the quota.

Source: National Bureau of Statistics.

Third, the growth dynamics and employment in the manufacturing sector were not significantly affected in the short term, but the possibility of lagged effects has not been ruled out, given the constraints that the epidemic imposed on foreign trade. In the construction industry, for example, the number of employees in 2003 increased by 7.5% year-on-year, while the employee growth rate in 2004 dropped significantly (see Figure 4.2).

Fourth, as far as the affected groups are concerned, those most affected are the informally and flexibly employed, with laid-off workers, migrant workers and college graduates constituting the three major groups. In the short term, SARS led to a reduction in employment opportunities for laid-off workers; in the medium and long term, market demand shrank and new employment decreased. Statistics show that within the first half of 2003, nearly 8% of the total rural migrant labor force returned to their hometowns, and the proportion of college graduates searching for employment reached 35.8%.

Fifth, the overall impact of SARS on the situation in urban areas has been relatively limited. The registered unemployment rate in urban areas increased by 0.3 percentage points year-on-year to 4.3% in 2003; by 2004, the unemployment rate had fallen back somewhat and has remained at around 4.2% since then (see Figure 4.3). The index of total wages of

Figure 4.2: Number of employees in construction industry enterprises.

Source: National Bureau of Statistics.

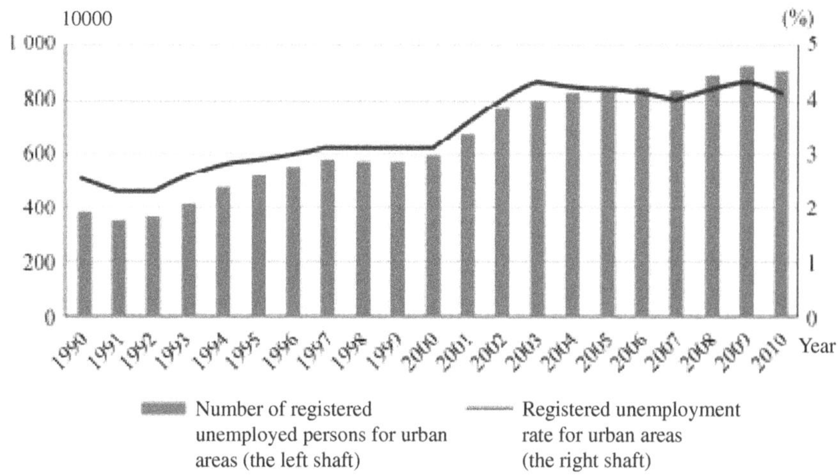

Figure 4.3: Number of registered unemployed persons and unemployment rate for urban areas.

Source: National Bureau of Statistics.

employed persons in urban work units still showed a certain upward trend in 2003 (see Figure 4.4).

Sixth, to address the possible biases of the above statistics, such as the "accession" dividend gained by joining the World Trade Organization and the human capital dividend created by the expansion of universities, we conducted empirical regressions using regional- and time-level differences between Beijing and Guangzhou, and found that there is no significant difference in the overall employment and unemployment rates before and after SARS for these two cities compared to other regions in China.

However, it is important to note that in 2003, China had just received the "WTO accession" dividend and was actively exploring the global market and moving into an investment-led development mode and was also in the demographic dividend window. At the time of SARS, China's economy was in a phase of acceleration from high growth (7–9%) to ultra-high growth (10%+), but currently, the Chinese economy growth rate is in a phase of gradual slowdown. China's tertiary sector, which was hit the hardest by the pandemic, contributed more than 60% to economic growth in 2019, much higher than the number 42% in 2002. Therefore, the short-term impact of the COVID-19 pandemic on the labor market is likely to be greater, and the medium- to long-term recovery is likely to be slower.

In addition, while the spread of SARS in 2003 was concentrated in a few areas, the current outbreak is widespread across the country, and the

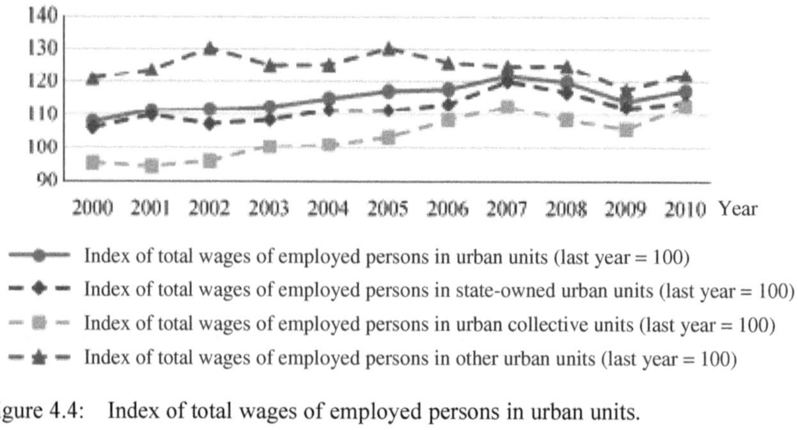

Figure 4.4: Index of total wages of employed persons in urban units.

Source: National Bureau of Statistics.

global spread of the pandemic may again affect China. This means that the pressure of pandemic prevention and the difficulties faced by enterprises in resuming work and providing employment for the workforce will be much more dire in this pandemic than during the SARS period.

4.1.7 Findings from micro-enterprise research

Teams from several leading institutions in China have conducted research on the current status of employment and resumption of work in micro enterprises. We have selected and summarized the findings related to workforce employment for analysis.

4.1.7.1 *Study on small and medium-sized enterprises*

The Chinese Enterprise Innovation and Entrepreneurship Survey (ESIEC) team asked enterprises in five provinces and two cities (Beijing, Shanghai, Guangdong, Zhejiang, Henan, Liaoning and Gansu) about their resumption of work and production and the various issues that threaten their survival status.

The results of the study show that the majority of enterprises delayed resumption of work, and the overall situation is very serious. Of 2344 representative samples of enterprises, only about 2% of enterprises (20.2%) resumed work before February 10. Breaking down the percentages by industry, the resumption rate of business services is relatively high, reaching 30%, while the resumption rate of heavy industry is the lowest, at about 10%. Among the 1,871 enterprises that have not resumed work, only nearly 40% of them (39.5%) are expected to resume work before mid-March, while nearly half of them (47%) are unable to determine their specific resumption time.

One of the major reasons for the failure to resume work is that employees cannot return to work in time. About 40% of enterprises (38.5%) have labor shortage problems, which are especially prominent in the industrial sector. Due to the need to cover fixed costs, this in turn leads to cash flow shortages for nearly 70% of enterprises (69.7%). In response, nearly 15% of the companies surveyed intend to ease the financial pressure by laying off employees, and nearly a quarter expect to lay off more than 30% of their workforce.

According to the report, the light industry faces the most serious problems, including rising costs, falling demand and broken industry chains. Heavy industry, on the other hand, faces challenges mainly due to labor shortage, for which a timely return to work is important. The business services industry, with the help of the Internet economy, can maintain or even catalyze new demand and recover relatively quickly. The residential services industry is directly affected by the weak consumer demand and faces greater pressure on rental costs.

4.1.7.2 *Study on medium and large enterprises*

In a study conducted by Professor Wang Yong's team at Tsinghua University School of Economics and Management, the sample enterprises were mainly private enterprises (accounting for more than 91%), covered a total of 12 industries and were distributed across 27 provinces, autonomous regions and municipalities in China. Most of the enterprises in this study are leading companies in their respective industries that have reached a mature level of development.

The questionnaire from the study showed that large and medium-sized enterprises in the consumer services and building and construction sectors are the most severely affected due to the enormous difficulties in resuming work and operations. 58.02% of the entrepreneurs surveyed believe that the pandemic has had a severe impact on them, with 29.72% reporting a heavy labor cost burden and 21.23% reporting a shortage of personnel. The problem of staff shortage is more prominent in the pharmaceutical, consumer goods manufacturing, industrial goods manufacturing, consumer services, agriculture, forestry and fishery industries.

However, despite the heavy burden of labor costs, these large and medium-sized companies generally responded positively to the challenges of the pandemic by giving adequate attention to human resources.

4.1.7.3 *Study on enterprises in the Hubei region*

Wuhan University's China New Private Economy Research Center, together with the Wuhan City Federation of Industry and Commerce, conducted research on 573 enterprises in Hubei Province (mainly in Wuhan). The results show that the survival of private enterprises in Wuhan is worrying: as many as 97.21% of the enterprises in the sample were still in a state of complete or partial shutdown at the time of the survey, and more than half of the enterprises were pessimistic about their development prospects, with another 6.34% planning to withdraw from Wuhan. State support policies have not yet been put in place, and the cash flow shortage problem remains difficult to solve: Only 11.87% of enterprises have received financial support from banks, and only 8.03% have received rent reductions of varying degrees.

The multiple dilemmas faced by enterprises in Hubei are particularly difficult. On the one hand, the shortage of funds, rising operating costs and lack of pandemic prevention materials directly caused by the pandemic, coupled with the threat of employee turnover and market loss brought about by the successive resumption of production in other provinces and municipalities, are enormous. On the other hand, the obvious decline in residents' income has led to a shrinking consumer market and overall demand, which has been transmitted to the supply side, again endangering the survival of local enterprises and amplifying the negative impact.

Therefore, the team recommends an orderly resumption of work in Hubei Province as soon as possible, with precise assistance to small and medium-sized private enterprises and medium- and long-term preferential support policies for key areas.

In summary, we can form the following three judgments about the impact of the pandemic on enterprises and employees: First, although enterprises in general are hit by the pandemic, SMEs in particular may essentially go bankrupt and close down as a result and therefore should be the focus of policy. Second, rescuing enterprises is equivalent to rescuing employees; it is only by supporting individuals and simultaneously prioritizing the resumption of work and production in enterprises as soon as possible that a sustainable effect can be produced. Third, the orderly resumption of work in Hubei Province should commence as soon as possible.

4.2 Response Measures and Suggestions

This section compares and summarizes the specific support measures introduced for groups heavily impacted by the pandemic, namely, small, medium and micro enterprises (SMMEs), migrant workers and recent college graduates, and provides suggestions.

4.2.1 Employment in small and medium-sized enterprises

Small and medium-sized enterprises can be supported to quickly resume production through social insurance fee waivers and deferrals, unemployment insurance refunds and subsidies to support enterprises to stabilize their jobs.

(1) *Financial support*: The CBRC and other departments issued a circular to grant temporary deferments for a certain period of time for the repayment of principal and interest on loans to small and medium-sized enterprises affected by the pandemic. At the same time, credit support was increased and loans were granted at preferential interest rates.

(2) *Social insurance contribution reduction*: Each region can, according to its own situation, exempt small and medium-sized enterprises from the three social insurance contributions. Enterprises severely affected by the pandemic can apply for a deferment of social insurance premiums, during which late fees will be waived; by the end of June, enterprises can apply for a deferment of the housing accumulation fund, and failures to make normal repayments of public reserve fund loans are not treated as overdue payments.

(3) *Tax support*: State administration of taxation announcement or notice: From March 1 to the end of May, small-scale taxpayers in Hubei Province are exempted from VAT, and the levy rate is reduced from 3% to 1% in other areas; commercial and industrial electricity prices are reduced by 5% in phases, except for high-energy-consuming industries; and off-season price policies for non-resident gas gate prices go into effect in advance.

(4) *Job stabilization subsidies*: The Ministry of Human Resources and Social Security and other departments issued a document indicating the increase of the unemployment insurance stabilization rebate and relaxing the criteria for enterprise layoff rates. At the same time, support for enterprises to carry out on-the-job training and enterprise training can be included in the scope of subsidized class training in accordance with the provisions.

(5) *Innovation support*: The Ministry of Industry and Information Technology clearly encourages SMEs to carry out technical research and production innovation for prevention and control of the COVID-19

pandemic and to do a thorough job on technical perfection, certification and testing, qualification applications and promotion and application of services. At the same time, support is provided for the digital transformation of enterprises. Internet platform services are promoted to enhance the level of intelligent manufacturing and the development of integration and innovation of large and small enterprises.

4.2.2 Addressing the employment of migrant workers

The impact of this pandemic on the employment of migrant workers is relatively obvious and direct. The central and local governments have introduced multi-channel measures to alleviate the employment difficulties of migrant workers.

(1) *Increasing employment stabilization subsidies*: First, enterprises should be encouraged to guide the adoption of salary adjustments, shortened working hours and rotating shifts to stabilize work positions. The Ministry of Human Resources and Social Security and other departments have also reduced the burden on enterprises and reduced or avoided layoffs through enterprise social insurance fee reductions, deferred payments and increased refunds for unemployment insurance stabilization. Second, guidance and supervision are provided to enterprises that do need to lay off employees to regulate layoffs and effectively protect the legitimate rights and interests of workers in accordance with the law.

(2) *Strengthening the guarantee that migrant workers will return to the cities*: The State Council revealed a series of initiatives to guarantee the return of migrant workers to the cities: (i) proactively carry out pandemic prevention and awareness for migrant workers and guide them to adopt scientific pandemic precautions and reasonably arrange their return to the city and their jobs; (ii) at the same time, strengthen the pandemic prevention and control measures for returning to work to ensure safe travel for migrant workers traveling for work: those who leave their hometowns to work will be educated about healthy travel and about the pandemic, those who do not leave home will be guided to participate in online learning and training and recommended to take up local jobs nearby, and those who have been infected or are still under observation will be prevented from going out; (iii) strengthen coordination between destination areas and

origin areas of migrant workers: migrant workers' places of origin should proceed according to local conditions, closely track the developments of the pandemic and do a thorough job of the centralized release of the main information related to enterprises in the local area; areas receiving migrant workers should enhance monitoring, dynamically grasp labor demand and ensure timely release of job information; labor-using parties should provide point-to-point travel services via shuttle buses and other means.

(3) *Broadening employment channels*: First, online recruitment activities should be continued and targeted labor collaboration should be organized. Second, returning migrant workers must be mobilized to join agricultural employment. Third, major local projects and construction tasks must be encouraged to absorb migrant workers for employment. Fourth, entrepreneurship should be supported and online entrepreneurial training, entrepreneurial services and financial support must be provided. Fifth, a number of temporary public welfare positions should be developed for the bottom-up placement of migrant workers who are temporarily unable to go out and have difficulties in living.

4.2.3 Addressing the issue of employment of college students

This year, recent college graduates are also one of the groups most severely affected by the pandemic. In response, the employment difficulties of graduates should be alleviated by increasing employment opportunities, expanding education channels, optimizing recruitment channels and providing guidance services.

(1) *Increasing employment opportunities*: First, a strategy should be adopted at the national level to actively encourage graduates to be employed in major national projects, construction tasks and important fields. Second, recruitment should be expanded in key areas, such as the employment of primary and secondary school teachers, and all of the publicly funded teacher trainees should be placed in teaching positions. Third, grassroots employment efforts should be guided. Education departments should implement a robust special post program for rural teachers and other grassroots employment projects, such as "college student village officials". SMMEs enterprises should be encouraged to absorb college graduates for employment. Fourth, military enlistment should be encouraged by optimizing the allocation of indicators, implementing early

medical examination and other initiatives. Fifth, newer areas of employment should be enriched. Graduates must be encouraged to search for employment and engage in entrepreneurship in production and life service industries as well as fields such as education, medical and elderly care that meet their urgent livelihood needs. Sixth, the scale of apprenticeship must be expanded. The market competitiveness of graduates can be enhanced through internships. At the same time, policy subsidies should be given to enterprises that open apprenticeship positions.

(2) *Expanding channels for further education*: The executive meeting of the State Council revealed that this year, the scale of master's degree enrollment and professional education will be expanded. Plans for graduate programs will focus on increasing the number of high-level professional degrees; for vocational undergraduate and applied undergraduate programs, there will be a pivot toward specialized and applied undergraduate programs, such as preventive medicine, emergency management, elderly service management, e-commerce and other majors.

(3) *Optimizing recruitment channels*: Recruitment services should be optimized and online recruitment activities should be increased. Once the pandemic has abated, the launch of industrialized, dedicated on-site recruitment should be quickly organized and mobilized. Employers must be guided to postpone interview and acceptance times and extend time limits for reporting and settling accounts for fresh graduates who have delayed leaving school. Two years of household registration and file trusteeship must be provided for unemployed graduates.

(4) *Providing guidance services*: College career guidance teachers, counselors and tutors must pay careful attention to enhancing personalized guidance and must actively guide graduates to find an appropriate career orientation. Online counseling guidance classes should be introduced and a psychological hotline should be set up to strengthen psychological guidance for job hunting.

(5) *Strengthening support for those facing hardships*: First, the focus should be on strengthening the support of key groups. Graduates with special circumstances should be provided with situation-specific support and a "one person, one policy" dynamic service, and should be given

priority for recommendation to employment positions. Second, we should strengthen support for college graduates in Hubei. The time frame for graduation defenses and degree audits for postgraduates should be extended, the number of degree committee meetings should be increased and degree conferral should be confirmed in phases and batches. At the same time, the Ministry of Education should increase policies oriented toward employment and graduation-related project plans. Third, the provision of services for all graduates should be guaranteed.

4.2.4 New opportunities arising from the pandemic: The digital economy and platform economy

First, during the pandemic prevention and control period, the digital economy entered a new stage of rapid development. Various platform enterprises were able to fully release their potential and expand, and the labor market also presented new business models and trends.

On the one hand, based on the new demand created, platform companies have created many mass service jobs. E-commerce platforms, new media platforms and social networking platforms have experienced extraordinary development. In addition, new business forms such as online medical care, online education and telecommuting have also gained massive recognition and popularity during the pandemic.

On the other hand, the use of various digital technologies by platform companies has increased technology-based productivity and strengthened the demand for skilled personnel (Acemoglu and Autor, 2011). The pandemic has also led to further improvements in the construction and application of new digital infrastructures.

Second, the pandemic has also accelerated the digitalization process of traditional industries, prompting enterprises to actively rely on digital platforms for transformation and upgrading, thereby partially alleviating the current labor market dilemma.

On the one hand, through the deeper integration of the online and offline worlds, the digital economy has given rise to new business models, expanded new demand markets and flexibly mobilized the workforce. Studies have found that the application of digital technologies can more effectively match employers with employees and buyers with sellers by reducing search costs (Goldfarb and Tucker, 2019; Kuhn and Mansour, 2014). For example, the "shared staff" model of Alibaba's Fresh Hema supermarket has alleviated short-term labor cost burdens and labor shortages, leading to the expansion of the online take-out business. In addition, new models such as "online premieres", live sales and online marketing have emerged.

On the other hand, digital technology also drives changes in the management style and organizational structure of enterprises. In the context of delayed return to work, telecommuting systems guarantee the orderly resumption and development of production and operation. Platforms and the interactive features of the digital economy will gradually come to the fore in the labor market, which is expected to give rise to a flatter and more decentralized enterprise architecture, along with further digitalization in various fields.

To summarize, the above-mentioned policies introduced by governments at all levels in a short period of time reflect a high degree of efficiency in decision-making. In general, the above policies are of universal benefit. How much individual workers or enterprises can benefit depends on other factors. These factors are often linked to market mechanisms. Some targeted policies for specific groups often come with certain conditions attached to their implementation, the difficulty of which is that the information asymmetry between enterprises and the government can easily lead to distortions such as wasted resources and poor implementation effects, which should be avoided.

4.3 Conclusion

The downward trend of the economy in 2019 already had a certain impact on the employment landscape, and the COVID-19 pandemic has further aggravated the labor market. On the one hand, the start and resumption of work by enterprises are generally delayed, and the return of workers to work is correspondingly delayed; on the other hand, the production and operation difficulties of small and medium-sized enterprises have increased, while recruitment demand in the market has generally decreased. The combination of the above factors has significantly impacted the labor market in the short term. The employment situation is most dire for the labor force of small and medium-sized enterprises, college graduates and migrant workers.

Stabilizing employment is the first of the "six stabilities", which is of great significance. The central and local governments have already introduced a large number of policies and measures to deal with the situation. These initiatives are highly specific to the situation at hand and should be implemented as soon as possible.

In light of historical data, we believe that the fundamentals of China's overall stable employment situation will not change, and the impact of the pandemic on the labor market will be short term and manageable. In particular, the digital economy and the Internet platform economy have a strong employment absorption capacity and wide coverage, which is a "heart booster" in the current downward economic environment. During the pandemic, the potential of platform enterprises was fully realized, and the labor market also gave rise to new industries and new trends. In the resumption of work and production, we should break down possible institutional barriers, continue to develop the digital economy, transform and upgrade traditional industries, accelerate the development of the service industry and cultivate new dynamic energy for economic development. At the same time, the pandemic is also forcing reforms, and this time, it is more necessary for the government to listen to the voices of grassroots enterprises, so as to effectively stabilize employment and promote growth in the medium and long term.

In general, the current epidemiological situation is still complicated, and the task of transforming the mode of economic development, optimizing the economic structure and cultivating new economic growth points is an urgent one. In the short term, governments at all levels should focus on key populations, take multiple measures to stabilize enterprises and employment and implement precise, targeted measures as soon as possible. In the long term, efforts should be made to turn crises into opportunities, seize the good opportunities for stable employment created by the Internet platform economy, continue to deepen supply-side structural reforms, improve the business environment, accelerate the transformation of old and new dynamics and realize the transition from the demographic dividend to the human capital dividend, so as to do a thorough job of stabilizing employment in the long term and provide institutional support.

https://doi.org/10.1142/9789811252921_0005

Chapter 5

The Impact of the COVID-19 Pandemic on Agriculture, Rural Areas, and Farmers and Policy Responses

Zhang Yuan and Duan Wen

School of Economics, Fudan University, Shanghai, China

5.1 Turning Point of the Pandemic and a Shift in Focus

The advent of the COVID-19 pandemic has had a serious impact on the national economy and social development. On January 25, 2020, General Secretary Xi Jinping chaired a meeting of the Standing Committee of the Central Political Bureau. It was decided that the Party Central Committee will organize a team of leaders to deal with the pandemic. Since then, several consecutive meetings of the Standing Committee were held to implement scientific, nationwide pandemic prevention and control. In February, a number of targeted economic and pandemic prevention and control policies were intensively introduced, and there was a major turnaround in the control of the pandemic, control of infection sources, and material security. The Huoshenshan and Leishenshan hospitals were constructed in an astonishingly short timeline, and public confidence was stabilized. With thorough scientific deployment and precise policies implemented by the Party Central Committee, and after two consecutive months of hard work by the majority of medical workers, prevention and control of the pandemic is now showing a clear trend for the better. By early March, the number of new confirmed cases in provinces, autonomous regions, and municipalities other than Hubei had dropped to single digits, and many provinces, autonomous regions, and municipalities saw zero new confirmed cases for many days in a row. Academician Zhong Nanshan said at a press briefing on February 27 at the Guangzhou Municipal Government Information Office that "we are confident that the pandemic will be under basic control by the end of April". Therefore, while prioritizing prevention and control of the pandemic, the Party committees and governments at all levels should not neglect other socio-economic development goals and tasks because of the pandemic, but should also strive to minimize the negative impact of the pandemic on other socio-economic development goals. At the same time, it is important to quickly heal the wounds caused by the pandemic and work to accomplish socio-economic development goals. In particular, regions which have had zero new confirmed cases for many days in a row should accelerate the pace of economic recovery to ensure stable growth and other socio-economic development goals.

This chapter first starts with a preliminary analysis of the negative impact of the COVID-19 pandemic on China's macroeconomy as compared to the SARS outbreak in 2003, and then focuses on the short-term negative impact of the current pandemic on poverty eradication, farmers' income growth, and the development goals proposed in the 2020 Central Document No. 1. Policies suggestions are then made for stabilizing economic growth in 2020, coping with the pandemic, and protecting the livelihoods of rural residents.

5.2 Conditions at the Time of the COVID-19 Pandemic and the SARS Epidemic are Quite Different

To analyze the extent of the impact of the COVID-19 pandemic on the Chinese economy, we compare the current Chinese economy with that of 2003, and then use the 2003 SARS epidemic as a frame of reference to determine the likely impact of the current pandemic. Compared to 2003, we believe that the current economy has changed significantly in at least the following five ways.

(1) The current structure of the national economy has changed significantly compared to 2003, and the short-term impact of the COVID-19 pandemic on the service sector, which accounts for a large share of the national economy, is greater.

The contribution of the service sector to GDP was only 39% in 2003, while it had increased to 61.5% by 2018, and the contribution of the secondary industry to GDP has decreased from 57.9% to 34.4%. Since the outbreak began before the Spring Festival, many areas blocked transportation and restricted the movement of people to control the outbreak, which prevented migrant workers from returning to work in a timely fashion after the Spring Festival on the one hand, and dealt a serious blow to the service industry on the other. At a time when the service industry has become the number one industry in the national economy, the impact on it may bring about a drop in national economic growth more severe than that in 2003.

(2) The current integration of China's economy into the global system with an industrial chain division of labor is much deeper than in 2003, and the pandemic will amplify the negative impact through supply chain linkages.

At the time of the SARS outbreak, China's formal accession to the WTO occurred just over 1 year earlier; by 2018 China's total exports had already grown to 4.52 times what they were in 2003, while total imports had grown to 4.12 times what they were in 2003. China's ties to the world economy have become closer through the division of labor in the industrial chain, and COVID-19 pandemic will have a significant negative impact on China's position in the global manufacturing supply chain, which will be transmitted to domestic upstream and downstream companies throughout the supply chain.

(3) The trend of counter-globalization started by the United States and the series of policies by the Trump administration to try to contain the rise of China are not conducive to China being able to make full use of its big-country manufacturing advantages in the global market.

Trump has tried to break the world's rules since taking office, initiating trade frictions against dozens of countries, including China. From curbing Huawei's 5G technology in the U.S. and Europe last year to not providing engines for China's C919 large aircraft this year, all of these are aimed at curbing China's economic rise. Despite the first phase of the U.S.–China trade talks agreement at the end of 2019, economists around the world generally believe that the trend of reverse globalization will be hardly changed in the coming years. The pandemic has given the U.S. an opportunity to take advantage of the situation, potentially moving some of its supply chain in China back to the U.S.

(4) The current economic policies available to China are very different from the choices faced after the SARS epidemic.

On August 31, 2003, the State Council issued the Circular of the State Council on Promoting the Sustainable and Healthy Development of the Real Estate Market, which concluded that there was no bubble in the real estate market and requested that "no policy barriers" be set up to stimulate the real estate industry to drive rapid growth in the national economy. But for the current Chinese economy, housing prices are already high, and the same policy tools are obviously not applicable to promote Chinese economic growth at the present time.

(5) Since early March, the COVID-19 pandemic has spread further globally due to insufficient awareness of the severity of the outbreak and inadequate control in some countries.

If these countries are unable to control the pandemic, China will inevitably have to resort to quarantining people from these countries to prevent and control the importation of the pandemic from abroad (such measures are expected to last at least 2 months on top of the existing ones). Such a situation would have serious consequences, further exacerbating the difficulties faced by China's supply chain, and making it more difficult for China to expand foreign demand and stabilize growth, employment, and foreign trade.

5.3 The Overall Impact of the COVID-19 Pandemic on the Chinese Economy

5.3.1 Preliminary assessment of the medium-term economic impact of the pandemic

The impact of the COVID-19 pandemic on China's economy should first be based on medical research on the progress of the pandemic. In terms of domestic pandemic control, academician Zhong Nanshan said at a press briefing on February 27 at the Guangzhou Municipal Government Information Office on pandemic prevention and control that "We are confident that the pandemic will be under basic control by the end of April". Therefore, the negative impact of the pandemic on China's economy as a whole remains manageable in view of the optimistic situation in the country. In 2003, the year of the SARS outbreak, GDP growth was 10.5%, and in 2004 it also reached 10.5%. However, China's GDP growth dropped to 6.1% in 2019. Based on the significant changes in China's current economy compared to 2003, our analysis and judgment is that the negative impact of this outbreak will exceed that of the SARS outbreak in 2003.

5.3.2 Challenges posed by the pandemic in the short term to rural livelihood in 2020

In order to prevent and control the spread of the pandemic, local governments have taken preventive and control measures to restrict the movement of people. Except for some of the main transportation channels that are still maintaining operations, most of the gross and fine transportation networks in counties, towns, and villages have been largely cut off, resulting in temporary interruptions in the flow of most people and materials. The process of resuming work in the urban sector is still slow. All these have a direct impact on the supply chain and the operation of the national socio-economy. At the same time, the pandemic will also have a direct negative impact on China's exports. We believe that, overall, the long-term impact of the pandemic on the farming industry is relatively small (of course, Hubei and other areas with serious outbreaks are a different story), mainly because agricultural production is in rural areas and is less affected by various pandemic prevention and control measures (e.g., blocking the movement of people), and although spring planting and sowing may be slightly delayed, their work will not be substantially postponed overall. There is a moderate impact on the farming sector, which is mainly attributed to the blockage of logistics and a depressed market demand. However, we should not overlook that the pandemic will pose a short-term challenge to national and local rural livelihoods in 2020 through the following five areas.

(1) A key challenge for rural areas is to delay the departure of nearly 300 million migrant workers to work, significantly reducing their working income in 2020 and greatly increasing the difficulty of poverty alleviation in 2020.

In 2018, there were 288 million rural workers nationwide, including 173 million migrant workers who left the countryside to work. The average monthly income of these rural workers was 3,721 yuan, with those who left the countryside having an average monthly income of 4,107 yuan (National Bureau of Statistics, 2019). This income level is comparable to or even slightly higher than the current poverty line level. This means that 1 farmer working away from home for 1 year can help lift 12 of his or her family members out of poverty. Some studies have found that working outside the home to increase non-rural income is an extremely important channel for rural households to escape poverty (Zhang Yuan *et al.*, 2012). However, the return of migrant workers to urban areas after the Spring Festival has come to an abrupt end under current pandemic prevention and control measures. Based on the current development of the pandemic, nearly 300 million migrant workers will earn roughly one month's salary less in 2020. This will not only drag down the growth rate of income of all rural households in 2020, but will also greatly increase the difficulty of eradicating absolute poverty under the current standard by the end of 2020.

(2) The pandemic has negatively impacted the service sector and residential consumption in the urban sector, which in turn has reduced the demand for rural labor in these sectors, leading to an increase in the unemployment rate of rural migrant workers.

On the one hand, the biggest impact from the pandemic on the domestic urban sector is in the service sector. Unlike in 2003, the proportion of migrant workers engaged in the tertiary sector has been as high as 50.5% in 2018, including 6.7% in accommodation and restaurants and 12.2% in residential services, repair, and other services (National Bureau of Statistics, 2019). These service industries have been greatly hit by the delayed return to work in the urban sector and the pandemic prevention and control measures. In 2003, the SARS epidemic led to a 0.2 percentage point increase in the urban-registered unemployment rate, and today, when the share of service industries is already significantly higher than in 2003, the impact of the current pandemic on service industries is likely to bring about higher unemployment rates. A 0.3 percentage point increase in the unemployment rate would mean that at least 500,000 new migrant workers would have to lose their jobs. This will reduce the remittance income received by the remaining farm households, discourage capital investment in agricultural production, and reduce the number of returning entrepreneurs, thus creating a negative impact on rural socio-economic development. On the other hand, the decline in consumption of agricultural and sideline products by urban residents will reduce the income from the sale of agricultural and sideline products by rural households and increase the difficulty of increasing income and escaping from poverty for those who stay behind in the countryside. Data published on the website of the National Bureau of Statistics 2020 show that in 2019, wage income accounted for 41.09% of the disposable income of rural households, while income from family businesses accounted for 39.96%. Because most urban residents are remaining at home and avoiding going out in order to prevent infection, a clear observation is that urban residents as well as the restaurant industry are now consuming significantly lower levels of agricultural and sideline products such as vegetables, fresh produce, and poultry, with a greater decline in demand for the restaurant industry in particular. The first and fourth quarters of each year are the two quarters when urban residents consume the highest percentages of food, tobacco and alcohol. The current pandemic will suppress urban residents' food consumption in the first quarter as well as the restaurant industry's demand for agricultural and sideline products, which will in turn reduce the family business income for rural households, which accounts for the second highest share of rural household income. Such a situation is detrimental to income growth and poverty alleviation among rural households.

(3) The outbreak of the COVID-19 pandemic will directly reduce China's export growth in 2020, lowering the demand for export orders and negatively impacting the stabilization of employment and rural residents' income.

The outbreak will undoubtedly directly reduce the demand for Chinese exports from other countries, reduce China's export orders, and reduce the demand for rural migrant workers in the export sector as well as their wage levels. In particular, the export sectors of traditional manufacturing industries such as textiles and household electronics primarily employ rural migrant workers. The lower external demand also constitutes a negative impact on poverty alleviation and on raising the income level for rural residents.

(4) Serious challenges are posed to rural socio-economic development in Hubei Province and other provinces heavily affected by the pandemic (Henan, Hunan, Zhejiang, Guangdong).

In addition to the provinces of Hubei, Guangdong, Zhejiang, Henan, and Hunan have also been heavily affected by the pandemic. Among them, Hubei, Henan, and Hunan are the main grain-producing and pig-farming provinces in the central region, and also serve as major labor exporting provinces; the pig stock and the number of rural migrant workers from these three provinces account for more than 15% of the national totals. Guangdong and Zhejiang are important regions for import and export in China, and their import and export totals in 2018 accounted for the first and fourth in the country, respectively, while the total import and export of the two provinces in 2018 accounted for 21.67% of the national total. The negative impact of the pandemic on imports and exports will reduce overseas orders for domestic firms, whereas Zhejiang and Guangdong export-oriented firms employ mostly rural migrant workers. Therefore, the pandemic will put pressure on the incomes of the nation's rural residents both directly and indirectly by impacting the socioeconomic development of these provinces.

5.4 Overview of Policies Introduced by the Central Government

5.4.1 The Central Government has introduced a series of fiscal policies

After the outbreak of the pandemic, the Party Central Committee and the State Council made scientifically-informed decisions and formulated a series of targeted response policies, which in general can be divided into three major areas: pandemic prevention and control, support for enterprises, and support for individuals. For example, the Ministry of Agriculture and Rural Affairs issued an initiative letter to farmers' cooperatives nationwide on January 31, proposing six initiatives to strengthen production and supply, ensure quality and safety, open up sales channels, operate honestly and faithfully, stringently manage pandemic prevention and control, and strengthen personnel protection. The letter also encouraged the reasonable production of produce, livestock, poultry, and other important agricultural products as well as maintenance of normal production order, so as to ensure the effective supply of "food basket" products. Proactive organization and rapid and orderly circulation of agricultural products was also encouraged in order to ensure that agricultural products could reach the shelves of city supermarkets. It was stipulated that if any difficulties arose in the production source or transport of agricultural products, the local government or agricultural and rural departments must be notified in a timely manner. There is a zero-tolerance stance toward people taking advantage of the opportunity to hoard, price gouge, publish false and misleading information, or commit other acts that disrupt the market order. Husbandry farmer cooperatives should regulate breeding production and not purchase, transport, or sell wild animals and products that are of unknown origin or illegally obtained. Shortly after the promulgation of these initiatives, the National Development and Reform Commission, together with relevant departments and financial institutions, set up a coordination mechanism for financial support and protection, in accordance with the spirit of the circular of the People's Bank of China, the Ministry of Finance, the Banking and Insurance Regulatory Commission, the Securities and Futures Commission, and the Foreign Exchange Bureau on further strengthening financial support for pandemic prevention and control. In close collaboration with departments and localities, the commission made the production of control appliances and supplies related to pandemic prevention and control, along with corresponding upstream key materials and components, a top priority for financial support, and implemented a list system for management of these key supplies.

On January 31, in the interest of comprehensive protection of the transport of living materials, the National Development and Reform Commission and Ministry of Commerce required that relief be given to enterprises facing difficulties in capital, labor, energy, industry chain support as they resume production. There should be active coordination and effective safeguards put in place; reliable channels should be established to ensure the supply of important materials, timely mobility for emergency transport needs, and protection for the transport needs of important living materials. Market monitoring for local produce, food, and other daily consumption needs should be enhanced, and supermarkets should be urged to replenish stock frequently and keep ample reserves of stock and produce. There will be a strict crack down on fabrication and dissemination of information intended to cause price increases, enable price gouging, hoarding, collusion, and other illegal acts. The market supply of essential goods such as grain and oil, meat, instant noodles and bottled water should be increased. Subsequently, various central departments have promulgated the *Guidance of the National Health Insurance Bureau, Ministry of Finance, General Administration of Taxation on Phased Reduction of Employees' Basic Health Insurance Premiums* (Health Insurance Issuance, (2020), No. 6), the *Circular of the Ministry of Human Resources and Social Security, Ministry of Finance, General Administration of Taxation on Phased Reduction of Enterprise Social Insurance Premiums* (Ministry of Human Resources and Social Security, (2020), No. 11), the *Notice from the Ministry of Housing and Urban-Rural Development, Ministry of Finance, and People's Bank Notice on the Implementation of Phased Support Policy for Housing Provident Fund in the Appropriate Response to the COVID-19 Pandemic* (Jianjin, (2020), No. 23), which implement policies of phased reduction or deferment of medical insurance, social insurance, and housing provident funds for enterprises employing workers, thus greatly reducing the burden on enterprises and the probability of bankruptcy due to cash flow breakdowns. On February 1, the People's Bank of China, the Ministry of Finance, the CBRC, the SFC, and the Bureau of Foreign Exchange jointly issued the *Notice on Further Strengthening Financial Support for the Prevention and Control of the COVID-19 Pandemic*, which stipulates the implementation of good counter-cyclical adjustment to provide sufficient liquidity through various monetary policy tools such as open market operations, standing lending facilities, re-lending, and re-discounting to maintain a reasonable abundance of liquidity in the financial market and promote reasonable growth of money and credit in response to the needs of pandemic prevention and control and the high maturity of funds after the holidays. In addition, other departments as well as local governments at all levels have successively formulated different response policies according to the needs of pandemic prevention and control and socio-economic development.

5.4.2 Agricultural policies introduced by the Central Government

Among the series of policies formulated by the central government in response to the pandemic, there are many directly targeting agriculture, rural areas, farmers, and poor households under the Targeted Poverty Alleviation program. For example, on February 14, the State Council Poverty Alleviation Office and the Ministry of Finance issued the *Notice from the State Council Poverty Alleviation Office and Ministry of Finance on Actively Responding to the Impact of the COVID-19 Pandemic to Strengthen the Project Management of the Public Financial Special Poverty Alleviation Funds to Ensure the Full and Timely Completion of the Target Tasks of Poverty Eradication* (Guo Kai Ban, (2020), No. 5), which formulated a series of policies to support poor households to resume production, enable people to restore their own production capacity, and increase rewards and subsidies. Conditions will be created that will encourage poor laborers to start their own business. Employment support will be strengthened, and appropriate arrangements will be made for making special poverty alleviation funds available for the organization of stable employment positions for the poor. As the need for labor in pandemic prevention and control increases, priority will be given to the employment of poor laborers for new temporary positions related to cleaning, sanitation, pandemic prevention and elimination, inspection and guarding, etc. Existing policies on public welfare jobs will be implemented. During prevention and control, poor laborers who leave home for work are given subsidies for transportation and living expenses in accordance with regulations, and incentives can be increased for certain areas on a conditional basis. The basic livelihood of the poor must be fully protected. For poor people who suffer from COVID-19, concentrated or home isolation, are unable to leave home for work, unable to carry out basic production, or whose income has been significantly affected (such as those living in poverty due to the pandemic), the existing support channels should implement targeted measures in a timely fashion to ensure that basic life needs are not affected.

On February 14, the Ministry of Finance and the Ministry of Agriculture and Rural Affairs issued the *Notice of the General Office of the Ministry of Finance and the General Office of the Ministry of Agriculture and Rural Affairs on Effective Support for the Work of Stabilizing Production and Ensuring Supply of Agricultural Products during the Prevention and Control of the COVID-19 Pandemic* (Cai Ban Nong, (2020), No. 6), which stipulates making full use of the role of the national agricultural credit guarantee system and promoting solutions to expensive financing for medium-scale agricultural business entities. From the date of issuance until the end of December 2020, the National

Agricultural Credit Guarantee Union Limited Liability Company will reduce by half the re-guarantee fees for provincial agricultural guarantee companies. Each locality should introduce policy credit guarantee business guarantee fee reduction measures in light of the actual situation on the ground in order to reduce the cost of financing the relevant new agricultural business entities affected by the pandemic. The pandemic has had a relatively heavy impact on family farms and farmers' cooperatives; each region should take advantage of the time available to begin the construction of cold chain logistics facilities for the refrigeration and preservation of agricultural products, and make use of the Central Government financial arrangements for the development of agricultural production funds. We must increase support for family farms and farmers' cooperatives, further refine the means of support, focus on improving the availability of cold facilities for fresh products, and continually enhance the resilience and flexibility of agricultural production capacity.

Premier Li Keqiang hosted a State Council executive meeting on February 18 to ensure that spring agricultural production remains normal during the farming season. The council decided to phase in the reduction of enterprise social security fees and the implementation of an enterprise moratorium on housing fund policy, and enact multiple measures to stabilize enterprises and employment. The meeting stressed that the farming season does not wait for people; in order to protect the summer harvest, each locality must take responsibility for its part in the spring agricultural production. Doing so will require a three-pronged approach. First, scientific guidance on the prevention and control of rural outbreaks should be refined and well categorized. We must guide and support each region to be well prepared for spring plowing and to optimize the field management of overwintered crops. We should support enterprises dealing with seeds, fertilizers, pesticides, feed, and other agricultural products to speed up the resumption of production, and promote the establishment of transport channels with point-to-point guaranteed agricultural supplies. This year, the minimum purchase price of rice should remain stable, and depending on the situation can be appropriately increased. Encourage areas that are able to do so to resume double cropping of rice. Second, we must keep a strong handle on livestock and poultry production. This can be done by granting extended loan repayment terms, relaxing loan guarantees, and other policy support to poultry farmers in key areas with large losses, and promoting coordination between farming households and meat processing enterprises. By adjusting the scope of loan subsidies for farm households from an annual slaughter of more than 5,000 head to more than 500 head, the recovery of pig production can be quickened and the national stock of frozen pork can be increased. Third, we must strengthen the prevention and control of major diseases and pests, strengthen monitoring, and make preparations for any necessary countermeasures. We must step up prevention and control for the highly pathogenic avian influenza, African swine fever, and other major animal diseases. On March 16, the National Development and Reform Commission and the Ministry of Agriculture and Rural Affairs jointly issued the statement *On the Support of Private Enterprises to Develop Pig Production and Related Industries*; the National Development and Reform Commission and the Ministry of Agriculture and Rural Affairs will work with relevant departments to create a healthy state of affairs by supporting private enterprises to accelerate the development of pig production and related industries and establish high-quality industry development, strong supply security, and stable and orderly prices.

5.5 Policy Recommendations

5.5.1 Policy recommendations for stabilizing growth

(1) Crack down on the illegal activities of selling forehead thermometers and infrared thermometers. Research found that such thermometers are purchased in bulk by certain criminal gangs and resold repeatedly to make high profits, resulting in the price paid by the real buyer being many times higher than the factory price. It is suggested that investigation departments in charge of industry, commerce, commodity price, economic issues, and public security increase efforts to combat the illegal behavior of malicious speculation of thermometer prices, and monitor WeChat use for trading and speculation by criminal gangs. In order to put an end to such malicious speculation, both buyers and sellers must provide supporting materials (buyers should provide an official letter with official seal issued by the neighborhood committee, village committee, business units, and purchases should be limited; sellers should provide the producer or seller of the product legal proof materials) so that underground traders in the gray market will have nowhere to hide.

(2) Take advantage of the UK's exit from the EU to strengthen economic ties with the UK and the EU and stabilize European foreign demand

for China. The UK's formal exit from the EU on January 31, 2020 entails a substantial rift in European economic integration, as well as the need for the UK to adjust its relations with the rest of the world. At this time, the UK intends to establish closer economic ties with China, and British economists generally support closer economic ties with China. Therefore, China should take advantage of this opportunity to conduct diplomatic activities and establish closer economic ties with the UK and the EU.

(3) Work diligently to establish economic ties with Japan and India to expand Asia's foreign demand for China. India is currently the world's second most populous country and has experienced rapid economic growth in recent years. The country holds a huge potential for market demand, especially for Chinese manufacturing products, which have a large market in India. After the outbreak of the pandemic, the Japanese government and the public expressed a strong signal of goodwill to China by donating medical substances to Wuhan, Hubei. With the U.S. besieging Chinese high-tech companies represented by Huawei, seeking cooperation from Japan in some areas of science and technology is a potential option; moreover, Japan and China complement each other in terms of industrial structure. Promoting China's ties with these two Asian economies could effectively expand foreign demand from Asia.

(4) The pandemic has revealed a serious shortage of hospital beds in China's medical sector, and it is recommended to take advantage of the opportunity to make up for the shortcomings of medical and elderly institutions in terms of hardware. In recent years, investment in the health, social security, and social welfare sectors in China has accounted for less than 0.5% of the total investment in fixed assets, which is highly relevant to two issues, namely "difficulty in accessing medical care" and "difficulty in providing for the elderly. " At the end of 2018, China's elderly population had reached 249 million, which is expected to reach 480 million by 2050. Such a large elderly population entails a huge market for healthcare and elderly care, and an urgent demand for the existing hardware that is in tight supply (beds). Quality nursing homes in good condition are always "hard to find". It is recommended that the National Development and Reform Commission formulate a plan to increase the proportion of social fixed asset investment in health, social security, and social welfare to more than 2% during the 14th Five-Year Plan.

(5) On the consumer side, encourage automobile consumption among urban residents, and introduce policies to encourage the deployment of agricultural vehicles to the countryside, increase subsidies for agricultural machinery. The boost to the consumption of automobiles and agricultural machinery will spur growth in related upstream and downstream industries. The auto industry is the jewel in the crown of modern industry and has a strong pulling effect on metallurgy, nonferrous metals, rubber, electronics, petrochemicals, steel, finance, insurance, advertising, marketing intermediaries, and other industries. However, China's auto consumption has been sluggish in recent years. Domestic residents' auto consumption grew at a year-on-year rate of –0.7% in the first three quarters of 2019, and profits of the above-scale auto manufacturing industry fell by 16.6% year-on-year. As the pandemic has reduced Chinese residents' consumption and travel demand, some researchers expect new car sales to fall 25% year-on-year in the first quarter of 2020. China's middle-income group has now exceeded 400 million, and they are the key target for expanding domestic demand. It is recommended that policies be introduced on the consumption side to incentivize urban residents to increase their consumption of middle- and high-grade cars, including reducing or waiving purchase taxes, providing subsidies to consumers, implementing trade-in subsidies, and eliminating traffic restrictions in small and medium-sized cities. For rural areas, it is recommended that automobile campaigns be introduced to the countryside to subsidize farmers' purchase of agricultural vehicles and large agricultural production machinery.

(6) Accelerate the transition from investment in "railway and public transportation" to investment in "new intelligent infrastructure" as a point of new economic growth. Based on the 5G network, intelligent transportation systems (supporting transportation facilities for driverless and shared cars), intelligent micro-grid systems (network facilities for optimal allocation of energy such as intelligent energy storage, charging, hydrogen refueling, and distributed energy) and other new intelligent infrastructures, which have the attributes of public use, positive externality, and strong spillover, as well as the advantages of advanced technology, good prospects, and sustainable debt, should be regarded as the new scope of infrastructure construction investment and the next stage of investment focus. The new intelligent infrastructure is characterized by large investment and a strong pulling effect.

Taking 5G technology as an example, it is expected that China's overall direct investment in 5G technology amounts to 1.2 trillion yuan, with an investment cycle that may exceed 8 years. The 5G industry chain and enabling industries (including smart transportation, smart cities, smart factories, smart education, smart agriculture, video entertainment, etc.) will also give rise to tens of trillions of yuan of investment.

5.5.2 Policy recommendations to support agriculture, rural areas, and farmers to cope with the impact of the pandemic

The idea of Targeted Poverty Alleviation proposed by General Secretary Xi Jinping at the end of 2013 carries very high scientific validity (Zhang Yuan *et al.*, 2019), and in practice has achieved good results, lifting more than 10 million people per year out of poverty for several consecutive years. Therefore, under the strong leadership of the Party and the ideology of Targeted Poverty Alleviation, China is fully capable of overcoming the pandemic and winning the final battle against poverty, and well poised to properly address the short-term negative impact of the pandemic on rural livelihoods. To this end, we make the following recommendations based on the above analysis.

(1) We should not waste time in giving ample attention to the shortage of medical personnel and supplies faced by the cities in close proximity to Wuhan and areas near Hubei severely affected by the pandemic so that we can win the battle against the pandemic, containing it as soon as possible. This will allow us to minimize the negative impact of the pandemic on poverty alleviation and other socio-economic development goals.

From February 5, prefecture-level cities near Wuhan, where the pandemic is more severe, and some prefecture-level cities in other provinces bordering Hubei also began to experience medical resource shortages, and on February 6, the pandemic prevention and control commands in Xinyang and Nanyang, Henan Province, faced a shortage of medical supplies and asked for help from the community. For this reason, it is recommended that while the whole country should support Wuhan and Hubei, other regions should also be mobilized in time to assist the plight of medical resource shortages faced by serious outbreak areas outside Hubei (that is, other provinces and cities bordering Hubei Province). After the pandemic has subsided, the infrastructure shortcomings faced by lagging regions due to the pandemic should be rectified in a timely manner on the basis of the 2020 Central Document No. 1, which already proposes to rectify infrastructure shortcomings in rural areas, whereas the insufficient number of hospital beds made evident by the pandemic also falls under the category of infrastructure. Therefore, it is recommended that, based on the 2020 Central Document No. 1, some funds must be used to increase the number of hospital beds in township and county-level health centers to improve the capacity of rural areas to respond to unexpected epidemics.

(2) Under the premise that the pandemic is basically under control, road closures will be lifted as soon as possible to free up logistics and ensure the smooth flow of transportation of products and living materials, and allow all links of the supply chain to begin resumption of operation. Provinces and municipalities where the pandemic is not severe should resume production as soon as possible, given that there is thorough screening of febrile patients.

On February 6, the Ministry of Commerce issued a document allowing some enterprises to start production; on February 8, the General Office of the State Council also issued a notice to maintain good traffic conditions to ensure smooth traffic flow, but at present, many township and village roads are still closed or interrupted, and many products, such as animal feed, cannot be transported from livestock breeders. It is recommended that the public security and road authorities also quickly release documents requiring grassroots governments, village committees, and neighborhood committees to lift the township and village road closure measures, otherwise the pace of resumption of production will still be sluggish.

(3) Increase policy support for labor-intensive SMEs, reduce the probability of SME bankruptcy, and maintain employment and livelihood stability through comprehensive support policies such as tax and rent reductions, delayed payment of employee social security, and extension of expiring loans.

The survival of SMEs is directly related to more than 80% of the nation's employment and the stability of society. It is recommended that simple measures such as one-time tax and rent reductions (e.g.,

1 month tax reduction), a one-month extension of employee social security payments, and a one- to two-month extension of bank loans if the loans are not repayable should be adopted for SMEs. It is recommended that the central government encourage local governments to allocate "real money" to support SMEs to survive the pandemic and to prevent the bankruptcy of SMEs from causing massive unemployment.

(4) To maintain the continuity of Targeted Poverty Alleviation policies, local governments at all levels are forbidden from arbitrarily interrupting various Targeted Poverty Alleviation initiatives because of the pandemic.

Poverty alleviation funds must not be squandered or misappropriated, and provincial-level finances must not cut off or reduce the input of various poverty alleviation funds and resources to lower-level governments because of the pandemic, but rather must maintain the consistency of poverty alleviation policies and poverty alleviation funds. At the same time, local governments at all levels should pay great attention to those who have suffered poverty induced by COVID-19 pandemic. It is recommended that urban civil affairs departments and rural poverty alleviation departments give ample attention to families in which the main provider of labor or income for the family has died in the pandemic, and families that become poor in this pandemic must be promptly included in the scope of protection of rural Targeted Poverty Alleviation and urban minimum living standards.

(5) It is suggested that the central grain reserve unit should acquire live pigs from Henan, Hubei, and Hunan provinces to solve the problem of reduced amounts of frozen meat reserves on the one hand, and to cope with the possible further increase of meat prices in the future on the other.

The decline in consumption in the catering industry and traffic blockage in some areas have led to many farmers in areas severely hit by the pandemic facing dual dilemma of not being able to bring in feed while also not being able to sell their pigs. This is the right time to increase the central reserve of frozen meat, which can make up for the drop in reserves caused by the Spring Festival, reduce the losses of farmers, and lay the foundation for the government to moderate meat prices and stabilize CPI in the future.

5.6 Conclusion

In the past two months, based on the central government's targeted measures and scientific response, China has achieved a phased victory in the battle against the pandemic, with several provinces and cities showing a positive trend of zero new confirmed cases for many days in a row. "We are confident that the pandemic will be under control by the end of April," said academician Zhong Nanshan at a press briefing on February 27, 2020 at the Guangzhou Municipal Government Information Office. In fact, as researchers, we have closely observed the policies of the Central Government during the pandemic and found that the timely response of policymakers and the scientific and targeted economic policies have been affirmed by many economists, and many of the targeted policies enacted are precisely what many economists consider to be the correct ones. Therefore, we are confident that China will be able to overcome this pandemic. What is worrisome, however, is the performance of neighboring countries in the fight against the pandemic. If a global outbreak of the COVID-19 pandemic were to occur, it would significantly dampen global economic growth, and even if China succeeds in overcoming the pandemic, the long war is not one that can be won alone.

https://doi.org/10.1142/9789811252921_0006

Chapter 6

Senior Services in the COVID-19 Pandemic

Peng Xizhe* and Wang Xuehui†

**School of Social Development and Public Policy, Fudan University, Shanghai, China*

†*Population and Development Policy Research Center, Fudan University, Shanghai, China*

By the end of 2019, there were about 254 million people aged 60 and over in China, accounting for 18.1% of the total population.[1] The overall health status of the elderly in China is not optimistic; in 2018, more than 180 million elderly people suffered from chronic diseases, accounting for 75% of the elderly sub-population, and there are about 40 million disabled and partially disabled elderly persons.[2] China is currently facing the challenge of a rapidly aging population, with a large number of elderlies suffering from chronic diseases and disabilities, who require extremely urgent healthcare services. In recent years, China has considered and vigorously supported elder care as a strategic and emerging industry. During pandemic prevention and control, the elderly care service industry is not only

[1]*National Bureau of Statistics: "Statistical Communiqué of the People's Republic of China on National Economic and Social Development in 2019"*, February 28, 2020.

[2]*"Text Record of the Press Conference of the Office of the Healthy China Action Promotion Committee on July 29, 2019"*, http://www.nhc.gov.cn/xcs/s7847/201907/520f21e5ac234785bcc363a286866fb0.shtml.

a high-risk enterprise, but also an industry that has suffered a huge impact in terms of development. This industry shoulders the important task of providing solutions to issues faced by large numbers of elderly people. At the same time, elderly care enterprises, represented by residential institutions, have also been faced with the difficult task of pandemic prevention and control. As regards the high-risk areas for COVID-19, the Ministry of Civil Affairs and the National Health Commission have successively issued pandemic prevention and control guidelines for "institutions providing both eldercare, medical services and those integrating both of these services", contributing to the effective control of the pandemic. The grim fact is that the elderly care service industry has been greatly impacted due to pandemic prevention and control measures, in particular, the supply of community home care services has been affected on a relatively larger scale, such that relevant enterprises face a huge risk of bankruptcy. This chapter aims to analyze the development status of China's elderly care service industry, analyze the impact of the pandemic on the industry, and evaluate the pandemic response strategies of different entities within the industry.

6.1 The Impact of COVID-19 on Services for the Elderly

6.1.1 The impact of COVID-19 on the elderly

The physical condition of the elderly continues to deteriorate as age progresses. The elderly often suffer from a variety of chronic underlying diseases, and undoubtedly belong to a high-risk group relevant to this pandemic. On February 19, 2020, based on data from more than 70,000 confirmed cases, the China Centers for Disease Control and Prevention released a report based on an analysis of the epidemiological characteristics of COVID-19. It showed that the proportion of cases in the elderly group over 60 years old accounts for 44.1% in Wuhan and 35.1% in Hubei province (including Wuhan). The percentage in the whole country (including Hubei) is 31.2%. Regardless of the confirmed cases in Wuhan, Hubei (including Wuhan), or the whole country (including Hubei), the percentage of confirmed cases in the elderly is the highest. In addition, cases of death mainly occurred in this group. The fatality rate of the elderly group is significantly higher than that of other age groups. The crude fatality rate is 3.6% for the 60–69 age group, 8.0% for the 70–79 age group, and 14.8% for >80 age group. The confirmed cases in the elderly often occurred in patients with existing comorbidities, and the report shows that the fatality rate of patients with comorbidities is much higher than that of patients without them. The fatality rate of patients with cardiovascular disease, diabetes, chronic respiratory disease, hypertension, and cancer is 10.5%, 7.3%, 6.3%, 6.0%, and 5.6%, respectively.

During the pandemic prevention and control period, community home care providers suspended services. The daily lives and care services provided to elderly people who live alone and/or have a disability were greatly affected. Elderly people living alone were not able to buy daily necessities and medicines due to the closed management of the community, and they needed the assistance of community staff. The disabled elderly who live alone have been the most vulnerable group during the pandemic. They do not live with their children and cannot live independently. Their personal safety is threatened. This population has a strong reliance and dependence on home care services.

6.1.2 The impact of COVID-19 on nursing homes

6.1.2.1 *The risk of pandemic transmission in nursing homes*

Nursing homes are places where the elderly live in close proximity. There is no doubt that it is a disaster once staff and/or elderly residents become infected. Hence, following the outbreak of the COVID-19, pandemic prevention and control measures in nursing homes has been a priority. From the perspective of transmission routes, the source of infection in closed nursing homes mainly comes from the outside community.

Hence, it is infected people who are moving from the community into the facility that most often introduce the virus. If a new senior citizen carries the virus, then people in the closed residential home may become infected. If a staff member (manager, caregiver, medical staff, logistics staff, cleaners) become infected outside the institution, he will infect other personnel or residents after entering the nursing home. Though the nursing homes are relatively isolated from the outside world, they do not exist in a vacuum. All kinds of daily necessities need to be brought in from outside, and staff enter and leave the facility throughout the pandemic prevention and control period. Thus, there is a greater possibility of the spread of the virus in nursing homes, which is a key area for the prevention and control of this pandemic.

6.1.2.2 *Problems and dilemmas faced by elderly care institutions during the pandemic prevention and control period*

After the outbreak of COVID-19, the Ministry of Civil Affairs required all elderly care institutions to implement strict measures for pandemic prevention and control. Despite some cases of infections occurring within elderly care institutions, there have been no large-scale infections in these institutions nationwide. The result of strict pandemic prevention has been remarkable. At the same time, some problems did occur, such as an insufficient stock of anti-pandemic resources, a lack of anti-pandemic professionals, and insufficient preparation of emergency plans. Currently, elderly care institutions across the country have implemented policies which forbid senior citizens from leaving the institution to prevent the spread of the pandemic. However, some urgent problems occurred at the same time.

(1) There were elderly people who needed urgent care and to return to hospital to receive professional care. Some elderly people who returned home for the Spring Festival did so because of the expectation of limited life expectancy. After the outbreak, these people had to remain at home because the original receiving institution did not allow senior citizens to be readmitted. In other cases, some elderly people left the facility to see a doctor, but after completing their treatment, they were turned away from nursing homes and had to return to their family's home.
(2) Institutions cannot admit the elderly into the nursing homes, and they dare not do so; during the COVID-19 pandemic, the elderly were a highly vulnerable group, and elderly care institutions, where elderly people live together, contain high-risks. This is especially true for nursing homes which provide care services for the disabled and demented elderly. Currently, most elderly care institutions do not have the good equipment and facilities for professional isolation and protection. If they admit the elderly without full consideration, it will create risks of pandemic spread.

(3) Elderly care institutions implemented the policy of not admitting new senior citizens, which impacted occupancy rates. Therefore, there were empty beds and at the same time income decreased and costs increased leading to financial problems in some institutions. A survey of some elderly care institutions found that during the pandemic, many institutions had beds available. Due to the pandemic, the elderly were unable to return to the facility in time after celebrating New Year at home. Pandemic-related expenditures including adding protective facilities and equipment, and purchasing protective equipment increased sharply, and the prices of food and other daily necessities also increased. In addition, during the pandemic, institutions stopped face-to-face cash collection and payment services, and most of the elderly and their families were not familiar with online payment procedures. Thus, they encountered problems when trying to pay remittances. Various factors have reduced institutional revenues and increased costs, leaving elderly care institutions in financial trouble.

6.1.3 The impact of COVID-19 on community home care services

COVID-19 is a major public health event. pandemic prevention and control guidelines from the Ministry of Civil Affairs required that home-based care services be stopped. At the same time, community facilities for the elderly, such as the community comprehensive elderly service centers, community day service centers, elderly care homes, and catering places for the elderly, were also shut down. These prevention and control measures achieved significant results in controlling the pandemic in the community, but they also brought many difficulties and challenges to the elderly at home and community home-based elderly care service enterprises.

6.1.3.1 *Significant increase in labor costs*

During the prevention and control of COVID-19, community home care services have been hit hard. All community service places for the elderly had been closed, and home care services had been reduced by more than half. Despite the sharp decline in business volume, employees cannot be dismissed on a large scale, and current employees still need to be paid basic wages and relevant insurance, which is a heavy burden for enterprises.

6.1.3.2 *The sharp drop in revenue may risk breaking the capital chain*

During the pandemic, home-based services have been suspended, and facilities like day care centers, and nursing stations have basically been in a state of stagnation. A few providers still have business operations, but the business volume is less than 25% of usual volume. For a large-scale nursing station chain company in Shanghai, the net loss in one month is about 20 million yuan. If business cannot be gradually resumed, the continuous loss of income from the branches will force the company to go bankrupt.

6.1.3.3 *The development of the industry has been severely impacted*

Many home-based service providers are facing difficulties in the funding chain, which will inevitably affect the payment of employees' wages. Some companies may even take measures not favorable to employees, leading to labor disputes. The general labor costs in community nursing stations engaged in home care services accounts for 70% of its total cost. If a large number of enterprises cannot ride out the difficulties, it will lead to an increase in the number of unemployed, which is not conducive to a stable labor market. In addition, the suspension of community home care services effects the care service providers in stages, it effects the quality of life of the elderly immediately and for a prolonged period. "Elderly care is not only a major livelihood of the people, but also a major industry." The realization of the goal of "Making elderly care services an important platform for promoting high-quality development and creating a high-quality of life and important growth opportunity for releasing consumption potential and cultivating development momentum" will be greatly impacted.

6.2 Strategies and Measures to Cope with Challenges

6.2.1 Policy response

6.2.1.1 *At the national level*

After the outbreak, the State Council, the Health Commission, the Ministry of Civil Affairs, and other national departments and relevant ministries and commissions issued a number of policies to prevent and control the pandemic. Closed management was implemented in nursing homes across the country. To prevent the spread of COVID-19 in elderly care institutions, the Ministry of Civil Affairs successively issued two editions of the *Guidelines for the Prevention and Control of Pneumonia pandemic Caused by COVID-19 in Elderly Care Institutions*. The second edition provides specific guidelines for the prevention and control of the pandemic in elderly care institutions from seven perspectives, including organizational leadership, access management, psychological comfort, protection of the elderly, internal control, pandemic management, and disinfection. In contrast to the first, the second edition puts forward new requirements for the implementation of systems in residential institutions during the period of closure, providing more specific and detailed regulations on pandemic prevention and treatment, and adding guidelines for residents to seek medical treatment during the pandemic period. The second edition strengthens the treatment ways in the elderly care institutions when senior citizens are diagnosed as suspected or infected, promoting the elderly care institutions to be able to deal with various diseases normally during the prevention and control period. The National Health Commission has also issued policy documents for the prevention and control of pandemics in elderly care and integrated medical care institutions, which strengthens the ability of elderly people to seek medical care during the pandemic and the prevention of the pandemic in key areas.

Based on these policy documents, prior to February, the focus of the policy in the elderly care sector was still on pandemic prevention and control. It gradually evolved to comprehensively covering and strengthening the pandemic prevention and control work of elderly care, medical care, and primary medical and health service institutions. The intensive policies introduced during the pandemic have effectively controlled the spread of the pandemic in closed elderly care service facilities, and ensured the safety of the lives of the elderly. Since March, the focus of the policy has been on the orderly restoration of services in elderly care facilities. On March 5, the Ministry of Civil Affairs issued the *Guiding Opinions on Precise Management of Pandemic Prevention and Control and Restoration of Service in Elderly Care Service Institutions by Division and Level*, adhering to the strategy of preventing the spread of the pandemic, especially imported cases. It proposes that after the approval of the local party committee and government, reopening can be resumed in an orderly manner, provided that the pandemic prevention and control is in place. At the same time, the policy also clarifies the corresponding preferential policies that senior care service institutions may qualify for, and encourages localities to introduce targeted support policies for senior care service institutions based on their actual conditions.

6.2.1.2 *At the local level*

In terms of supporting the development of the elderly service industry during the pandemic, places such as Sichuan, Anhui, Jiangsu, Shandong, and Shanghai have introduced various supporting policies. On March 4, 2020, the Sichuan Provincial Department of Civil Affairs and the Department of Finance issued the *Notice on Issuing One-time Operating Subsidies to Elderly Care Institutions in the Province During COVID-19*, which allows elderly care institutions that are operating normally and implementing closed management during the prevention and control of the pandemic throughout the province to receive a one-off operating subsidy. On March 5, 2020, ten departments, including the Department of Civil Affairs of Jiangsu Province, jointly issued the *Guiding Opinions on Actively Responding to COVID-19 and Promoting the Stable and Healthy Development of Elderly Care Services*, proposing eight measures to help the elderly care service industry overcome the difficulties of the pandemic, including reducing the tax burden of elderly care service companies, reducing the rent costs of elderly care service organizations, subsidizing the operating costs of elderly care services, allowing elderly care organizations to reduce, exempt, or postpone some fees, strengthening financial support for the development of elderly care services, helping elderly care institutions resume normal operations, ensuring the supply of necessary materials for elderly care institutions, and actively developing

"Internet + elderly care services". On March 7, 2020, the Shanghai Municipal Civil Affairs Bureau issued the *Notice on Implementing the Supporting Policy Guidelines for Elderly Care Service Institutions in the City During COVID-19*. The document focused on amalgamating a number of enterprise support policies issued by the State Council, relevant ministries and commissions, and Shanghai, which elderly care institutions can refer to for the implementation. On March 11, Shandong Province issued the *Notice on Several Measures to Actively Respond to the New Coronary Pneumonia Pandemic to Support the Development of the Elderly Service Industry*, clearly issuing 11 specific measures including operating subsidies, credit financing support policies, tax reductions and exemptions to support the industry in strengthening pandemic prevention and control, overcoming operating difficulties, and healthy and stable development. On March 13, 2020, the Shanghai Municipal Civil Affairs Bureau and Bank of China Shanghai Branch jointly launched the exclusive financial service program "Jin Jiu Tiao", established the first 3 billion yuan of special credit funds, and fully supported the resumption of work and production in Shanghai's elderly care service industry.

6.2.2 The corresponding measures of elderly care service companies

Compared with other fields, the elderly care service industry has always been a relatively stable industry that is resistant to the economic cycle, which has been well reflected during the pandemic. During the pandemic, the advantages of the elderly care service institutions have been clearly revealed. The huge opportunity for the development of this industry has also been highlighted. However, for home care service companies that are just at the initial stage of development, this pandemic is strong enough to push them to the brink of bankruptcy. To minimize the losses caused by the pandemic and realize the healthy and sustainable development of the industry in the future, elderly care service companies must develop timely response strategies.

6.2.2.1 *Coping strategies of elderly care institutions*

(1) *Elderly care institutions should transform temporary responses into emergency management systems*: Illness, weakness, dementia, and

other problems are common among the elderly, who are prone to emergencies due to diseases, sudden deaths, and nosocomial infections. Therefore, emergency management is an important part of the daily management of elderly care institutions. These institutions should have plans in place to deal with sudden natural disasters, accidents, and public health emergencies, conduct effective daily assessments intervention in and mitigation of various risks, establish systems and sound mechanisms, to be able to deal with emergencies in an orderly manner. In addition, emergency incidents often trigger many derivative problems, expanding the scope and impact of incident response. For example, psychological counseling of the elderly highlighted in the prevention and control of the pandemic, good communication and coordination between the institution and families, and the management of nosocomial infections, are all important contents of the daily management and service of the institutions, as well as the supporting elements included in the emergency management system.

(2) *Elderly care institutions actively establish close ties with community health service centers*: In response to the medical care needs of the elderly, elderly care institutions should establish normalized contact with community health service centers, and actively obtain permission from the health and civil affairs departments to promote their services, including remote guidance, health promotion, and medical transfer from community health service centers to elderly care institutions. These institutions should ensure that once health problems arise, they obtain telemedicine guidance from the community health service center and provide professional services such as home delivery of medicines and physical examinations as needed.

(3) *Senior care institutions should strengthen their health management services*: In addition to the demand for medical care, the demand for health management services in the elderly is more important. During this pandemic, there have been many rumors, causing panic and anxiety among the elderly. Health managers of elderly care institutions should immediately clarify rumors and fallacies, disseminate pandemic prevention knowledge, and provide psychological comfort and guidance. In the daily management of elderly care institutions, health management expertise, such as scientific medication guidance, dietary and nutritional advice, and exercise should all play an active role.

6.2.2.2 *Coping strategies of community home service companies (institutions)*

(1) *Multiple measures have been taken to effectively reduce business operating costs*: Cost control is the basis for the sustained and stable development of elderly care service companies faced with cyclical economic fluctuations, but simple cost reduction strategies will inevitably affect the work efficiency and service quality of the company. Therefore, cost reduction measures of community-based home care service companies are not only about reducing expenditure on personnel and materials but also about reducing unnecessary costs and refining the optimal working mode and optimal service mode under the premise of ensuring necessary operating costs. The normal operation of the service and management model is the principle to ensure the sustainable development of elderly care service enterprises during the economic downturn. At the same time, companies can seek government financial support and short-term capital bridging support from financial institutions to ensure that cash flow is not interrupted due to the pandemic.

(2) *Long-distance nursing skills training should be carried out for the families of the elderly*: During the pandemic prevention and control period, children will replace professional nursing staff as important caregivers. When it is not possible to enter the home to carry out front-line care services, the community home-based service companies and smart elderly care companies cooperate with families to provide online training services through intelligent information platforms, and strengthen the nursing skills and knowledge of caring within families, hoping to improve the quality of life of the elderly at home during the special period of the pandemic.

(3) *Home care service companies actively integrate with community care facilities' resources*: In the "post-pandemic era," the elderly will stay at home more for health and safety reasons, especially those with underlying diseases. Whether it is door-to-door services, nursing services, remote consultations, and 24-hour safe and automatic attendant services, development opportunities will be ushered in, and home care services will be more valued. The mode of operation of community elderly care service centers or residential homes may need to be partially adjusted. These community elderly care facilities may become

community support points, with their primary mission being to support and export services to the home-based elderly population located in the surrounding community. The care centers provide service personnel, resources, and equipment for the elderly in their homes, while also helping with the purchase of food supplies, daily necessities, and other commodities. Home care service companies have taken this opportunity to actively develop cooperation with the main body of community care services, while functioning as a shopfront in the community to reduce service radiuses and costs.

6.3 Conclusion

6.3.1 Elderly service industry under COVID-19

The intensification of an aging population and the yearning of older people to have a better life will continue to generate huge market demand. This social background is important for the future development of China's elderly care service industry. Throughout this pandemic, it has been clearly realized that there is a huge opportunity for the development of the health care service industry. China is gradually becoming an aging society. By 2025, there will be close to 300 million elderly people, and by 2050 it will reach 500 million. This population and the accompanying demand for services to meet the needs of this group contain unlimited business opportunities in the "silver economy". According to *Several Opinions of the State Council on Accelerating the Development of the Elderly Service Industry,* this industry is one of the pillars of the transformation and upgrading of China's economy. At present, the main problem restricting the development of the elderly service industry is the limited ability of the elderly to pay. People born in the 1960s are gradually entering the life stage of "being elderly", and China has made efforts in a variety of ways, such as pension finance and a pension insurance system, to rectify this financial limitation. Thus, the payment system for the elderly care service industry will gradually be established and improved.

The elderly care service industry is not one in which people gain high returns in a short period. However, continuous cash flow after stable operation will attract the flow-on resulting from social capital. The pandemic has had a huge impact on tertiary industries, which are dominated by service industries, and offline services have suffered a huge impact. For the elderly care service industry, a greater impact has been experienced in the home and community care sector, with residential care institutions being less severely affected. Although the profitability of residential care and nursing homes is not high, they do enjoy a high degree of stability, provided that pandemic prevention is in place.

The Fourth Plenary Session of the Nineteenth Central Committee of the Communist Party of China redefines the positioning of homes, communities, and institutions in elderly care services, strengthening the need to "speed up the construction of an elderly care service system that coordinates home and community institutions, and combines medical care, health, and wellness." After this pandemic, the state will pay more attention to the development of residential care facilities, and the development of the management level of home-based care services which will achieve a qualitative improvement, providing an opportunity for the overall development of this sector. It is certain that, after the pandemic is over, a new round of growth will be ushered in in this industry.

6.3.2 Future development trends of China's elderly care service industry

6.3.2.1 *Development trends demand for services*

Due to the sharp drop in China's birth rate and the continuous increase in life expectancy, the trend of an overall aging of the population will accelerate up until the middle of the 21st century. The potential demand for care services for the elderly depends on this trend, and the acceleration of this trend will accelerate at the same time increased demand for services. Thanks to social and economic development and the continuous improvement of the old-age security system, the overall spending power of older people in China has gradually improved. In the next 10 years, people born in the 1960s are entering the stage of being senior citizens. People born in the 1960s are the first generation of parents having only one child. Many of them have relatively stable finances and mature consumption habits. However, the family pension model is becoming more and more difficult to maintain, and societal or government pensions have become an inevitable reality. This group will become the most important consumers in the elderly care industry. In addition, the consumption ideas of Chinese older citizens have also changed over time. This generation pays more attention to health, values, and has optimistic attitudes. These changes will provide good opportunities for the vigorous development of this service industry.

Most elderly people are unwilling to leave their families and familiar environments. Home care will continue to be the mainstream service care model in the future. Those older people living at home have needs for daily nursing, chronic disease management, care and companionship, meal delivery, and housekeeping services. Those elderly with disabilities and dementia, and those in need of rehabilitation and long-term care, are most in need of residential care in specially purposed facilities. The ongoing nature of an aging population in China, and the increase in the proportion of the elderly with disabilities and dementia, is likely to blowout the demand for long-term care options.

6.3.2.2 *Development trends for supply*

In terms of supply, the current development model of the elderly care service industry is relatively simple. At present, in China this industry has clearly shown the characteristics of government-led leadership, in which the government has undertaken certain public service and social welfare responsibilities. This development model may lead to employment agencies focusing on government land use planning and financial subsidies, while paying insufficient attention to improving the quality of their services to the elderly, and excessive reliance on government policies, resulting in the industry's current overall low level of development and unclear profit models. The supply trends also show that there is still a lot of room for development and improvement in the industry. These are entrepreneurial opportunities; the state has made it clear that it will fully liberalize the elderly care service market and support social capital investment in the establishment of elderly care institutions. In the future, the development model of the industry will be more diversified. In-depth integration with the health, tourism, cultural entertainment, and catering industries will further tap into and release the development potential and continue to enrich the new models and new formats of the elderly care service industry.

The development of the elderly care service industry is an important part of the development of China's aging and elderly industry. The vigorous development and close integration of elderly real estate, elderly finance, elderly insurance, elderly health, elderly health tourism, and smart elderly care will drive the development of related industries, create a better external environment for the development of the elderly service industry, and promote the sustainable development of the elderly care service industry in the broader social service system.

https://doi.org/10.1142/9789811252921_0007

Chapter 7

The Impact of the COVID-19 Pandemic on the Service Industry and Policy Responses

Rui Mingjie

School of Management, Fudan University, Shanghai, China

Since the outbreak of COVID-19, the entire country has mobilized huge forces to fight against the pandemic. Various measures, including the measures to suspend work and production of enterprises and institutions, and stay-at-home measures are all showing great effects. The number of newly diagnosed cases nationwide is gradually decreasing, and the number of people cured is increasing. Calculating how to restore the economy, resume work and production, adjust industrial policies, and respond to corporate crises while continuing to fight the pandemic has become a particularly important issue. Stabilizing the service industry so as to stabilize the economy of our country and various localities is really a top priority.

7.1 The Service Industry is the Most Important Industry in the National Economy

Since the outbreak of COVID-19, people have rarely gone out to consume, and mostly stay at home. Although some enterprises and institutions have gradually begun to resume work and production, people still need to reduce contact and avoid gathering in public places to prevent cross-infection. As a result, in addition to the necessary basic consumption of water, electricity, coal, food, and communications, the normal level of consumption of work, life, and special arrangements for holidays will definitely decrease. This also includes the current consumption of non-essential durable consumer industrial products, such as automobiles, household appliances, mobile phones, clothing, daily necessities, and service products, especially the consumption of tourism, transportation, hotels, catering, shopping, entertainment, fitness, vehicle services, and government public services. The reduction in household consumption has a huge impact on the consumer goods industry, or on enterprises connected to the consumer goods industry. Faced with a sharp decline in consumer demand, many companies engaged in consumer services and consumer manufacturing have no orders, hence businesses cannot progress and the dilemma of a financial crisis is faced. They do not have enough capital funds, and cannot generate enough income. Once the crisis spreads, the whole economy will face danger. What is the cause of this?

7.1.1 Consumption has become the main contributor to China's economic growth

Since 2013, China's economic growth model has undergone major changes. It has changed from a model of investment-driven economic growth in the past to a model of consumption-driven economic growth. The latest data released by the National Bureau of Statistics shows that the contribution rate of final consumption expenditure to GDP growth in 2019 was 57.8%, the contribution rate of total capital formation is 31.2%, and the contribution rate of net exports of goods and services is 11.0%. According to Figure 7.1, consumption is already one of the main forces of China's economic growth and development.

Final consumption (see Figure 7.2) consists of two parts: household consumption expenditure and government consumption expenditure. From 2010 to 2019, final consumption increased year by year, and the growth rate stabilized at around 10%, with its contribution to economic growth averaging 60%. However, in 2019, its contribution dropped to 57.8%, and the year-on-year growth rate was 12.29%. From 2010 to 2019, both household consumption expenditure and government

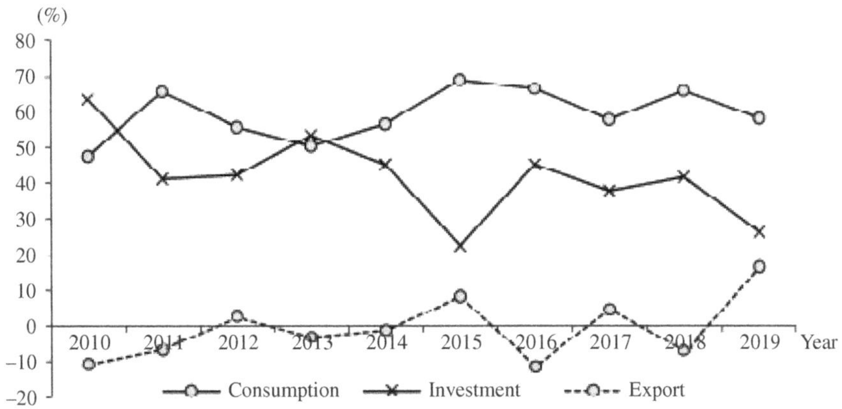

Figure 7.1: Changes in the contribution of consumption, investment, and exports to economic growth (2010–2019).

Source: National Bureau of Statistics.

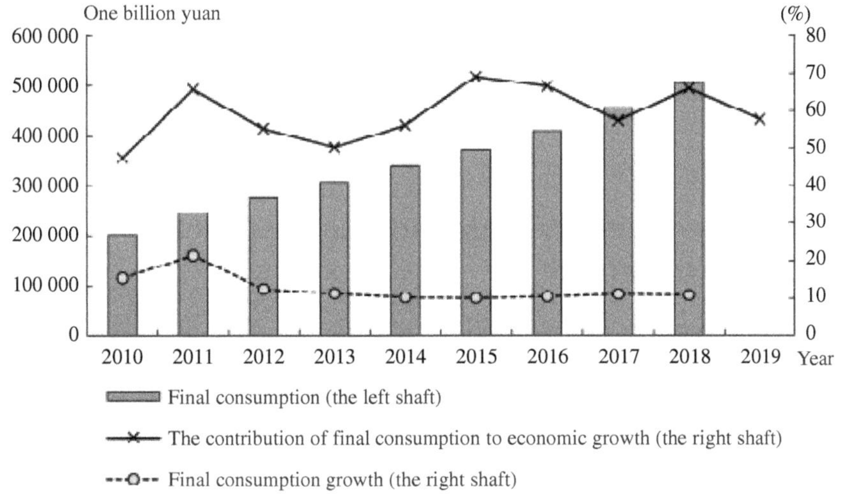

Figure 7.2: Changes in the contribution of final consumption to economic growth (2010–2019).

Source: National Bureau of Statistics.

consumption expenditure increased year by year, and the growth rate basically stabilized at around 11%. From a structural point of view, the proportion of government consumption expenditure of final consumption stabilized at around 30%.

Resident consumption expenditure includes two major aspects: consumption of consumer goods and consumption of consumer services. Consumer goods consumption directly corresponds to the consumer goods industry, which refers to the industry that provides consumer goods to meet people's material and cultural needs. The consumption of consumer service products directly corresponds to the consumer service industry, which mainly includes the life service industry and the public service industry.

The life service industry is an industry that directly provides residents with material and spiritual consumption products and services. The products they produce are service products, which are used to meet the various needs of life. The current vigorous development of the life service industry mainly includes key areas such as the business service industry, cultural industry, tourism, health service industry, legal service industry, family service industry, sports industry, the elderly service industry, and the real estate industry. Public service industry is also a necessary industry for residents' work and life, and service products are mainly provided by the government and public service organizations.

7.1.2 Tertiary industry[1] is the cornerstone of stable economic growth

Since the initiation of reform and opening-up, China's economic development has had impressive achievements. The industrial system is becoming increasingly comprehensive, and the industrial structure has undergone tremendous changes. China has transformed from a major agricultural country to a major manufacturing country. At present, the service industry (tertiary industry) has become the most important industry, making a large contribution to GDP and employment.

---

[1] The service industry.

Data released by the National Bureau of Statistics shows that China's economy continues to develop, and the service industry is already the most important industry in China's economy and society. From 2010 to 2019, the proportion of GDP in primary and secondary industries gradually declined, while the proportion in tertiary industries increased. For the entire year of 2010, the added value of the primary industry accounted for 9.33% of the GDP; it then declined slowly over the course of 10 years, and fell to 7.11% in 2019. The proportion of the secondary industry declined more dramatically, from 45.96% in 2010 to 38.97% in 2019, going down 7 percentage points. The proportion of added value of the tertiary industry has steadily increased in the past 10 years, from only 44.41% in 2010 to 53.92% in 2019 (see Figure 7.3).

Take the data at the end of 2018 as an example; in 2018, the workforce in China's industry totaled 770.586 million, of which 22.577 million were employed in the primary industry sector, 21.395 million were employed in the secondary industry sector, and 35.938 million were employed in the tertiary industry sector, accounting for 46.3% of the national employed population. From the perspective of changes in the employment population,

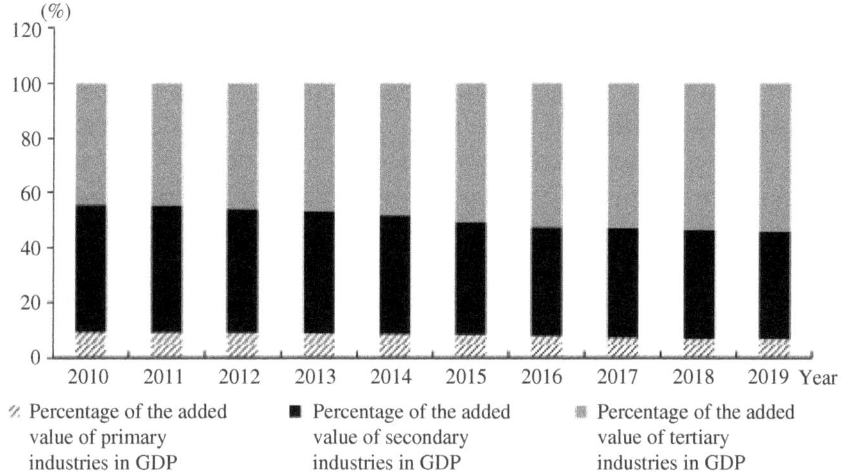

Figure 7.3: Percentage of the added value of primary, secondary, and tertiary industries in GDP (2010–2019).

Source: Drawing based on data from the National Bureau of Statistics.

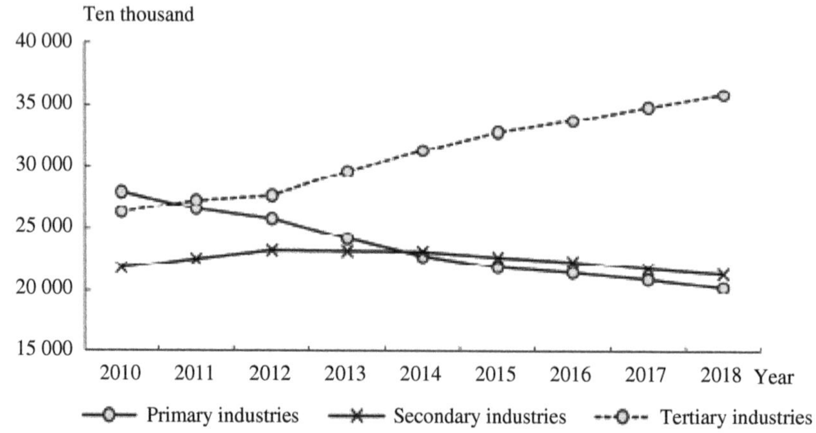

Figure 7.4: Changes in the employment-absorbed population of primary, secondary, and tertiary industries (2010–2019).

Source: National Bureau of Statistics.

the number of employees in primary industries continued to decline from 2010 to 2018. The number of people in secondary industries remained basically stable, and the number employed in tertiary industries increased rapidly (see Figure 7.4).

This change in the industrial structure complies with Petty Clark's Law, which stipulates that with the growth of per capita GDP and the improvement of economic development, the structure of the tertiary industry sector of a country or region will be adjusted accordingly, and the tertiary industry's contribution to GDP will gradually increase. The highest percentage of contribution can even exceed 70%. The contribution of the manufacturing industry will gradually drop to 20–30%, while primary industries will decrease to less than 5%. The tertiary sector has gradually become the industry that absorbs the largest number of employed people.

7.1.3 The current consumer service industry contributes more to GDP than the production service industry

The service industry in the modern industrial system includes two important components: one is the service industry that offers various services to consumers, called the "consumer service industry", which comprises daily life services and public services. Life services such as clothing, food, housing, transportation, communication, information, learning, and finance are typical examples. The other is the service industry for producers, that is, the services provided for producers in the primary, secondary, and tertiary industries, especially manufacturing companies, usually called "productive services". Examples can be found in financial, supply chain, maintenance, human resources, professional consulting, and distribution services.

The consumer service industry is very important and directly relates to various aspects of consumers, such as work and life, leisure and entertainment, and health and hygiene. The types and quality of service products provided by the consumer service industry, together with the types and quality of industrial consumer goods, have become the most important aspects that directly affect the material and spiritual quality of life of residents, and are closely related to a happy life. The producer service industry is also very important; it is a key industry that supports the transformation and upgrading of the manufacturing industry. The purpose of upgrading is to maintain the continuity of the industrial production process, promote industrial technological progress and industrial upgrades, improve production efficiency, and provide guarantee services. Meanwhile, it is a support service industry directly related to the manufacturing industry. It is an emerging industry independently developing from the internal production service sector of the manufacturing industry. The producer service industry is dependent on manufacturing companies, and runs through the upstream, midstream, and downstream links of corporate production. It uses both human capital and knowledge capital as the main inputs, and introduces increasingly specialized human capital and knowledge capital into the manufacturing industry. It is a key link for accelerating the integration of the secondary and tertiary industries. Producer services can be divided into two categories: the first category is basic production services, which provide general necessary services for the production and operation of enterprises and institutions, such as credit fund services, education and training, law, management consulting, distribution agencies, and intermediary services. The other is embedded production services, which are services embedded in the manufacturing process of manufacturing enterprises, such as supply chain management, supply chain finance, the industrial internet, innovation platforms, data collection and analysis, and timely maintenance.

In developed countries, the added value of the tertiary industry's contribution to GDP can reach beyond 70%. Of these, the added value of the consumer service industry's contribution to the economy is generally only 30% of the service industry's added value, while the contribution of the added value of the producer service industry can be as high as 70% of the added value of the entire service industry. The tertiary industry, especially the producer service industry, is already the most important pillar of the national economy of developed countries. China is a developing country; in 2019, its per capita GDP barely exceeded US$10,000. However, the industrial structure is undergoing changes. The service industry's value-added GDP ratio is generally on the rise; the proportion of consumer service industry in GDP rose from 27.45% in 2010 to 31.12% in 2017, and the production service industry rose from 16.28% in 2010 to 20.35% in 2017. The entire service industry contributed 51.47% to the GDP of the year in 2017, which is more than half, as shown in Figure 7.5.

According to the data for 2019, in China's tertiary industry sector, namely service industries, the consumer service industry still accounts for the bulk of added value, accounting for about 60% of the service

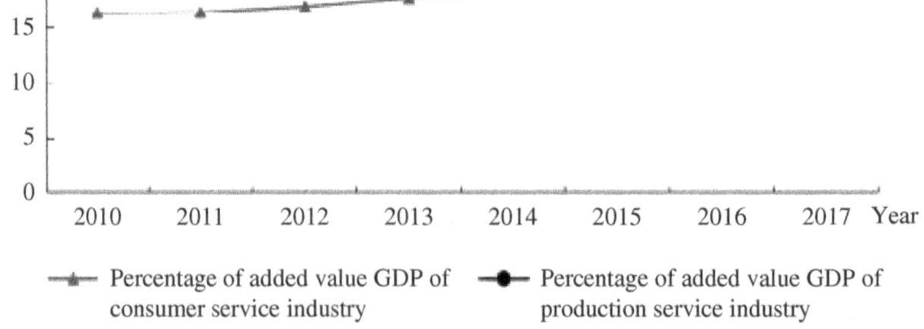

Figure 7.5: Percentage of added value GDP of consumer service industry and production service industry (2010–2017).

Source: Drawing based on the *China Statistical Yearbook* over the years.

industry's added value, while that for the producer service industry is 40%. Based on the internal proportional structure of China's service industry, the consumer service industry involving the lives and work of citizens is the core industry for economic stability and growth.

7.1.4 Service products in the service industry have their own characteristics

The COVID-19 pandemic has led to a substantial reduction in household consumption, which has had an impact on the consumer manufacturing industry. In the short term, these products, such as cars, televisions, and air conditioners were barely consumed. However, since these products are easily temporarily stored in warehouses after production, when consumption increases after the pandemic, losses incurred by enterprises during the pandemic will be rectified. However, in the service industry, especially the life service industry, reduced consumption during the pandemic cannot be compensated by increased consumption after the pandemic. This is determined by the difference in the characteristics of the service products of the service industry and the industrial products of the manufacturing industry.

Service products have two important characteristics. Firstly, production and consumption are simultaneous. The production process of these products is also a consumption process. Typical examples include hairdressing, beauty, catering, drama, sightseeing, car use, shopping, production maintenance, and material supply. These services are produced by producers at the same time as consumers receive services for consumption. Therefore, there is no need for service production without service consumption. The production and consumption processes of industrial products can be separated. Consumption happens after production. Mobile phones, cameras, daily necessities, steel, and automobiles are cases in point. The second characteristic is non-storability. Once the service is produced, it must be consumed. It cannot be stored. For instance, it is impossible to store services such as hairdressing, beauty, catering, drama, sightseeing, car use, shopping, distribution, and law. Consumers cannot buy them first and use them later. For example, restaurants can store some meals as finished or semi-finished products, but consumers can't enjoy the food cooked on site and their catering service.

Therefore, the production of service products in the service industry is not like the production of industrial products in the manufacturing industry. It is impossible to produce and store service products and then wait for the pandemic to pass before distributing them to consumers for consumption. During the pandemic, the decline in the demand for service products by residents and enterprises is the destruction of the production capacity of the service industry, causing losses in production of the service industry.

7.1.5 The main size of service industry enterprises is small, medium, and micro

At present, the main service providers of the service industry, especially the life service industry, are a large number of small, medium, and micro enterprises, among which the majority are private individual enterprises. These are small in size, small in capital, and widely distributed. They provide basic life services to a large number of people. Compared with the number of enterprises in the secondary and tertiary industries, the number of legal entities in the secondary and tertiary industries has increased year by year, however, the growth rate of the tertiary industry is faster than that of the secondary industry. As of 2017, the number of legal entities in the secondary industry was 4,731,300, and the number of legal entities in the tertiary industry was 1,560.70, as shown in Figure 7.6.

Since the outbreak of the pandemic, it has not been possible for the public to enjoy normal consumption: pandemic prevention has required that all residents stay at home. Therefore, these small, medium, and micro enterprises have had to close and wait. Although some companies were allowed to start operations at the end of February, normal service consumption has needed time to recover, and the return to normal production and operation of a large number of small, medium, and micro service companies has been very difficult. Even large-scale catering chain companies like Xibei cannot shut down for a month. During the pandemic, the fixed expenditures of enterprises, such as rent and employee salaries, have remained stable, whereas normal service income has been greatly reduced. Thus, the financial situation of enterprises has been prone to problems, and corporate crises have easily arisen. A large number of small, medium, and micro enterprises in the service industry have had to shut down or stop operations due to lack of demand. This will inevitably lead to the emergence of a large number of temporarily unemployed

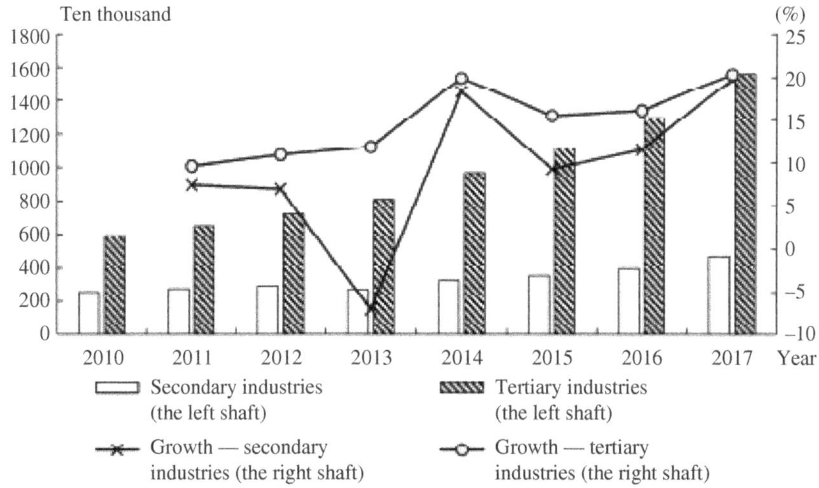

Figure 7.6: Number of legal entities in the secondary and tertiary industries (2010–2017).

Source: National Bureau of Statistics.

Note: Statistics on the number of enterprises in different industries as of 2017.

people, which may affect social stability. The same is true for the producer service industry. The manufacturing industry has fewer employees, and as a result, production service enterprises must also under employ. Therefore, the current loss of the entire service industry is already a loss. Even if there is a rebound after the pandemic, the economic downturn in 2020 is inevitable. The question is not whether there will be less growth, but by how much will growth be reduced.

7.2 Analysis of the Scale of Damage and the Flow-on Effects to the Service Industry During the Pandemic

How much impact will this pandemic have on the service industry? What flow-on mechanisms will affect China's economy? Can the correct ideas and countermeasures to reduce losses and promote development be found? These are very important and urgent questions that need to be answered, but they are difficult to answer, because the essence of these questions and their answers is to be found in how this pandemic will evolve, and it is still difficult to make accurate judgments.

7.2.1 Judgment of the duration of the pandemic

The duration of the pandemic is a key variable in determining its impact on the service industry and the economy. Only when the pandemic is over can residents resume normal work and life. Generally speaking, the longer the pandemic lasts, the greater the impact on the work and life of residents, and the greater the impact on the service industry and the economy. The duration of the pandemic is not only related to the characteristics of the new coronavirus, but also to the current prevention and treatment methods, diagnosis and treatment technology, and the status of pharmacological equipment.

The coronavirus that caused this pandemic is a new type of virus, and very little is known about it. People are still in the process of conducting research. At present, there are no particularly effective drugs and treatment plans, but it is necessary to continuously collate and distribute the latest in prevention and treatment practices during this period. For example, the National Health Commission has released the 7th edition of the diagnosis and treatment plan. On March 2, the Shanghai New Coronavirus Prevention and Control Expert Group released the "Shanghai Plan" for diagnosis and treatment. This shows that the medical and pharmaceutical industries are actively working and researching, hoping to win the battle against the pandemic. From the perspective of prevention and control, in early March, the pandemic in all provinces, autonomous regions, and municipalities across the country has achieved phased success. With the exception of Wuhan, Hubei, the number of newly confirmed cases has dropped significantly. The number in many provinces, regions, and cities has dropped to zero for many days.

If January 23 is taken as a reference point, then before this day China was still in a stage where the coronavirus was rapidly spreading, with Wuhan as the main prevention and control area. After this day, especially after human-to-human transmission of COVID-19 was confirmed, strict prevention and control measures began to be adopted in various places. During the Spring Festival, residents across the country stopped going out and ceased to attend gatherings. Instead, people fought against the pandemic by staying at home. Enterprises and institutions also halted work and production. Most provinces, autonomous regions, and municipalities continued to adopt strict measures until February 23. Although some enterprises began to resume work during this period, the whole month from January 23 to February 23 was a month that residents across the country stayed at home, and also a month for companies, especially service companies, to close their doors. Starting from February 24, the number of enterprises resuming work increased, and residents began to return to work. An optimistic estimate stipulated that the pandemic generally would end at the end of April, except for Hubei, Wuhan. A conservative estimate placed this date at the end of May.

If January 23 and February 23 are taken as a node, the pandemic period can be divided into three stages. The first stage covers the day before January 23, which was during the outbreak and rapid spread of the pandemic in Wuhan and other parts of Hubei. The second stage, from January 23 to February 23, is the period when the pandemic spread across the country, and all provinces, autonomous regions, and municipalities began to take strict measures. The pandemic at first spread and then gradually came under control. The third stage is when many people resumed work, and people gradually returned to normal work and life. In this stage, the pandemic was finally under control. This stage is estimated to last between one to three months. The domestic pandemic should be over by the end of May 2020.

7.2.2 Estimating the impact of the pandemic on the service industry

The pandemic has had a huge impact on the service industry overall, but the specific impact is distinct on different types of service industries and different sub-service industries. The consumer service industry has been directly impacted, because residents stayed at home, which reduced consumer services on a large scale, directly leading to the reduction of the production and operation of these service providers, or even the closure of businesses. The impact on the production service industry has been indirect. The consumption of industrial products has been reduced while people are at home. At the same time, because the workforces of manufacturing companies are at home, manufacturing companies reduced or even totally stopped production. As a consequence, the production service industry that serves the manufacturing industry has had to reduce its services or even close its business. Of course, because of stay-at-home orders, employees of production and service companies have also had to suspend work.

According to the degree of impact of the pandemic, sub-industries of the consumer service industry can be divided into four major categories.

The first category is severely affected industries. In the second stage of the pandemic, as mentioned above, there was an almost 70% or more turnover loss, occurring in industries like tourism, catering services, hotel, performance and exhibition, vehicle travel service, hairdressing and beauty, housekeeping service, and real estate agency services. For example, the impact of the pandemic on the domestic tourism industry has been calculated by the China Tourism Research Institute; it is estimated that in the first quarter of 2020 and throughout the year, domestic tourist arrivals will decrease by 56% and 15.5%, respectively. There will be a year-on-year decrease of 932 million person-times. Domestic tourism revenues will have a negative growth of 69% and 20.6%. The annual revenue reduction will be 1.18 trillion yuan. On February 12, the China Culinary Association released the *Report on the Impact of the New Coronary Pneumonia Pandemic on China's Catering Industry in 2020*, showing that within 7 days of the Spring Festival holiday in 2020, COVID-19 caused a loss of about 500 billion yuan in the retail sales of the catering industry. Ninety-three per cent of catering companies chose to close their stores.

The second category consists of generally affected industries. In the second stage of the pandemic, there was almost a 50% turnover loss, especially in industries like logistics and distribution, legal services, railway transportation services, aviation travel services, and retail. It is estimated that the main measures for the prevention and control of the pandemic began after January 21. From this date, the passenger flow of Spring Festival travel began to decline, and the passenger flow during the Spring Festival was greatly reduced. The daily passenger flow of civil aviation and railway travel has dropped by more than 80% year-on-year. Thirty days before the Spring Festival travel season (January 10–February 8), a total of 1.35 billion passengers traveled nationwide, showing a decrease of 40% year-on-year. Among them: railways fell 32.9% year-on-year, aviation fell 33.1%, and highways fell 41.2%. Since New Year's Eve, overall passenger traffic, railway, aviation, and road passenger traffic has dropped by 78%, 77%, 67%, and 79% year-on-year, respectively.

The third category refers to those slightly affected industries. In the second stage of pandemic prevention and control mentioned above, there was an almost 20% loss in turnover. Examples of industries in this category are financial and insurance services, consulting and intermediary services, water, electricity, and coal service. These industries are basically free of losses, or have suffered less losses. For example, the hydropower and coal service industry were slightly affected, because the demand for industrial production declined in February, while the demand from residents remained basically unchanged.

The fourth category points to industries that are basically unaffected or had room for development. In the second stage, there was almost no loss of turnover, and there were even varying degrees of increase. Typical examples can be found in communication services, network services, the cable television service industry, online education, data service industries, and the online gaming industry. The Yibang Power Research Institute issued a report on February 20, 2020, saying that after conducting a survey of nearly 200 companies, it was found that from the perspective of major online retail platforms, logistics distribution, and supply chains recovery will determine the rise and fall of transaction volume. WeChat Mini Program Mall transactions have grown faster.

7.2.3 Estimates of the overall impact of the pandemic on the service industry

On February 28, 2020, the National Bureau of Statistics officially released the National Economic and Social Development Statistical Bulletin for 2019. According to the report, the gross domestic product in 2019 was 99,086.5 billion yuan, showing an increase of 6.1% over the previous year. Among them, the added value of the primary industry was 7,046.7 billion yuan, reflecting an increase of 3.1%. The added value of the secondary industry was 3,8616.5 billion yuan, showing an increase of 5.7%. The added value of the tertiary industry was 534233 trillion yuan and the increase amounted to 6.9%. The added value of the primary industry sector accounted for 7.1% of the GDP, while that for the secondary and the tertiary industries were 39.0% and 53.9%, respectively. For the sake of simplicity, China's total GDP in 2019 was about 100 trillion yuan, of which the added value of the tertiary industry was 53.4 trillion yuan. If the added value of the tertiary industry is the same every month, then the added value of the tertiary industry (the service industry) is 4.45 trillion yuan every month in 2019. If the added value of the tertiary industry in 2019 is used as the basis of the annual added value of the tertiary industry in 2020, and the damage to the service industry caused by this pandemic is judged according to this, possible losses can be estimated in the three stages of the pandemic, which add up to the total loss caused by the pandemic.

In the first stage of this pandemic, there was only a partial outbreak in Wuhan and other parts of Hubei. The impact on the national service industry and its sub-sectors was minor, with the Spring Festival holiday occurring in the first half of the second phase. The holiday was extended, so the average overall impact on the service industry segment may have been as high as 90%. In the second half of the second phase, the situation gradually improved, but the prevention and control measures were relatively strict. The resumption of work began gradually. Therefore, the overall impact on sub-sectors was 70%, and the average was about 80%. The third stage was the stage that started in early March. It was optimistically estimated that it would take 1–3 months to end the pandemic. Due to the resumption of work and the gradual normalization of residents' lives, it is estimated that the impact on service industry segments at this stage was roughly 20% on average. Most of the manufacturing industry did not resume production for a long time, so the normal operation of the producer service industry was affected. Some service industries have played a special role in the fight against the pandemic. They have suffered no losses and have even seen increases. The impact of the pandemic on the tertiary industry may be slightly less than 4.5 trillion yuan (the added value of the service industry in the first month of 2019). The losses may reach 4 trillion yuan. This is not a small number.

Assuming that there is no such pandemic in 2020 and economic development is on par with previous development, there should be a 6% growth in GDP. By the end of 2020, China's total GDP should be 106 trillion yuan. However, the pandemic has caused a loss of about 4 trillion yuan. Assuming that the service industry has recovered relatively well after the pandemic, it is estimated that the economic growth rate in 2020 should reach 2–3%. If this is the case, it is still a very remarkable achievement. The above is only a rough estimate and not very accurate.

7.3 Measures to Stabilize the Service Industry and Employment, and Promote Growth

Optimistically speaking, if overall economic loss throughout the pandemic is 5 trillion yuan in total (we estimated that the service industry will lose 4 trillion yuan in the previous section), it is still a huge number, which will have a significant impact on economic growth and industry in 2020. Therefore, the pandemic must be fought with all our strength and all must strive to end the pandemic as soon as possible. At the same time, minimizing economic losses, stabilizing the overall economic situation, and stabilizing social development must be considered. How can this be done? From a strategic point of view, the service industry, small, medium, and micro enterprises, and the labour force in the service industry must all be stabilized. Once we promote consumption, the overall situation of China's economy in 2020 will be stable.

7.3.1 The basic logic of emergency policy design

As of early March, governments and departments at all levels from the central to local governments issued a series of policies to combat the pandemic and stabilize the economy. The most important are those emergency policies that support small and medium-sized enterprises, because the small, medium, and micro enterprises were affected by the pandemic in the very beginning. The pandemic influenced the survival and development of these enterprises which are closely related to the country's overall economic situation. The central bank, the Ministry of Commerce, the State Administration of Taxation, and other departments issued emergency policies. Beijing issued several measures to fight the pandemic and support enterprises. Shanghai issued the "28 Measures" to support the service industry on February 8, 2020. Guangdong has introduced 10 measures, while Fujian has introduced the "12 Measures" for stabilizing the economy and supporting enterprises. Suzhou introduced policies to provide supportive assistance to small and medium-sized enterprises at the beginning of the pandemic.

After combining and summarizing these policies, the current policies mainly include the following four aspects: (1) Financial support: such as the extension of bank loans, newly-needed bank loans, and lower loan interest rates. (2) Tax deductions: such as VAT deductions for small-scale taxpayers, life service industry VAT exemptions, and income tax deductions; for corporate charitable donations, all can be paid before tax. The period for companies to digest losses this year can be lengthened from 5 to 8 years; social insurance premiums for employees are reduced or exempted. (3) Financial subsidies: financial discounts for loans to small and micro enterprises, reduction or exemption of state-owned asset rents, and reduction or exemption of customer rents by referring to state-owned assets for other investors, with reference to the reduction or exemption of real estate lease tax to reduce electricity and gas prices. (4) Support measures for individual industrial and commercial households. On the whole, these policies are basically policies to solve financial difficulties, reduce operation burdens, and stabilize the survival of enterprises. These policies have covered various aspects such as finance and taxation. The promulgation of these policies has been welcomed by the majority of small, medium, and micro enterprises. These policies in particular have enhanced the strength and confidence of service companies in overcoming difficulties, and have provided these small, medium, and micro enterprises with good policies and good expectations for the future.

However, these policies targeted at enterprises are actually aimed at service supply, not at service demand. What the service industry really lacks is household consumption and the lack of demand of service products. Generally speaking, until the pandemic is over, people cannot go back to their normal lives and service demand cannot be restored. Therefore, it is impossible for small, medium, and micro enterprises in the service industry to resume normal operations. In order to stabilize the economic growth of the service industry, the basic logic, design, and introduction of the government's emergency policies is set out below. Firstly, in the short term a large number of small and medium-sized enterprises in the service industry should be stabilized. They can stop operation in the short term but will not go bankrupt. However, these companies have a poor ability to resist risks, so if there are no customers or business for a month or two, the businesses may close. Secondly, large-scale unemployment of service workers should be prevented while at the same time labor costs of enterprises must be reduced. Third, from a longer-term perspective, the growth of household consumption (including consumption of service products and consumption of industrial products) should be stimulated. Although the key to consumption growth is the end of the pandemic, in the third stage of the fight against the pandemic, that is, early March, some policies to stimulate consumption could be introduced. Fourth, we have to encourage small, medium, and micro enterprises to actively respond, be innovative in their business models, expand their business space, and build self-reliance.

7.3.2 Government actions to further stabilize the service industry

7.3.2.1 *Recovery and development of the service industry ecosystem and industrial value chain*

Although the service industry is downstream from the entire industry chain and basically belongs to the field of final consumption, the status of the service industry is actually closely related to the collaborative ecosystem of various sub-sectors of the service industry and upstream related industries of the service industry, such as various manufacturing industries. For example, the status of the tourism industry is not only related to the status of scenic spots, but is also related to the overall status of service industries such as catering, accommodation, entertainment, souvenirs, transportation, communications, tour guides, ticketing, and shopping involved in the tourism ecosystem. Therefore, it cannot be said that the tourism industry will resume after the pandemic is over and the attractions are opened. Policies to support travel agencies and scenic spots are undoubtedly very important, but without overall support for the entire ecosystem of this industry, it may take a long time to even restore let alone develop the tourism industry. This is not only the case in the tourism industry, but in other industries such as catering, hotel, vehicle travel services, aviation services, and production services. In addition, the recovery and development of the service industry also depend on the status of upstream industries in the industry chain, such as the recovery of the manufacturing industry. For example, the producer service industry is an industry closely related to the manufacturing industry. The manufacturing industry has stopped production or underperformed due to the pandemic, as a result the producer service industry has experienced various problems. Therefore, it is necessary to consider implementing or adjusting existing emergency policies from the perspective of the service industry's sub-industry ecosystem, and the service industry's entire industry value chain.

7.3.2.2 *Provide temporary unemployment relief to support the basic life necessities of the unemployed*

The service industry employs a large number of people. It is dominated by small, medium, and micro enterprises, which usually hire many temporary or part-time workers. For example, the domestic service industry is very typical. At the start of the pandemic, almost all domestic workers became unemployed and had no income. If the pandemic continues, workers in domestic service have no means of support. This is the case not only in the domestic industry, but also in many other service industries such as tourism, catering, beauty salons, and vehicle travel services. Therefore, it is recommended that a temporary unemployment relief policy be introduced. According to the records of these service industry employees who have paid social insurance in the past, relief for one to two months will be given. The specific amount could be indexed to the income standard of local minimum monthly wage. Relief for the period of temporary unemployment of many service workers can stabilize their lives. At the same time, it also helps these small, medium, and micro enterprises reduce their fixed costs while also increasing consumption.

7.3.2.3 *Introduce emergency policies to stimulate consumption and stabilize the service industry*

At the beginning of March, the pandemic eased and enterprises and institutions began to resume work. However, great care was still needed. Therefore, the demand for services was not very large, and structural changes had also occurred. In order to stabilize and restore the service industry and the economy as soon as possible, through the production and operation of the consumer goods manufacturing industry the introduction of policies to stimulate consumption is recommended. For example, subsidies for new energy vehicles can be restored. Real estate purchase tax can be reduced or exempted. Consumer credit interest rates can be lowered and the old household appliances can be exchanged for new products.[2]

[2] When peasants buy new household appliances, their old household appliances can offset part of the money.

This mode of consumption is usually undertaken once it is easy to maintain social distancing guidelines. If consumption by a large number of residents occurs, the recovery of the production capacity of related manufacturing industries is guaranteed. The recovery of the manufacturing industry can drive the recovery of the production service industry and gradually drive the growth of the consumer service industry. At the same time, it is conducive for China to rejoin the global division of labor system as soon as possible to ensure the position of the manufacturing industry in the global industrial chain. China's manufacturing industry is already a key link in the global industrial value chain. Without recovery, related industries and companies in other countries in the industrial chain will certainly not be able to suspend work for a long period, and this may result in their industrial chains being restructured.

7.3.2.4 *Give full play to the emergency leadership mechanism and provide effective assistance to the service industry*

Generally speaking, the existence of support policies for the service industry does not mean that the development of a large number of small and medium-sized enterprises will be stable, or the industry itself will be stable. Substitutions for some service needs are possible, such as catering. Some service requirements are temporarily not necessary, such as tourism. In contrast, some service needs are necessary, such as water, electricity, coal, and supplies of all those materials that sustain life. To this end, policy executors need to have emergency operation plans for specific industries, especially to actively assist in solving the difficulties of small and medium-sized service companies in different industries, and provide emergency policy consultation and assistance. However, different service industries are led by different departments. For example, many consumer service industries are under the control of the Department of Commerce, while the producer service industries are under the supervision of different departments, such as the Economic and Information Commission, Department of Taxation, Department of Human Resources, and Department of Unemployment Relief. It is recommended that a temporary emergency leadership organization be established to stabilize the development of the service industry, and to provide unified command and effective assistance to help tide over small and medium-sized enterprises in the service industry.

7.3.3 Emergency self-reliance measures for small and micro enterprises in the service industry

This pandemic is a sudden corporate externality crisis for service companies. How should service companies respond? The companies' reactions show whether they have crisis awareness, and good management system and strategy for coping with their own or external crises. Therefore, although the government has issued many support policies, the majority of service industry companies cannot wait to be rescued. Instead, they should conduct self-rescue measures. They should put survival as the top priority ahead of development.

7.3.3.1 *It is necessary to carefully study and judge the direct impact on the economy and industry as pandemic trends change*

At present, the emergency situation of the pandemic has eased. The resumption of work and production has begun, and people's lives and working conditions are returning to normal. As a result, the demand for the service industry will gradually increase. The service industry has struggled through its most difficult stage and is expecting a promising future. However, the overall situation of the economy and industry will to a certain extent fluctuate. In particular, if the current pandemic situation worsens in overseas countries and regions, it will inevitably affect global markets, including global capital markets. The volatility in the European and American securities markets that began in early March has already illustrated the problem. Attention must be paid to judging whether or not it is a short-term or long-term impact. It is hoped that this pandemic will not change the long-term trend of China's economy, but companies must have strategies to respond to negative situations in the short-term.

7.3.3.2 *It is conducive to good practice to study market changes and adjust business strategies*

It is expected that the entire consumer and consumer service market may be in a downturn for a considerable period of time. Even if the pandemic is quickly suppressed (we hope so), it may take a while for people who have been traumatized by the pandemic to psychologically adapt to normal production and life. It is estimated that normalcy will fully return in June this year. Therefore, during this period, small, medium, and micro enterprises should make appropriate strategic adjustments, carry out production and operational adjustments, implement a human resources response, and develop capital strategies and other crisis responses. The most important thing is to ensure the safety of the capital chain. If necessary, temporary suspension of business is also possible. The purpose of temporarily going out of business is to eliminate or reduce the losses caused by the pandemic crisis and save the company. Survival is a must, otherwise, development is impossible.

7.3.3.3 *It is important to be creative and improve business and service products to adapt to changes in demand*

Service industry companies should carefully study the changes in residents' service consumption needs and create ways to achieve consumption, that is, improve and innovate service businesses and service products, such as shifting from centralized and non-isolated production and services to decentralized and socially distanced production and services. Restaurants should be equipped with distanced dining seats, and beauty salons should also have separate service functions. Express deliveries can adopt a form of contactless delivery. Some services have adjusted from offline services to internet online services and delivery, such as takeaways. The projects being invested in to observe future market changes need to be adjusted or postponed in order to protect the security of the capital chain. It is also important to stabilize the existing corporate service ecosystem and upstream and downstream partnerships in the industrial chain, or develop better strategic alliances to overcome difficulties.

7.3.3.4 *It is encouraged that business down time caused by the pandemic be taken advantage of to learn how to improve the level of business management*

A large number of small, medium, and micro service companies are small in size and have a poor ability to resist risks. Their overall service level and the quality of service products need to be improved. There is a gap between people's pursuits of a promising life and the quality of service products. For this reason, it is necessary for the survival and development of small, medium, and micro enterprises that they improve their internal skills, strengthen their production and operation capabilities, and improve their service levels. Therefore, an excellent choice to make the best use of business down time caused by the pandemic is to acquire new skills and competencies to improve business acumen, analyze existing problems and their causes within the enterprise, and conduct targeted research and improvement to facilitate resilience to fight further battles. In the future, opportunities for the development of the service industry and the development of the service product market will favor those companies that are well prepared and competitive.

7.4 Conclusion

The sudden emergence of the pandemic caused by the new coronavirus in 2020 disrupted our country's normal social and economic activities. Preventing the spread of the pandemic is the most important task at present, but at the same time, minimizing economic losses, stabilizing the overall economic situation, and stabilizing social development have to be considered, to lay the foundation for economic growth throughout 2020 and thereafter. The service industry is already the most important industry in terms of contribution to the economy of our country. How can we stabilize the service industry and the employment population in the service industry in order to promote the economy for better growth? This has become the most important issue nowadays.

In response to this problem, two parties need to work together. Firstly, the government should provide a suitable package of targeted emergency policies, which must contain temporary support policies for small, medium, and micro enterprises in the service industry, as well as policies to stimulate and promote household consumption and drive the recovery of the service industry and manufacturing industry. In addition, assistance should be provided to temporarily unemployed service workers to guarantee the security of their normal lives. Apart from government aid, enterprises in the service industry, especially small, medium, and micro enterprises, cannot wait for help, and they should prioritize self-reliance. Following the premise of ensuring the safety of the capital chain, they should strive to learn how to improve business capabilities, analyze changes in market demand, make business adjustments and product innovations, and explore new markets in the service industry. They should seek survival before seeking development. If the majority of service industry enterprises, which are the cornerstone of the overall economy, deal with this crisis properly under the correct leadership of the government, the service industry can be stabilized in the short term and even develop better in the future.

https://doi.org/10.1142/9789811252921_0008

Chapter 8

The Impact of the COVID-19 Pandemic on the Logistics Industry and Policy Response

Xu Yifan and Jianlin Liu

School of Management, Fudan University, Shanghai, China

The COVID-19 outbreak has put a halt to the stable development of China's economy: the market, which should have prospered because of the coming of Chinese New Year, was depressed with economic activities coming to a near halt.

As an old saying goes, when disaster strikes, help comes from all sides. Under the unified leadership of the CPC Central Committee, the whole country promptly dispatched personnel, medical supplies, and daily necessities to Hubei, especially to Wuhan, which fully demonstrated the advantage of China's political system in motivating all sectors and pooling resources. With unremitting efforts, the pandemic has been contained and society has gradually stabilized. Furthermore, since enterprises resumed work and production in an orderly manner, the economy has begun to recover.

Integrating industries such as transportation, warehousing, processing, distribution, freight forwarding, and information, logistics is a complex industry that is inter-industrial, inter-departmental, inter-regional, and highly permeable. It plays a basic and strategic role in supporting the development of the national economy, which has also been fully demonstrated in this pandemic. However, it should be noted that the problems and shortcomings that have been exposed are also salient, and are waiting at the soonest possible opportunity to be addressed.

In the coming "post-pandemic era", it would be of great significance to systematically analyze and evaluate the impact of the pandemic on the logistics industry and accordingly set out measures and provide suggestions. By doing so, China's logistics industry can enjoy more robust development.

8.1 Analysis of the Impact

As an important part of modern service industries, logistics has a reciprocal relationship with the economy, with each influencing and supporting the other. An E–L model is constructed (Figure 8.1) as follows to analyze the impact of the pandemic on the economy.

According to the *Covid-19 Diagnosis and Treatment Plan (Trial Eighth Edition)*, this pandemic should be included in the Class B infectious diseases stipulated in the *Law of the People's Republic of China on the Prevention and Treatment of Infectious Diseases,* and should be managed as a Class A infectious disease. Its epidemiological characteristics are as follows:

(1) Source of infection. The main sources of the infection are COVID-19 patients including asymptomatic COVID-19 patients. The virus is infectious even during the incubation period, and it is more contagious 5 days after infecting its host.

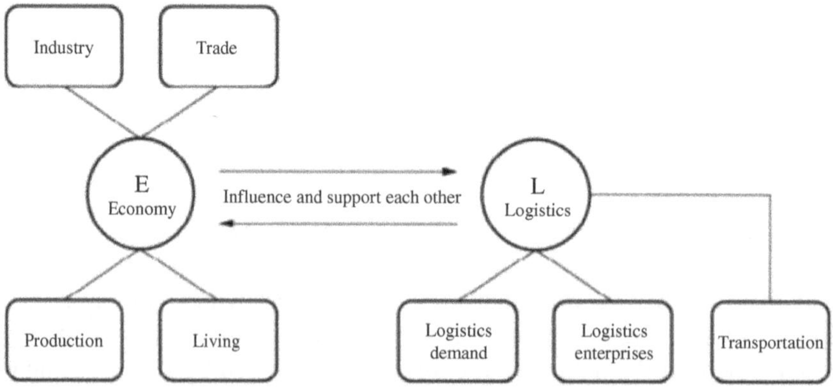

Figure 8.1: Simple E–L analysis model of the economy and logistics.

(2) Mode of transmission. Respiratory droplets and close contacts are two main modes of transmission. Contact with objects contaminated with the virus can also cause infection.

Aerosol transmission is possible if one is exposed to high concentrations of aerosols in a relatively closed environment for a long period of time.

Since the Novel Coronavirus has been detected in the feces and urine of some patients diagnosed with COVID-19, human excrement should be prevented from polluting the environment, causing either contact transmission or aerosol transmission.

(3) Susceptible population. The vast majority of the population is generally susceptible. Immunity can be acquired to some extent after being infected by the virus or vaccinated, but the duration of immunity is still unknown.

Therefore, the impact of the pandemic on the logistics industry is quite clear, since it is built directly on services calling for human interactions.

8.1.1 The short-term impact

In the short term, according to the E–L model (Figure 8.2), the impact of the pandemic on the development of the economy and logistics is reflected in the productivity of companies and people's usual daily activities, while that on logistics is solely reflected by logistics demands, logistics enterprises, and transportation. These five aspects will be analyzed.

8.1.1.1 *On production*

During the pandemic, production has mainly been focused on the manufacture of protective equipment and anti-pandemic products, supplemented by products which meet people's basic needs. The key is to ensure an integrated industrial chain, the smooth flow of both upstream and downstream of the supply chain, and the security, stability, and maintenance of the normal flow of the three basic links (inbound logistics, in-plant production, and outbound logistics).

(1) Major risks: If a COVID-19 close contact or an asymptomatic COVID-19 patient enters the site, the production or logistics

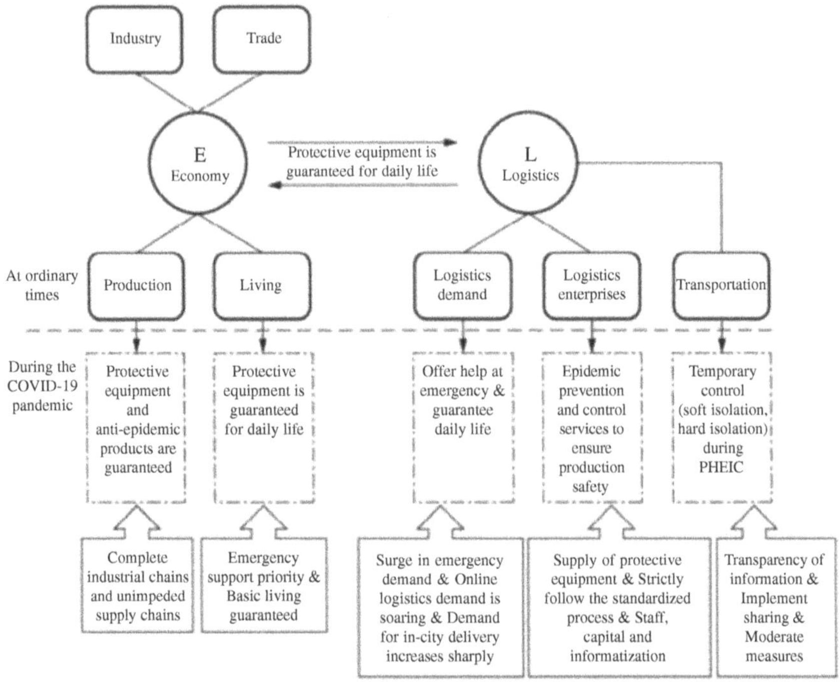

Figure 8.2: The E–L model for short-term impact analysis of PHEIC on economic and logistical development.

processes will be disrupted, and the supply chain will be disrupted as a result.

(2) Main effects: Production costs have increased due to the investment in protective equipment and temporary anti-pandemic teams; furthermore, the disruption of the supply chain in some industrial chains has caused production to be temporarily blocked and costs to rise sharply.

8.1.1.2 *On people's daily activities*

The COVID-19 virus is managed as a Class A infectious disease. During the pandemic, though priority has been given to guarantee the provision of emergency supplies to frontline workers, basic supplies for residents should also be taken into consideration. The lack of daily protection and disinfection products, and the lag time in the provision of emergency resources guarantees and management systems have made logistics distribution a heatedly-discussed issue. However, another consumer avenue emerged during this period — online shopping, which was suddenly thrust into the spotlight. After comparing the consumption data during the statutory Spring Festival holidays in 2019 and 2020, it was found that the pandemic had changed people's consumption style: consumption was postponed to some extent, but the demand from individuals was not eliminated.

(1) Major risks: The unrestricted movement of close COVID-19 contacts or asymptomatic COVID-19 patients may lead to the spread of the pandemic; the interruption of the supply chain on the supply of daily necessities may lead to a gap between supply and demand.
(2) Main effects: Since consumer demand has been extremely, though temporarily, suppressed, service suppliers may suffer huge losses in the short term; the failure to effectively match the supply and demand of fresh products such as fruits and vegetables caused by interruption to the local supply chain may further lead to huge losses for both suppliers and consumers.

8.1.1.3 *On logistics demands*

As a large and complex system, emergency rescue logistics systems need to be deployed and operated in coordination. Major logistics demands include but are not limited to the following four categories: (1) emergency logistics demand for special materials for disaster relief and assistance; (2) logistics demand for the procurement, transportation, storage, and transfer of raw materials which are for the production of special emergency supplies, such as pandemic prevention and disaster relief, as well as transportation and distribution of finished products; (3) logistics demand for people's basic necessities of life, especially intra-city distribution; and (4) logistics demand for the delivery of protective and disinfection supplies and other necessities, needed by people who have shopped on-line to purchase anti-pandemic products.

Though the logistics demands during the pandemic are typically characterized by emergency rescue, guaranteeing and meeting the basic logistical demands to guarantee the supply of the necessities of normal life is also important to maintain social stability and win the overall war against the pandemic.

(1) Major risks: The logistics of large-scale short-term emergency rescue have not been matched by effective logistics service supply, which may result in the failure of the emergency logistics system.
(2) Main effects: The emergency rescue logistics system has temporarily lost efficacy; the logistics system providing daily necessities is not smooth and at times has even been disrupted.

8.1.1.4 *Logistics enterprises*

If logistics is the blood of the economy, then logistics enterprises are the red blood cells. During the pandemic, logistics enterprises have needed to overcome "three obstacles" before starting and resuming work: (i) in terms of employees — employees should be protected when they returned so that may continue to work in their post safely; (ii) in terms of capital — the sustainable provision of capital and cash; and (iii) in terms of informationization — whether information technology can realize or meet the need of information exchange in the context of pandemic prevention and control.

(1) Major risks: The obstacles in terms of employees and capital make it more difficult for enterprises to start and resume work. The level of informatization will directly affect enterprises' participation in large logistics systems during the pandemic. What's more, the shutdown of operations will dry up cash flow.
(2) Main effects: During the pandemic, the cash flow and short-term profits of logistics enterprises have been significantly affected by the shutdown of operations. When the pandemic is over, on the one hand, logistics enterprises will operate in a more standardized way to establish emergency operation plans and allocate resources accordingly. On the other hand, logistics enterprises will invest more in their own information infrastructure

8.1.1.5 *Transportation*

Unlike the hard disruption of transportation infrastructure due to war or large-scale natural disasters, the soft disruption during the pandemic has usually been caused by transportation control aimed at preventing transmission. Adopting a "one-size-fits-all" approach to implement reckless hard blocking in the name of fighting the pandemic is actually sloppy and perfunctory, because the free flow of goods is essential both for pandemic prevention and for guaranteeing people's basic necessities.

(1) Major risks: Traffic will be clogged due to interruption of normal flow.
(2) Main effect: Supply chains are disrupted

In short, the short-term impacts of the pandemic on logistics can be summarized as follows:

(1) Production will be temporarily adjusted due to changes in demand. Though daily demands will be temporarily suppressed due to pandemic prevention and control, online shopping has been rapidly boosted. Logistics demand to ensure the provision of necessities for people's daily lives have always been the foundation for the survival and development of logistics enterprises.
(2) With a surging demand in emergency logistics, enterprises operating in line with pandemic prevention will play a significant role. However, those enterprises that fail to address the "three major obstacles", especially the first two obstacles (in terms of staff and capital), will sooner or later be eliminated.
(3) During the pandemic, control measures should be taken that are different from those taken in wartime or in large natural disasters, and avoid blocking deliberately. Special attention should be paid to the situation that a large number of small, medium, and micro enterprises (not only logistics enterprises) have been unable to resume work for an extended period or have even gone bankrupt, because their cash flow and short-term profits have been hugely impacted by the pandemic.
(4) In the post-pandemic era, devising strategies to boost consumer confidence as well as further promote consumption, and to ensure supplying people's basic needs during the pandemic deserve our attention and in-depth discussion.

8.1.2 The long-term impact

To understand the long-term impact of the pandemic on logistics, it is necessary to first see whether the pandemic has damaged the foundation of economic development, which can be analyzed from two aspects: first, whether the overall structure and pattern of industry and trade have undergone systemic large-scale collapse; the second factor is the duration of the pandemic as well as the extent of its impact. To this end, we built an E–L analysis model (Figure 8.3).

According to the *Catalogue for the Guidance of Industrial Structure Adjustment (2019 Version)* issued by the National Development and Reform Commission on October 30, 2019, there are 47 nationally encouraged industries (a total of 821 sub-items), which are the pillars of China's economy (Table 8.1).

At present, though domestic industries have resumed work in an orderly manner and the economy has gradually picked up, great uncertainties are still being faced in the development of international trade and the flow of international supply chains. It is difficult to conduct in-depth enterprise research and interviews, and data collection and communications are also limited. Qualitative analysis methods have largely been adopted to analyze the long-term impact of the pandemic on the economy and logistics, with the effects to be tested by time.

Having analyzed the relationship between logistics, the economy, and the law governing its development, and having built upon our understanding of the pattern of infectious diseases, the following four basic viewpoints are proposed relating to the long-term impact of the pandemic on the economy and logistics.

Viewpoint 1: In the long run, the trend of sustained and stable economic growth, as well as the accompanying growth trend in the logistics industry will not change.

Recently, many institutions have analyzed and predicted the impact of the pandemic on China's economy. The vast majority of the comparative analyses have been conducted based on the data of retail catering, movie and entertainment, transportation and tourism, real estate, and online shopping, which have been significantly affected by the pandemic in the short term, or based on how the economy was affected by the SARS outbreak in 2003.

Through analysis, it has been found that none of these reports considered that the structure of industry and trade, as well as investors' confidence, may have an impact on the sustainable development of the economy. In fact, according to the statistics of national GDP, it is the increased investment in industry and trade that plays a pivotal role in economic growth, rather than final consumption. As can be seen from

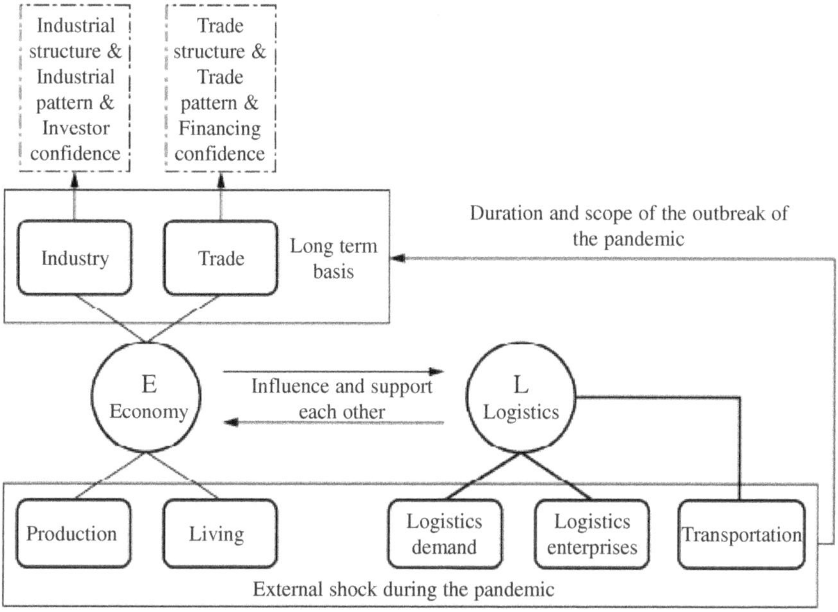

Figure 8.3: The E–L model of long-term impact analysis of PHEIC on economic and logistical development.

Table 8.1: Catalogue for the Guidance of Industrial Structure Adjustment (2019 edition) (details of encouraged categories).

Encouraged industries
agroforestry (57) water conservancy (25) coal (18) new energy (16) nuclear power (13) oil and gas (10) steel (13) non-ferrous metals (6) gold (3) petroleum (17) building materials (14) pharmaceuticals (6) machinery (63) urban rail transit equipment (10) automobiles (7) shipbuilding (15) aerospace (17) light industry (32) textiles (13) construction (13) urban infrastructure (26) rail (18) highway and transportation (including urban passenger transport) (20) waterway transport (15) air transport (7) integrated transport (8) information (51) modern logistics (10) financial services (14) technology services (16) business services (8) commerce and trade services (9) tourism (2) postal service (9) education (4) health (8) culture (9) sports (11) elderly care and childcare services (17) domestic industry (6) other services (14) comprehensive utilization of environmental protection and resource conservation (45) commercial explosive industry (69) civil explosives products (7) human resources and human capital services (7) artificial intelligence (15)

Table 8.1, the six industries affected by the pandemic only account for 0.7% of the encouraged industries. As long as there is no systemic collapse in the pillar industries or in the structure of domestic and foreign trade, China's economy will maintain sustained and steady growth. What's more, as China's industrial and trade structure focuses more on higher quality development, our economy will become more resilient and have greater potential for growth.

According to the data released by the Ministry of Commerce on February 17, both China's actual use of foreign capital keep steady growth, and high-tech industries have maintained a relatively high increase in foreign capital absorption, which illustrates investors' confidence in China's economic development.

In summary, since logistics serves the economy, as long as economic development keeps its momentum, the logistics industry will grow accordingly.

Viewpoint 2: How the economy and logistics are affected by the pandemic is closely related to its duration and scope.

In consideration of the epidemiological characteristics of COVID-19, the most effective measures to contain its spread are to cut off transmission routes and at the same time protect vulnerable populations.

(1) When facing the pandemic, the more decisive and stricter in taking measures, the better the outcome. In order to deal with this sudden outbreak, 31 provinces, autonomous regions, and municipalities in China have successively launched the level-one response to major public health emergencies, not to mention that Wuhan has carried out the "lockdown" with great self-sacrifice, in its efforts to contain the potential source of infection within the city. Other parts of the country have also tried their best to restrict the flow of people. All these measures have proved to be effective and bought valuable time and space for both China and the world to fight the pandemic.

    By March 23, a total of 26 provinces, autonomous regions, and municipalities had downgraded the level one response. As COVID-19 prevention and control has increased, a phased victory is within reach. However, with a tough situation abroad, China needs to strictly guard its borders and actively participate in the global fight against the pandemic, because only when the danger is eliminated worldwide will it be called a final victory. By doing so, China will demonstrate how a big country shoulders its rightful responsibilities and builds a community with a shared future for mankind. What's more, by then, people will be able to travel and consume assuredly, trade can be conducted freely and globally, and the world economy will be restarted, accelerated, and developed sustainably.

(2) Production should be resumed in a timely fashion. The more detailed and adequate the contingency plans, the safer the resumption of work will be and the less impact the pandemic will have on the economy. Based on the epidemiological characteristics of COVID-19, three key points should be emphasized: to control the source of infection, cut off transmission routes, and protect vulnerable groups. Though the epidemiological characteristics of COVID-19 have been updated in, the eighth edition, apart from updates to diagnosis and treatment plans and the pathological characteristics of the infected, few upgrades were made to the three key points aimed at prevention. Therefore, they are still the main principles to be followed, and it is both safe and necessary to orderly resume work on the premise of targeted prevention and control of the pandemic.

Industries should set up pandemic prevention and control teams according to their specific conditions, and formulate guidelines for employees in strict accordance with the latest *COVID-19 Diagnosis and Treatment Plan* to ensure that employees who return to work are healthy. The workplace shall be disinfected according to the prevention and control requirements to ensure the safety of the working environment. Furthermore, pandemic prevention and control plans shall be formulated and specific drills carried out. As long as management measures are properly designed and truly implemented, the safety of the resumption of work can be guaranteed. After all, only the resumption of work and production can stop economic losses.

(3) The shorter the pandemic and the smaller its scope, the lesser the impact on economic development. The larger the opportunity for development to resume normal production and the earlier the return to work, the lesser the impact the pandemic will have on the economy.

Most are aware that economic globalization brings with it the globalization of industrial chains and supply chains. At present, the situation abroad is not optimistic, our international trade and supply chains have been severely restricted, which effects overall recovery and stable development of the domestic economy. It is of great significance that our successful experience in fighting the pandemic, as well as our confidence, has been passed on by China to those countries and people in need, to help them fight against the pandemic, not only demonstrating Chinese values, but also contributing to the recovery of the global economy.

Viewpoint 3: Whether in the sphere of production or of the provision of services needed for daily life, logistics plays an indispensable role as a foundation and a means of connection. Therefore, logistics should be resumed in accordance with the resumption of production.

To put it simply, logistics includes various services whose function is to complete the flow of goods between the supplier and the buyer. Firstly, logistics services are provided only when demand for them exists, which means that logistics services are synchronized with the demands of production and consumers. Secondly, in comparison with the logistics involved in the provision of life-related necessities, that of production-related goods account for more than 80% of total annual logistics, which is the key motivator for the resumption of production.

Viewpoint 4: In the logistics ecosystem, small, medium, and micro logistics enterprises are largest in number, but the weakest in their ability to resist risks.

The logistics industry is an ecosystem composed of numerous logistics and related enterprises that provide direct or indirect services like logistics information, technology, equipment, finance, legal affairs, and taxation services to enterprises (as shown in Figure 8.4). According to estimates, by the end of 2019, the core of this ecosystem was composed of 41 listed companies, more than 800,000 logistics companies, over 11 million vehicles, and more than 30 million truck drivers.

In this logistics ecosystem, the vast majority of enterprises are small, medium, micro, or owner-operated enterprises. During the pandemic, a large number of these workers have been waiting for work or even temporarily unemployed. If this situation cannot be turned around in time, under greater pressure, bankruptcy is a possibility for some.

In the long run, the impact of the pandemic on logistics can be summarized as follows:

(1) The pandemic will not change the overall structure of China's industry and trade. The economy will maintain stable and sound growth, as will the logistics industry.

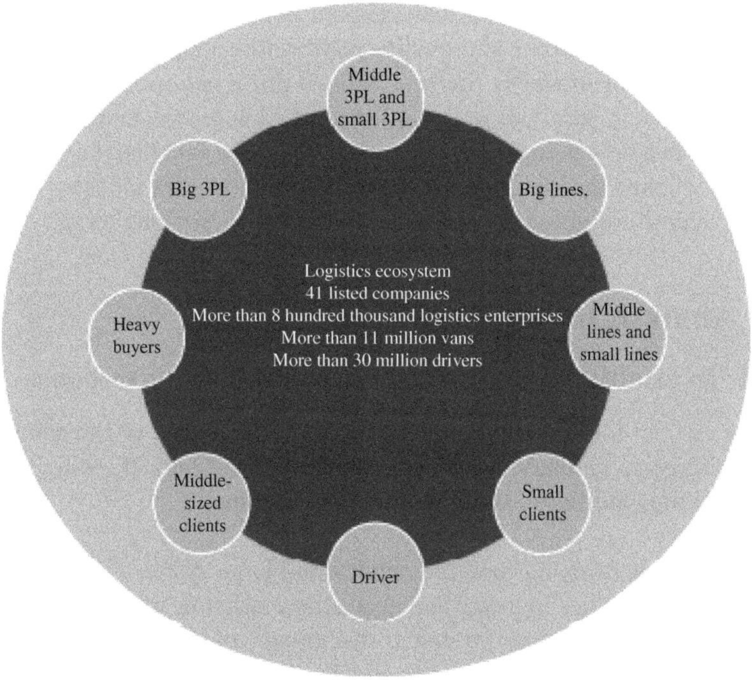

Figure 8.4: Overview of logistics ecosystem.

(2) However, the impact of the pandemic will be largely decided by its duration and scope. While domestically, it is expected that comprehensive success will be achieved in fighting the pandemic, the uncertainty of the situation abroad is increasing. Therefore, it is imperative that China's experience and confidence are passed on to countries in need. In the next phase, the focus will shift from strict prevention of and fighting the spread of the virus within China to strict prevention of the virus being spread into China from abroad and assisting in fighting the pandemic outside China.
(3) The sooner the effective measures are taken and the pandemic is contained, the sooner the favorable conditions are created for an orderly resumption of work and production, and hence the sooner the negative impact of the pandemic on the economy will be stopped. However, the orderly resumption of work and production calls for a safe and stable logistics system that is both reliable and effective.
(4) Small, medium, and micro logistics enterprises are large in number, but weak in their ability to resist risks, and this needs a high level of

attention by the relevant management departments. In the long run, joining an organized and quality platform or adopting an innovative development model is the best actions these enterprises can take to ensure their survival, and platform-based logistics enterprises will usher in a new period of development. It can be said that the pandemic may change the structure and pattern of the logistics industry, but not its overall trend toward stable development in the long term.

8.2 Analysis on the Response

8.2.1 To establish a multi-faceted comprehensive response

In order to put forward a targeted response to the impact of the pandemic on the logistics industry, systematic thinking, long-term thinking, scientific thinking, and bottom-line thinking are required.

(1) Systematic thinking: within complex and large systems, consisting of emergency relief logistics and production systems, global trade logistics and supply chain systems, the impact of the pandemic on the development of the economy and logistics. Only by aiming at the main objectives, grasping the main factors and finding out the main contradictions can we formulate effective strategies.
(2) Long-term thinking: that is to believe the impact of the pandemic is temporary in time and limited in scale. Once effective scientific strategies are formulated, they must be firmly implemented because in the long run, the better they are implemented, the better the outcome. To bear temporary losses is fundamental to long-term interests.
(3) Scientific thinking: believing in and respecting the laws of science are fundamental to both the prevention of and treatment of patients in the pandemic and it is important that all decisions are made accordingly.
(4) Bottom-line thinking: With the basic protection of people's health and safety and a basic guarantee for people's well-being as the bottom line, the pandemic should not only be prevented and fought, people's basic needs should also be met efficiently.

The current situation is very relevant in the short-term analysis, however, overall trends are more pivotal in long-term analysis. In consideration of the developmental characteristics of China's logistics industry, the analysis framework for dealing with the impact of the pandemic on the logistics industry is summarized in Figure 8.5.

First of all, in terms of the main characteristics of the development of China's logistics industry at the present stage, various platforms are gradually expanding having an ever more far-reaching influence; the supply chain and its management are becoming increasingly popular and widely practiced; more attention as well as investment are being given to enterprise informatization; and standardized development and operation have become mainstream. In general, with a strong sense of social responsibility, logistics enterprises have gradually optimized their global layout, and grown more mature in international operation. However, despite its large scale, the industry is not robust, with relatively low market concentration, and most enterprises are small, medium, and micro logistics companies. During the pandemic, it has been shown clearly that those platform-based enterprises with international layout, advanced information technology, and standardized operation play a crucial role.

Second, though the pandemic has now been effectively contained in China, and people's work and livelihoods have gradually returned to normal in an orderly manner, prevention and control measures have not slackened. The situation abroad is not optimistic, so the pressure of preventing and controlling imported cases needs to be faced, which has been and will continue to be the focus of our job. In the long run, the pandemic will not have a fundamental impact on China's industrial structure and pattern. International trade, especially the trade with countries along the "One Belt One Road" initiative, is gradually recovering. The logistics

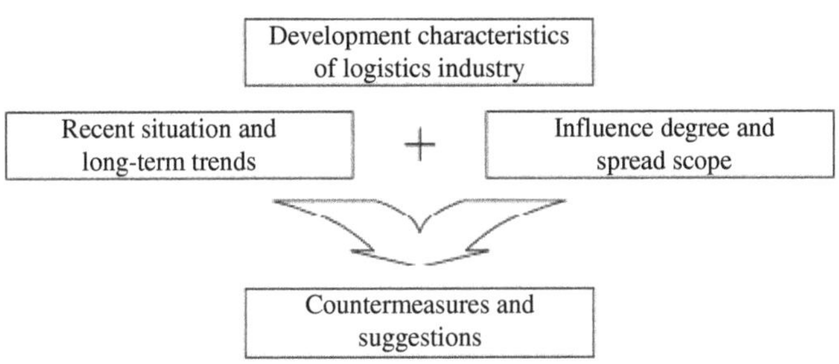

Figure 8.5: Schematic diagram of the analysis framework.

industry will maintain its long-term development, but the overall structure and pattern of logistics will be changed.

Thirdly, in the short term, six industries have mainly been affected by the pandemic, accounting for only 0.7% of the encouraged industries, so the fundamentals of economic development will not be much affected. With the orderly resumption of work and production, and a new round of investment in new infrastructure worth trillions represented by 5G, artificial intelligence, the industrial internet, and the internet of things, the pandemic's impact on our realization of this year's economic target is quite limited. However, due to the uncertainties abroad, it is necessary to assess the risks and possible losses in advance and develop as soon as possible a scientific response plan that is effective and feasible.

Finally, in the ecosystem of the logistics industry, small, medium, and micro enterprises are large in number but weak in their ability to resist risks. As the base of China's logistics industry, they have to be consolidated.

8.2.2 Measures and suggestions

Based on the above analysis, we put forward the following measures and *suggestions.*

8.2.2.1 *Advocate logistics enterprises to be independent and strengthen their foundation*

Though the development of logistics enterprises has largely benefited from industrial policies, their survival and development cannot completely rely on these policies. Instead, enterprises should step up efforts to improve standardized management and enhance scientific governance capacity, especially in terms of cash flow management and capital allocation, join other platforms or build their own platforms, and strive to improve their digital and information capabilities.

8.2.2.2 *Lead logistics enterprises to establish standardized development*

The standardized development of enterprises is not only conducive to improving the overall service quality of the logistics industry, but also beneficial to the government in that it can adopt precise policies and management practices to strengthen standardized development, especially in enterprises' operation, taxation, and legal affairs. For example, the government can guide, lead, and encourage logistics enterprises to standardize their development by implementing the brand strategy and establishing a credit system.

8.2.2.3 *Support logistics enterprises to grow better and stronger*

As a basic and strategic industry in China, state and local governments have attached great importance to logistics, and have issued many supporting policies and introduced encouraging measures. At present, various fiscal, tax, and financial policies that have been issued should be further integrated, implemented, and refined. All localities should be encouraged to build block-chain, industry chain, and supply chain financing service platforms that are public, or headed by leading enterprises, and innovate financing methods through multiple channels. A fair and orderly market environment should be built to support innovation, start-up businesses, and smart upgrading. Meanwhile, the assessment and evaluation system should be dynamically revised to encourage logistics enterprises whether built on either platforms or supply chains, whether global or international, to grow bigger, stronger, and more refined. For enterprises affected by the pandemic, feasible tax reduction and exemption policies should be formulated to help them overcome difficulties.

8.2.2.4 *Establish a comprehensive emergency security system*

Needless to say, during this pandemic, certain problems have been exposed in the emergency logistics system, for example, the insufficient reserve of emergency supplies, especially the key materials for pandemic prevention and control, namely personal protective equipment, including medical masks, protective clothing, goggles, and medical equipment, the lack of which has led to tight supply for a period of time. Other problems include delayed production of emergency materials, impeded emergency logistics, the difficulty of trans-regional and trans-departmental scheduling and coordination, and low efficiency in the distribution of transshipment warehouses. After the pandemic, government departments should step up and establish a national reserve system to classify comprehensive emergency support and supplies, a production and supply system of emergency materials, and an emergency logistics system for transportation, warehousing, and distribution. A big data platform is needed to provide corresponding control and support to improve the standard process of emergency material handling, coordination, and distribution, and optimize relevant emergency laws and regulations. A white list system of emergency logistics enterprises should be established, and standardized and large-scale logistics enterprises should be included in the management system, so as to improve the service capacity of emergency logistics.

8.3 Conclusion

By constructing the E–L model of the economy and logistics, this chapter analyzes the impact of the pandemic on the logistics industry, including both short-term and long-term effects. The conclusions are as follows.

Conclusion 1: In the short term, the pandemic has had a strong but limited impact on logistics. Special attention should be paid to the situation abroad.

Production will be temporarily adjusted to changes in demand. Though the normal activities of people's lives may be temporarily suppressed due to pandemic prevention and control measures, online shopping consumption has sprung up everywhere, which promotes the development of logistics.

Since the demand for emergency logistics will surge, logistics enterprises operating in line with pandemic requirements will play an important role, but those companies which fail to manage the "three major hurdles", especially the first two (in terms of staff and capital), will be eliminated sooner or later.

In short, as long as the control measures are appropriate and well implemented, the pandemic, if of short duration and small scope, will have a limited impact on economic and logistics development.

Conclusion 2: In the long-term, the overall trend and stable development of logistics will not be influenced by the pandemic, but its structure and pattern will be. The sharing of both experience and confidence in fighting the pandemic are not only conducive to combatting the pandemic globally, but are also good for the long-term development of the economy and logistics.

In the long run, the pandemic has had little impact on the overall structure of China's industry and trade. China's economy will maintain its long-term stable growth. Therefore, the logistics industry whose development is in line with economic development will also maintain long-term stable and sound growth.

At a time when domestically our control of the pandemic is expected to achieve complete success, uncertainty about the situation abroad is increasing. Therefore, the main task of the next phase will shift from concentration on domestic containment, that is, strictly preventing the coronavirus from spreading within China to strictly preventing the coronavirus from entering China and assisting containment efforts outside China. The sooner effective measures are taken and the spread of the virus is contained, the sooner favorable conditions will be created for the orderly resumption of work, production, and markets, and the sooner the negative impact of the pandemic on the economy can be stopped.

Platform-based logistics enterprises will usher in a new period of development with more opportunities. The pandemic will not change the overall development trend of the logistics industry, but will change its structure and pattern. After the pandemic, enterprises are expected to be more standardized in management, more scientific in governance, and more robust in growth.

Finally, the chapter puts forward suggestions from these four aspects: advocating logistics enterprises to be independent and strengthen their foundation, leading them to establish standardized development, supporting them to grow better and stronger, and establishing a comprehensive emergency security system.

Acknowledgement

This study was funded by the Key Project of National Natural Science Foundation of China (71531005).

https://doi.org/10.1142/9789811252921_0009

Chapter 9

The Full Impact of the COVID-19 Pandemic on China's Tourism Industry and Policy Responses

Sun Yunlong

Department of Tourism, Fudan University, Shanghai, China

9.1 Trends and Characteristics of China's Tourism Industry in Recent Years

9.1.1 *Trends*

Being one of the top five "happiness industries", tourism plays an important role in meeting people's ever-growing need for a better life, as well as improving public services, promoting the equal distribution of cultural and educational resources, and strengthening cultural exchange. Recent years have witnessed sustained development of China's tourism industry. The average annual growth rate in both the number of tourists and tourism income has been higher than that of GDP. In the same period, tourism has gradually grown into a strategic pillar industry in the national economy, employing more than one-tenth of the country's total work force. It is not only a new driving force for economic development, but also a stabilizer for the national economy and people's livelihood. It has incomparable advantages in expanding domestic demand, stimulating consumption, increasing employment, promoting innovation and transformation, revitalizing rural areas, and alleviating poverty.

In recent years, China's tourism industry has developed with great vigor. Guided by the policy of integrating culture and tourism, the concept of "promoting tourism through culture, and enhancing culture through tourism", has led to the cultural and tourism industry developing in concert, drawing on each other's strengths, and driving the overall development of related industries, as well as social and economic activities. A series of new business forms, products, and models have arisen, such as red tourism, sports tourism, research tourism, rural tourism, health tourism, and urban micro-tourism. According to the Ministry of Culture and Tourism, from 2014 to 2019, the comprehensive contribution of tourism to China's GDP rose from 6.61 trillion yuan to 10.94 trillion yuan, and the proportion of tourism of total GDP rose to 11.05%. In 2018, 79.87 million people were directly and indirectly employed in tourism, accounting for 10.31% of the country's total employed population.[1]

According to the *2019 Statistical Communique of the People's Republic of China on National Economic and Social Development* released by the National Bureau of Statistics, the number of domestic tourists in 2019 reached 6.01 billion, an increase of 8.4% over the previous year; the revenue from domestic tourism was 5.725.1 billion yuan, up 11.7%; inbound tourists totaled 145.31 million, up 2.9%, and international tourism revenue was $131.3 billion, up 3.3%. Chinese residents made 16.921 million outbound trips, up 4.5%. Among them, 16.211 million were made for private purposes, up 4.6%, and 102.37 million were made to Hong Kong, Macao, and Taiwan, an increase of 3.2%.[2]

Recent years have seen a significant growth in outbound tourism: Chinese tourism consumption accounts for 16% of international tourism consumption, among which, more than half of the tourism GDP in the Asia-Pacific region is contributed by Chinese tourists. According to the National Immigration Administration, in 2019, 670 million inbound and outbound visits were made, up 3.8% year on year, and a total of 36.235 million vehicles for inbound and outbound transportation were inspected by the national border inspection authority, up 3.4% year on year. In 2019,

---

[1] *Basic Situation of the Tourism Market in 2019*, official website of Ministry of Culture and Tourism of the People's Republic of China, March 10, 2020: https://www.mct.gov.cn/whzx/whyw/202003/t20200310_851786.htm.

[2] *2019 Statistical Communique of the People's Republic of China on National Economic and Social Development*, official website of National Bureau of Statistics, February 28, 2020: http://www.stats.gov.cn/tjsj/zxfb/202002/t20200228_1728913.html.

350 million inbound and outbound visits were made by mainland residents. People from Hong Kong, Macao, and Taiwan made 160 million, 53.587 million, and 12.278 million trips to and from the mainland, respectively, and foreigners made 97.675 million trips to and from the mainland.[3]

It can be seen from the above data that China's tourism industry is growing robustly, making increasingly significant contributions to the national economy, social development, and foreign exchange.

9.1.2 Characteristics of the industry

As a highly sensitive, interconnected, and generally resilient industry, tourism is still vulnerable to public events in terms of politics, the economy, military actions, and health, as well as natural disasters, of which pandemics are the most destructive having the most significant impact. Since the tourism industry relies heavily on people' mobility, when a pandemic occurs, the common prevention measures of reducing both the gathering and flow of people curbs the development of the industry, suspends business temporarily, causes cash flow to run out, and even endangers the ability of companies to continue operations, inducing a wave of bankruptcy across the whole industry. However, boasting a relatively high resiliency, the tourism industry is often one of the sectors where demand recovers fastest after a crisis is over. According to a study conducted by the World Tourism and Travel Council (WTTC) on four types of crises, between 2001 and 2018, the recovery time for tourism was reduced from an average of 26 months to 10 months.[4]

As a labor-intensive industry, tourism has low barriers to entry, small-scale enterprises, a high degree of homogenization, diversified business, a low market concentration rate, and fierce competition, caused by its development stage as well as the characteristics of the industry. Because of its focus on life services, the tourism industry is highly sensitive to changes in consumer demand. Recent years have witnessed the birth of a large number of "small but nice, refined or specialized" enterprises, whose development has brought new vitality and focus to the industry.

---

[3]1. *670 million inbound and outbound visits in 2019,* National Immigration Administration, January 17, 2020: https://s.nia.gov.cn/mps/tztg/202001/t20200117_1178.html.

[4]Crisis Preparedness, Management & Recovery, WTTC, November 2019: https://www.wttc.org/priorities/crisispreparedness/.

As for the overall trends, large enterprises and small and micro enterprises coexist; head effects and long tail effects synchronize, and standardized products are complemented by niche designs. According to statistics, there are about 38,000 travel agencies, mainly consisting of small, medium, and micro enterprises in China; there are around 480,000 accommodation facilities of all kinds, including 26,000 hotels in the top 50 Chinese hotel groups, accounting for only 5.4% of the total; and nearly 10,000 A-level scenic spots of which around 65% are small and medium-sized scenic spots of AAA or below. In addition, a large number of scenic spots that have not entered the A-level range also form an important part of the tourist attractions market. Further, millions of travel-related enterprises such as catering, shopping, entertainment, transportation, and performance, which are mostly small, medium, and micro enterprises, have created a large number of jobs.[5]

9.2 The "Freeze" and "Acceleration" of Tourism in the Context of the Pandemic

9.2.1 *Industries built on "liquidity" suffer a "liquidity" freeze*

As the essence of the service industry is to create value based on human relationships, the orderly operation of the service industry relies on people's social interaction. The tourism industry not only depends on interpersonal connections, but also needs flow in various sectors, including logistics, capital, and information driven by the flow of visitors. However, in response to a public health event, the most essential emergency measure is to suspend social mobility, such as extending holidays, shutting down production, conducting quarantine, and setting travel restrictions. Though the cost of these measures is huge, they are necessary in an emergency. Only by stopping the flow of people can the virus be effectively isolated and mode of transmission blocked. In this regard, the novel COVID-19 pandemic, and the corresponding emergency measures, hit the life service industry hard especially the tourism industry, because the stagnation of flow means the suspension of the industry.

On January 23, 2020, the Ministry of Culture and Tourism issued a document requiring all localities to strengthen pandemic prevention and

[5] On statistical data released by the Ministry of Culture and Tourism in recent years.

control, step up publicity and guidance, and further manage foreign activities. Since January 24, scenic spots have been successively closed in several places including Beijing, Shanghai, Hangzhou, and Sanya. On January 25, the China Association of Travel Agents, directed travel agencies and online travel companies across the country to suspend group Tours and "air ticket + hotel" products. The sudden COVID-19 outbreak brought social interaction and mobility to a temporary standstill, rapidly freezing demand, and thus rendering a state of shutdown in the industry as a whole.

9.2.2 Industry reshuffle was accelerated with market demand rebounding quickly after the pandemic

A strong growth trend will be maintained in China's tourism industry despite the COVID-19 pandemic. In fact, this crisis is an opportunity to accelerate industry consolidation. In recent years, with the fast-paced development of society, tourism services have gradually become a strong demand of urban residents. Though the overall outlook of tourism is good, as characterized by multi-level and diversified development, many "small, dispersed, and weak" travel agencies still exist, with low market concentration rates. In the long term, the pandemic has only temporarily suspended activities of the tourism market. The previous experience of the SARS pandemic showed the tourism industry rebounding quickly after the pandemic, and enterprises which manage to withstand the test of the pandemic will embrace a faster development cycle. The COVID-19 outbreak is therefore an opportunity to accelerate industry transformation and eliminate inefficient capacity. At present, it seems that enterprises that attach importance to cash management, cost control, organizational flexibility, and business innovation in their daily operations will survive the pandemic. The realization of the internet and technology replacing human labor will be further accelerated, and unprecedentedly, more emphasis will be given to cultivating the ability to resist risk in enterprises and industries.

9.3 Analysis of Different Sectors

9.3.1 *Hospitality services*

Because of the COVID-19 pandemic, the travel data during the 2020 Spring Festival was appalling. Following the guidance of national policies, travel agencies returned a large number of tour fees; access to scenic spots were suspended, and travel restrictions were imposed in some severely affected areas. Over the years, tourism income during the Spring Festival Golden Week has played an important role, accounting for about 9% of total annual tourism revenue, hence the label "Golden Week". Taking the 2019 Spring Festival Golden Week as an example, the number of trips nationwide reached 421 million, and national tourism revenue reached 513.9 billion yuan, accounting for nearly 10% of the total in that year. For small, medium, and micro enterprises, the proportion would reach about 30%. During the Spring Festival in 2020, service industries including aviation, tourism, catering, retail, and entertainment were severely hit by the pandemic, with the number of visits together with sales revenue falling off a cliff: A total of 13 million air tickets and more than 60 million train tickets were canceled across the country from January 24 to February 4. According to a conservative estimate, tourism revenue during the Spring Festival holiday was reduced by 500 billion yuan.[6]

Because of the strict control of travel, nearly all tourism sectors suffered a serious blow, with travel agencies suffering most. On January 24, 2020, the General Office of the Ministry of Tourism issued an urgent notice, requiring all travel agencies and online tourism enterprises to temporarily suspend the promotion and the sale of group tours and "air ticket + hotel" products, for both domestic and outbound travel, and that pre-sold products were to be refunded. However, travel agencies may not be able to obtain refunds for the advance deposit and pre-purchased inventory of upstream and downstream partners, including transportation, hotel, catering, scenic spots, and ground transportation. This is true especially for those involved in the outbound tourism business, as costs need to be reduced by chartering flights and cruises, and so on. Compared with travel agencies, the situation faced by the management of scenic spots is slightly better, because they did not have to bear huge losses caused by the refunds from the supply chain. However, due to the policy that temporarily stopped access to scenic spots, business volume plummeted to zero. Even after later reopening, results were not satisfying, because tourists have been severely discouraged from traveling, and in the meantime fixed expenses such as labor and rent have to be paid. The pandemic has also greatly affected the hotel industry: many hotels have witnessed a 10%

---

[6]Publicly available data from the Ministry of Transport, the Civil Aviation Administration, and the China Academy of Tourism.

drop in their occupancy rate. According to the *Analysis on the Impact of the Pandemic on the National Hotel Market* jointly released by China Hospitality Association and Hotel Strategy (HK) Management & Consulting Limited, compared with the same period in 2019, hotels lost an average of 67.81% of their operating revenue in the spring of 2020, resulting in a total of 1.23 billion yuan in operating losses, including the expenses of canceling bookings, operations, and pandemic prevention.[7]

9.3.2 Shipping sector

According to the International Civil Aviation Organization (ICAO), global airline revenues are expected to fall by $4 billion to $5 billion in the first quarter of 2020 due to the COVID-19 pandemic. A report conducted by the Research Institute of Guotai Jun'an Securities claims that China's aviation industry lost 15 billion to 21 billion yuan in the first quarter, and further losses are expected. Passenger demand will recover slowly after the pandemic with domestic airlines recovering faster than international ones, and business travel recovering faster than leisure travel. The growth rate of demand may turn positive in the third quarter, while the industry will not fully return to normal growth until 2021.[8]

Figures released by the OAG show that total capacity on scheduled civil flights in mainland China has fallen rapidly from more than 14m seats a week at the end of January to about 4m. Recently, domestic transport capacity has recovered slightly, but the occupancy rate remains low. At present, in the global aviation industry, the Chinese mainland is still the region most affected by the pandemic.[9] Airline companies in Hong Kong and Macao have been hit as hard as those on the mainland: Hong Kong's overall capacity has fallen by as much as 70% from 840,000 on January 20 to 240,000 in early March 2020. The capacity of Cathay Pacific Airways Limited, a leading airline, has been reduced to a quarter of that before the pandemic, and the same has been seen in airlines in Macau. In an effort to minimize losses, many airlines in Hong Kong and Macao have

---

[7] http://www.chinahotel.org.cn/forward/enterSecondDary.do?id=b92ba90011ef4de3a786d86fbe161f20&childMId1=b92ba90011ef4de3a786d86fbe161f20&childMId2=&childMId3=&contentId=9b166d6cbb0b42d6973c7a51fff412ce.

[8] https://www.sohu.com/a/374379458_169306.

[9] https://www.oag.com/coronavirus.airline.schedules.data.

taken unconventional measures such as laying off workers, cutting wages, and granting unpaid leave.

To encourage airlines to increase capacity and reduce losses, the Civil Aviation Administration and the Ministry of Finance recently issued the *Notice on Financial Support Policies for Civil Aviation Transport Enterprises during COVID-19 Prevention and Control Period* to reward international flights that resume operation or do "non-stop" flights during the pandemic. Even so, airline companies with heavy assets and high leverage are still struggling and operating under enormous pressure.

9.3.3 The cruise industry

Recent years have witnessed the rapid rise and explosive growth of the cruise industry in domestic tourism. It is obvious that China's cruise market enjoys a huge capacity for development. According to the *2018 Market Report of Asia Cruise Industry* released by the Cruise Line Association International (CLIA), the number of cruise passengers in Asia hit a record high of 4.24 million in 2018, of which Chinese tourists accounted for 55.8%. Meanwhile, the global cruise industry market is worth about 46 billion US dollars, and about 26 million people around the world take cruise vacations every year.[10]

However, the hidden risks of the cruise industry were fully exposed during the COVID-19 pandemic. Several international luxury cruises were suddenly transformed from "sea resorts" to "hotbeds of the virus", among which the "Diamond Princess" cruise ship captured the most attention, with a total of more than 700 people infected while onboard.

Due to the pandemic, on February 3, the Cruise Lines International Association (CLIA) issued the strictest ban, suspending the travel of crew members from China and prohibiting any individual departing from or passing through China during the past 14 days from boarding the ship, including passengers and crew. On March 4th, the travel ban was extended to South Korea, Iran, and northern Italy. On March 7, Malaysia banned foreign cruise ships from docking. On the same day, the US Centers for Disease Control and Prevention (CDC) issued a "stop order" to Princess Cruises. On the night of March 8, the US State Department issued a warning that Americans, especially those with underlying health problems,

[10]https://www.cruising.org.au/Regulatory/Research.and.Reports.

should avoid taking cruise ships during the COVID-19 pandemic because of the higher risk of contracting the virus on board. As countries became increasingly wary of international cruise ships docking, a growing number of routes were suspended and canceled, and more ports began to refuse cruise ships. It was estimated that cruise companies would lose $3 million to $4 million each time they canceled a trip. According to *China Cruise Market Report 2020* compiled by Cruise Industry News, it is estimated that, without the pandemic, there will be about 3.905 million inbound and outbound Cruise passengers in China in 2020.[11] Based on China's current domestic control and the spread of the pandemic abroad, domestic cruise passengers are estimated to be reduced by 30%, about 1.2 million, and the loss of the cruise industry in the Chinese market will exceed 3 billion yuan.

9.3.4 Small, medium, and micro enterprises

During the pandemic, small, medium, and micro tourist businesses had a particularly difficult time, many of which tottered on the edge of bankruptcy. The reasons for their low risk-resistance are as follows.

(1) Generally speaking, small, medium, and micro enterprises in the tourism industry are usually characterized by the following features: single product, poor bargaining power, light assets, weak profitability, and insufficient financing channels.
(2) In these enterprises' cost structures, fixed costs account for a relatively high proportion, which includes costs associated with staff salary, "five insurance and one fund" (endowment insurance, medical insurance, unemployment insurance, work-related injury insurance, childbirth insurance, and housing provident fund), house rent, and equipment rent.
(3) Because of the pandemic, the regular services of tourist businesses shut down, and the flow of operating cash was interrupted, which made it difficult for enterprises to pay fixed expenses and operation costs.
(4) As Spring Festival Golden Week is the most important sales season of the year, many enterprises had purchased inventory in advance and

[11] https://www.cruiseindustrynews.com/flip/2020china/.

invested a lot in advertising to promote sales. However, most orders were canceled due to the shutdown of the industry, so profits were not generated, thus resulting in losses.

To sum up, facing the triple blow of business revenue suspension, fixed operational expenditure, and cash flow interruption, small, medium, and micro tourist businesses are in a tough situation. If the pandemic is not effectively controlled and enterprises are not provided with financial support, a series of chain reactions will be triggered, including lost jobs, negative effects on both upstream and downstream enterprises, market confidence will be lost, fiscal revenue will shrink, social income will decrease, and demand will decline, all of which will hinder the industry's recovery. Small, medium, and micro enterprises are hidden champions in the national economy as well as indicators of economic vitality. If sustainable operation is not maintained by the majority of these enterprises, in the short-term, the vitality of the industry and people's livelihood will be directly affected.

9.4 Analysis of the Response

9.4.1 *On emergency policies for the tourism industry*

After the COVID-19 outbreak, the central government recognized the plight of the tourism industry. To boost people's confidence in the industry, both central and local governments have introduced targeted rescue and emergency policies to help tide over enterprises dealing with difficulties and promote the healthy and sustainable development of the industry.

On January 26, 2020, required by the *Notice on Strengthening the Coordination of Financial Services of Banking and Insurance Industry for the Prevention and Control of COVID-19 Pandemic* issued by the China Banking and Insurance Regulatory Commission, loans must not be blindly withdrawn, cut off, or restricted for industries greatly affected by the pandemic, including wholesale and retail business, accommodation and catering, logistics and transportation, and cultural tourism, as well as enterprises that have promising prospects but are temporarily affected by the pandemic. Methods like appropriately lowering loan interest rates, improving policy arrangements for renewing loans, and adding both credit loans and medium- and long-term loans are encouraged, to support enterprises in overcoming the impact of the pandemic.

On February 3, a notice issued by the China Tourism Association (CTA) stated that "In an effort to reduce economic losses caused by the pandemic, the membership fees will be waived for its 212 members for 2020."

On February 5, the General Office of the Ministry of Culture and Tourism issued the *Notice on Suspension of Part of the Deposit for Tourism Service Quality to Help Travel Agencies Combat Business Difficulties*. The decision was made to temporarily refund part of the deposit for the tourism service to travel agencies which have paid the deposit in accordance with the law and obtained their business licenses. The standard for the temporary refund is 80% of the current payment. Liu Kezhi, director of the market management department of the Ministry of Culture and Tourism, said that as of February 25, 35,200 (or 90%) of the country's 39,000 travel agencies, had asked for a temporary refund of the deposit. The amount totaled 8 billion yuan, of which 3.462 billion yuan had already been refunded by February 25. Such a policy was launched in a timely and precise way, which effectively alleviated the pressure of insufficient cash flow of travel agencies.

On the evening of February 5, at the State Council executive meeting, it was proposed that the value-added tax on express delivery and transportation be suspended, as well as the Civil Aviation Development Fund. Specifically, "Key materials needed in transportation, prevention, and control as well as income from public transport, life services, and postal delivery are exempt from VAT. The civil aviation development fund paid by civil aviation enterprises is also exempt". According to CICC, if the cancellation of the Civil Aviation Development Fund is applicable nationwide, within a half-year period, the net profit of Air China and China Eastern Airlines is expected to increase by 400 million to 500 million yuan (about 4–6% of the net profit in 2020). The net profit of Spring Airlines and Juneyao Airlines is expected to increase by 70 million yuan (about 3–4% of the net profit in 2020).

On February 6, the Ministry of Finance and the State Taxation Administration issued the *Notice on Tax Policies to Support the Prevention and Control of COVID-19 Pandemic*. According to the fourth article, for industries and enterprises greatly affected by the pandemic, including transportation, catering, accommodation, and tourism (consisting of travel agencies and related services as well as scenic management), the maximum carryover period of their losses in 2020 will be extended from the original 5 years to 8 years.

On February 10, according to the Ministry of Human Resources and Social Security, all local human resources and social security departments would resolutely implement the central government's decision on winning the prevention and control war against the COVID-19 pandemic, actively respond, and introduce a series of favorable policies for enterprises and the people. It was also pointed out that insured businesses which had laid off no or few workers will be returned 50% of their actual unemployment insurance premiums paid in the previous year. The Ministry of Human Resources and Social Security further stressed that payment of social insurance premiums by the insured enterprises could be paid later if the personal rights and interests of the insured workers were not affected, with payment procedures being completed within three months after the end of the pandemic.

On March 3, the Civil Aviation Administration of China issued the *Notice on Financial Support Policies for Civil Aviation Transport Enterprises during the COVID-19 Pandemic Prevention and Control Period*, according to which central finance shall provide financial support to Chinese and foreign airlines that operate scheduled international passenger flights between domestic destinations (not including Hong Kong, Macao, and Taiwan) and overseas destinations, as well as airlines that are deployed to carry out major transport missions in accordance with the joint prevention and control mechanism of the State Council. Rewards shall be given to international flights that are not grounded or resume operations during the pandemic, and preferential policies will be provided for flights which are operated by only one airline.

In addition to the above emergency responses conducted by the central government and ministries, local governments have also issued successive rescue policies to meet the unique characteristics of their region, most of which involve stabilizing employment, increasing financial support, reducing operating costs of enterprises, reducing tax burdens on enterprises, and optimizing government services. If implemented well, these policies will accurately and effectively help enterprises turn the corner and prepare them for the recovery of the market.

9.4.2 Suggestions on the measures to promote the industry's recovery

9.4.2.1 *Short-term policies*

(1) Implement financial support policies. As mentioned above, small, and medium enterprises in the tourism industry usually hold light assets and lack collateral. Meanwhile, faced with the suspension of business, it would be difficult for them to get loans from banks. It is suggested to classify these enterprises according to the tax they paid and their business flow data during normal operations and select and fund the best.
(2) Establish a special rescue fund for small, medium, and micro tourism enterprises to relieve their financial pressure. Provide green channels for approval and preferential interest rates and help the enterprises recover from the pandemic as soon as possible.
(3) Further promote the social security fund to stabilize society and provide mutual aid. Social insurance fees for some severely affected enterprises shall be reduced, and those for employees who have taken "unpaid leave" shall be refunded.
(4) Give full play to the collaboration within the industry to promote cooperation among enterprises of all sizes so that they can go through the difficulty together.
(5) Attach more importance to personnel training and skill training. Subsidies shall be given to the training expenses of small, medium, and micro enterprises which have continued their cooperation and actively conducted staff training during the pandemic.
(6) Add public holidays and issue travel vouchers to stimulate consumer demand.
(7) Develop emergency and revitalization plans, for tourism as soon as possible for tourism revitalization.

9.4.2.2 *Suggestions on long-term policies*

(1) Develop better emergency responses to risks to travel and optimize prevention and control mechanisms. Tourism is high-risk industry. Therefore, risk assessment shall be carried out for different tourism scenarios, behaviors, and products, and on this basis, emergency plans and safeguard measures shall be formed.

(2) Solve the financing problems of small, medium, and micro tourism enterprises. In the context of block chain and supply chain finance, a credit system for small, medium, and micro enterprises shall be established, on which basis, a mutual guarantee and financing mechanism can be explored to solve financing problems.
(3) Drawing from international experience, a mandatory insurance mechanism targeted at the high-risk nature of the tourism industry shall be established to strengthen the resilience of small, medium, and micro enterprises.
(4) Boost innovation in private enterprises, promote the application of new technologies and new modes of service, and reduce the impact of emergencies on labor-intensive enterprises.
(5) Implement a system of paid vacations to ensure that the demand for tourism is stable and the supply can be flexible and diversified.
(6) Give full play to the important role of industry organizations. Communication and collaboration shall be strengthened, and risk awareness shall be enhanced. The whole industry shall be self-regulated to protect the rights and interests of consumers and promote the healthy development of the industry.
(7) Promote the training of new tourism professionals. A key to revitalizing the tourism industry lies in professional development training, including the successful establishment of a Master of Tourism Management program which shall be reviewed and encouraged. Its goal is to ultimately build a professional development training platform integrating manufacturing, study, and research, and produce highly competent and skilled professionals equipped with both theoretical and practical abilities needed for revitalization of the industry.

9.5 Conclusions

Crises often consist of opportunities. After decades of ups and downs, China's tourism industry is facing the challenges brought about by a global pandemic. The enterprises which have survived are having the most difficult time in this industry-wide and society-wide war against the pandemic. They push through the old and bring forth the new: innovating in marketing, expanding sales channels by introducing influencers to conduct live broadcasts; providing high quality services, meeting the demand of high-end consumption shifting from outbound tourism to domestic tourism; and integrating cultural elements into tourism. The tourism industry is driving the overall upgrading of destinations, products, and services. It is predicted that in the post-pandemic era, China's tourism industry will usher in a strong wave of transformation and upgrading.

https://doi.org/10.1142/9789811252921_0010

Chapter 10

The Impact of COVID-19 Pandemic on the Digital Economy and Policy Responses

Zhou Guangyou

School of Economics, Fudan University, Shanghai, China

The unexpected outbreak of COVID-19 has spread not only across the country but the whole world, and has had a relatively huge impact on China's social economy. Confronting this pandemic and realizing sustainable economic development are important tasks at hand. In recent years, with the quick development of big data technology, many countries have highlighted the prospect of a "digital economy" as an important development on their strategic agenda . President Xi pointed out in a report at the 19th National Congress of the Communist Party of China (CPC) that China should "promote the intensive integration of the internet, big data, artificial intelligence, and the real economy, develop new growth points and new momentum in fields like middle- and high-end consumption, innovative leadership, green and low carbon, sharing economy, modern supply chains, and human capital services." Based on the analysis of the impact of the pandemic on the digital economy, this chapter suggests the implementation of precise policies from the perspective of the digital economy, and proposes countermeasures and suggestions to support the development of the digital economy.

10.1 The Digital Economy and its Development Patterns

The digital economy is a more advanced and sustainable economic form, exerting influence on various aspects of the social economy through technical methods of information communication (Pei Changhong *et al.*, 2018).

10.1.1 The meaning of the digital economy

The concept of the digital economy dates back to the mid-90s of the 20th century. There are still many controversies concerning what exactly is "a digital economy", and a widely acknowledged definition has yet to be agreed upon. However, according to the statement made at the G20 Hangzhou summit, the digital economy refers to a series of economic activities that employ digital knowledge and information as a key production factor, utilize modern information networks as an important carrier, and utilize the efficient application of information communication technology for the optimization of economic structures. Driven by a new generation of information technology, including Cloud Computing, the Internet of Things and Artificial Intelligence, the reach of the digital economy keeps expanding, from digital industrialization in the narrowest sense, to industrial digitization in the broadest, covering traditional information industries like basic telecommunication, electronic and information product manufacturing, software services, and the internet; this is in addition to penetrating other non-information industries, and playing an important role in Intelligent Manufacturing, modern agriculture, and "Internet +" (Zhang Hui and Shi Lin, 2019).

Encompassing the areas of digital industrialization, industrial digitization, and digital governance, the digital economy is a new component of the economy and society, as well as an inevitable outcome of the development of networking and digital intelligence. The digital economy is an economic model that promotes economic development and social progress through digital means. The operation of this economic model essentially follows and is governed by the three major laws: Davidow's Law, Moore's Law, and Metcalfe's Law. Therefore, the digital economy has the basic properties of data dependence, high liquidity, interactive penetration, convenience and high efficiency, and virtual concealment/network externality. The digital economy is a new economic form that differs from the agricultural economy and the industrial economy; it possesses unique characteristics from that of the traditional economy. These are mainly manifested in the following respects: data resources have become the key production factors, with "cloud + network + terminal" being the core infrastructure, the platform economy has become the mainstream business model, diverse personalities become the new consumption concepts, and knowledge and intelligence characteristic of the economy form of the digital economy. Furthermore, multiple co-governance has become a scientific governance method for the digital economy (Yang Peiqing, 2020). Some scholars also believe that the digital economy has four characteristics: economies of scale, economies of scope, reduced transaction costs, and "creative destruction" (Pei Changhong *et al.*, 2018).

10.1.2 The development patterns of the digital economy

The digital economy has received extensive attention from scholars since its initial introduction. In foreign countries, the use of big data, cloud computing, and artificial intelligence has greatly changed people's lifestyles and provided them unprecedented extraordinary services and benefits (Watanabe *et al.*, 2018). However, contrary to these achievements, the productivity of industrialized countries has declined significantly (Watanabe *et al.*, 2018). At the same time, the sharing economy in the digital economy has also received widespread attention and is regarded as a discontinuous innovation, which creates more wealth in the entire society (Andrea, 2018). Studies have also found that mobile payment is one of the main factors driving family entrepreneurship in the digital economy (Yin *et al.*, 2019). Domestic research has found that the development of the digital economy and digital finance has helped to improve the entrepreneurial behavior of rural residents and brought new entrepreneurial opportunities (Zhang Xun *et al.*, 2019), the development of digital financial inclusion has significantly boosted household consumption (Yi Xingjian, 2018), and financial technology innovation serves the financing of small and micro enterprises by exerting inclusive effects and forming inclusive value (Zhou Guangyou *et al.*, 2020). However, in the era of the digital economy, the risk of new financial formats has more obvious spillover effects on systemic risks and financial uncertainties in the formal financial market. Therefore, technological dimensions must be added to the traditional financial supervision dimensions to shape a bi-dimensional supervision system to better respond to the risks inherent in financial technology and the regulatory challenges it provokes (Yang Dong, 2018; Li Cangshu and Shen Yan, 2019).

As an economic format, the digital economy can be traced back to the information economy that emerged in the 1940s. The development process of the digital economy falls into five phases (see Table 10.1).

Table 10.1: The development history of the digital economy.

Stages	**Time**	**Main characteristics**
The first stage: Embryonic stage	1940s–1960s	The initial stage of the digital economy was from the 1940s to the 1960s. In 1946, the US Department of Defense developed the world's first general-purpose computer, ENIAC, which marked the official beginning of the digital economy era
The second stage: Start-up stage	1970s–1990s	From the 1970s to the 1990s, with the emergence of large-scale integrated circuits, the size of computers was further reduced, and their performance was further improved, and they began to spread to small and medium-sized enterprises and residents
The third stage: Rapid development stage	1990s–the beginning of the 21st century	With the development of personal computers and network technology, the network economy developed rapidly. It is generally believed that since 1995, the digital economy entered the Internet era
The fourth stage: Comprehensive coverage stage	2001–2015	With the acceleration of the computing speed of the personal computer, storage scale, and net speed, the continuous advancement of mobile communication technology and the emergence of smart phones, the once-shattered network economy, driven by new technologies represented by the mobile Internet, welcomed another wave of prosperity, with the PC Internet entering the mobile Internet era. In the field of mobile communication, mobile communication technologies such as 3G and 4G have been gradually put into use. People started to use smart phones, and Cloud Computing was proposed

Table 10.1: (*Continued*)

Stages	Time	Main characteristics
The fifth stage: Transformation and adjustment stage	2016–Now	the digital economy has developed in the direction of the Internet of things, cloud computing, big data and intelligence with cloud computing entering an explosive stage. Big data was formally proposed in 2008 and has now been widely used in government decision-making, transportation, logistics, finance, advertising, telecommunications, medical care, entertainment and agriculture. Intelligence has developed rapidly in recent years, from traditional mobile phones and tablet computers to robots, virtual reality, wearable devices, smart cars, smart homes, smart cities, and artificial intelligence. Block chains, platform economies, sharing economies, and other new formats have successively emerged

The White Paper on China's Digital Economy Development and Employment (2019) issued by the China Academy of Information and Communication Technology showed that China's digital economy has continued to develop rapidly. In 2018, the scale of the digital economy reached RMB 31.3 trillion, with a nominal increase of 20.9% on a comparable basis, accounting for 34.8% of GDP. The rapid development of China's digital economy is mainly manifested in the following three aspects.

(1) China attaches great importance to the development of the digital economy, and regards it as the focus of the government's work. The world's first worldwide digital economy policy document *G20 Digital Economy Development and Cooperation Initiative* was adopted at the G20 Hangzhou Summit in July 2016. In October of the same year, General Secretary Xi Jinping emphasized the important role of the digital economy in promoting economic development. In 2017, content related to the digital economy was written into the *Report on the Work of the Government* for the first time, proposing to "promote the in-depth development of 'Internet+', and accelerate the growth of digital economy." Since then, General

Secretary Xi Jinping has repeatedly emphasized on different occasions to vigorously support the development of a digital economy, and has issued a series of guiding documents, such as *Guiding Opinions on Actively Promoting the "Internet +" Action, Development Plan on Smart Manufacturing (2016–2020)* and *Development Plan for New Generation Artificial Intelligence*. He has also successively established the China Integrated Circuit Industry Investment Fund and the China Internet Investment Fund to provide support from various aspects including funds and talents.

(2) Internet infrastructure continues to improve, and the number of Internet users continues to increase. On the basis of network users, according to the CNNIC's *China Internet Development Statistics Survey*, as of June 2019, the number of Internet users in China has reached 8.54 million, an increase of 25.98 million from that at the end of 2018. Also, the rate of Internet penetration reached 61.2%, up by 1.6 percentage points, compared with the end of 2018.

As is shown in Figure 10.1, the number of Internet users in China has increased from 710 million in June 2016 to 854 million in June 2019, an increase of 144 million in three years. The Internet

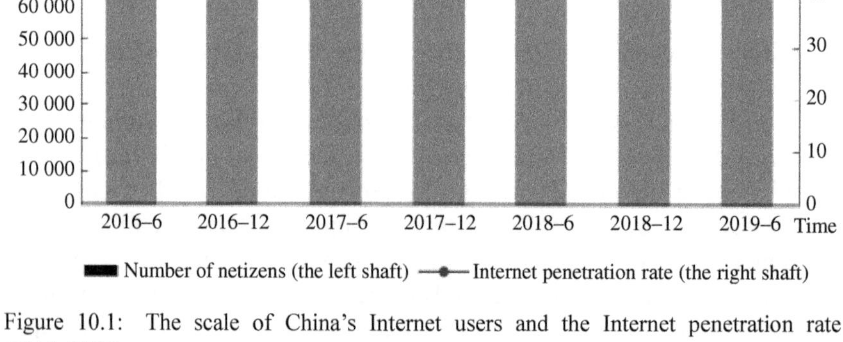

Figure 10.1: The scale of China's Internet users and the Internet penetration rate (2016–2019).

Source: *CNNIC Statistical Survey* on the Development of Internet in China.

penetration rate increased from 51.74% in June 2016 to 61.2% in June 2019, an increase of 9.5 percentage points. It shows that China's network user base has been continuously strengthened.

(3) There are obvious regional differences in the degree of development of the digital economy, which primarily depends on the degree of regional economic development. The most developed areas in terms of the digital economy are mainly located along the Yangtze River Delta, the Pearl River Delta, and within the Beijing–Tianjin–Hebei region, represented by Beijing, Guangdong, Shanghai, Zhejiang, and Jiangsu. Central and western regions represented by Hubei and Sichuan are developing rapidly, but other regions are lagging behind. In terms of specific cities, several tiers have been established, with Beijing, Shanghai, Shenzhen, and Hangzhou belonging to the first tier, and Chengdu, Guiyang, Wuhan, and Xi'an belonging to the second, however, it should be noted that there is a huge distance between the two tiers.

10.2 The Impact of the COVID-19 Pandemic on the Digital Economy

The COVID-19 pandemic has had both short-term and long-term, as well as positive and negative effects on the digital economy. An in-depth analysis and scientific research are needed on these effects.

10.2.1 Short-term effects

10.2.1.1 *Consumption has been greatly impacted, with online consumption replacing offline consumption at an accelerating rate*

The COVID-19 pandemic affected consumption, which fell sharply during the Spring Festival. During this festival the closing of cinemas, the shutting down of tourist attractions, and the shortened business hours of shopping malls and supermarkets all significantly impacted the relevant consumption market. The slowdown in consumption growth will continue for at least two quarters. At the same time, closures create conditions for accelerated development of emerging business models related to the Internet economy such as online consumption, which will accelerate the rate of its replacement of offline consumption. In 2019, the online retail sales of physical goods reached 20.7% of the total retail sales of consumer goods. It is expected that during the pandemic period, the substitution of online consumption for offline consumption will be accelerated.

10.2.1.2 *The pandemic has affected the pace and structure of investment, and the scale of investment has declined and retreated*

An important point is the investment delay caused by the pandemic has been expected to be about three weeks, which will affect the pace of investment and production. Its main manifestation is in the decline of investment scale and an overall backward shift, which may affect the total investment scale for the year. During the spread of the pandemic, the postponement of large-scale production leads to simultaneous contraction of supply and demand, which has had a greater impact on business investment expectations and investment scale, but the extent of the impact will depend on the duration of the pandemic. Another point is, the impact of the pandemic on corporate investment has also had obvious structural features, mainly manifested in the acceleration of investment in medical projects and basic living materials, and the slowdown of investment in other industries.

10.2.1.3 *The pandemic has increased business operating costs, restricted business development, and exerted a negative influence on trade*

The continuous spread of the COVID-19 pandemic has increased the operating costs of companies, has affected export business relationships established through the endeavors of companies over many years, and triggered concerns about China's import and export trade. First, due to delayed resumption of construction, manufacturing, and production in many provinces, autonomous regions, and municipalities, some companies may not be able to fulfill contracts and hence encounter financial penalties due to delayed delivery. In addition, the postponement of the resumption of work has also increased the operating costs of companies and put more pressure on their cash flow. Second, the impact of the pandemic on future business development is also expanding.

10.2.1.4 *With various kinds of the "Zhai"[1] economy rising, consumption demand in the digital economy is booming*

Due to an overlap of the Spring Festival holiday and the pandemic prevention and control period, various types of *Zhai* economies have quietly emerged, and consumption demand in the digital economy has surged. The online entertainment industry (games, reading, video, and other online content) witnessed explosive growth, and online booking consumption platforms (online travel OTA) are confronting the test of a short-term consumption window and the efficiency of the industry's operating model. E-commerce platforms have provided a buffer, minimizing the impact of the pandemic on consumption, and the market for online collaborative offices, remote diagnosis and treatment, and online education has rapidly expanded. In addition, the application and popularization of online transactions and online financial services are very extensive. Although, people's consumption needs and the amount of capital circulation to a certain extent are smaller than those before the pandemic, compared with the severe impact traditional businesses have suffered, the digital economy has gained opportunities for expansion and development This is especially so for those retirees who had not used the Internet prior to the pandemic, but have gradually begun to understand online financial management, payment, and consumption.

10.2.2 Long-term effects

The short-term negative impact of the pandemic on China's economy is inevitable. However, due to the sound foundation at the base of China's development of the digital economy, it has already played an active and important role in the transformation of the national economy, thus

[1]"Zhai economy" is a new word with the rise of Internet, which mainly means working at home, working part-time, working at home or doing business at home. At the same time, spending at home is also an indispensable part of home economy.

offsetting to a great extent the negative impact of the pandemic. However, the long-term impact of the pandemic on the economy is profound.

10.2.2.1 *The digital economy remains a strong backup force for the fight against the pandemic*

According to calculations by the China Academy of Information and Communications Technology, the scale of China's digital economy in 2019 is expected to reach RMB 35 trillion, accounting for 35.4% of the GDP. The digital economy has become a new engine for China's economic growth, and China's economy is upgrading from "integration of industrialization and informationization" to the model of "integration of digital economy and real economy". In other words, China's economy has basically achieved systematic transformation of momentum from old to new. This new momentum of economic development mainly depends on the steady growth of the digital economy, and it has not undergone qualitative changes due to the impact of the pandemic. Therefore, the stable development of the digital economy has provided strong backing for the successful fight against the pandemic, showing that the fundamentals of China's long-term and high-quality economic growth will not change in the future (Liu Gongrun, 2020).

10.2.2.2 *The pandemic will cause a new round of "consumption sinking" in the digital economy*

The impact of the pandemic has forced companies to actively seek change. Due to their long-term properties of "path dependence" and "high trial-and-error costs", SaaS (Software-as-a-Service) software, online office, and online sales have had highest acceptance in start-ups or Internet companies. However, large enterprises or traditional enterprises that need to improve efficiency and reduce costs only scratch the surface. Due to the special scenario of the pandemic prevention and control period, as well as the delay in resuming work, companies were forced by cash flow pressure to actively seek services, and move their work places online to minimize the negative impact on income. The pandemic will also lead to changes in long-term living and consumption habits. For example, the pandemic may become a turning point for fresh food e-commerce, and it has also resulted in a period of expansion of online financial services. The pandemic has raised people's attention to food safety, more young people choose to cook at home, and the middle-aged and elderly have also increased their price tolerance for fresh food e-commerce. Taking this opportunity, fresh food e-commerce companies have successfully oriented themselves to target customers, and the average daily active users during the Spring Festival in 2020 exceeded 10 million. If e-commerce can accelerate the improvement of the cold chain, and boost logistics and transportation systems to form a virtuous circle, such user habits are expected to continue. Online financial services have also reached those retirees who had not used the Internet prior to the pandemic, but have gradually begun to understand online financial management, payment, and consumption, due to the pandemic. Offline bank branches used to be the gathering place for retirees to withdraw pensions. During the pandemic, people rejected gatherings, and retirees are beginning to understand online financial management and payment (Cheng Shi, 2020).

10.2.2.3 *Digital economies promote the transformation from offline consumption to digital consumption*

Due to the impact of the pandemic, shopping malls, movie theaters, restaurants, tourist attractions, and other popular consumption venues have basically closed down, but thanks to the digital economy, people have switched to digital consumption. First, new growth has occurred in digital industries such as mobile games, live broadcasting, and online shopping, and new changes have occurred in the new retail industry. New-generation information technologies such as artificial intelligence, virtual reality, big data, cloud computing, and the Internet of things have been effectively applied in e-commerce to promote online 3D shopping, physical store self-checking, and 24-hour unmanned supermarkets, which can better match people's personalized consumption demand. Second, traditional financial institutions have gradually launched "contactless financial management". At the same time, the pandemic has brought traditional financial institutions and digital economy companies represented by Alipay into the cooperation version 2.0. More than 300 fund agencies, banks, securities agencies, and other financial institutions have agreed that Alipay fully manage finances in categories such as deposits, pension insurance, and bank financing. Third, the digital economy has also given birth to "fast track" financial support to entity enterprises, providing precise assistance to small and micro enterprises and contributing to their ultimate victory in the fight against the pandemic.

10.2.2.4 *The pandemic forces traditional industries to accelerate digital transformation*

Crisis and opportunities always accompany each other. Similar to the start of China's golden age of e-commerce, with the rise of e-commerce giants during the SARS period, this pandemic has forced traditional industries to accelerate the digitalization process and promote digital transformation. Traditional companies will pay more attention to purchasing and sales through digital platforms, and will also more widely apply emerging technologies such as 5G, artificial intelligence, industrial Internet, and virtual reality, whereby the industrial structure will be further optimized. There are digital-based online business models, such as network telecommuting, online education, and provisions to "purchase things on behalf of others". Personal contact is also reduced in social governance systems, such as urban management, transportation and logistics, and medical services, as well as smart cities, the industrial Internet, and large consumption methods. The application of these services has fully demonstrated the vitality and advantages of the digital economy. It is foreseeable that many traditional industries will increase their support and investment in the digitalization process, vigorously promote the development of new technology such as big data, the Internet of things, artificial intelligence, and block chains, and accelerate the application of 5G technology. The digital economy will also become the core force driving the transformation of industries. In addition, the digitalization of the industry, such as office models and online education, will change the industry's thinking model. Therefore, the pandemic has forced people to seriously examine the feasibility of industrial digital transformation. In the process of pandemic prevention and control, many traditional industries have begun to try to overcome spatial barriers through digitalization to provide users with precise services, and broad prospects for the application of digital technology have been implemented. Responding to the pandemic as an opportunity, if digital technologies such as big data, artificial intelligence, block chains, cloud computing, and the Internet of things are applied to industrial development, the digitalization of traditional industries will be accelerated.

10.3 Analysis of Countermeasures

With the widespread use of digital technology, the economic benefits of the digital economy in the social economy are gradually being tapped, and many governments have also begun to increase investment and support for the digital economy. The application of digital technology will have a great driving effect on future economic development (Zhang Hui and Shi Lin, 2019).

10.3.1 Short-term countermeasures

Since the outbreak of the pandemic, digital infrastructure (such as 4G and 5G), a new generation of information technology (such as artificial intelligence, big data), new models and new formats (such as contactless delivery services, online consultations and diagnoses, real time teaching, remote instant maintenance), and new formats of the digital economy (such as high-efficiency and transparent governance supported by digital technology) have all provided a steady stream of motivation to win the battle against the pandemic, demonstrating the important role of data in pandemic prevention and control (Yin Limei, 2020). Therefore, it is very important to give full play to the special role of the digital economy in fighting the pandemic.

10.3.1.1 *Give full play to the role of digital infrastructure construction in guaranteeing the ultimate victory over the pandemic*

It is necessary to strengthen the construction of digital infrastructure represented by 5G, accelerate response times in the information and communication industry in important departments, such as hospitals, and meet the communication needs of remote control, remote consultations, and diagnoses, remote surgery, and data transmission. Give full play to the special role of digital technologies such as 5G, artificial intelligence, big data, and the Internet of Things in pandemic prevention, monitoring, and response. Appropriately adjust the fiscal and monetary policies in digital economy-related fields, strengthen counter-cyclical adjustments in the field of people's livelihood, and provide appropriate subsidies to some emerging digital economy companies to help tide them over difficulties.

10.3.1.2 *Mobilize the enthusiasm of enterprises to fight the pandemic and work hard to restore normal life*

First, actively guide telecom operators, like Baidu, AutoNavi, and other companies to use location service information to carry out big data analysis of population flow, and provide supporting services. Companies such as WeDoctor, Dingxiang Doctor, Ping An Good Doctor, and Chunyu Doctor can use online consultation platforms to provide services to match medical resources. Neusoft, Huawei, and other companies can provide technical support for the development of telemedicine. JD, Alibaba, Meituan, Multipoint, and other companies can focus on prevention and control, and supply and dispatch of daily necessities. Tencent, ByteDance, and other content companies can strengthen big data analysis, and do a good job of online public opinion guidance and publicity. Second, make innovative use of the internet, information, and software technologies to create smart software platforms such as online teaching and online office, encourage companies to adopt flexible and effective working methods, and improve the skills of employees. Guide and support schools and educational training institutions to make full use of live teaching and other methods to carry out education and teaching, and take solid steps to resume normal production and life.

10.3.1.3 *Promote digital government and smart cities, and correct shortcomings in governance as soon as possible*

The role of digital government is not only for the convenience of the people, but more importantly, for the government to more accurately grasp data and improve the ability to deploy resources. At present, cities such as Shanghai and Hangzhou have succeeded in using digital technology to strengthen crisis response and urban governance, and these experiences should be promoted nationwide. First, in terms of data platform construction, it is recommended that block chains and other technologies be used to connect the information islands of various government departments and realize information sharing; second, in terms of intelligent decision-making, the ability of big data analysis will be further expanded from the use of convenient applications to many areas of social management, such as infectious disease prevention and treatment, intelligent traffic regulation, emergency supplies dispatch, social governance, and public safety protection giving full play to the role of big data; third, online office software can be fully utilized, and an efficient platform for the government's external information disclosure and internal office collaboration can be built to improve office efficiency; fourth, strengthen the application of information for community pandemic prevention and control by establishing community grid platforms, investigating data lists, strengthening dynamic monitoring and real-time management of data, and timely updating and reporting to achieve the goal of precise prevention and control and compensate for the shortcomings of governance as soon as possible.

10.3.2 Long-term countermeasures

The resilient "replacement" of the digital economy in the pandemic demonstrates its important position in promoting the transformation of China's economic momentum from old to new, and promoting high-quality economic development. In a sense, whether the digital economy withstands the impact of the pandemic, whether it supports macroeconomic stability and even leads the economic development of the "post-pandemic era" will be a vital test of the success of China's economic structural transformation. From a long-term perspective, once the pandemic is effectively controlled, the market will regain confidence, the scale of investment in the digital economy will continue to increase, and the digital economy will be the best choice for China's economic development in the "post-pandemic era". To this end, we propose the following countermeasures.

10.3.2.1 *Strengthen the construction of laws, regulations, and standard systems, and build a sustainable market system*

Our country is currently facing problems such as high market entry barriers and inadequate institutional mechanisms in the digital economy, which largely restrict the further development of the digital economy (Wang Weiling and Wang Jing, 2019). Therefore, the construction of laws, regulations, and standardized systems should be strengthened in accordance with the inherent requirements for the development of the digital economy, and the establishment of a market system that fits the long-term sustainable development of the digital economy should be explored (Pang

Jian and Zhu Xinmin, 2013). First, speed up the implementation of the *State Council Institutional Reform and Function Transformation Plan*, which orders to cut down the number of non-administrative approval and qualification licensing in the field of digital economy, strictly implementing related matters, and improving the efficiency of administrative approval. Second, increase the government's support for information technology innovation and business innovation. For economic activities that use information services as the main carrier, the government must establish the principle of "development-oriented" when formulating regulatory policies, suspending supervision, or adopting a market-based supervision method. Third, further break down industry monopolies and entry barriers, especially to introduce market mechanisms in the fields of social management and public services, giving full play to the joint efforts of the government and enterprises, and vigorously promote the development of smart cities.

10.3.2.2 *Accelerate the digital transformation of enterprises and enhance their competitiveness*

Accelerating the digital transformation of traditional enterprises is an inevitable requirement for enterprises to maintain their competitive vitality and their social and economic development in the external environment (Zheng Xiyu, 2019). From one perspective, the digital transformation of enterprises mainly includes business model and corporate culture transformations. Traditional enterprises should speed up the construction of their own digital platforms and reduce their operating costs through the indiscriminate replication capabilities of digital technology. For companies that do not have inhouse technical capabilities, the government acts as an intermediary to strengthen the transformation and cooperation between technology companies through government endorsement, and jointly promotes the construction of corporate digital platforms. Of course, in order to ensure the improvement of the quality of the digital transformation of enterprises, it is necessary to strengthen the daily digital management of the transformed enterprises, and at the same time pay attention to the transformation of corporate cultural concepts. In contrast, companies should focus on digital marketing and strive to build digital brands. Compared with traditional media, digital media has richer content and stronger interactions with consumers. Therefore, companies should have the skills to use social media to promote corporate cultural concepts and products. At the same time, it is necessary to ensure the consistency of offline and online services to achieve seamless connection between offline and online consumption. Product selection and customization are completed online, and product experience and after-sales services are achieved offline.

10.3.2.3 *Fully develop and effectively use digital technology to provide financial services for small, medium, and micro enterprises*

During the pandemic, small, medium, and micro enterprises suffered an unexpected hit, and many enterprises faced serious financial difficulties. Using this as an opportunity, a long-term mechanism can be built that alleviates the long-standing financing difficulties of small, medium, and micro enterprises by making full and effective use of digital technology and internet platforms. First, commercial banks can implement an "online" strategy by developing joint loans with financial technology companies, to provide financial support to small, medium, and micro enterprises. Second, give full play to the advantages of small, fast, and flexible financing of small and medium-sized banks, and promote their digital and online transformation through business solutions such as applets and cloud back offices, improve their own online operating efficiency and reduce operating costs, and provide long-term stable online services for small, medium, and micro enterprises. Third, combine the characteristics of small, medium, and micro enterprises with weak anti-risk capabilities and low financial management levels. Therefore, financial technology companies and banks should propose targeted comprehensive financial service solutions such as credit, insurance, cash management, wages, and supply chain finance, to improve the level of their assets and liabilities and the ability to respond to risks.

10.3.2.4 *Leverage on high-tech advancements to drive the rapid development of an unmanned economy*

As representative, it is of the pioneers of strategic emerging industries, the unmanned economy is also an important embodiment of the strategic high-tech industries of various countries. To a large extent its capacity for sustainable development determines its capacity for the sustainable development of strategic high-tech industries in various countries. Therefore, the unmanned economy is one of the most important elements of the national sustainable development strategy. The rapid development of digital technology has become another major driving force for the rise of the unmanned economy. High-tech support such as big data, the internet of things, and artificial intelligence are inseparable from the emergence of the unmanned economy. Together, they promote the reform of the unmanned economy, and create favorable conditions for its rapid marketization. Compared with traditional business models, the unmanned economy not only reduces business costs and increases profitability, but also obtains rich information and data through various high-tech means, thereby providing consumers with diversified services. First, in view of the current situation in China, it is necessary to create a new economic form with great potential for development, one that is full of vitality and leads to win–win for all parties through improving innovation, expanding innovation resources, optimizing economic structures, and transforming development methods. The rapid development and widespread use of new technologies such as artificial intelligence and the internet of things have created favorable conditions for an unmanned economy. Second, because of the influence of both national policy guidance and market forces, the unmanned economy has greatly changed people's production, lifestyle, and consumption patterns. Of these, the core competitiveness of the unmanned economy exerts the greatest influence, which is data perception in three core technologies: customer recognition and tracking, dynamic shelf tracking, and independent terminal settlement. The widespread application of related technologies, such as mobile payments, face recognition, and product tracking, has also laid a good technical foundation for the development of the unmanned economy, and has had a pivotal impact on China's economic and social development (Zhu Zongqian *et al*., 2019).

10.3.2.5 *Increase financial technology innovation, and give full play to the role of financial services in the real economy*

10.3.2.5.1 Financial technology promotes technological innovation of enterprises and promotes economic growth

Financial technology promotes technological innovation within enterprises, improves the all-factor productivity of real enterprises, promotes the transformation and upgrading of the real economy, and promotes economic development.

First, accurately locate customers' needs and carry out technical updates and product upgrades in a timely manner. Innovative technologies such as big data, cloud computing, and artificial intelligence in the financial sector help entity companies realize accurate positioning and reasonable prediction of customers' needs, design products that are more suitable for long-tail groups, and realize the changes of products from standard models to personalized customization. The upgrading of enterprise products means that traditional production technology, production equipment, and production methods will be updated, which directly optimizes the production model and resource utilization efficiency of the enterprise, and the development of the enterprise moves toward a more advanced production form.

Second, improve product structure and quality, and promote the transformation and upgrading of physical enterprises. Relying on mobile internet and big data technology, financial technology transfers innovative elements, such as knowledge and technology, to physical enterprises, which have the characteristics of low-cost diffusion, diminishing marginal returns, and increasing returns of scale, helping to optimize the product structure and quality of enterprises, thereby promoting the transformation and upgrading of physical enterprises. At the same time, the technological innovation and product innovation functions of financial technology improves the production structure of physical enterprises, further reduces the proportion of traditional production, and accelerates the upgrading of the industrial structure.

Third, share business information and improve the efficiency of resource allocation. Financial technology promotes the function of financial communication, improves the efficiency of resource allocation of physical enterprises, and allows financial communication to break through the constraints of time and space. New technologies such as block chains and cloud computing automatically enter customers' information, transaction records of enterprise users, demand queries, and other information into the cloud system, and finally integrate them into a data system that cannot be tampered with. Financial institutions use big data modeling and artificial intelligence analysis to intelligently judge the default probability of target customers based on history data recorded in the cloud, such as borrowing records, payment orders, and consumption records, and cooperate with relevant government departments to establish a credit rating system, reduce the risks of capital allocation, and improve its efficiency.

10.3.2.5.2 Financial technology innovates financial products and service methods to promote the growth of the real economy

First, give full play to the creative effect, form product values, and broaden investment and financing channels. Financial technology creates new financial assets, financial tools, and innovative service methods through the combination of technological innovation and finance, forming new products and service values, and promoting economic growth. For example, financial technology innovation has brought about new financial products, new service methods, and even new financial formats, such as digital currency, financial products, intelligent investment consultations, mobile payments, and P2P online loans. While compensating for and expanding the shortcomings of traditional investment and financing models, diversified investment, financing, and wealth management requirements of enterprises and individuals are met with the characteristics of flexibility, speed, and efficiency, broadening investment and financing channels, and promoting economic growth.

Second, give play to information effects, form information values, and reduce investment and financing costs. Financial technology innovation has given birth to new information mechanisms and expanded information application fields, reducing information asymmetry, filling information gaps, and forming information value. The Internet platform shaped by financial technology innovation, with its professional, comprehensive, fast, and low-cost advantages, provides information sharing services for small, medium, and micro enterprises and individuals, reducing costs of corporate information search, transaction, and financing, and enabling enterprises to obtain the financial support required for development, thus serving the development of the real economy.

Third, give play to the inclusive effect, form inclusive values, and promote inclusive economic growth. The creative and information effect of financial technology work together to increase financial products and enrich financial service methods, reduce the cost of information acquisition and application, benefit a wider area and more types of enterprises and individuals, expand the scope of financial services, and form inclusive value. Specifically, financial technology innovation serves small and micro-enterprises financing by comprehensively exerting its inclusive effect and forming inclusive value, promotes innovation and entrepreneurship, increases income and alleviates poverty, narrows the gap between the rich and the poor, and promotes inclusive economic growth.

10.3.2.5.3 Financial technology promotes the development of electronic payments, consumer demand, and economic growth

From one perspective, great importance must be attached to the role of consumption in economic growth, and the promotion of electronic payments to stimulate consumer demand. In 2019, China's total retail sales of consumer goods was RMB 41.2 trillion, a year-on-year increase of 8%, and the rate consumption contributed to economic growth was 57.8%, driving GDP growth by 3.5 percentage points, ranking first as the driving force in economic growth for six consecutive years. At the same time, the application of modern information and network technology for payments has brought about unprecedented innovation in payment tools. Traditional transaction media are gradually being replaced, and retail payment tools are changing with every passing day. As an important stage in the consumption process, payments have a direct impact on consumer demand, through promoting consumption and consumption impulse, by reducing payment costs, and providing consumer credit, thereby promoting economic growth. Therefore, it is necessary to give full play to the special role of electronic payments, in increasing online consumption and promoting economic development. Electronic payment has the characteristics of being low cost, fast, and convenient. Compared with traditional payment methods, it also has the special function of remote payment. In recent years, the rapid development of financial technology and electronic currency has created favorable conditions for the widespread use of electronic payments, and has also provided the possibility of electronic payments stimulating consumer demand. Therefore, the situation should be taken advantage of by increasing investment in infrastructure, such as network communications, increasing the application scenarios of electronic payments, expanding the scope of applications, and giving full play to the special role of electronic payments in driving consumer demand, thereby contributing to the promotion of economic growth.

10.4 Conclusion

In summary, the impact of the COVID-19 pandemic on the economy is unavoidable and cannot be ignored, and it has had both short-term and long-term effects on the digital economy, both positive and negative. The pandemic has had an impact on the digital economy, but this impact can be viewed as an opportunity. The following findings are found through research.

(1) The digital economy is an inevitable consequence of the development of networking and intelligence reaching a certain stage. It follows and is governed by three major laws: Davidow's Law, Moore's Law, and Metcalfe's Law. The digital economy has the basic properties of data dependence, high liquidity, interactive penetration, fast speed and high efficiency, virtual concealment and network externality, and has the four basic characteristics of economies of scale, economies of scope, reduction in transaction costs, and "creative destruction" .
(2) The digital economy experiences all five stages: embryonic, start-up, rapid development, comprehensive coverage, and transformation and adjustment. At present, the digital economy is facing unprecedented opportunities and is accelerating into the fast lane. In recent years, China's digital economy has developed rapidly, which has been mainly manifested in: China attaching great importance to the development of the digital economy, making it the focus of the government's work; continuously improving internet infrastructure, and at the same time generally increasing the number of internet users. However, due to the imbalance between economic development in the eastern and western regions of the country, there are obvious regional differences and heterogeneity in the development of the digital economy in China.
(3) The pandemic has had both short-term and long-term effects on the digital economy. The short-term impact is mainly manifested in: (i) The impact on consumption, namely the fast paced replacement of offline with online consumption; (ii) The scale of investment declining and shifting; the increase in corporate operating costs limiting

business development, which has had a negative effect on trade. With the rise of various types of "Zhai" economies, consumer demand in the digital economy has surged. The long-term impact of the pandemic on the digital economy is mainly manifested in the following: the digital economy still provides strong backing for the fight against the pandemic. In the long run, the pandemic will lead to a new round of "consumption sinking" in the digital economy. The digital economy promotes the transformation of offline consumption to digital consumption. The pandemic has forced traditional industries to accelerate their digital transformation.

(4) At the same time, short-term and long-term strategies have been proposed for the digital economy to respond to the pandemic and to continue its own development. In the short term, full play should be given to the role of digital infrastructure in laying a solid foundation for the ultimate defeat of the pandemic; the enthusiasm of enterprises to fight the pandemic and to restore normal life should be mobilized; digital government affairs and smart cities should be promoted as soon as possible to compensate for shortcomings in governance; market order should be stabilized, market confidence ensured, and financial support increased. From a long-term perspective, the establishment of a system of laws, regulations, and standards should be strengthened to build a sustainable market system by accelerating the digital transformation of enterprises and enhancing their competitiveness; making full and effective use of digital technology to provide financial services for small, medium, and micro enterprises; leveraging high-tech advances to drive the rapid development of the unmanned economy; increasing financial technology innovation and giving full play to the role of financial services and the real economy.

https://doi.org/10.1142/9789811252921_0011

Chapter 11

Financial Markets in the Pandemic: Effects and China's Policy Responses

Qian Jun and Gu Yan

Fanhai International School of Finance, Fudan University, Shanghai, China

Since the outbreak of COVID-19, the Central Committee of the CPC has attached great importance to delivering instructions and strategic plans for pandemic prevention and control, as highlighted by General Secretary Xi Jinping's various meetings and delivered speeches. Temporary "city closures", travel restrictions, delays in work resumption and return to school, and other preventive and control measures have hit all sectors of the country, especially the service industry. Finance, as an important part of the modern service industry, has also been severely impacted. Moreover, financial markets are highly sensitive to information change developments. In the face of the combined impact of the pandemic at home and abroad, policy adjustments, and market expectations, how will financial markets such as stocks, bonds, and futures perform? How should this performance and its influence on China's financial industry be evaluated? What measures should the Chinese government and the financial industry itself take to actively respond to this? These questions will be discussed and analyzed in the following sections.

11.1 Impact of the Pandemic on Global Financial Markets and China's Financial Sector

11.1.1 Pandemic shock and global financial markets' responses

Risk aversion induced by pandemic shock is the first reaction of financial markets, but the responses are also influenced by a variety of factors such as macro policies and market expectations. Soon after Zhong Nanshan, a renowned respiratory expert, stated that human-to-human transmission of COVID-19 was confirmed on the night of January 20, the Shanghai Composite Index plunged 1.41% the next day; on January 23, the Chinese government commenced a lockdown on Wuhan, and the Shanghai Composite Index shed 2.75%. During the Spring Festival holiday, the number of confirmed cases of coronavirus disease increased exponentially in China and on February 4 alone the highest peak was recorded with 3,887 new confirmed infections registered. At the same time, the State Council announced a three-day extension of the holiday to contain the novel coronavirus outbreak, and the stock market would not resume trading until February 3. There was some controversy over whether to open the market on that day or to continue the delay due to fears of extreme volatility, and the market did see a 7% tumble when opened as scheduled. However, the A-share market strongly rebounded the next day and recovered the losses in less than three weeks with massive liquidity injection by the central bank to cushion the coronavirus impact until positive signs in the pandemic were being recorded. In contrast, the domestic bond market showed a more pronounced risk aversion effect. In terms of interest rate bonds, since the market opened for trading after the Spring Festival, Treasury yields dropped all the way down and as of the morning of March 9, the 10-year Treasury active bond was quoted at 2.53%, an all-time low since July 2002. Due to the shock brought about by the pandemic, consensus expectations for economic growth seemed pessimistic, and risk aversion quickly heated up. Interest rates decreased rapidly, and this was coupled with the central bank's monetary policy maintaining a sound and slightly accommodative stance after the holiday. As for credit bonds, there was a certain divergence, with high-grade bonds continuing the downward trend in yields which started before the holiday, while the yields of low-grade bonds rose steadily. The growth in spread suggested that bond defaults would pick up, and debt-issuing companies were facing higher financing costs or even difficulties in financing.

Compared with domestic financial markets, the performance of international financial markets seemed to attract more attention. Owing to the spread of the pandemic and the oil "price war", global stock markets generally plummeted. In the U.S. stock market, a global weather-vane, the Dow Jones Industrial Average, S&P 500, and NASDAQ Composite all fell by more than 25% compared to their peak at the beginning of 2020 and entered bear markets in March. From March 9 to March 13, the U.S. stock market triggered two circuit breakers in a single week, which was unprecedented in its history. At the same time, stock markets in Canada, Brazil, Thailand, the Philippines, Indonesia, Pakistan, Kuwait, Mexico, and other countries also experienced circuit breakers. In contrast, the U.S. Treasury yields in this period continuously slid to fresh record lows with the yield on the benchmark 10-year U.S. Treasury plunging to a record low of 0.32%. Moreover, a yield curve inversion between the 3-month Treasury bill and the 10-year note occurred, as a result the market displayed strong risk aversion, and gold prices exceeded $1,700 per ounce. However, as the recession continued to deepen, gold began to weaken along with U.S. stocks, demonstrating a trend similar to the synchronized changes during the 2008 financial crisis.

11.1.2 Impact of the pandemic on the development of China's financial sector

11.1.2.1 *Credit risks increase in banks*

For a long time, indirect financing led by commercial banks has been the main financing mode of China's financial system. In recent years, with the L-shaped economic downturn and the breaking of rigid payments, the risk of bank loans to enterprises has increased, and the non-performing loan rate in the banking industry has continued to rise. Since the outbreak of the pandemic, due to travel restrictions and delays in resuming work, there has been a considerably large decline in consumer demand and the real estate industry in particular has suffered serious setbacks. In view of this, it is inevitable that loans to traditional large and medium-sized industrial enterprises and the real estate industry will be delayed in phases. In the meantime, given the need for stabilizing employment, which is most important in securing people's livelihoods, under the guidance of pandemic prevention and control, many banks have significantly increased inclusive loans to small and medium-sized enterprises (SMEs) during this period.

These changes have brought about two main adverse effects on the banking industry. First, the increased inclusive loans may have a (phased) higher non-performing rate in the future. After all, SMEs themselves have higher loan risks, and the impact of the pandemic has further increased this potential risk. In fact, the bond market has already reflected these fears, and low-grade credit spreads have increased significantly after the Spring Festival. Second, policies such as interest rate cuts and preferential loans were prevalent during this period, leading to the narrowing of the net interest margin of loans granted by banks, which also reduced to a large extent the loan profit ratio of many banks. However, influenced by the trend of Internet finance in recent years, the main businesses of commercial banks, such as deposits and loans, have largely been processed online, which made it possible to avoid the direct impact of the pandemic on banking business. More importantly, the large and medium-sized banks currently dominating the Chinese financial system are capable of managing their risks of on- and off-balance sheet assets. In addition, negative effects such as bad loans caused by the pandemic are seen as temporary, especially considering that the country is adopting a proactive fiscal policy and a flexible monetary policy for countercyclical regulation. It is believed that the banking system as a whole can generally maintain stable development and will not be subject to systemic risks triggered by the pandemic.

11.1.2.2 *Structural market effects — brokerages and funds*

The capital market is most sensitive to information, and it did respond quickly when the pandemic broke out. Prior to the Spring Festival holiday, A-shares fell by more than 1% on January 21 and 23, 2020, and both Hong Kong and U.S. stocks that opened for trading on January 31 also registered significant declines. Considering the potentially devastating effects of the pandemic on the capital market, many investors expressed doubts of the market opening for trading on February 3 after the holiday. However, when the A-share market withstood the pressure and opened as scheduled, its performance was beyond expectations. Instead of the prolonged slump that most people had feared, it rebounded rapidly after the plunge on the first trading day, with three major indexes across the board having already recovered from their decline. However, affected by the general sharp decline in the international market, the A-share market also suffered some turbulence, yet it was still the best-performing market compared with other major global stock markets during this period.

The robust performance of the A-share market after the Spring Festival has driven the rapid growth of domestic brokerage businesses, and the average daily turnover of many brokerage firms has increased month-on-month; meanwhile, fund businesses involved in secondary market transactions have also grown substantially. However, in the short term due to the pandemic, it is difficult to fully carry out investment banking services such as on-site investigations, and due diligence of brokerage firms, while PE/VC-related businesses have also been greatly affected. In addition, with the slowdown in IPO review and listing (except for the Shanghai Stock Exchange Sci-Tech Innovation Board or SSE STAR Market), all primary market-related businesses would be influenced to some extent. However, the Sci-Tech Innovation Board, with information disclosure at its core, has fully demonstrated the advantages of more inclusive and market-oriented listing rules. Recently, the strong stock prices of several medical and sci-tech companies listed and traded on the Board have stimulated the development of these companies and industries. It also brings benefits to related financial service industries including brokerage firms, funds, and investment institutions; more and more companies from these industries are expected to be listed on the STAR Market. In addition, based on the experience with SARS, which showed that the overall IPO market tended to show compensatory growth in the second half of the year, when the pandemic was largely eradicated. From an annual perspective, the difficulties in the primary market are likely to be temporary, and the pandemic should have limited impact on brokerage firms and fund-related businesses in the medium and long term.

11.1.2.3 *Exposure of insurance supply shortcomings*

In recent years, China's insurance industry has developed significantly, and by the end of 2018, the market scale was ranked second in the world for three consecutive years, with a compound annual growth rate of 27% from 1979 to the present. However, insurance density and depth are still low compared with developed worldwide markets. In 2017, the national insurance density was RMB 2,632 per person and the insurance depth was 4.42%, ranking only 45th and 36th, respectively, among 88 countries and regions in the world. In China, the severe threat of the COVID-19 to the lives and health of the public has once again exposed the shortcomings of insurance market supply.

With the institutional advantage of socialism with Chinese characteristics, in order to better carry out pandemic prevention and treatment, the relevant functional departments of the Chinese government have issued several documents and generally established that the cost of coronavirus treatment is covered by social security (including social insurance and assistance) and finance at all institutional/government levels. Financial underwriting certainly reflects institutional advantages in dealing with major crises, but it also reflects to a large extent the current problem of inadequate supply in the insurance market. The costs of treatment and property damage, corporate bankruptcies, and unemployment, all require the insurance industry to be more closely involved and proactive. However, it has only played a very limited role in disaster management. In addition, since the outbreak of the pandemic, some insurance companies have leveraged malicious hype to dupe unsuspecting customers and launch exclusive insurance products, which were eliminated by the China Banking and Insurance Regulatory Commission.

11.1.2.4 *Demands for asset management are created*

Over the past 40 years of reform and opening-up, China's economy has maintained rapid growth, and household income has grown at a faster rate, accompanied by a significant increase in residents' demand for wealth management. According to the Global Wealth Report 2019 released by the Credit Suisse Research Institute in October 2019, aggregate global wealth rose by 2.6% to $360 trillion in 2018; wealth per adult reached $70,850, an increase of 1.2% compared to mid-2018; the United States, China, and Europe contributed $3.8 trillion, $1.9 trillion, and $1.1 trillion, respectively, becoming the largest contributors to global asset growth. In addition, the report also shows that China currently has 4.4 million millionaires, second only to the United States; China is second to the United States with 18,132 ultra-high net worth individuals with wealth exceeding $0 million.

Relying on the rapid economic development brought about by reform and opening-up, as well as the loose liquidity environment created by macro-control measures after the financial crisis a decade ago, China's asset management industry has experienced several years of fast growth. By the end of the second quarter of 2019, the scale of the asset management industry reached RMB 115.83 trillion. However, compared with the still rapidly expanding demand for asset management, there is still much room for the industry to grow, especially considering that there are still few investment channels for Chinese investors. Meanwhile, in the same period the stock market has long been unable to reflect economic growth, the collapse of P2P lending and corporate debt defaults have been frequent, and alternative investments such as REITS have just started, which means that the market still has huge potential demand for the development of the asset management industry to enhance asset preservation through professional investment and research teams.

New asset management regulations introduced in April 2018 represent a concerted attempt to unify regulatory standards and transform the asset management industry. During the same period, bank wealth management subsidiaries were established and net worth products were issued, marking a new stage for the development of the industry. In the midst of COVID-19 pandemic, companies shut down or suspended their operations and cut salaries, and many residents suffered from wage income loss. At the same time, the severe volatility in stocks, bonds, commodities, and derivatives markets have also affected residents' property income. It is expected that financial awareness and the financial needs of Chinese residents will be further amplified after the pandemic to remain financially resilient, and steadily increase income. Considering the downturn in short-term interest rates and the possible increase in inflation, the asset management industry should enhance the ability to respond to emergencies in the medium and long term. In the meantime, the asset allocation and risk management needs of Chinese residents and enterprises will be further expanded, generating development opportunities for the asset management industry.

11.2 China's Economic and Financial Policy Response to the Pandemic

11.2.1 Strengthening countercyclical macro-control and support for SMEs in key industries

(1) *Countercyclical macro-control policy based on short-term pressure and mid- to long-term upbeat outlook should be strengthened*: The

pandemic showed a shock effect for a short period and should have a limited impact on China's economy in the medium and long term. Based on this judgment and the current situation of the pandemic at home and abroad, it is recommended that in response to the downward pressure on the economy in the first and second quarters, a more proactive fiscal policy should be adopted at the macro level. In addition, more substantial tax and fee cuts, delayed payments of social security, and other necessary measures should be adopted for SMEs in industries that are able to create greater avenues of growth after short-term shock to effectively reduce their business operating costs. An appropriately accommodative monetary policy (with the central bank as the core decision-making body) should be implemented to guarantee the liquidity supply for the national economy and the capital market. In addition, central and local governments should further increase investments and purchases to maintain economic demand. Macro-control policy initially loosens and is then normalized. In the first half of the year, a proactive fiscal policy complemented by a flexible and accommodative monetary policy should be put in place, and imports should be increased to an appropriate level, while in the second half of the year, excessive credit stimulus should be avoided.

(2) *Building up the mechanism of SME protection and emergency relief*: The pandemic has dealt a heavy blow to SMEs that are highly dependent on short-term cash flow and has also greatly damaged China's macro economy, where the proportion of the service industry is increasing. In this regard, the government should in the short term take advantage of fiscal means for timely blood transfusions, and further strengthen the construction of relevant support and protection systems in the long term, including social security and financial protection systems, so as to provide emergency protection for the secure operation of SMEs together with ensuring sustainable employment. It should be noted that the pandemic has promoted the rapid growth of e-commerce and consumer industries in online transactions. This growth has not only dominated a part of traditional industry markets but has also eased employment pressure with its expansion in production, logistics, and services in the context of traditional industry depression. When old industries are replaced with new ones under market-based regulation, the government should respect fair market competition, welcome positive changes, and, except for solving

employment problems, not expend resources on bailouts for industries and enterprises without medium- and long-term development prospects. Government intervention should also be implemented when market-based regulation fails (e.g., when financial institutions cannot extend maturing loans).

(3) *Comprehensively reinforcing the "stabilization of foreign trade and investment" through expanding imports and opening-up*: The agreement reached in the first phase of the U.S.–China trade negotiations pointed out that both sides should consider resuming negotiations in the event of risks from uncontrollable factors. It is suggested that the central and local governments at all levels make plans for managing trade risks. For example, the procurement of healthcare resources be increased to compensate for the decline in domestic demand for aircraft, automobiles, and other manufacturing products. At the same time, full use be made of the Lin-gang Special Area of the Shanghai Pilot Free Trade Zone (SHFTZ) to attract more high-quality foreign institutions to invest in Shanghai with comprehensive, high-level financial opening-up characterized by greater depth, broader range, and increased strength, minimizing the risk of falling foreign investment in Shanghai and the whole country. In this regard, the government must further ramp up policy support for foreign trade companies in Lin-gang Special Area, such as offering more tax incentives, providing credit support, and giving priority to their work resumption. In the medium and long term, the pandemic may affect the position of some Chinese companies in the global value chain, including those in the Yangtze River Delta region. Learning from the experience of Japanese companies in coping with the crisis, Chinese companies can consolidate and enhance their position in the global value chain through increased R&D and innovation. In addition, considering the impact of the global pandemic on various economies, China seeks to guarantee or even boost trade with South Korea, Japan, Italy, and other severely affected countries and regions. On the one hand, it is to maintain the existing global trade order, reflecting its responsibility as a major country in the international community and international affairs; on the other hand, it is also a necessary guarantee for its own economic and trade development as the global economy is closely intertwined with China's. After all, a healthy and stable global economic environment is an essential foundation for China's economic development.

(4) *Enhancing information exchanges with other economies to guide reasonable expectations in the global market*: In the global prevention and control of the pandemic, under the guidance of the World Health Organization, it is necessary for all countries to maintain transparency and openness of information so as to end the pandemic as soon as possible. By the same token, one of the lessons learned from the 2008–2009 global financial crisis is that major economies must strengthen the communication and coordination of macro-control policies to contain the spread of the crisis and facilitate effective crisis management. In recent years, China has continued to open up its economy, especially in terms of financial openness. The capital market is highly sensitive to information, which requires the Chinese government and regulatory authorities to clearly and promptly inform other core stakeholders in other major markets of China's policies and regulatory measures to further enhance policy transparency and guide global participants to establish reasonable expectations.

11.2.2 Improving the construction of financial markets to prevent and address risks and support science and technology innovations

(1) *Establishing and securing a regular operating mechanism for the financial market*: During the Spring Festival holiday, the central and local governments generally made the decision to postpone the start of work and school in view of the threat of the pandemic, but whether financial market trading should also be postponed aroused considerable controversy before the A-share market reopened on February 3rd. The operating experience of mature markets shows that one of the most important functions of a healthy capital market is to maintain regular operation to protect the liquidity needs of investors, and to guide the deployment of social resources through continuous market transactions and price adjustments. If an emergency occurs, especially one with a significant negative impact, then the postponement of the opening-up of the market will not reduce the short-term loss of investors but will instead increase the uncertainty of investors about the future economic situation, which may in turn lead to excessive adjustments (including panic selling) when the market eventually resumes. In fact, the A-share market opened with a sharp drop on February 3rd,

but it soon recovered and rebounded. This example indicates that the establishment and maintenance of a regular operating mechanism for the financial market not only helps investors to establish more rational expectations, but also plays a positive role in improving the financial market system in China.

(2) *Further expanding the opening-up of China's financial market*: The A-share market plummeted more than 7% on February 3 as it opened as scheduled amid an ongoing pandemic. Despite the plunge, institutional investors at home and abroad have taken advantage of the sell-off and bought a net 18.2 billion yuan of shares via Hong Kong's links with SSE and Shenzhen Stock Exchange, the highest single-day net inflow in history. Based on the performance of the A-share market, institutional investment funds for medium and long-term value investment have played a vital role in stabilizing the market. Therefore, measures should be taken to further expand the opening-up of China's financial market, for instance, restoring and stepping up the development of "Shanghai-London Stock Connect", exploring new options for capital project management such as "Tobin tax" in the SHFTZ (especially the Lin-gang Special Area), developing more functions for free trade accounts with unified domestic and foreign currency, and promoting the construction of offshore markets. Through attracting more medium and long-term international investors and institutions to participate in the construction of China's multilevel financial market in the form of establishing wholly owned institutions headquartered in Shanghai, small and medium-sized domestic investors enjoy the favorable products and services provided by international institutions, while competition with excellent international institutions can stimulate domestic institutions to push forward their development.

(3) *Building the Sci-Tech Innovation Board and piloting the registration system to promote technological innovation in the financial market*: Since its launch on the SSE in July 2019, the Sci-Tech Innovation Board has had remarkable achievements supporting hi-tech enterprises and has continued to exert its strength amid the coronavirus outbreak. On the one hand, it provides financial support for biomedical companies that require large-scale early stage R&D investment through listing to promote the medium and long-term development of these companies; on the other hand, it facilitates the further development of emerging technology companies such as e-commerce, online

education, and telecommuting prompted by the pandemic. Through the Sci-Tech Innovation Board and the registration system, the listing of these sci-tech companies and the successful exit of investors are encouraged, in an effort to attract more foreign institutions and capital to invest in domestic start-ups, accelerate science and technology innovation, and upgrade industrial structure in the medium and long term.

(4) *Improving the insurance and financial derivatives market to prevent and defuse risks*: The pandemic has presented stronger requirements for development and improvement of the financial and insurance markets. Insurance is the most important and direct financial tool to prevent and resolve risks. At present, in addition to life and property insurance that cover general risks, catastrophe insurance designed to provide protection against disasters has also emerged internationally. In contrast, China's insurance market is still far from mature. In particular, as an international financial center, Shanghai needs to launch more financial and insurance products to hedge risks, including, but not limited to, "production interruption insurance" for SMEs, insurance coverage for unknown diseases, and accident insurance covering public health events. At the same time, the establishment of the Shanghai Reinsurance Center should be implemented. Drawing on the idea of catastrophe insurance bonds, the financial market should explore the development of basic products and derivatives based on insurance products to achieve further risk diversification.

(5) *Driving the internationalization of asset management to strengthen the product and service offerings of domestic asset management companies*: To meet increasing asset management needs during the pandemic, apart from cultivating local asset management companies, it is also of great importance to attract through greater openness, global company headquarters or Asia-Pacific headquarters to China. Shanghai should take advantage of the Lin-gang Special Area to pilot a cross-border capital pool of both domestic and foreign currency, enticing more international asset management companies to do business and set up exclusive subsidiaries in Shanghai. The biggest concern of international companies entering the Chinese market is the uncertainty of capital flow. In this regard, medium and long-term institutional asset management companies should be encouraged and supported, and more market-oriented capital management tools

should be adopted to reduce this kind of uncertainty. Meanwhile, Shanghai should welcome commercial banks to set up wealth management subsidiaries and encourage insurance asset management companies to establish professional asset management subsidiaries. In the Lin-gang Special Area, wealth and asset management companies can invest in the form of equity in industries such as healthcare and digital technology that have a huge potential for vigorous development. In addition, it is essential for Shanghai to introduce more RMB interest rate and foreign exchange derivatives including RMB interest rate options, enrich the varieties of domestic and foreign currency transactions and risk management measures, and strengthen the ability of enterprises to manage financial risks of interest rates and exchange rates.

11.3 Conclusion

The sudden outbreak of the COVID-19 pandemic took a substantial toll on domestic and international economic and financial markets. Under the strategic deployment of the Central Committee of the CPC, the dedicated efforts of healthcare workers, and the effective national response plan of temporary closures and travel restrictions, the pandemic in China has been fully controlled. However, global coronavirus cases have shown a spike around the world. The rapidly deteriorating situation has also caused turmoil in the global financial market with risk aversion on the rise among global funds. In the light of the demand-side impact and the possible supply-side risks, some institutions and organizations have started to discuss whether the pandemic will cause, if it has not already caused, a global financial crisis.

In the face of shock and subsequent possible risks, China's financial industry needs to pay close attention to their impact on the financial market and various financial sectors. Compared with other major economies in the world, the financial industry has seen rapid growth in terms of scale. However, there is still a significant gap in important functions such as resource allocation and risk prevention. As a result, China must further strengthen countercyclical regulation in its macroeconomic policies, provide support for SMEs in key industries, and reduce the credit risk of dominant banks in the financial system. Furthermore, the financial industry should advance opening-up with greater strength and higher quality, introduce more international leading institutions in brokerage, asset management, insurance, banking, and other fields, improve the quality of products and services of local companies through more effective competition, and establish a more open, mature, innovation-supportive, and internationally consistent operating mechanism for the financial market.

https://doi.org/10.1142/9789811252921_0012

Chapter 12

The Impact of the COVID-19 Pandemic on China's Financial and Real Economy and Policy Responses

Wang Yongqin and Han Yu

School of Economics, Fudan University, Shanghai, China

Before analyzing the impact of the COVID-19 pandemic on the Chinese economy, its current state should first be examined. Since 2008, China's economy has undergone significant changes with four main characteristics; first, the GDP growth rate exceeded 8% for the first time in 2012; second, total factor productivity (TFP) growth has declined sharply since 2008; third, debts have increased across the board with local debt, household debt, and corporate debt growing more than government debt; and fourth, the changes in GDP growth, TFP growth, and debt growth have not been smooth transitions but have occurred as a series of increases and plateaus (steps) as shown in Figures 12.1, 12.2, and 12.3, respectively.

The above characteristics are crucial to understanding China's economic landscape. Views concerning the current economic situation are categorized into two types: the first is the view that China is faced with structural economic problems and that the economy has entered a new normal, requiring an adaptation to this new model of economic development, while the other view holds that these problems are cyclical and "abnormal" and that a stop must be put to the downward economic and financial spiral. In our view, the Chinese economy is now on a downward path in the leverage cycle, and we should adopt different strategies to address the economic problems revealed by this cyclical phenomenon.

12.1 Leverage Cycle

The financial cycle is mainly manifested as the leverage cycle, or the debt cycle. Stocks have limited effect on the economic cycle, while debt,

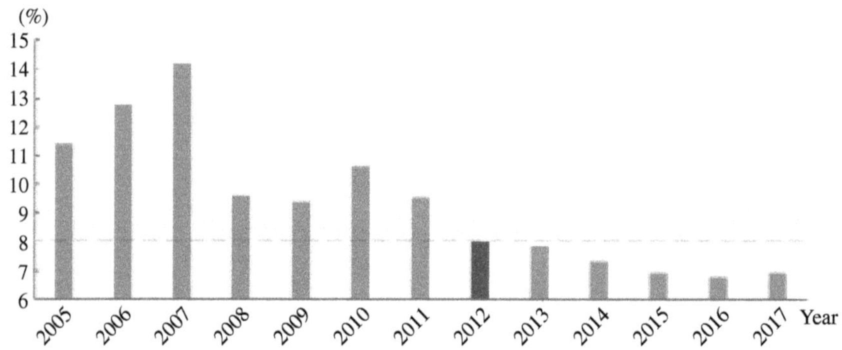

Figure 12.1: Annual growth rate of China's GDP.

Source: Bloomberg.

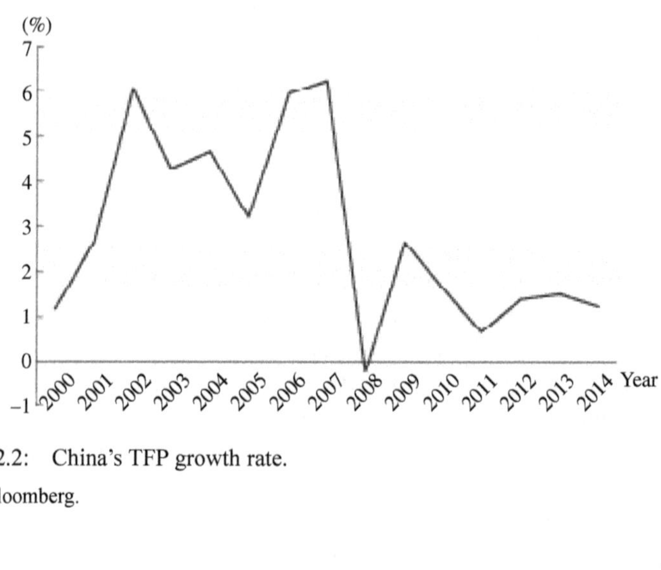

Figure 12.2: China's TFP growth rate.

Source: Bloomberg.

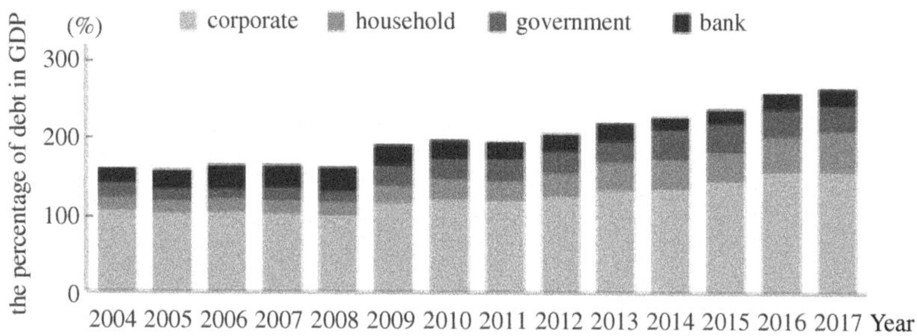

Figure 12.3: China's debt stock.

Source: Bloomberg.

especially household debt, has a profound impact. Leverage is one of the most fundamental and important ideas of the modern financial system, and it is closely linked to collaterals. The modern financial system (especially the shadow banking system) is constructed by layers of collateral assets such as land→home mortgage loan→MBS→CDO→CDS. Each additional layer of collateral and leverage mobilizes the value of the underlying assets. Adding leverage is not really a problem, but the question of who is using leverage and for what purpose is important.

Asset prices in the financial market are determined by optimistic marginal buyers who have a higher opinion of the value of the asset. Optimistic buyers tend to get more money through leveraging, to drive prices up with their opinion being fully expressed. If there is short selling, their opinion will not be reflected in prices, which may cause the asset to be overvalued (Geanakoplos, 2010).

Leverage is the reciprocal of one minus the loan-to-value (LTV) ratio, and the LTV ratio determines the use of leverage and the level of financing. How is the LTV ratio set in an economy? How does it affect economic behaviors?

Uncertainty (the degree of panic) determines the LTV ratio. The LTV ratio is set to prevent the risk of future changes in the value of collateral assets. When the uncertainty of the asset return is high, the LTV needs to be low enough to cover the losses in the worst cases.

The booming economy with low future uncertainty forms a virtuous circle of "stable economy–increased leverage–rising asset prices–increased production and consumption". However, when the economy weakens, rising uncertainty leads to falling LTV ratios. Highly leveraged optimists do

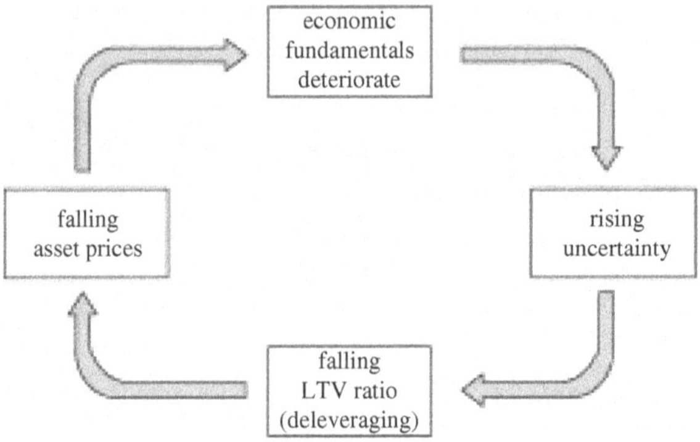

Figure 12.4: Vicious cycle in the downward phase of the leverage cycle.

not have enough collateral and go bankrupt. Hence, the marginal buyers become much less optimistic, and the asset prices decline, creating a vicious cycle as shown in Figure 12.4.

12.2 Leverage Cycle of the Chinese Economy: Household Debt and Corporate Debt

Why does leverage have a serious impact on the economy? For incomplete financial markets (insufficient risk sharing), debt acts as an anti-insurance system with large macro externalities: the most vulnerable households have to bear the risk of economic downturn and are forced to cut back on consumption, resulting in insufficient effective demand and at last economic recession. The problem lies on the demand side where the existence of debt overhang makes monetary policy ineffective. Debtors burdened with debt service obligations will obtain capital to repay their debts rather than to invest or consume. As shown in Figure 12.5,[1] China's debt growth rate, leverage growth rate, and GDP growth rate generally show a positive relationship. China now faces a huge backlog of household and corporate debt, and government debt is also accumulating, but the current situation is still manageable because the government has various soft budget constraints. At present, corporate bankruptcy law is not

[1] *Note*: The data are compiled from Wind and Lianxun Securities, and the leverage ratio and debt data are from the Center for National Balance Sheet (CNBS).

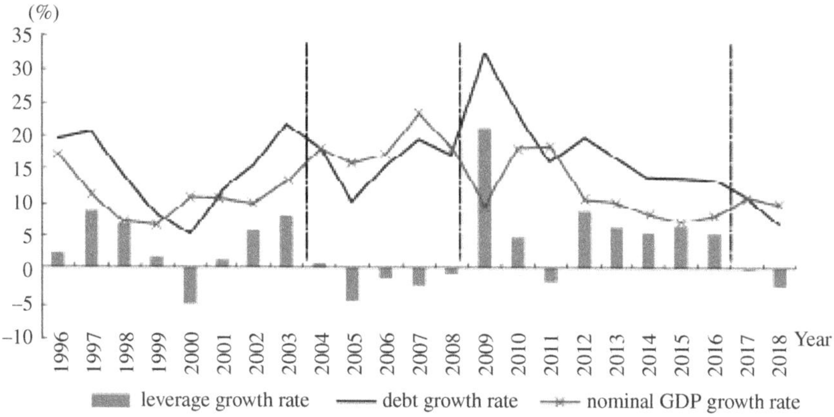

Figure 12.5: Leverage ratio, debt, and nominal GDP growth.

Source: Li, Q.L. *et al.*, In-Depth Analysis of China's Leverage Ratio, Special Research on Lianxun Securities, April 26, 2019.

well developed and there is no personal bankruptcy law in China, so in this context, the impact of household debt problems is very rigid and procyclical, which has exacerbated the economic downturn.

The sudden drop in China's TFP growth after 2008 may also be related to the debt problem. The RMB 4 trillion stimulus package adopted by China was to release liquidity (actually more than 40 trillion yuan) through bank lending. Waves of money flowed into real estate through shadow banking, while local government debt accumulated, and the increase in real estate mortgage loans pushed up household debt. This has resulted in the current scenario of "households not consuming and enterprises not investing." As Figure 12.6 demonstrates, housing prices and TFP growth rate are negatively correlated after 2008.

As can be seen in Figure 12.7, 2012 was a key turning point when GDP growth fell below the total annual interest payable for the first time. Overall, China is now in a downward phase of the leverage cycle, a vicious cycle among deleveraging, tightening liquidity, and decline in real economic activity.

The drop in collateral values has contributed to this process. In China, there is a scarcity of safe assets to use as collateral, and when the collateral value falls, people tend to use houses or equities as collateral to obtain financing, forming hidden danger similar to the 2015 stock market crash.

Figure 12.6: House price growth rate and TFP growth rate in China, 2001–2007.

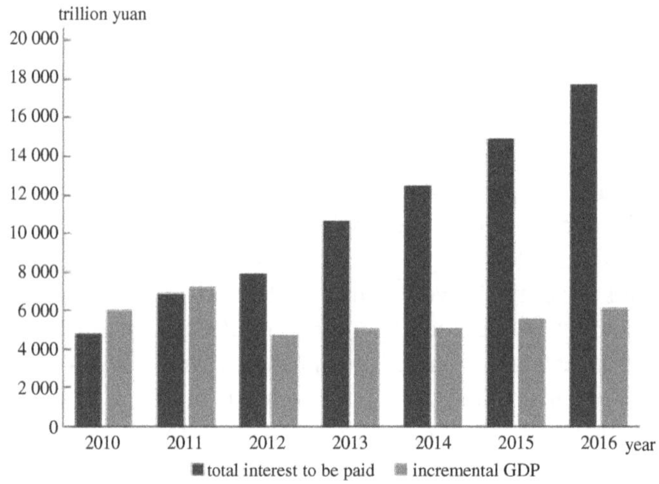

Figure 12.7: Incremental GDP and total interest to be paid from 2010 to 2016.

The heated equity pledge market reflects in essence the current situation of insufficient collateral in the economy. The only way to avoid such a cascade of problems is to reform the system and guarantee the availability of collateralizable assets at the source.

12.3 Economic Implications of Increased Uncertainty

"Normal" bad news that only brings first-order shocks has relatively little impact on the economy, because the LTV ratio remains unchanged, and the fall in asset prices can be mitigated by improvements in leverage. However, the bad news (first-order shocks) accompanied by rising uncertainty (second-order shocks) increases the volatility of asset yields, reduces the LTV ratio, and leads to a decline in leverage, creating a vicious circle of "decreasing leverage–falling asset prices–decreasing leverage ratio...", and falling into the crisis stage of the leverage cycle.[2] Taking the United States as an example (Figure 12.8), the occurrence of almost every leverage cycle is associated with an increase in economic policy uncertainty (EPU).

The outbreak of the pandemic has brought great uncertainty to the global economy, having a huge impact on financial markets and the real economy. A variety of forward-looking metrics, including macro

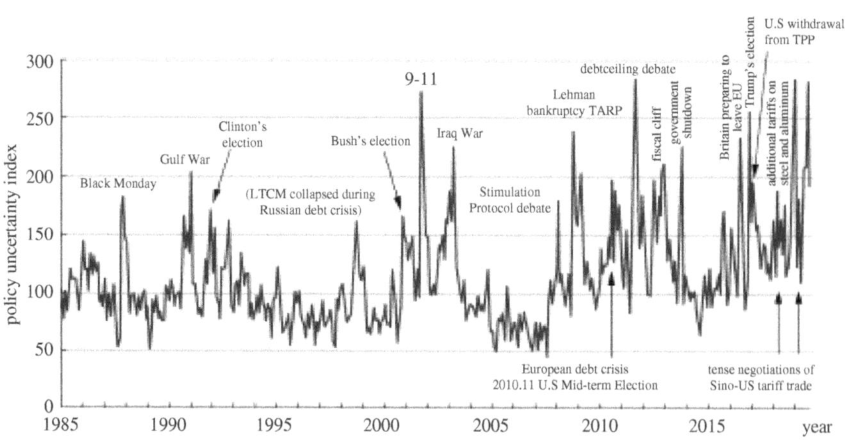

Figure 12.8: U.S. economic policy uncertainty index.

Source: Baker, S.R., Bloom, N., and Davis, S.J. Measuring Economic Policy Uncertainty, Updated at www.policyuncertainty.com, data normalized to 100 at the beginning of 2010.

[2] John Geanakoplos, "The Leverage Cycle".

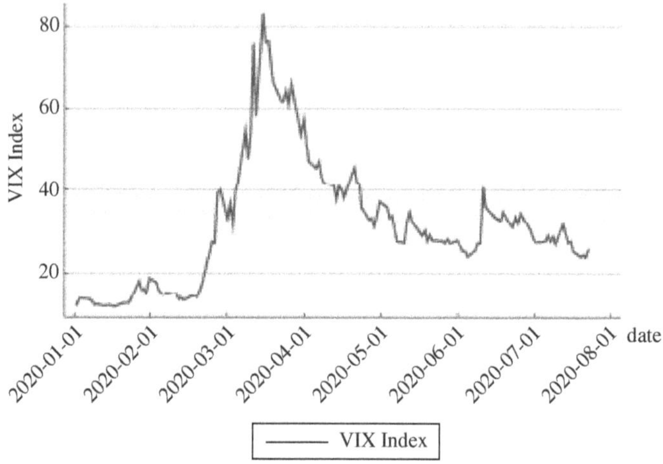

Figure 12.9: VIX index.

Source: U.S. Federal Reserve Economic Database (FRED).

uncertainty and micro dispersion, show that global uncertainty has risen sharply. From a macroeconomic perspective, the Chicago Board Options Exchange Volatility Index (CBOE Volatility Index or VIX) (Figure 12.9) continued to climb after late February and reached its apex around March 20th, second only to that of the Lehman Brothers' bankruptcy. Although there was a drop in the third quarter, it was still substantially above its level at the beginning of the year. China's EPU has fluctuated and risen since the government took the initiative to deleverage in 2016, and the index has remained at a high level after the onset of the pandemic (see Figure 12.10). The above indicates that uncertainty in China and the world is on the rise, and market concerns are also growing, which may accelerate the downward trend in China's leverage cycle. At the micro-firm and consumer level, surveys in the U.S. and the U.K.[3] suggest that companies have increased divergence in expectations about business conditions. The uncertainty of cash flow causes companies to curtail production for prudential reasons; the uncertainty of income pushes consumers to increase

[3] Survey of Business Uncertainty (SBU) and Decision-Maker Panel (DMP) Report on the One-Year-Ahead Expectations of Businesses for Sales, Investment, and Employment Growth.

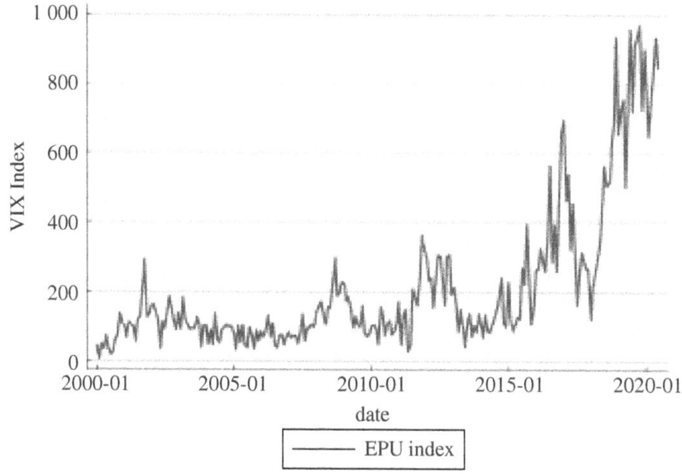

Figure 12.10: China economic policy uncertainty index.

Source: "Economic Policy Uncertainty in China" by Scott R. Baker, Nicholas Bloom, Steven J. Davis and Sophie Wang (2013) at www.PolicyUncertainty.com.

precautionary savings, resulting in a lack of effective demand (Bloom, 2009). Investment and consumption are particularly hard hit when there is a debt backlog. In the following, the impact of rising uncertainty due to the pandemic on the financial and real economy from the perspective of debt (including bond market, banking sector leverage, corporate and residential leverage), stocks, real estate, and the international market will be analyzed.

12.4 Pandemic Outbreak Increases Risk and Uncertainty in the Financial Market

12.4.1 Impact of the pandemic on debt: Rising financing costs for the real sector and insufficient effective demand from households

Debt in the economy can be roughly divided into two types: bonds and bank loans. The following section examines the impact of the pandemic on debt in the real economy from the aforementioned two micro perspectives as well as from the macro leverage perspective.

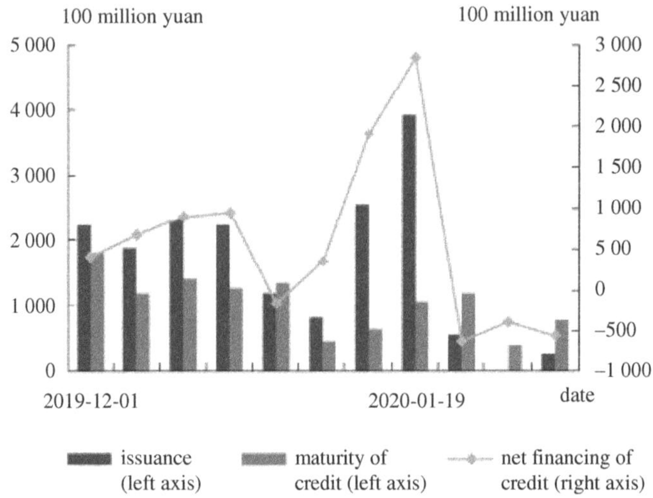

Figure 12.11: Weekly issuance, maturity, and net financing of credit in the primary market.

Source: Transcript of the First Week After the Holiday: How is the Pandemic Pulling the Credit Market?, Ruizhe Fixed Income Research, February 9, 2020.

Through the uncertainty of the pandemic, bond market deleveraging has affected the prices of different bonds. As demonstrated in Figure 12.11, the supply side almost stagnated after the Spring Festival, with the amount of credit financing in the primary market being negative in the first quarter. In the secondary market, safe assets such as Treasury bonds and policy bank bonds have been sought out, while credit spreads for corporate bonds and enterprise bonds have risen. The industries are classified into two categories according to the extent of the impact caused by the pandemic. Corporate bonds after the Spring Festival (after the closure of Wuhan) saw a general increase in spreads of information technology, energy, raw materials, real estate, non-essential consumer goods represented by hotels, and distribution and other industries (Figure 12.12). Enterprise bonds are reflected in the rising spreads of transportation infrastructure, real estate, and automobile industries (Figure 12.13) due to stagnant industrial production and shrinking demand in the service sector amid social isolation. Since March 12, when the World Health Organization declared COVID-19 a "global pandemic", global supply and demand have shrunk, information technology has been integrated into global supply chains, and air and maritime transport

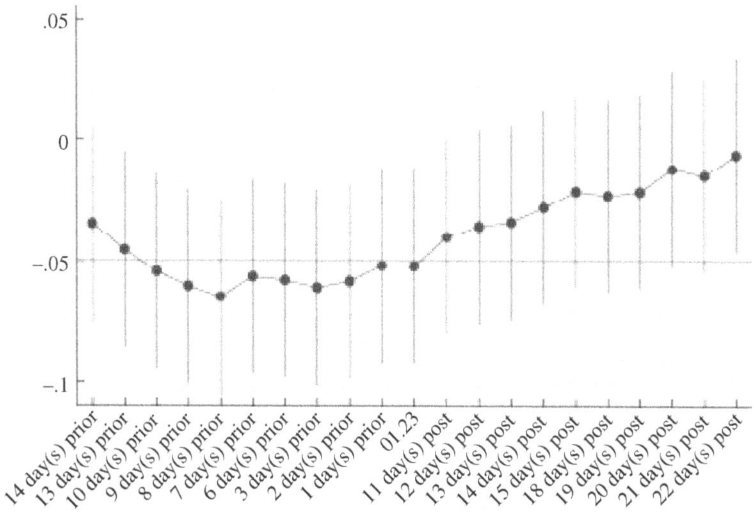

Figure 12.12: Corporate bond spreads around the Spring Festival (January 23).

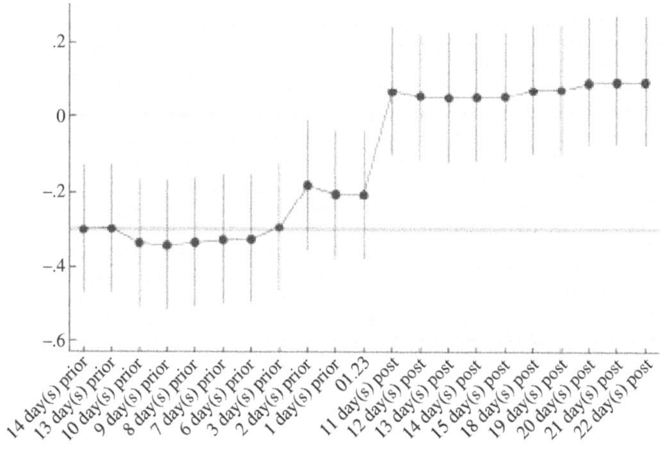

Figure 12.13: Enterprise bond spreads around the Spring Festival (January 23).

involving transnational operations and financial services have increased significantly (Figure 12.14).[4]

[4] *Note*: Net credit financing amount = credit issuance amount-credit maturity amount, data from Wind and China Merchants Securities

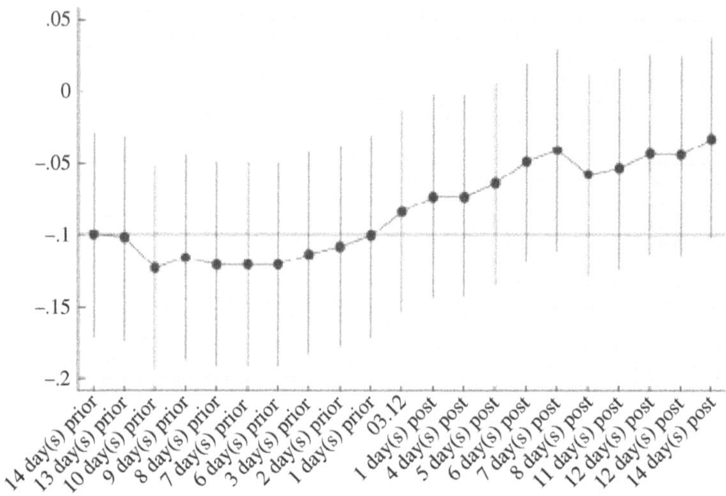

Figure 12.14: Corporate bond spreads around March 12.

Source: CSMAR and Wind.

Note: The first tier of the GICS structure are sectors greatly affected by the pandemic. Figure 12.12 [28.6%] shows information technology; telecommunications services; consumer staples; energy; materials (metals, non-metals, and mining); industrials (aerospace III, aerospace, and defense III, electrical equipment, marine III, machinery); financials (real estate management and development, diversified financial services); consumer discretionary (media III, hotels, restaurants, and leisure III, integrated consumer service III, auto parts, consumer goods distributors III, diversified retail). Figure 12.13 [17.48%] includes industrials (transportation infrastructure, general category III); financials (real estate management and development); consumer discretionary (automobiles). Figure 12.14 [17.71%] illustrates information technology; materials (metals, non-metals, and mining); industrials (aviation III, marine III); financials (diversified financial services). Industries in the third tier of the GICS structure are shown in parentheses, and the proportion of total bond transactions in square brackets.

Bank loans include both corporate loans on the supply side and household debt on the demand side. More than 50% of Chinese corporate financing relies on bank loans. According to the theory of credit rationing under asymmetric information (Stiglitz and Weiss, 1981), in order to avoid adverse selection and moral hazards, banks will preferentially lend to dominant enterprises. Small and medium-sized enterprises (SMEs) have difficulty in obtaining loans because they have less publicly available information and relatively lower collateral quality. Therefore, SMEs usually rely more on their relationship-based financing with specific banks. After the pandemic, the banking industry has lowered its leverage and preferred to lend to state-owned enterprises and large private enterprises

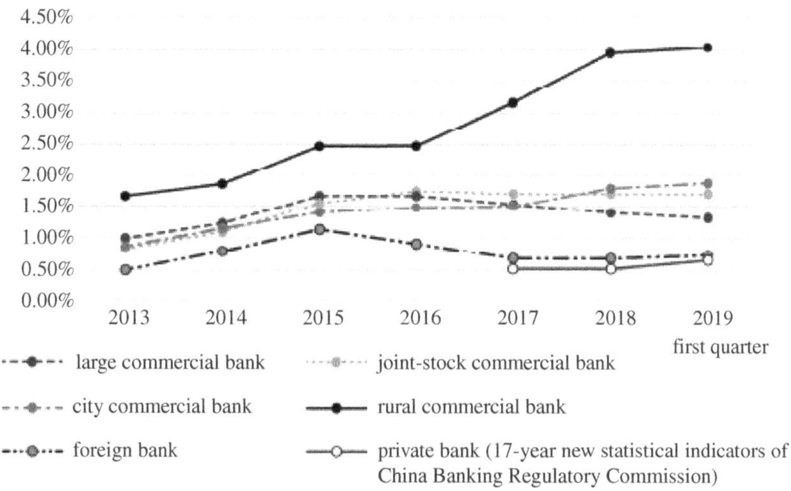

Figure 12.15: Non-performing loan ratio of commercial banks.
Source: "Mainland China Securities Survey 2019", KPMG.

with good qualifications and strong anti-risk capabilities. Urban and rural commercial banks targeting SMEs recorded a high rate of non-performing loans on the asset side (Figure 12.15). Systemic risks are increased as they have the possibility of demanding early repayment from enterprises to reduce the liability side of their balance sheets. Banks and enterprises are closely interdependent. Once enterprises go bankrupt due to cash flow shortage, non-performing assets still need to be disposed of by banks. Such assets have poor liquidity and greatly reduced value and confidence in the banking industry, leading to a vicious cycle. A positive leverage adjustment should focus on increasing capital, cutting non-core assets, and disposing of non-performing assets. In order to solve the problem of indiscriminately calling in loans in advance, it is essential to build confidence in the banking sector, provide a favorable policy environment for enterprises, alleviate future economic uncertainty, and form a virtuous circle of business development, good corporate credit, and high-quality bank loans.

The pandemic not only affects bank lending and the bond transactions of financial institutions, but also highlights the debt backlog in the downward phase of the leverage cycle. With supply and demand shrinking at the same time, the negative impact of reduced demand will be even greater in China's service-oriented economic structure.

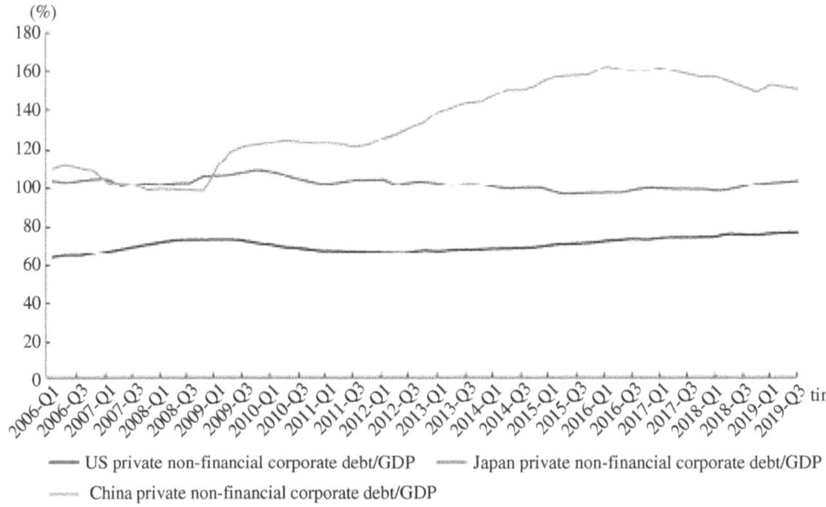

Figure 12.16: Debt asset ratio of non-financial corporations in China, the U.S., and Japan.

Source: Bank for International Settlements (BIS).

From a supply-side perspective, leverage in the non-financial corporate sector has increased by about 50% in 10 years. In terms of non-financial corporate debt across countries, as in Figure 12.16, China has a higher debt asset ratio than that of the U.S. and Japan. Highly leveraged companies (especially those with short-term debt) will be hit even more severely; revenues on the asset side are decreased due to the drop in demand for final products or intermediate products; large short-term debt on the liability side coupled with financing difficulties have caused companies to be trapped in a liquidity dilemma, including many high-quality companies with long capital turnover time. Investors only pay attention to cash flow and ignore the fundamentals, which will diminish the efficiency of resource allocation in the whole society.[5]

(1) Household debt: household loans in the domestic and foreign currency credit balance sheets of financial institutions, including consumer loans and business loans.

[5]Dalio, R., My Thoughts About the Coronavirus, http:// WWW.Linkedin.Com/pulse/my-thoughts-coronavirus-ray-dalio?articleId=6640623255357005825#comments 6640623255357005825.

(2) Non-financial corporate debt: loans to non-financial corporations and organizations in the domestic and foreign currency credit balance of financial institutions as well as entrusted loans, trust loans, undiscounted bank acceptance bills in the stock of social financing scale, corporate bonds less the stock of government debt in the form of non-government bonds in the balance of local government debt with addition of overseas loans.
(3) Government debt: balance of Treasury bonds along with balance of local government debt (local government debt includes a portion of financing platform debt before 2018, and the part that overlaps with non-financial corporate debt has been removed from the non-financial corporate sector).
(4) Financial sector asset side: other depository corporations' claims on other depository corporations and financial institutions.
(5) Financial sector liability side: other depository corporations' liabilities to other depository corporations/financial institutions and bond issuance.
(6) Nominal GDP: Rolling sum of four quarters.

Figure 12.17 further demonstrates that resource allocation on the supply side is problematic. The output value generated by the total assets of non-financial corporations has continued to decline over the last decade, indicating a misallocation of resources in the economy with traditional overcapacity sectors receiving large amounts of resources but marginal productivity decreases, and the current pandemic is likely to exacerbate the extent of resource misallocation.

From a demand-side perspective, leverage in the household sector has exceeded that of the government sector since 2015. In terms of absolute debt levels, China's household debt was RMB 4 trillion in 2007 and has now increased to RMB 50 trillion. Such a high level of debt has reduced the funds available for consumption, resulting in insufficient effective demand. Since 2020, the past-due rate of personal auto loans and consumer loan asset-backed securitization products (ABS) has risen (Figure 12.18), reflecting the decline in the quality of underlying assets. With demand-side residents facing deleveraging, consumer demand has been squeezed. China's tertiary sector, also known as the service sector, has made an increasing contribution to GDP with the percentage exceeding 50% in 2018. In a service-based economy, consumption is the primary driving force for economic growth, and a shortfall of effective demand is more devastating than inefficient resource allocation on the supply side.

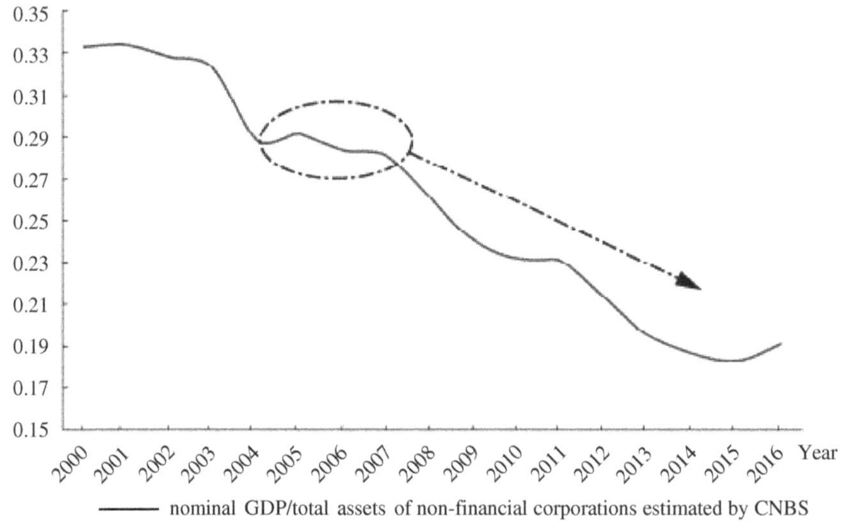

Figure 12.17: GDP output per unit of total assets of non-financial corporations in China.

Source: CNBS, Wind, and Lianxun Securities. Note: The estimated total assets of non-financial corporations are from the "National Balance Sheet of China" published by the Chinese Academy of Social Sciences.

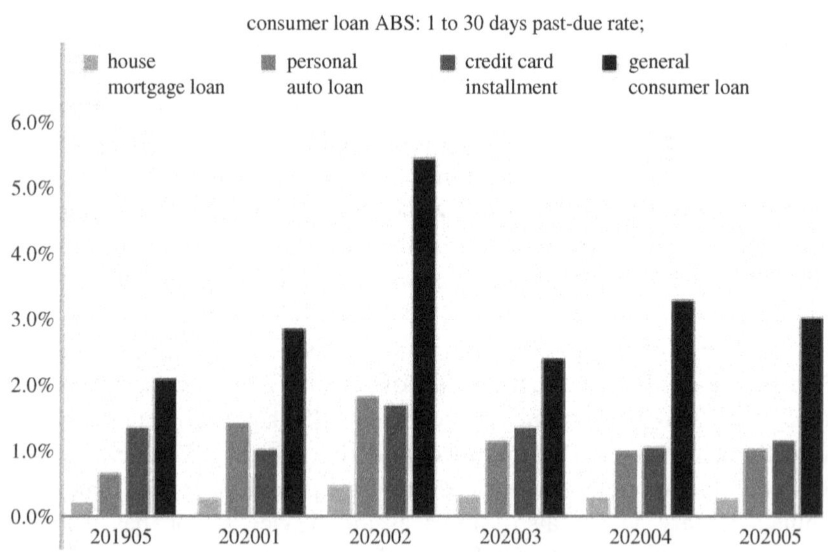

Figure 12.18: Consumer loan ABS 1 to 30 days past-due rate.

Source: "Tracking the Performance of Consumer ABS Market", China Asset Backed Securities (CNABS).

12.4.2 Impact of the pandemic on the stock market: High risk implicit in equity pledges

The stock market is highly sensitive to information, and negative news first caused a fall in stock prices in the financial market. As shown in Figure 12.19, the Shanghai Composite Index saw the biggest drop on the first trading day after the Spring Festival (February 3). Other major stock indexes plummeted worldwide in March. Market-wide circuit breakers were triggered in the U.S. stock market on March 9th, 12th, 16th, and 18th, respectively, four times within two weeks. The uncertainty brought about by the pandemic has increased the second-order volatility in stocks. In the first part, the VIX index based on U.S. stocks rose sharply. Figure 12.20 that follows shows increased volatility in returns of major stock indexes in China, the United Kingdom, Japan, and the United States.

The drop in stock prices caused by the pandemic is, on the one hand, transmitted from the financial system to the real economy through Tobin's Q theory; on the other hand, as equity is also collateral, the risk of transfer of corporate control implied by equity pledge may reduce operational efficiency. Tobin's Q value is the market value of a company divided by its assets' replacement cost. The theory holds that investment is

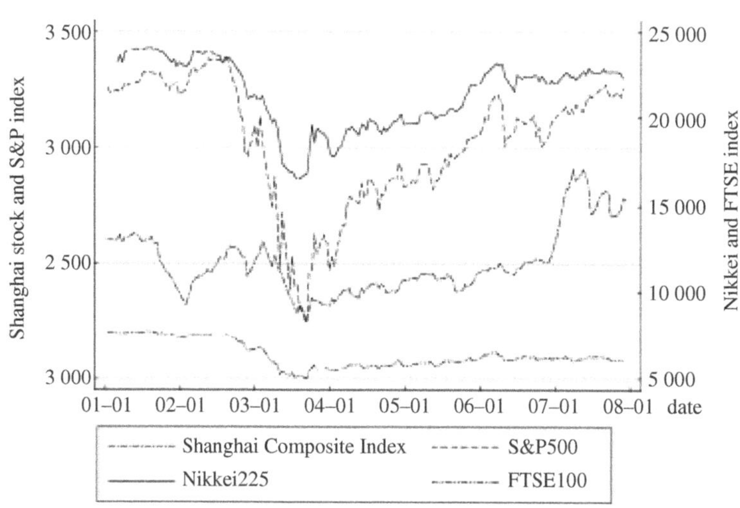

Figure 12.19: World major stock indexes.

Source: CSMAR.

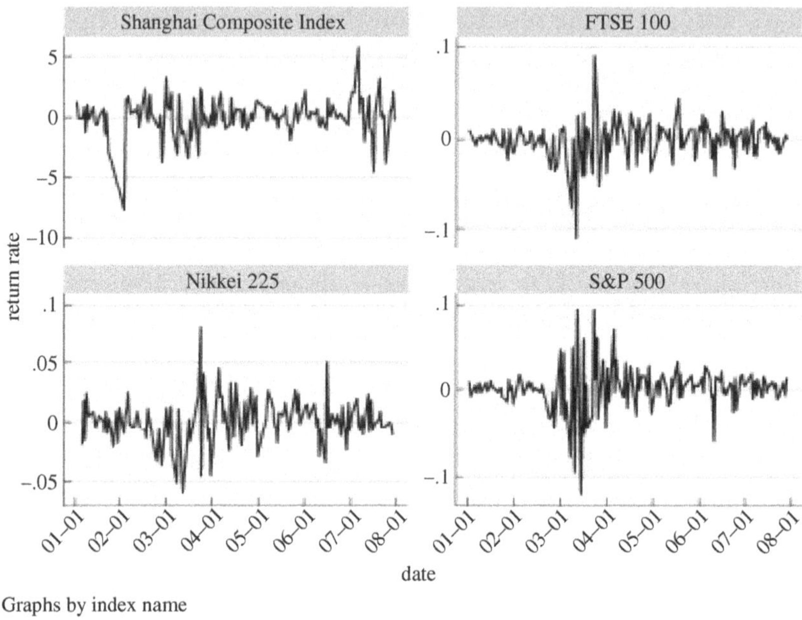

Figure 12.20: Return rate of world major stock indexes.
Source: CSMAR.

proportional to cash flow expectations, reflecting whether each unit of investment has a positive effect on the company. Since the replacement cost is difficult to estimate, in practice a simplified Q ratio is calculated as the equity market value divided by equity book value. When $Q > 1$, the value added per unit of investment is greater than the cost, encouraging companies to increase investment; when $Q < 1$, the rate of investment is negative, and the return is not enough to cover the cost, and no investment will occur. Stock prices have fallen since the Spring Festival with companies' market value shrinking and being undervalued. Low market value has caused the Q ratio to drop below 1, and companies have suspended investment. In addition to the reduction in investment, companies may also choose to sell their stocks to boost profits, increasing the risk of forced liquidation of pledged shares as described in what follows.

In recent years, equity pledge as a financing method has been widely adopted by major shareholders of listed companies. As of the end of July 2020, a total of 2,866 A-share listed companies have equity pledges, accounting for 77% of all A-share listed companies. As shown in Figure 12.21, since the end of 2014, the proportion of pledged A-shares

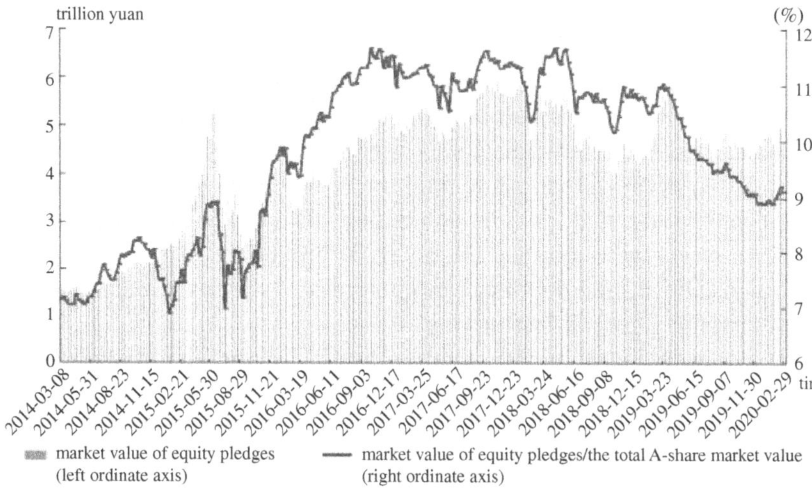

Figure 12.21: A-share pledge rate.

Source: CSMAR.

Note: Market value of equity pledges = market value of a single pledge × total number of A-share listed companies = total number of single pledges (including limited and unlimited sales) × single stock weekly closing price × total number of A-share listed companies. Market value of equity pledges refers to the left ordinate axis, and the proportion of market value of equity pledges to the total A-share market value refers to the right ordinate axis.

has been on the rise, climbing from 7% of the total A-share market value to around 11.5% at the beginning of 2018. It fell back to about 9% at the start of 2020.[6]

Despite the decline in the overall market value of equity pledges, its impact still cannot be overlooked. At the end of July 2020, the market value of equity pledges was similar to that of a year ago, but the number of pledges dropped from 50,000 to 30,000, as a single pledge bears high risks. When the pledge rate of controlling shareholders is too large, forced liquidation will result in the transfer of corporate control. Securities, banks, and trusts make up 90% of pledgees, and they hope to sell their shares at a discount for ready cash, not caring about the business operation, which will consequently lead to a decline in productivity. The

[6]On March 12, 2018, in order to regulate equity pledges of listed companies, the "Measures for Stock Pledged Repurchase Trading and Registration and Settlement Business (Revised 2018)" was officially implemented, and the proportion of pledged A-shares began to decline.

market's response to information is non-linear and stock prices overreact to bad news. In the absence of sufficient fundamental news, bad news is likely to trigger a panic sell-off by investors (Bloom *et al.*, 1998). Other financial institutions will also begin to sell their shares at a reduced price (fire sale), and the stock prices will keep dropping. A number of equity pledge defaults can spread panic, with more and more pledges facing the risk of liquidation, and stock prices falling off a cliff, forming a vicious cycle. As stock prices plunge, the assets of brokerages, banks, and other institutions shrink, and debt asset ratio increases, which can easily trigger a debt crisis in financial institutions.

The current equity pledge situation offers discouraging prospects. As of the end of July 2020, a total of 74 A-share companies have pledged shares accounting for more than 50% of total share capital, the majority of which were private and foreign-owned SMEs with a total market value of less than 10 billion yuan. Major shareholders with a high pledge rate are mostly companies with poor performance, meager or negative net profits. In 2019, the cumulative pledge rate of major shareholders of 996 listed companies exceeded 70% of their holdings.[7] The real estate sector took the first place in the total pledged equity and the eighth place in the average pledge rate, reflecting the hidden risks of the real estate market. It is worth noting that the average pledge rate of international trade and diversified finance exceeds 20%, which is among the top ten industries with the highest pledge rate. The spread of the global pandemic may increase the vulnerability of China's stock market.

12.4.3 Impact of the pandemic on exchange rates, international trade, and international financial markets: Uncertainty drives a decentralized global supply chain; the U.S. dollar remains the main safe-haven currency, and U.S. dollar debt pushes up the risk for real estate enterprises

Figure 12.22 displays the trend of the benchmark exchange rate of RMB against the U.S. dollar in the past year. With the prevention and effective control of the domestic pandemic in the first half of 2020, the exchange

[7] Song, G.Y., "2447 listed companies pledge equity with 90 pledge over 50%", http://www.ryanbencapital.com/2020/03/06/15342858d1/2020.03.06.

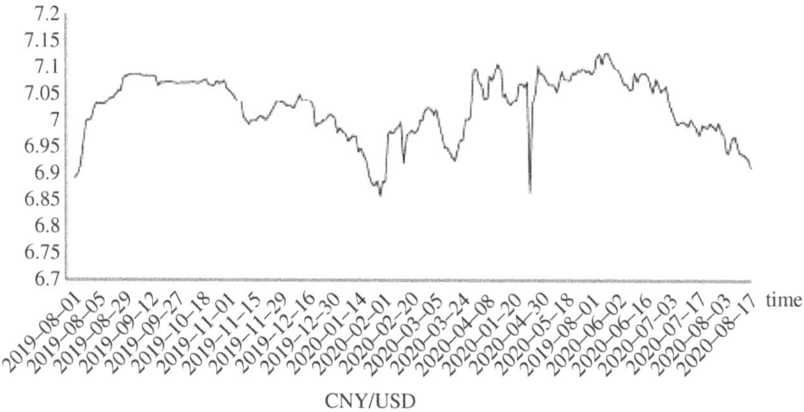

Figure 12.22: CNY to USD exchange rate.

Source: CSMAR.

Note: The figure shows the central parity of the RMB exchange rate expressed by indirect method, and the time unit is in days.

rate of the U.S. dollar against the RMB first rose and then fell. However, the U.S. dollar remains the dominant safe-haven currency, and the current exchange rate is at an all-time high around 7.

The impact of exchange rates on the economy is mainly reflected in two areas, international trade and international finance. Unlike the traditional theory of international trade, global supply chains account for more than 50% of total international trade. Moreover, the products manufactured by different countries are all part of the supply chain of multinational companies, and the importance of price has declined for export goods. Figure 12.23 shows that China's manufacturing exports have accounted for nearly 20% of the global manufacturing market share in the past five years, while Figure 12.24 suggests that the proportion of China's export goods used as intermediate products has increased from 23% in 2001 when it first joined the WTO to 32% in 2018. This implies that China's manufacturing sector has been deeply integrated into the global supply chain, and an insufficient supply of upstream products or lower downstream demand might depress the volume of international trade.

Against the backdrop of high uncertainty caused by the pandemic, China is exposed to the risk of supply chain shifts. The 2008 financial crisis raised our awareness of tail risks in financial markets, and the 2020 coronavirus pandemic has increased concerns about tail risks in the supply

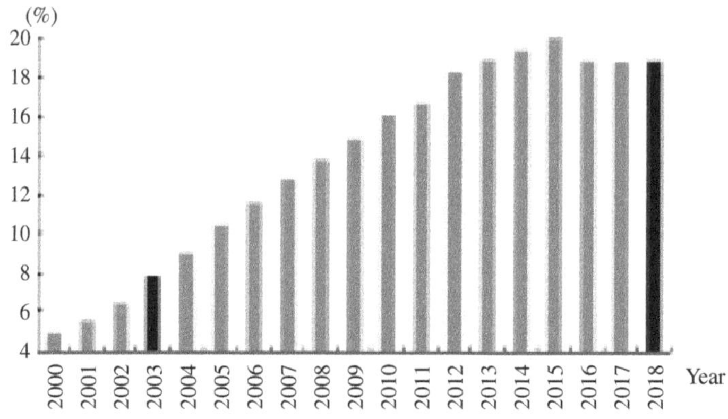

Figure 12.23: Global market share of China's manufacturing industry.

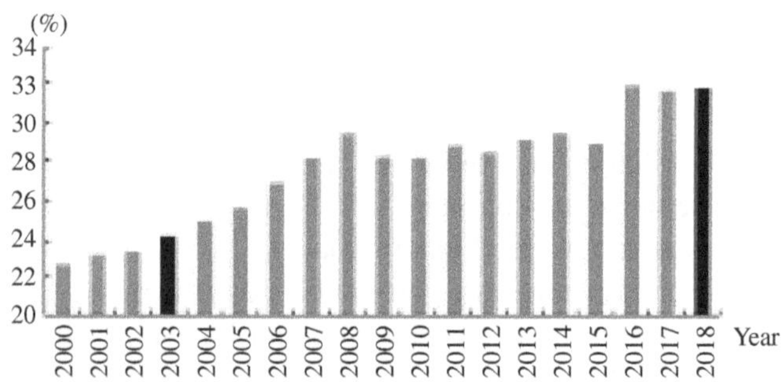

Figure 12.24: Proportion of intermediate products in manufacturing exports.

Source: Natixis and the UNCTAD-Eora GVC database.

chain. For the purpose of risk diversification, multinational companies may decentralize their supply chains, and set up factories in multiple locations around the world within the same supply chain. Although costs may rise, these measures improve the resilience of supply chains to ensure smooth operation if one factory is not working. In the future, the supply chain will shrink inward, showing trends of localization and regionalization, and China faces potential risks of shifting supply chains. China's labor costs are increasing at a faster pace than in the past. The country is now putting more emphasis on environmental conservation, and is seeking to upgrade the supply chain. In addition, under the pressure of Sino-US trade frictions, companies may have increased incentives to

Figure 12.25: Product space of China's export products.

Source: The Observation of Economic Complexity, https://oec.world.

move the supply chain out of China to other economies (such as Southeast Asia and India). However, with China being a traditional manufacturing country, it is difficult to reduce global supply chain reliance on China.

First, China succeeded in bringing the pandemic under control, creating favorable conditions for production. Second, China is the only country in the world that possesses all the industrial categories listed in the International Standard Industrial Classification, with sound infrastructure and a relatively complete supply chain system. The network diagram (see Figure 12.25) reflects the product space of China's exports by connecting products that can be exported together. The denser the network, the greater the product space, and the more likely it is to be in the same supply chain (such as the various parts that make up the same product). The same color represents the same industry. China's electronic components and mechanical equipment form a relatively complex industrial chain structure, and it is difficult to restructure this chain in other regions. Therefore, the traditional positive impact of exchange rate depreciation on stimulating exports will be offset or even replaced by the impact of the decentralization of the supply chain.

With the pandemic under effective control in China by March, production in domestic enterprises began to recover. However, the pandemic has continued to ravage Europe and the United States, and the movement of people and goods has been restricted, posing the risk of supply chain rupture. Figure 12.26 shows the risks faced by upstream and downstream

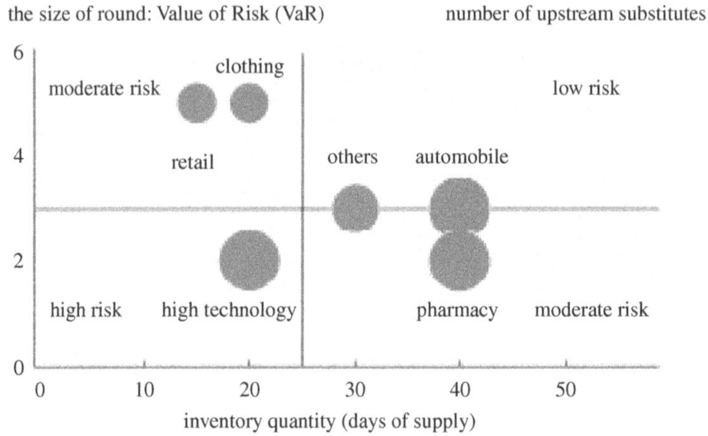

Figure 12.26: Risks of downstream enterprises in the supply chain.

Source: COVID19 and Trade: A Deadly Disease Disrupts, The Economist, 20200215, p. 28; Llamasoft: Goldman Sachs Global Investment Research.

Note: The horizontal axis represents inventory quantity. The closer to the right, the higher the quantity, and the lower the risk of its downstream companies; the vertical axis represents the number of substitutes. The more substitutes in the previous link, the lower the risk of downstream manufacturers.

companies in the global supply chain during the pandemic. The pandemic has shocked both the supply and demand sides of the world economy with inadequate production capacity of core components in Japan, South Korea, Europe, and the United States and insufficient demand for downstream products in the market. In summary, the pandemic has depressed China's export market, making it difficult for the export sector to become a driving force for economic growth during the declining period of the domestic leverage cycle.

From the perspective of the financial market, exchange rate fluctuations increase risks on the liability side of U.S. dollar bond issuers. Major issuers of U.S. dollar bonds are real estate enterprises, and the stock of U.S. dollar bonds issued by real estate companies are mainly short-to-medium term (5 years or less) (see Figure 12.27). On September 30, 2014, since the introduction of the "Notice of the People's Bank of China and the China Banking Regulatory Commission on Further Improving Housing Financial Services" (PBOC, (2014), No. 287), the domestic financing channels of real estate enterprises have been restricted and a small climax of offshore U.S. dollar bond issuance emerged with most bonds having a maturity of 3

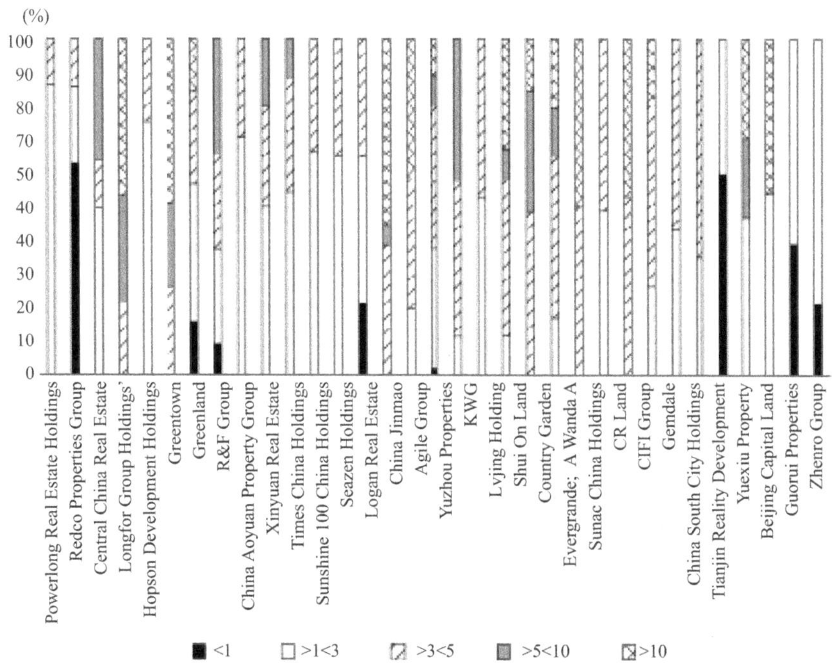

Figure 12.27: Maturities and stock of U.S. dollar bonds by real estate enterprises.

Source: Wind.

Note: Maturities of U.S. dollar bonds by major real estate enterprises is weighted by the stock of U.S. dollar bonds. The data are as of October 2018.

or 5 years. The year 2020 happens to be the peak of debt repayment for this batch of 5-year U.S. dollar bonds, with the maturity of offshore bonds concentrated at the beginning of the year (see Figure 12.28). The 3-year bonds swapped in 2016 will also face the pressure of debt repayment in the second half of 2020. Moreover, in accordance with the "Notice Concerning Requirements in Relation to Application, Filing and Registration of Foreign Bond Issuance by Real Estate Enterprises" (NDRC Foreign Investment, (2019), No. 778), the funds raised from offshore bonds can only be used to swap out medium or long-term foreign debt maturing within the next year. Debt swap channels are constrained, putting real estate enterprises under liquidity pressure as they can only repay U.S. dollar debts through their own funds or domestic bond financing.

Due to cash flow pressure, a number of real estate enterprises took the initiative to issue additional U.S. dollar bonds, with some interest

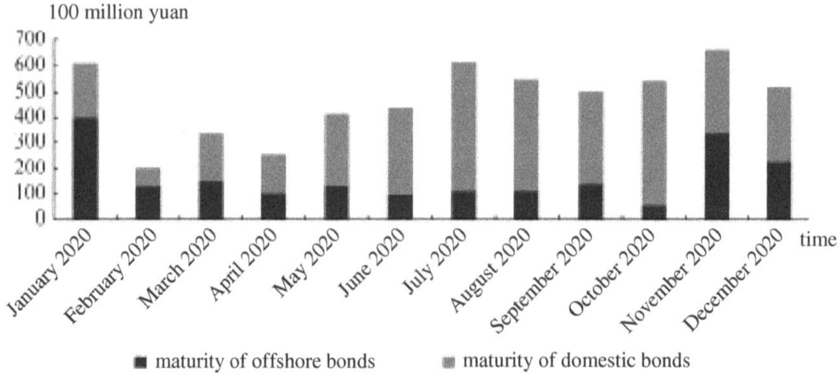

Figure 12.28: Real estate debt maturities in 2020.

Source: China Real Estate Information Corporation (CRIC) and www.fangchan.com

rates exceeding 10%. In January 2020, the overall amount of overseas financing in the real estate industry increased, with single-month offshore bond issuance reaching a record high of USD 18.1 billion (approximately RMB 126.7 billion), an annual increase of 83%. Net financing in a single month was also as high as RMB 95.1 billion, the largest amount in history.[8] The financing cost of Zhenro Group and Hopson Development Holdings was about 6%, while the number for China South City Holdings and Modern Land was more than 10%. Affected by exchange rate fluctuations, the large amount of U.S. dollar debt and high interest rates will place an increasingly heavy burden on real estate enterprises.

12.4.4 Impact of the pandemic on the real estate market: Assets and liabilities of the industry to which the core collateral belongs are under pressure

The real estate industry affects the Chinese economy in two respects: as the pillar industry of non-tradable goods, and as collateral that provides stable and continuous financing for the economy and promotes a virtuous economic cycle.

[8] Luo, M., "Go Overseas to Find Money: Real Estate Companies Keen on U.S. Dollar Debt with the Scale Hitting a Record High in January", *Securities Times*, February 21, 2020.

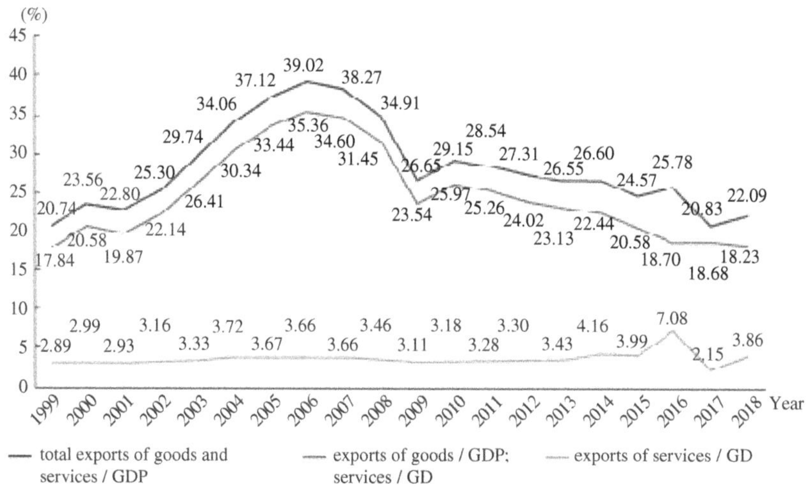

Figure 12.29: China's exports of goods and services as a share of GDP.

Source: 2000–2018 data from "China Statistical Yearbook", FRED.

Note: Prior to 2016, trade in services was only measured in U.S. dollars. Therefore, the annual average exchange rate data published by the Federal Reserve was used to calculate the amount of RMB-denominated trade in services.

In recent years, China's economy has become more dependent on non-tradable goods. As shown in Figure 12.29, China's foreign trade dependence has been on a downward trend since 2006. Among non-tradable goods, real estate accounts for a significant proportion. Figure 12.30 demonstrates that from 2010 to 2019, the real estate sector added 0.8% to GDP growth. After each major shock (such as the 2008 global financial crisis, the 2013 money shortage, and the 2015 stock market crash), the contribution of real estate to GDP has risen sharply. Figure 12.31 shows that the average contribution of real estate to GDP exceeds 30%.

However, the pandemic has frustrated the real estate industry, real estate agents, as a whole, have also been affected. As depicted in Figure 12.32, on the asset side, real estate development funding has become increasingly dependent on sales in the past five years, which provide about 50% of the funding for development and construction. Cash flow shortages brought about by the decline in sales will put companies under huge debt pressure. Figure 12.33 reveals that compared with

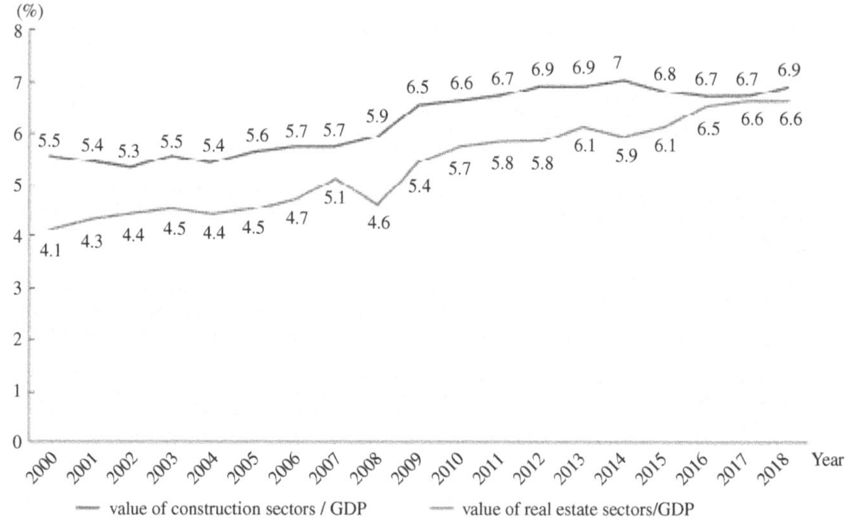

Figure 12.30: Contribution of the construction and real estate sectors to GDP.

Source: China Statistical Yearbook (2019).

Note: The figure shows the value added of the construction and real estate sectors as a share of the GDP for the year.

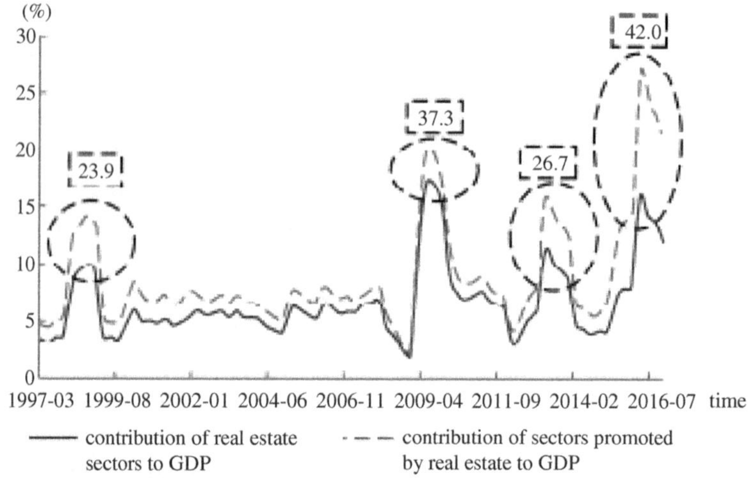

Figure 12.31: Contribution of real estate to GDP.

Source: Chinese Input-Output Association, Wind and Guotai Junan Securities.

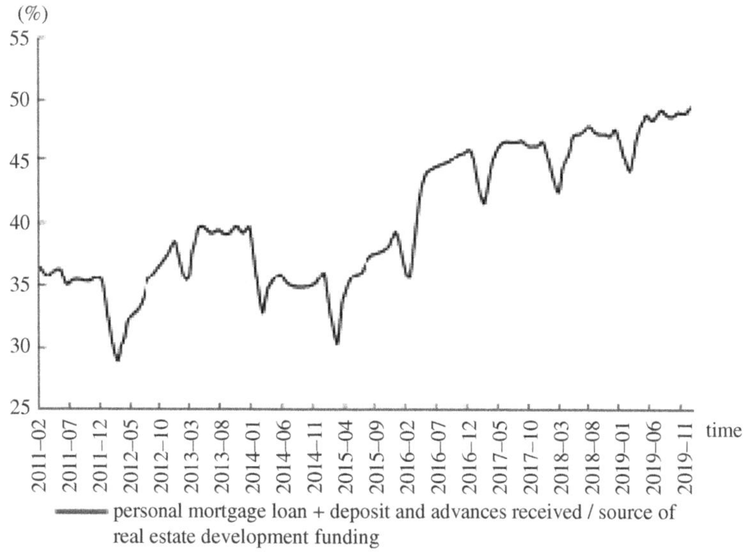

Figure 12.32: Sales as a percentage of real estate development capital.

Source: Li, Q.L. *et al.*, "Four Trends to Focus After the pandemic", *chinatimes.net.cn*, February 25, 2020.

Note: Data from Wind and Yuekai Securities.

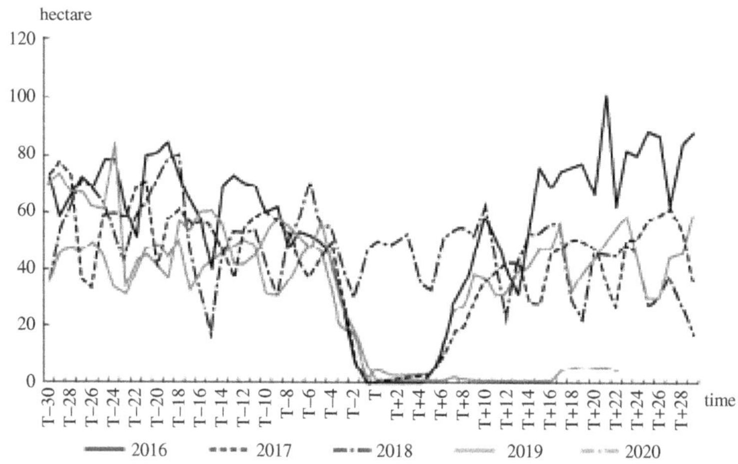

Figure 12.33: Area of commercial housing transactions in 30 large and medium-sized cities after the Spring Festival.

Source: Li, Q.L. *et al.*, "Four Trends to Focus After the pandemic", chinatimes.net.cn, February 25, 2020.

Note: Data from Wind and Yuekai Securities. T day represents the Spring Festival.

the previous four years, no potential buyers appeared after the Spring Festival in 2020, despite diverse real estate companies having discounts and promotions. With the effective control of the pandemic, sales figures within large real estate companies have picked up, but there are still 210 real estate companies going bankrupt in the first half of 2020, mainly small and medium-sized real estate companies in third-and-fourth tier cities. As the real estate market in China is characterized by a high turnover rate and high debt, many real estate companies complete a cycle from start-up to sales within one year. On the debt side, Chinese real estate companies have the highest debt in the world, including a large amount of U.S. dollar debt, and are thus exposed to exchange rate risks.

In addition to debt burden, the impact of the pandemic is conducive to the reshuffling of the real estate industry. Small and medium-sized real estate companies are numerous in China, with an average of one real estate agent per 10,000 people. After business transformations, there are still about 30,000 domestic real estate agents, while the United States in comparison only has about 500 real estate agents (data from the America Real Estate Association). The bankruptcy of some small and medium-sized real estate companies with operating difficulties during the pandemic can be helpful to the healthy development of the real estate industry.

The real estate market is an important financial market, and priority should be given to stabilizing house prices. Over the past decade, the surging house prices in China have not only been determined by accelerated urbanization and housing shortages, but also by the value of property as collateral for assets. The stability of real estate prices is of great significance to economic development. As real estate is an important collateral for the financing of SMEs and private enterprises, maintaining stable house prices will help maintain the stability of collateral value, reduce uncertainty, and increase the LTV ratio. Enterprises can raise enough funds to expand production, and increase leverage with confidence, so as to break the downward phase of the leverage cycle. Once the price of real estate, or the underlying asset fluctuates, the LTV ratio of real estate will decrease, enterprises and households will actively deleverage, and the price of real estate will fall again, leading to a vicious cycle: loss of collateral value–economic fundamentals deteriorate–uncertainty rises–real economy continues to deleverage. Thus, the entire real estate-based financial system would be in danger of collapse. Real estate is also an important part of household assets, accounting for an average of over 40% of household assets in China and 30% in the United States. If house prices fall, household assets will shrink, causing households to cut consumption.

12.4.5 Interaction between various financial markets

Increased uncertainty following shocks to the economy and growing risk aversion have triggered the phenomenon of flight to quality in the financial market, with capital flowing from the stock market to the safer and more liquid bond market. Combining Figures 12.34 and 12.35, on the first trading day of February, the yields of 10-year Treasury bonds and high-liquidity CDB bonds fell by more than 15 basis points in a single day, reflecting the concentrated release of risk aversion accumulated during the Spring Festival; credit spreads rose, with low-grade credit spreads growing more, but the overall increase was relatively moderate owing to more resilient bond market liquidity. In addition, as shown in Figure 12.36, according to the calculations of transaction intermediaries, more urban investment bonds had transaction prices higher than their

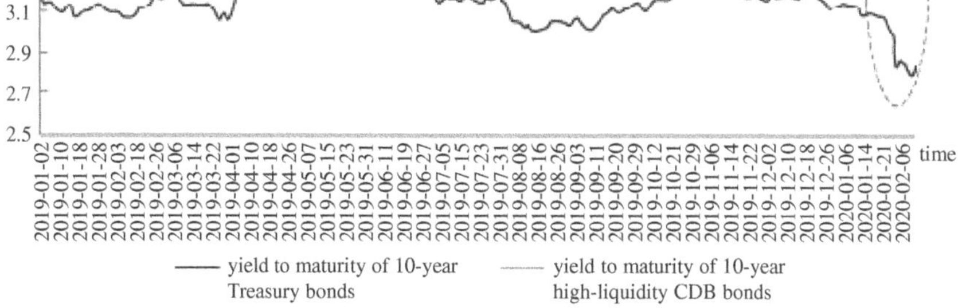

Figure 12.34: Changes in interest rate bond returns.

Source: Wind and Golden Credit Rating.

Figure 12.35: Trend of credit spreads by grade.

Source: Wind and Golden Credit Rating.

valuations, indicating that urban investment bonds are still an important choice for hedging risks. A large volume of funds flowed to the government's infrastructure department, squeezing corporate credit, limiting production capacity, and reducing the overall efficiency of social resource allocation; enterprises are burdened with operational difficulties, putting pressure on workers' wages. A lack of consumption has led to insufficient effective demand, which will have a greater negative impact on economies dominated by the service sector.

Supply chain trade is also closely related to the financial market. In the real economy, with the rapid development of the industrial chain, supply chain finance plays an increasingly important role in serving the real economy and solving the financing difficulties of SMEs. Supply chain finance provides financial services for core enterprises and their upstream and downstream partners, mostly SMEs with low information transparency and difficulties in obtaining bank credit loans. Besides, these SMEs do not have enough collateral such as Treasury bonds and real estate and cannot secure enough loans to meet their needs, but it is precisely these enterprises that need cash flow support. Supply chain finance allows inventories, prepayments, and accounts receivable of

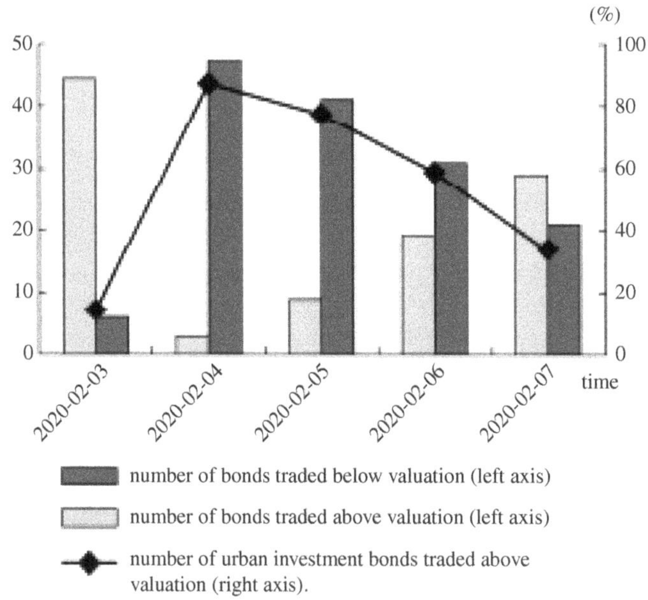

Figure 12.36: Number of urban investment bond transactions above valuation in early February.

Source: Transaction intermediaries, Wind and China Merchants Securities.
Note: The sample comprises the 50 bonds with the largest trading deviation on the day (ranked in descending order); the proportion of urban investment bonds traded above valuation = the number of urban investment bonds traded above valuation/the sample bonds with the above deviation.

upstream and downstream enterprises to be used as collateral for loans, which can activate the collateral in the industry chain and broaden the financing channels for SMEs. One of the severe setbacks of the pandemic was a break in supply chains, which caused the value of collateral in supply chain finance to fall and the amount of financing to decrease. Enterprises that have difficulty in recovering cash flow through sales were hit harder. Industrial chains whose core enterprises are central and state-owned enterprises (SOEs) will accelerate growth at the moment. Companies with government endorsement have a low default probability, and it is easier for them to secure loans and higher financing, with SOEs' accounts receivable providing collateral compared with those using private enterprise accounts.

12.5 Policy Response: Stabilize Expectations, Adopt Structural Monetary Policy, and Release Liquidity for Sectors Affected by the Pandemic

Since 2012, China's economy has entered the downward phase of the leverage cycle, with a sharp rise in various debts (especially corporate debt and household debt), a sustained decline in GDP growth, and a drop in TFP growth. The COVID-19 pandemic has brought new challenges to the Chinese economy. By taking an overview of the above arguments and the impact of the pandemic on different financial markets, we believe that the pandemic has had a far more disastrous impact on the Chinese economy than SARS in 2003.

First, the uncertainty brought about by the pandemic has had a stronger influence. China's EPU has risen since 2016; information about the pandemic is disseminated through social networks, fueling people's fear. Second, the growth rate of China's economy has slowed down in the past eight years. Compared with the economic upturn when China joined the WTO in 2003, the economy may be sinking deeper into the downward leverage cycle. Third, from the perspective of debt, the amount of incremental GDP after 2012 is less than the interest required to repay the debt, and the debt backlog of supply-side companies is increasing. Household debt is now 10 times higher than it was before the financial crisis, and effective demand is insufficient. Fourth, although stocks are not affected by the economic slowdown, stock prices are volatile. Equity pledges based on unstable collateral values can easily trigger a sell-off of companies that hurts corporate value, directly leading to a decline in the real economy. Fifth, with the formation of global supply chains, the breakage of supply chains, and shrinking demand expanding around the world, the growth of the Chinese and global economy is inhibited. Sixth, the international environment is not as favorable as it was when China first joined the WTO and the Sino-US trade frictions have already weakened economic growth in China.

After the pandemic, the low level of interest rates may cause the following problems: first, the "flight to quality" in the financial market has already reflected low interest rates in the pricing of Treasury bonds and other bonds, and there is limited room for interest rate cuts; second, in the face of uncertainty, companies are less sensitive to interest rates, which in turn reduces the effectiveness of monetary policy; third, low interest rates have led to higher corporate valuations and the expansion of production capacity by large companies, which would exacerbate their monopoly power; and fourth, the present discounted value of liabilities increases with low interest rates. Insurance companies and banks facing operational difficulties are prone to look for high-risk investments off-balance sheet to maintain operations, which will expose them to greater risks and increase the vulnerability of the financial system. Another negative effect is that the financial market becomes more fragmented, increasing systemic risks and returning to the cycle of strong uncertainty and deleveraging. Therefore, given that China is currently in the downward phase of the leverage cycle, the government should adopt more targeted and structural policies to deal with the adverse impacts of the pandemic.

12.5.1 As rising uncertainty is at the root of the downward trend in the leverage cycle, boosting confidence is the core strategy to weaken the negative impact and reverse the downward trend

Confidence is based on the value of collaterals. In conjunction with the above analysis, stabilizing the real estate market and stock market is to stabilize the value of collaterals. The central government and the central bank can use the "forward guidance" of unconventional monetary policy, which promises that low interest rates will be maintained for a longer period in order to boost market confidence, stabilize financing cost expectations, and encourage companies to increase leverage on production. At the same time, expectations management should be implemented in the real estate market (see the second point). In July 2012, President Draghi of the European Central Bank (ECB) delivered a famous speech and vowed to do "whatever it takes" to defend the euro, which has been relatively successful in stabilizing market expectations and easing the European debt crisis. With reference to the practical experience of Europe and the United States in the last financial crisis, and considering the strong influence and appeal of the Chinese government, clear forward-looking guidance is a cost-effective and efficient approach for China.

12.5.2 Strengthening expectations management in the real estate industry to reduce the risk of real estate price fluctuations

With a view to curb excessive price expectations, it is necessary to send a signal to the market to reduce speculative purchases; on the other hand, it's time to bring an end to the land finance model. Such an action would effectively weaken the motivation of local governments to raise land prices. It is suggested that local governments should obtain financing through the issuance of bonds. In this way, real estate prices are controlled and the financing costs of local companies are diminished through low-cost government debt.

12.5.3 Due to the rigidity of debt, debt accumulated by leveraging when economic fundamentals are strong imposes a heavy burden on debtors in a downward period, and both the supply (investment) and demand (consumption) sides are suppressed, so it is also critical to reduce tax burdens and appropriately write off debt

The government (especially the financial department) can consider tax cuts for regions and industries severely affected by the pandemic, especially inefficient taxes that are burdensome for enterprises. In the past, the government used to divest non-performing assets and offer debt relief (debt write-offs) to enable the economy to rid itself of the debt problem and continue development. We are currently in a downward phase of the leverage cycle and debt relief is also needed to promote growth. In the U.S. subprime mortgage crisis, the high degree of securitization and the wide dispersion of creditors made it hard to negotiate debt relief. China's unique situation allows it to more easily achieve debt relief. Similarly, tax cuts also reduce the backlog of household and corporate debt.

In an international context, China's national debt as a percentage of GDP is still relatively low. The issuance of special Treasury bonds alleviates the problem of insufficient collateral in the currency and financial markets, and reduces overall financing costs. In addition, it is also an opportunity to gradually employ other forms of currency issuance, such as special bond issuance and central bank purchases.

12.5.4 Attaching more importance to the role of finance in coping with pandemic shocks

In addition to undertaking tax cuts as indirect debt relief, fiscal spending should also be appropriately increased to improve social security. Tax cuts are conducive to reducing the burden on supply-side companies, but have little effect on household debt. Quality social security mitigates household uncertainty about future income, helps reduce resident concerns, stimulates consumption, and boosts aggregate demand.

12.5.5 In terms of monetary policy, the central bank should adopt the collateral framework of the structural monetary policy (e.g., MLF) to directly purchase corporate and local government bonds in sectors affected by the pandemic

The core of monetary policy is to provide liquidity that stems from stable collateral value. Therefore, a collateral-based monetary policy reduces the fluctuations of asset values and reverses the downward trend of the leverage cycle. If liquidity is widely released, under the circumstances of high uncertainty, the liquidity brought about by loose monetary policy will not flow to the real economy. For example, after the global financial crisis in 2008, a large volume of capital rushed into real estate enterprises rapidly driving up real estate prices. Structural monetary policy can increase the LTV ratio and leverage the ratio of assets in a targeted manner, so as to directly inject liquidity into companies hit hard by the pandemic and sectors with tight credit constraints, effectively alleviating their financing difficulties.

Structural monetary policy has proven to be effective. The Federal Reserve launched the Term Asset-Backed Securities Loan Facility (TALF) in late November 2008 to purchase up to USD 1 trillion in collateralized asset-backed securities (ABS) and loans guaranteed by the Small Business Administration. After the European debt crisis, the ECB launched the Long-Term Refinancing Operation (LTRO) in November 2011 to extend collateral eligibility to include euro-area sovereign debts and SME loans. China's Standing Lending Facility (SLF) and Medium-Term Lending Facility (MLF) have served the same purpose. Existing research indicates that structural monetary policy can reduce the financing costs for target sectors by more than 50 basis points (Fang *et al.*, 2020).

12.5.6 Similar to unconventional monetary policy, "forward guidance" is also a tool used for unconventional fiscal policy

In contrast to conventional fiscal policy that focuses on tax cuts, unconventional fiscal policy coordinates economic activities through commitments to future policy actions to promote economic development, such as tax cuts on the supply side, higher fiscal spending on infrastructure construction, and tax increases on the demand side that generate inflation expectations to stimulate current consumption. This policy has proven to be effective internationally. For example, in November 2005, Germany announced an increase in consumption tax that would start in 2007, and the willingness to buy durable goods rose by 34% after the announcement.

Conventional fiscal policy includes tax suspension, deferral of social charges payments, loan guarantees, and subsidies for unemployed and temporary workers in Eurozone countries. The United States government introduced a strong fiscal measure on March 17th that would push for a $1.2 trillion stimulus package, possibly to include $1,000 direct payments to individual Americans within two weeks. After the policy was unveiled, U.S. stocks rebounded sharply. On March 17th, the three major stock indexes rose by more than 5%, which was in stark contrast with the circuit breaker the day before, reflecting the market's confidence in fiscal policy. In China, various regions have issued consumer vouchers to stimulate demand.

12.5.7 Regarding the international market, as many enterprises issue offshore U.S. dollar debt, financial operations such as foreign exchange forwards should be promoted to resolve exchange rate risks and ease the liquidity constraints in these sectors

In terms of the international market, as many companies (including many real estate and financial companies) issue offshore U.S. dollar debt, the liability side is exposed to the risk of exchange rate fluctuations. Thus, appropriate policy support should be in place to promote foreign exchange and ease liquidity constraints of these sectors.

https://doi.org/10.1142/9789811252921_0013

Chapter 13

Waging Financial War on the Pandemic and Countercyclical Monetary Policy Responses

Zhang Zongxin

School of Economics, Fudan University, Shanghai, China

The global COVID-19 pandemic has been a major shock to the world economic and financial system, and Chinese economic and financial markets are currently facing severe challenges. The 2003 SARS pandemic, whose impact on the financial market was mainly in the stock market, was characterized by local, phased, and manageable risks. However, the impact of the current pandemic on the financial system is significantly more complicated because of the intertwining of the exchange rate market, stock market, credit market, and the real economy. The financial system will become more fragile if another wave of the pandemic occurs.

In response to the heavy blow of the pandemic, the People's Bank of China (PBOC) and other relevant departments acted immediately to protect and support the financial market, striving to minimize the disruption of COVID-19 pandemic on the economy and finance and prevent negative impacts spreading further. On February 1st, the PBOC, the China Banking and Insurance Regulatory Commission, Ministry of Finance, China Securities Regulatory Commission, and State Administration of Foreign Exchange jointly issued the "Notice on Further Strengthening Financial Support for the Prevention and Control of the Novel Coronavirus

Pneumonia" (the "30 Financial Measures") to strengthen financial support for the prevention and control of the disease. Financial policy portfolios such as the "Thirty Financial Measures" have initially achieved positive results. On February 3 after a short period of large fluctuations, the stock market and exchange rate stabilized quickly, not only reflecting the strong resilience of China's financial market, but also indicating the rapid restoration of investor confidence.

Meanwhile, regulators have also eased restrictions on corporate financing and issued a series of regulations to extend support for enterprises in areas hard hit by the pandemic. Credit regulators have assisted enterprises by providing special funds, preferential interest rate loans, and loan renewal, while bond regulators have helped enterprises gain access to refunding, liquidity support, rollover, and deferred repayment of principal and interest. These timely measures have effectively protected enterprises from credit risk contagion, and have made a significant contribution to the prevention of systemic risks.

China's central bank and other financial institutions responded rapidly to the pandemic, systematically implementing countercyclical monetary policy and prompting a reduction in the cost of funds while maintaining accommodative liquidity. The central bank injected RMB 1.2 trillion worth of liquidity into the financial system via reverse repo operations, and lowered interest rates by 10 basis points on February 3. After that, the volume of funds provided by reverse repos began to decline and from February 4 to February 17, a total of RMB 1.6 trillion was injected. On February 29, no more reverse repo activities were carried out, but the financing period was extended with RMB 200 billion being injected through one-year MLF loans. At the same time, the central bank cut the one-year MLF rate by 10 basis points, leading the financial market interest rates and corporate financing costs to fall. The yields on one-year Treasury bonds and 10-year Treasury bonds declined by 25 and 40 basis points, respectively, while LPR dropped 10 basis points. The monetary policy transmission mechanism was relatively smooth and the cost of funds decreased. At the end of February, the impact of the pandemic began to ease, resumption of work and production gradually proceeded, and the financial system was stabilized. China achieved good results in the first stage to prevent the pandemic.

Unlike the stable situation in China, the COVID-19 pandemic began to spread on a global scale at the end of February, triggering strong

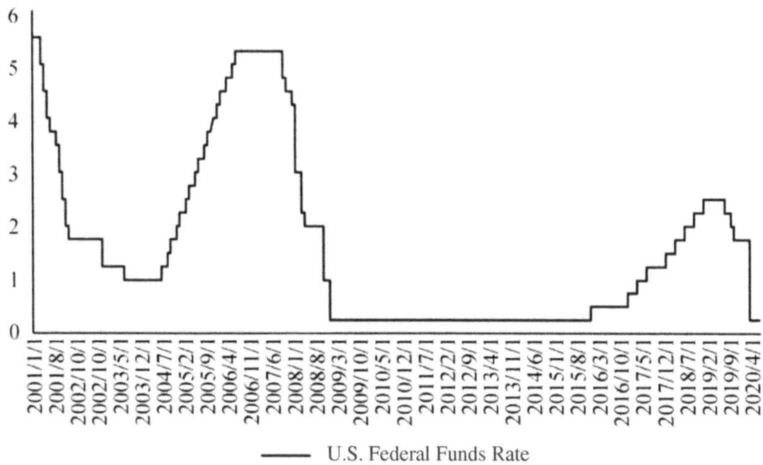

Figure 13.1: Trend of the U.S. federal funds rate from January 2001 to June 2020.

Source: Bloomberg.

negative emotions among global investors with risk assets falling sharply. In response to the impact of the pandemic on the U.S. economy, the Federal Reserve began to adopt monetary policies to stabilize the market. In March, it decided to lower the target range for the federal funds rate by 150 basis points to 0–0.25%. Figure 13.1 shows the trend of the U.S. federal funds rate from January 2001 to June 2020.

13.1 Impact of the COVID-19 Pandemic on China's Financial System

The widespread impact of the COVID-19 pandemic has brought systemic risks to the financial system. Due to the delay in work resumption and other factors, the fundamentals of the real economy have been affected, the operations of micro-economic entities have been disrupted, and securities issued by companies have not been immune to the impact of the pandemic; moreover, a rapid contagion of investor sentiment occurred, causing turbulence and amplifying risks within the stock market, bond market, commodity market, exchange rate market, and the real economy.

13.1.1 Impact of the pandemic on the industrial economy: PMI index hitting a record low

The pandemic has taken a toll on China's industrial economy, which can be reflected in the PMI index. In January, the manufacturing PMI index was 50.0, a decrease of 0.2 from the previous month, and the non-manufacturing business activity index was 54.1, an increase of 0.6 from the prior month, indicating that the industrial economy was running smoothly in January and not affected by the pandemic outbreak. The data in February demonstrates that the industrial economy experienced a sharp decline battered by the pandemic. In February, the manufacturing PMI was 35.7, down 14.3 from the previous month, and the non-manufacturing business activity index was 29.6, a sharp drop of 24.5 from the previous month. Both indexes dropped to historic all-time lows, with the manufacturing PMI breaking the previous record low of 38.8 in November 2008 during the global financial crisis. The impact of the pandemic has been immense, far exceeding that of the global financial crisis, and the integrated effects of pandemic shock and economic lockdown during the Spring Festival holiday have posed greater risks to enterprises (see Figure 13.2).

13.1.2 Impact of the pandemic on the financial market system

While the financial market reflects the real economy being hit hard by the pandemic, it also reflects a rapid diffusion of relatively pessimistic investor sentiment, which will inevitably have a significant negative impact on global financial markets, as Nobel Prize winning economist Robert J. Shiller warned, "the direct effects on the global economy are initially limited. But the virus has suddenly raised awareness of the far greater risks that will weigh on global financial markets."[1]

For China's financial markets, the pandemic has wreaked havoc on capital markets, but the A-share market has remained strong in spite of global financial market volatility. During the pandemic, the A-share

[1] "The Novel Coronavirus Pandemic: Nobel Prize Winner Robert Shiller Warns of Downward Spiral Risks", quoted in Reference News on March 3, 2020. The original text was published in the German newspaper Handelsblatt on February 28.

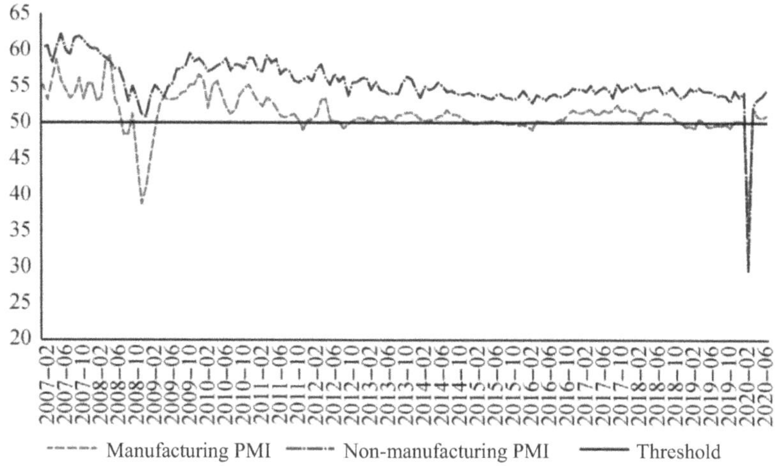

Figure 13.2: China's PMI index from January 2007 to June 2020.

Source: RoyalFlush.

market in February showed great resilience despite violent fluctuations. The Shanghai Composite Index fell by 3.23%, while the Shenzhen Composite Index and the ChiNext Index rose by 2.80% and 7.46%, respectively, continuing the upward trend of tech stocks relative to other stocks in January impacted by exogenous shock. The changes in the stock market can be divided into three stages. The first stage in early February, when the situation was more severe, market pessimism continued to rise during the Spring Festival holiday, and a sharp drop in stock prices was recorded on the first day the market opened on February 3. The next phase saw valuation depression in the stock market, and after the plunge was highlighted by foreign institutional investors pumping funds into the stock market. Coupled with the improvement in the pandemic situation, the government introduced relevant industrial policies to support micro-enterprises. Market expectations gradually shifted toward economic recovery and the stock market resumed its upward progression, attracting funds from investors which produced a rapid rebound to higher than pre-holiday levels. Finally, the global spread of the pandemic has witnessed the tumbling of overseas risk assets led by U.S. stocks, causing contagion of investor sentiment and a pullback in domestic stocks.

The impact of the pandemic on China's bond market has seen an obvious seesaw effect in the stock market, with an easing of monetary policy and overall good performance of the bond market. Specifically, the bond market rose significantly in February, with a major increase in interest rate bonds supplemented by the rise in credit bonds. The 10-year Treasury bond yield fell by 26 basis points, and the ChinaBond Total Return Index rose by 1.23%. The ChinaBond China 1–30 Year Sovereign and Quasi-sovereign Bond Index grew by 1.41%, and the ChinaBond Credit Bond Total Return Index increased by 0.98%. Changes in the bond market can also be divided into three stages. Unlike the stock market, bonds are more sensitive to monetary policy. Therefore, more focus needs to be given to changes in monetary policy. First, the first day the bond market opened after the Spring Festival, the central bank injected RMB 1.2 trillion into the markets through reverse repo operations, including RMB 900 billion of 7-day reverse repos at an interest rate of 2.40% and RMB 300 billion of 14-day reverse repos with rate of 2.55%. Both were 10 basis points lower than the previous open market operations. The rise in liquidity and the fall in the cost of funds successfully stimulated the bond market. Second, the fall in interest rates and the release of liquidity were less than expected, and the rising prices of pork and petrochemical products led to inflationary expectations. In order to respond to the concerns of bond investors, the bond market began to adjust. Finally, at the end of February, due to rising concerns about the pandemic overseas, the central bank continued to adopt loose monetary policies, allowing the bond market to re-enter the upward channel.

In terms of commodities, an overall sharp decline was observed as a result of the pandemic as the bulk commodity market was generally affected by the economic environment and the international market. In February, the indicator of the domestic commodity market, the Nanhua Commodity Index, fell by 7.62%; the precious metals market fulfilling a hedging function exhibited a completely different trend with gold rising by 5.49%. Other commodities experienced large declines to varying degrees, of which crude oil was the most prominent with prices dropping into negative territory in April for the first time in history. Except for gold, the trend of other commodities was similar to that of the stock market, but slightly weaker. Affected by the pandemic, investors were more pessimistic about the short-term economy, with corresponding product demand decreasing significantly in early February. As the domestic pandemic was controlled, and supportive policies were introduced by the government, the commodity market bottomed out. However, later commodities had another downturn because resumption of work and production were not satisfactory, transportation and logistics were impeded, sales of finished products were blocked, and inventories increased. In contrast, the trend of gold is similar to that of bonds and the opposite of other commodities, which is mainly based on hedging strategies.

13.1.3 Impact of the pandemic on the foreign exchange market: Maintaining the stability of the RMB exchange rate

In the context of the gradual opening of the domestic capital market, the flow of funds is smoother and more convenient. Changes in the exchange rate because of the impact of the pandemic largely reflect the flow of international funds and risk aversion. The U.S. Dollar Index rose from 97.68 at the end of January to 98.13 at the end of February, an overall increase of 0.46%. This trend was mainly divided into two stages: in the rising stage, the U.S. dollar mainly demonstrated its safe-haven characteristics, with the massive influx of funds causing the dollar to rise amid the spread of the pandemic; in the falling stage, the outbreak of the pandemic in the United States triggered investors' concerns about the fundamentals of the economy. At the same time, the prospect of the Federal Reserve cutting interest rates to hedge against an economic downturn provoked a stampede out of the dollar and prompted investors to flee to safer assets, which resulted in a depreciation of the U.S. dollar, as shown in Figure 13.3(a).

Pummeled by the pandemic, the RMB exchange rate in February fluctuated periodically with changes in global risk sentiment, ranging from 6.95 to 7.05 against the U.S. dollar. However, with the support of fundamentals, the overall fluctuation was relatively small, and no significant depreciation was observed. In March, amid the global surge of COVID-19 cases, the Federal Reserve implemented a loose monetary policy. In addition, pandemic prevention and control progressed steadily in China, resumption of work and production accelerated in the real economy, and market confidence in the fundamentals of the Chinese economy increased. In this context, the RMB exchange rate saw a significant appreciation as shown in Figure 13.3(b).

(a) US Dollar Index

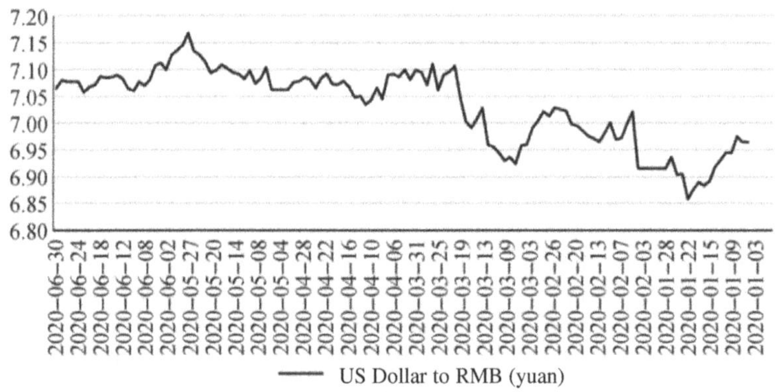

(b) RMB Exchange Rate

Figure 13.3: U.S. dollar index and RMB exchange rate from January 2020 to June 2020.
Source: RoyalFlush.

13.2 Response and Effect of Monetary and Financial Policies

In the post-pandemic era, it is necessary to advance the countercyclical monetary and financial policy packages. For example, "financial market stability before monetary policy easing" and "aggregate instruments before price instruments". By giving full play to the structural function of targeted financial services and innovating capital market financing tools, the policy package is intended to effectively resume regular economic and financial operations.

13.2.1 Establishing a financial defense mechanism and a financial stability mechanism to strictly defend the bottom line of "no systemic financial risks"

In response to the potential impact of the pandemic on the financial system, the central bank and other departments promptly established a financial defense mechanism and a financial stability mechanism to prevent domino effects and systemic risks in the financial system. Due to the uncertainty of the pandemic, the central bank applied a dynamic optimization of countercyclical monetary and financial policy packages to hedge against the negative impact of the pandemic. In addition, jointly with various departments it introduced financial prevention policies and basically followed the principle of "financial market stability before monetary policy easing" and "aggregate instruments before price instruments". The implementation of the financial defense and stability mechanism is reflected in the following three aspects: first, the central bank and five other departments promulgated the "Thirty Financial Measures" to strengthen financial support for the prevention and control of the pandemic, sending strong policy signals to stabilize the market and investor confidence; second, increasing the supply of liquidity in the financial system through monetary easing; third, providing credit support for enterprises affected by the pandemic by way of reducing the cost of funds and improving credit availability; in addition, promoting direct financing in the capital market and financing support for pandemic-stricken enterprises through the issuance of "pandemic prevention and control bonds" and the establishment of a "green channel" that would fast-track bond sales.

13.2.2 Implementing countercyclical monetary policy to boost liquidity in the financial system

In view of the damage inflicted by the pandemic on the real economy, as well as the uncertainty and a possible recurrence of the pandemic, the central bank dynamically assessed the future possible influence of the pandemic on the overall economy based on the negative shock seen in January 2020. In addition to introducing policies to promote corporate financing, it also conducted countercyclical monetary policy adjustments and maintained reasonable and sufficient liquidity to offset the ravages

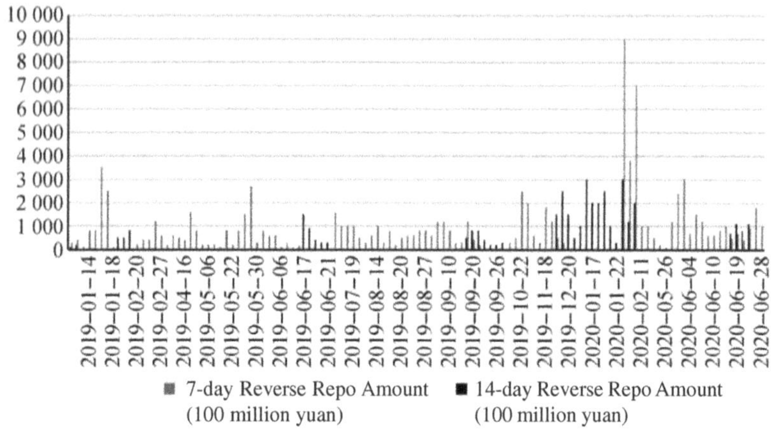

Figure 13.4: Liquidity support from January 2019 to June 2020.

Source: RoyalFlush.

of the pandemic. The central bank implemented a flexible and accommodative monetary policy in an orderly and steady manner, using liquidity tools in accordance with the policy orientation of "aggregate instruments before price instruments" to inject liquidity in the financial system through reverse repo and open market operations. By coordinating the "degree" and "flexibility" of the easing of monetary policy, the central bank in a timely manner soaked up liquidity, maintained sufficient liquidity, and avoided "overflow" and real estate price rebound. In February, the central bank issued the "Report on the Implementation of China's Monetary Policy in the Fourth Quarter of 2019", which clearly stated that China would step up countercyclical adjustments and maintain reasonable liquidity in the financial system to provide sufficient liquidity support for the real economy and the financial market system (see Figure 13.4).

13.2.3 Leveraging loan prime rate (LPR) reform and implementing market-based "interest rate cuts"

After injecting liquidity into the market and lowering financial market interest rates, the central bank further promoted the LPR reform, continued to unleash the potential of financial institutions to reduce loan interest

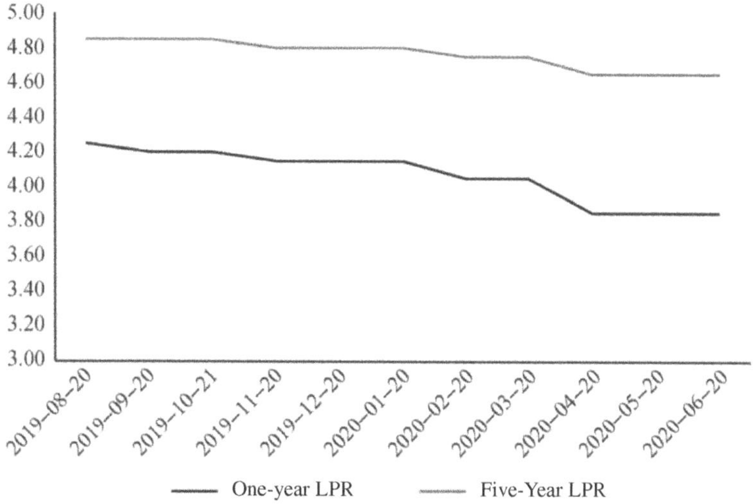

Figure 13.5: China's LPR interest rate trend from August 2019 to June 2020.
Source: RoyalFlush.

rates, facilitated a significant drop in the real interest rate of loans, and ensured steady progress in addressing financing difficulties and expensive financing for small and micro enterprises. In the "Report on the Implementation of China's Monetary Policy in the Fourth Quarter of 2019", the central bank displayed the intention of marginal easing of monetary policy in the future. On the premise of stabilizing investor expectations, on February 20, the one-year LPR was lowered by 10 basis points to 4.05%, and the five-year LPR was cut by 5 basis points to 4.75%, with the pricing benchmark for existing floating rate loans being converted into LPR from March 1. The high efficiency of the central bank demonstrates its determination to mitigate the financial pressure on the real economy. The decline in LPR will help reduce the cost of debt financing such as credits and bonds, and improve corporate financial stability (see Figure 13.5).

13.2.4 Encouraging commercial banks to provide credit to the real economy

The pandemic will cause a massive and rapid shock on commercial bank credit. If no effective measures are taken for policy intervention, commercial bank credit is expected to fall "off a cliff". The credit increase of commercial banks in the first quarter of each year accounts for approximately 35% of the total new credit increase for the year; bank credit from February to March must remain at a relatively reasonable level in order to ensure stable economic growth throughout the year. In an attempt to ensure the stability of credit volume, the China Banking and Insurance Regulatory Commission, the central bank, and other departments promptly took measures to launch the "Notice on Strengthening Financial Services in the Banking and Insurance Industry and Cooperating with the Effective Prevention and Control of the COVID-19 Outbreak" and the "Thirty Financial Measures", to increase credit support for fields related to pandemic prevention and control. For industries affected considerably by the pandemic as well as those enterprises with development prospects but experiencing temporary difficulties, loans shall not be blindly limited, rescinded, or reduced, and may be extended or renewed. At the same time, it is necessary to prevent the collapse of enterprises by appropriately lowering loan interest rates and increasing credit loans and medium- and long-term loans. Moreover, the central bank played a proactive role with policy-based financial institutions and issued the "Notice on Releasing Special Refinancing Loans to Support Matters Related to the Prevention and Control of COVID-19 Outbreak". Deputy Governor of the PBOC at the press conference held by the *Joint Prevention and Control Mechanism of the State Council on Responding to the Pandemic* stated that large special refinancing funds should be allocated first to increase loanable funds for commercial banks, thereby improving corporate financing; in addition, according to the list drafted by the government, low-cost loan interest rates should be implemented for enterprises contributing to pandemic prevention and control, in order to help them reduce corporate financing costs and cash-flow pressure.

13.2.5 Focusing on the effective combination of fiscal and financial policies

In dealing with the pandemic, the Ministry of Finance has actively exerted the economic stabilization effect of the countercyclical fiscal policy from two perspectives: first, the combination of fiscal policy and monetary policy has raised the tolerance level of the central government deficit, and increased interest subsidies for bank credit; second, on the basis of credit risk assessment of local debt, local governments have stepped up to make further tax and fee cuts and increase the scale of financing guarantees. Through a combination of fiscal and monetary policies and with the introduction of the "Notice on Supporting Financial Strengthening Services and Prevention and Control of COVID-19 Pandemic" and other supporting policies, new loans will be granted to key enterprises that guarantee supplies for pandemic prevention and control, and special refinancing from the PBOC helps provide preferential interest rate credit with interest subsidies at 50% of the PBOC's refinancing rate. Financial institutions are encouraged to provide credit loan support to key enterprises and small and micro enterprises hit hard by the pandemic, and improve the efficiency of all levels of governmental financing guarantee and re-guarantee institutions. For small and micro enterprises unable to repay, local government financing guarantee institutions shall perform their compensation obligations in a timely manner, appropriately extend the time limit for recovery depending on the impact of the pandemic, and write off compensation losses in accordance with regulations. Various methods, such as increasing targeted interest subsidies, loan guarantees by governments at all levels, and reduced taxes and fees have been adopted to efficiently coordinate monetary policies to support small and medium-sized enterprises.

13.2.6 Taking advantage of targeted financial policies to offer "targeted blood transfusion" and "targeted irrigation" to specific regions and industries

As the impact of the pandemic happens at regional and local levels, structural damage to the economy induced by the pandemic needs to be resolved structurally. At the same time, considering the difficulties of maintaining price stability and managing inflation expectations, the central bank did not inject liquidity into the real economy on a large scale despite the uncertainty brought on by the pandemic. Instead, it mainly took advantage of "targeted blood transfusion" and "targeted irrigation" to target finance to help severely affected areas such as Hubei, specific service industries, small and micro enterprises, and private enterprises.

The central bank also made comprehensive use of structural monetary and financial policy tools, such as targeted RRR cuts and special loans to provide targeted financial support. In the meantime, it gave full play to the interest sharing mechanism between enterprises and banks to restore normal production and maintain a stable and sound economic operation. Currently, these policies have achieved remarkable results on the premise of avoiding "overflow". According to the "Thirty Financial Measures" and the "Notice on Releasing Special Refinancing Loans to Support Matters Related to the Prevention and Control of the COVID-19 Outbreak", credit policies have been tilted toward severely affected areas, specific service sectors, small and micro enterprises, and private enterprises to achieve the outcome of a "structural" monetary policy conditional on controlling the aggregate liquidity.

13.2.7 Emphasis on capital markets to repair damage to the economy and making timely adjustments to capital market policies to support the real economy

13.2.7.1 *Recognizing the importance of the self-repair function and the promotion of resilience in capital markets, within the economic system*

Influenced by the negative exogenous shock of the pandemic, capital market-based economies featured faster economic recovery and stronger resilience compared with bank-based economies, which was beneficial to the endogenous stability of the macro economy. Capital markets use market-based instruments to redeploy resources and direct the flow of resources to areas that facilitate economic development, helping to maximize allocative efficiency, enhance economic resilience, and speed up economic recovery. Numerous academic studies have proven the superiority of capital markets in the process of economic recovery. International Monetary Fund economists Allard and Blavy (2011) examined countries with different financial systems in the Organization for Economic Cooperation and Development and found that market-based economies exhibit broader economic flexibility and recover faster than bank-based economies in the case of exogenous shocks, indicating the consistency of economic flexibility and capital market resilience.

In coping with the impact of the pandemic, China's financial policy-making authorities have introduced many financial defense policies concerning credit, bond, and stock markets to promote corporate financing and give full play to the interaction between the bank credit sector and capital markets. These policies have not only increased the protection of micro-entities in the market, but also provided more financing options for enterprises, maximizing economic flexibility and resilience.

13.2.7.2 *Innovating capital market financing tools, establishing a "green channel" for bonds, issuing "pandemic prevention and control bonds", and providing efficient financing support for the real economy*

Amid the outbreak of the pandemic, regulatory authorities unveiled policies such as the "Notice on Further Improving the Debt Financing Instrument Market to Serve the Pandemic Prevention and Control" and the "Notice on Properly Handling Enterprise Bonds during Pandemic Prevention and Control" to provide multi-channel support for the reasonable and direct financing needs of the corporate sector or local governments in pandemic-stricken areas through the "green channel" of the capital market. In response to the financing needs of different entities in the real economy, enterprises or local governments that meet the requirements are encouraged to issue "special credit bonds" and "targeted professional bonds", and small and micro enterprises are encouraged to issue "private placement bonds". For financing entities with lower credit ratings but controllable risks, credit guarantee should be provided by credit enhancement agencies. In particular, the bond market should provide support for enterprises from multiple dimensions such as issuing "pandemic prevention and control bonds" and preventing bond defaults. Meanwhile, the regulatory authorities should also streamline the registration and issuance process, including speeding up the approval process and extending the validity period of the approval document. In addition, methods such as allowing maturing bonds to refund, rollover, and defer repayment of principal and interest have alleviated the liquidity difficulties of relevant enterprises, prevented default risks, and diminished market impact.

13.2.7.3 *Relaxing regulatory policies, loosening refinancing of listed companies, and further evaluating the transition period for new asset management regulations*

Unlike debt financing, equity financing provides companies with long-term and cost-free funds. Pairing equity financing policies with credit and bond financing policies improves policy consistency and flexibility to help companies counter the impact of the pandemic with various sources of funding. On February 14, the China Securities Regulatory Commission launched the "Decision on Amending the Measures for the Administration of Securities Issuance by Listed Companies", "Decision on Amending the Interim Measures for the Administration of Securities Issuance by Companies Listed on ChiNext", and "Decision on Amending the Implementation Rules for the Non-Public Offering of Stocks by Listed Companies". The new refinancing regulations relaxed restrictions on the directional issuance of shares by companies listed on the Main Board and the ChiNext, including the restrictions on the subscription period, the number of targeted subscribers, the maximum rate of discount, and the pricing benchmark date. It is believed that these new regulations have played an important role in deepening the structural reform of financial supply, improving the market-based restraint mechanism for refinancing, enhancing the ability of the capital market to serve the real economy, and supporting listed companies to fight the pandemic, increase capital, and resume production.

In the context of the pandemic, Deputy Governor of the PBOC, at a press conference held by the Joint Prevention and Control Mechanism of the State Council said that technical assessment of the new asset management regulations was underway, and suggested the possibility of extending the transition period if financial institutions were having difficulty transforming their businesses to comply with the regulations. It is essential to maintain a moderately loose regulatory policy to avoid systemic risks and prevent the spread of the pandemic to the financial system. On the one hand, against a background of economic downturn, companies may struggle to restore their profitability. In addition, the new asset management regulations and other deleveraging policies have made corporate financing more difficult and capital flow tighter. With credit default risks accumulating, strict regulatory policies are likely to lead to a break in corporate cash flow, which is not conducive to preventing risk contagion. On the other hand, banks have encountered many difficulties in the disposal of stock assets and it is not practical to strictly implement the scheduled transition period. The impact of forced disposal may overlap with that of the pandemic, resulting in increased risks.

13.2.7.4 *Promoting the exchange rate stabilization mechanism to become the basic policy orientation for maintaining the stability of the RMB exchange rate*

With a view to preventing and mitigating the negative impact of the pandemic, it is necessary to pay attention to foreign exchange management and market stability. Since the outbreak of the pandemic, the State Administration of Foreign Exchange has put forward the "Notice on Establishing Green Channels of Foreign Exchange Policies to Support the Prevention and Control of the Coronavirus Pandemic" to assist in the fight against the pandemic by facilitating the import of pandemic prevention materials and meet the demand for foreign exchange. It also simplified the procedures needed for handling foreign exchange payments for imported pandemic prevention materials and foreign exchange receipts and settlement of donations, relaxed prior documentation requirements for the settlement and payment of capital accounts related to pandemic prevention and control, promoted cross-border financing, satisfied individual needs to conduct normal foreign exchange transactions, and provided effective help to combat the pandemic.

13.3 Conclusion

The COVID-19 pandemic has dealt a heavy blow to China's industrial economy. The delay in resuming work and production has prevented most enterprises from generating profits, while rigid expenditures such as wages and interest payments have caused cash flow difficulties, especially for small and micro service enterprises with light assets and capital. Being less able to withstand adverse exogenous shocks, these enterprises suffered the largest financial losses in the unfavorable environment. As a barometer of the economy, the financial market rapidly reflects damages to the economy. Coupled with negative investor sentiment, crossover and contagion effects spread among various markets, amplifying the fundamental risks.

In an effort to hedge against the negative impact of the pandemic, the central bank and five other departments jointly issued the "Thirty Financial Measures", which took the lead in setting a more flexible tone in monetary and financial policies. Under the premise of ensuring sufficient aggregate liquidity, the countercyclical monetary policy lowered interest rates, leading to a downward adjustment of financial market interest rates and corporate financing costs to reduce the burden on enterprises. Against this backdrop, in coordination with the central bank's monetary policy, other regulatory authorities also introduced various supporting policies for credit, bond, and stock markets by providing loan renewal, liquidity support, refunding, and preferential interest rates to effectively alleviate the difficulties of enterprises. At the same time, the strong policy support of various regulatory authorities enabled the financial market to recover and rebound quickly from the short-term shock experienced by the market after opening post the Spring Festival, demonstrating the strong flexibility and resilience of the financial market. By the end of February, the impact of the pandemic weakened, and the "financial war" against the coronavirus was largely won.

Considering the rapid spread and the uncertainty of the pandemic overseas, it is necessary to be vigilant against a second wave of shocks and the disruption of work resumption by imported coronavirus cases, and also to guard against market volatility due to contagion of investor sentiment. The robustness of monetary policy is of critical importance, and timely and flexible monetary and financial policies have become the basic orientation and first choice to use to hedge against the negative impact of the pandemic. In the short term, the most important thing is to stabilize expectations, especially by using monetary policy to make countercyclical adjustments to boost market confidence, prevent abnormal fluctuations in the financial market, and fend off systemic financial risks. In the long run, it is necessary to analyze and manage debt risks. Given that banks hold more claims on small and micro enterprises, non-performing loans in the banking industry may become a greater uncertainty factor affecting economic recovery. Due to the impact of the pandemic, it is expected that the non-performing loan ratio of the banking sector will rise in the short term, but the increase will be limited and banks have shown strong ability to withstand risks. At present, the scale of non-performing loans in the banking industry is nearly RMB 3 trillion, but loan loss provisions amount to around RMB 6 trillion, twice the size of non-performing loans; and the capital of the banking industry is as high as RMB 23 trillion, which is sufficient to resist risks. Furthermore, it is also necessary for the regulatory authorities to take the objective impact of the pandemic into account, appropriately improve regulatory tolerance, and provide enough policy space to deal with the possible "black swan" event of the pandemic.

In the event of a possible recurrence of a pandemic and other exogenous shocks, it is essential to prevent systemic risks through handling overseas uncertainty and building a financial risk prevention system. On the one hand, as the global spread of the pandemic may trigger a global economic recession, China's monetary and financial policies should reserve enough space for the uncertainty of the pandemic. With the effects of the current crisis remaining largely uncertain, the economic and financial system are poised to suffer massive hits. Therefore, it is imperative to continuously evaluate the countercyclical monetary and financial policy packages, and constantly plan for the optimization of policy portfolios so as to maintain stable economic and financial operations, ward off the instability of the pandemic and prevent the next possible large-scale influence on the economy and finance. On the other hand, a financial risk prevention system should be constructed to guarantee the safety of the financial system. The negative impact of the pandemic on the macro economy in 2020 (especially in the first and second quarters) is relatively enormous. However, it is still hard to evaluate the impact on the real economy and financial markets. In this regard, it is necessary to establish a financial stability mechanism to prevent potential risks from turning into systemic financial risks, to adopt a series of combined measures to block the "risk contagion chain", to avert the spillover risks from fluctuations in the international financial market to the domestic financial market, and to take strict precautions against the contagion chain of "COVID-19 pandemic → economic pandemic → financial risks" amid different financial markets.

https://doi.org/10.1142/9789811252921_0014

Chapter 14

The Impact of COVID-19 Pandemic on Insurance Markets and Policy Responses

Xu Xian

School of Economics, Fudan University, Shanghai, China

China's insurance industry has grown rapidly; the scale of premiums increased from RMB 159.6 billion in 2000 to RMB 38 trillion in 2018, with a compound annual growth rate of 19.26%. China's insurance market has become the world's second largest insurance market, thus forming an important part of the domestic financial landscape. At the same time, its development has had a huge influence on the overall scale of the global insurance industry. China's current insurance assets have exceeded RMB 20 trillion yuan, and the long-term nature of insurance funds makes insurance assets an important part of China's capital market. In 2019, China's premium income accounted for 4.31% of total GDP, and the growth rate of premiums reached 12.17%, which was much higher than the 6.1% growth rate of GDP.[1]

The insurance industry has become an important driving force for China's economic development providing a large number of jobs. As of 2018, the number of insurance agents in China had jumped to 7.64 million, accounting for 1.76% of the urban employed population. This huge number of jobs provided by the insurance industry is of great significance to alleviating employment pressure. At the same time, the essence of the

[1] Data from the National Bureau of Statistics.

insurance industry relates to business risk with this industry providing risk protection for the entire society. The insurance payments of China's insurance industry in 2018 amounted to RMB 122.9787 billion, providing risk protection for the whole society worth RMB 689,704 trillion.[2]

In summary, the stable development of the insurance industry is related to the development of the national economy, the stability of the capital market, the expansion of employment, and social progress. According to mainstream academic opinion, the function of insurance covers three areas: compensation for losses, financing, and social management (Skipper and Kwon, 2008; Mayers *et al.*, 2012; Rejda and McNamara, 2019). The economy is growing in the modern world, and insurance is generally considered to play a role in improving risk distribution, protecting existing wealth, accumulating capital, promoting financing, providing management advice, and alleviating fiscal pressure. As a key financial industry in China, the insurance industry also plays these important roles. The COVID-19 pandemic has affected the development of all walks of life. A serious question is: what is the impact of the COVID-19 pandemic on the insurance industry and will this impact affect overall economic and social development? Assessing the impact will help the insurance industry actively respond. Also, it helps to assess the impact of the COVID-19 pandemic on the entire society and the national economy from the perspective of a sub-industry.

The COVID-19 pandemic, one of the most urgent public health events, has had a great impact on social security and economic development. The first industry to bear the brunt has been the transportation industry. Between January and February 2020, the income from urban rail transit dropped sharply, and transportation pressure increased in the later stage of the pandemic (Feng Xujie, 2020). The banking, catering, tourism, and other service industries have all suffered relatively large negative impacts in the short term (Wang Guojin, 2020). There have been few articles focusing on the impact of the COVID-19 pandemic on the insurance industry. However, the 2003 SARS pandemic was a public health emergency with some similarities to the COVID-19 pandemic, and the research conducted at that time still has important findings of significance to present circumstances. Zheng Wei and Sun Qixiang (2003) made a

[2]The Compensation Expenditure of China's Insurance Industry in 2018 amounts to 12 Trillion Yuan, *China News Network*, March 14, 2019: https://baijiahao.baidu.com/s?id=1627989378901709978&wfr=spider&for=pc.

systematic analysis of the behavior of insurance companies during the SARS period proposing at that time that the insurance industry should learn from it to achieve a balance between finance, production, and life. Zhang Xiangxian *et al.* (2003) believed that the SARS pandemic brought both positive and negative impacts to the insurance industry. The positive impacts included the accelerated development of health insurance, the development of new types of insurance, and the improvement of the image of the insurance industry; the negative impacts included the decline in new life insurance business, a hindrance on the development of the marketing team, and the impact on related businesses. The research of Zhang Xiangxian *et al.* (2003) provided a good analytical framework and comparative perspective for analyzing the impact of major public health emergencies on the insurance industry. However, due to the rapid development of China's insurance industry in recent years, there are also significant differences in the size of the insurance market and the ability to resist risks with differences in the impact of the 2003 SARS pandemic and COVID-19 pandemic on the insurance industry. This chapter will focus on analyzing the long-term and short-term impact of the COVID-19 pandemic on the insurance market, consider how the insurance industry has responded, and give suggestions for future development. This will help the insurance industry turn dangers into opportunities to better partner China's social progress and economic development.

14.1 Analysis of the Impact

14.1.1 The short-term impact

14.1.1.1 *Income effects*

The short-term impact of life insurance is reflected in the increase in demand for health and life insurance, and the decline in demand for short-term accident insurance. The spread of COVID-19 has stimulated residents' awareness of their own health and insurance needs, which will increase health insurance premium income in the short term. Life insurance companies extend product liability to COVID-19, which is in line with residents' short-term incremental risk protection needs and will further stimulate the increase in residents' demand for health insurance. The cancellation of travel plans will lead to a decline in accident insurance sales in the short term and extending the scope of accident insurance liability to COVID-19 is expected to mitigate this negative impact. Personal accident insurance such as Aviation accident, train accident, and travel accident insurance are mostly related to the travel of the insured. As the pandemic spreads around the world, the need for business travel and personal travel have been greatly reduced, thus suppressing the growth of accident insurance premium income. In addition, because accident insurance can be purchased in advance, the pandemic will also affect the insurance policies that insurance companies have already sold, worsening the short-term surrender rate of accident insurance. Since China's accident insurance premiums have accounted for 3–4% of the overall life insurance industry since 2000, the short-term negative impact of COVID-19 pandemic on accident insurance will not bring much shock to the overall life insurance industry.

The short-term impact on property insurance is manifested in the decline in demand for new orders of cargo transportation and motor vehicle insurance and the increase in the demand for business interruption insurance. Export trade has declined, and domestic production has not yet fully recovered, resulting in a decline in the demand for short-term cargo transportation insurance. However, the proportion of freight insurance in the entire property industry is not high. In 2018, China's freight insurance premium income was RMB 174.1 billion, accounting for only 16% of property insurance. Hence, the overall impact on China's property insurance is relatively small. At the same time, restrictions on the purchase of new motor vehicles have led to a significant short-term decline in new auto insurance business. According to China Banking and Insurance Credit Data, from January 23 to February 17, 2020, the cumulative number of inquiries for vehicle insurance nationwide was 22.5 billion, showing a year-on-year decrease of 36%. The cumulative number of signed orders was 13 million, with a year-on-year decrease of 34%. In addition to new order income generated by the purchase of new cars, most auto insurance premium income is from the renewal business of existing insurance policies. Therefore, due to the impact of the pandemic, short-term renewal may be limited. However, the rigid demand of commercial auto insurance will only be postponed until the pandemic is over. Therefore, the overall impact is controllable. Factors such as the development of the pandemic and the potential risks of companies resuming work will give rise to related demands for business interruption insurance. Business interruption insurance, also known as loss of profits insurance, is an insurance product that protects the insured against the risk of loss due to material property damage or third-party disasters that cause the insured's business to be temporarily interrupted. Although business interruption insurance does not account for a high proportion of China's property and casualty insurance market, it has ample room for growth. Business interruption insurance is an additional insurance for corporate property insurance. In 2019, the original premium income of corporate property insurance was RMB 46.4 billion, accounting for only 3.6% of the annual property insurance income.[3] In the short term, due to the prevention and control measures of the pandemic, tourist attractions, playgrounds, entertainment clubs, and restaurants have been forced to close, causing them to suffer loss of profits. If companies had previously purchased business interruption insurance, they would be able to get compensation in this pandemic, reducing the loss of income caused by forced closure; at the same time, to prevent a second wave in the spread of the pandemic, the postponement of the resumption of work during the Spring Festival has led to continuous delays of the start date. The inability of employees in the hardest hit areas to return to work has led to the lack of employees in their positions, which will also cause indirect losses to the company. Business interruption insurance can also help to cover these losses.

14.1.1.2 *Demand effects*

Since compensation for the costs involved in facing the risk of this pandemic are mainly borne by national medical insurance and government financial support, the short-term impact of the pandemic on insurance compensation is limited. As far as health insurance is concerned, the significant difference between the COVID-19 and SARS pandemic is that the state bears all medical expenses for suspected and confirmed patients without compensation from commercial insurance, which eases the pressure on commercial health insurance. The cost of testing and treatment before the patient is identified as a confirmed patient is borne by medical insurance, but the amount of compensation is relatively low. In terms of life insurance, the national mortality rate for COVID-19 pandemic is

[3] *Property Insurance Company Operating Status Sheet*, China Banking and Insurance Regulatory Commission website, January 22, 2020: http://www.cbirc.gov.cn/cn/view/pages/ItemDetail.html?docId=887994&itemId=954&generaltype=0.

relatively low, and the incremental payments of term life insurance and whole life insurance are generally controllable. Many patients in Hubei were exposed to the first-generation virus at the beginning of the pandemic, so the morbidity and fatality rate were relatively high in this province. In other places, the mortality rate from COVID-19 pandemic is relatively low, about 2–3%. Combined with the nationwide coverage ratio of life insurance, the increase in death liability compensation has had minimal impact on the insurance industry.

The insurance industry's donation of insurance to groups such as police officers and medical staff will trigger incremental compensation and increase the cost of compensation. As of March 3, 2020, 26 medical workers were infected with COVID-19 and passed away.[4] As of February 24, 3,000 medical staff had been infected with COVID-19.[5] The donated insurance for medical staff connected directly to the designated hospitals, with almost all staff being covered. Thus, the donated insurance may have triggered incremental compensation. According to statistics from the Public Security Department of Hubei Province, as of February 25, 404 police officers had been infected and 4 had died.[6] Based on the estimated death liability of RMB 400,000 yuan and the liability of infection of RMB 200,000 per donated insurance, an incremental compensation of RMB 7.7 billion may be triggered. In 2019, the original insurance compensation expenditure of the insurance industry was RMB 13 trillion, and the incremental proportion was about 0.06%.

14.1.1.3 *Investment perspective*

The short-term investments of insurance companies mainly involve equity assets and fixed income assets. In terms of equity assets, the reform of the

---

[4]Benevolent hearts work hard for the national disaster: the number of deceased medical staff and nurses in the country has reached 26, Caixin.com, March 1, 2020: http://china.caixin.com/2020-03-01/101519796.html.

[5]Text Record of the Press Conference of the China–WHO Joint Expert Investigation Team on Novel Coronavirus Pneumonia, National Health Commission website, February 25, 2020: http://www.nhc.gov.cn/gjhzs/s3578/202002/1fa99f55972740f681d47cde0d1b2522.shtml.

[6]404 civilian auxiliary police officers in Hubei were infected with new coronary pneumonia, and the proportion of police officers in police stations was relatively high, *The Paper*, February 26, 2020: https://www.thepaper.cn/newsDetail_forward_6171993.

capital market is deepening and the IFRS9 accounting standards are converting. High-dividend equity assets are a high-quality choice. In terms of fixed income assets, the economic pressure brought about by the pandemic will increase the default probability of credit bonds. The weak stability in the macro economy, together with continued capital market reform policies, is conducive to equity asset allocation. China's macroeconomic weak indicator has gradually emerged. In November 2019, the PMI of China's manufacturing industry was 50.2, which means it was above the line of prosperity.[7] This lasted until January 2020, when the PMI fell sharply in February due to the impact of the pandemic. The stability of China's macro fundamentals is conducive to the sound development of the equity market. Meanwhile, the initial outbreak of the COVID-19 pandemic has quickly been controlled. As an external event shock, the pandemic has mostly short-term effects on China's economy. Overall, the current relatively loose monetary policy has controlled the impact on the economy. The reform of the multi-level capital market is progressing steadily. The sci-tech innovation board registration system reform has been successfully implemented. The reform of the GEM registration system has been implemented steadily, and the attractiveness of equity assets has gradually increased. Superimposed on the background of IFRS9 accounting standards conversion, equity assets with high dividends and low valuations are high-quality choices for the allocation of insurance assets, which improves the stability of investment yields while providing a considerable rate of return for insurance assets.

On the investment side of insurance companies, there is also the risk of an increase in the default rate of credit bonds. COVID-19 has aggravated national economic pressures. The income situation of the worst-hit industries has severely deteriorated. Small and medium-sized enterprises with cash flow difficulties and large-scale enterprises with short-term obstacles to capital turnover may experience bankruptcy liquidation and debt defaults, which in turn will trigger credit debt defaults and increase the risk. In an environment of increasing volatility in the conventional bond market and continued decline in interest rates, insurance companies must actively expand bond-related derivatives, bulk commodities, and other alternative assets, increasing the scope of insurance capital allocation, and giving full play to the long-term advantages of insurance capital.

[7] *Source*: Wind.

14.1.2 Long-term impacts

14.1.2.1 *Business logic*

From a long-term perspective, the COVID-19 pandemic will first reconstruct the business logic of the insurance industry's "good start". "A good start" has been a feature of China's insurance industry for a long time. Major insurance companies will launch corresponding "good start" products in the first quarter of each year to compete for the new year's premium market and use good development trends to foretell the year's good luck. Table 14.1 analyzes the "good start" phenomenon in China's insurance industry in the past ten years. Each year January sales accounted for a large proportion of the annual performance of the insurance industry. In addition, the original premium income in the first quarter accounted for more than 30% of the annual premium income, and it has been raised to around 40% since 2016.

COVID-19 has had an obvious negative impact on the "good start" of China's insurance industry in 2020. A-share listed insurance companies provide a good example. In January 2020, CPIC increased by 0.6% year on year; PICC fell by 6.78% year on year, and Ping An fell by

Table 14.1: "A good start" phenomenon in China's insurance industry from 2010 to 2019.

Year	January premium (100 million yuan)	First quarter premium (100 million yuan)	Annual premium	January premium (100 million yuan)	First quarter premium (%)
2010	1642.98	4541.36	14527.97	11.31	31.26
2011	1716.98	4517.16	14339.25	11.97	31.50
2012	1891.76	4834.81	15487.93	12.21	31.22
2013	2011.87	5150.59	17222.24	11.68	29.91
2014	3367.38	6999.78	20234.81	16.64	34.59
2015	4.005.56	8425.37	24282.52	16.50	34.70
2016	6376.73	11979.12	30959.10	20.60	38.69
2017	8553.40	15866.02	36851.01	23.21	43.05
2018	6851.92	14084.36	38016.62	18.02	37.05
2019	8500.00	1632.00	42645.00	19.93	38.27

Source: China Banking and Insurance Regulatory Commission.

13.74% year on year. The performance of non-listed insurance companies in January generally suffered. From a global perspective, there is no "good start" concept in the foreign insurance market, and the sales plans of insurance companies will vary and focus on different aspects at different times throughout the year. In fact, the business logic of Chinese insurance companies` "good start" has certain drawbacks. For example, insurance companies concentrate a lot of operating pressure at the beginning of the year. Excessive pressure in the short term is not conducive to the sustainable development of the company and its employees, with insurance company employee training systems targeting and evaluating the short-term business sprint capabilities of insurance salespersons, ignoring their long-term capabilities. The pandemic has become a hindrance to the "good start" of the insurance industry. However, the realization that success does not follow the business logic of the "good start" will enable the achievement of full-year performance, helping insurance companies to find that premium growth is healthier and more scientific, and to gradually break away from a dependence on the "good start" in the long run.

14.1.2.2 *Product innovation*

As a major public emergency, the COVID-19 pandemic has tested the ability of insurance companies to carry out rapid product innovation and marketing, which will help the insurance industry to better innovate products in the future. To enable these products to better meet the needs of society during the pandemic, insurance companies have carried out a series of product innovations within one month, involving different aspects such as insurance liability, risk groups, product additions, and insurance claims (see Table 14.2).

Future product innovation will be based on the valuable experience accumulated during the pandemic. The following experience will be used as a reference for future product innovation: In terms of insurance liability, the scope of insurable risks has been flexibly expanded, making China's insurance products increasingly capable of responding to emergencies; in terms of risk groups, further development of products to meet their needs of sub-groups will promote the differentiated development of China's insurance products. In response to product additions, the quality

Table 14.2: List of product innovations of insurance companies during the pandemic.

Insurance liability	Risk groups	Product additions	Insurance claims
Additional insurance claims for insurance liability risk group products. Insurance products include COVID-19 in the scope of insurance liability.	Differentiated insurance products have been developed for different risk groups, such as insurance for workers in small and micro enterprises to return to work, taxi driver accident insurance, and drug development liability insurance for COVID-19.	Additional insurance services have been added for COVID-19 prevention, such as medical examinations and mask delivery.	Exclusive green claim channels for COVID-19 have been created.

of service has been improved, and insurance products are further shifted from focusing on *ex-post* compensation to prior risk management; in insurance claims, attention is paid to consumer experience, aimed at improving the efficiency and quality of claims, innovating claims processing, and speeding up claims process.

14.1.2.3 *Development model*

After COVID-19 pandemic, the country will further strengthen the construction of the public health system. At present, China's public health system is mainly based on social insurance, and the role of commercial insurance is limited. The disadvantages of this status quo are the high financial burden on the country, the inefficient use of funds, and the difficulty in meeting people's individual needs. During the COVID-19 pandemic, the positive role of commercial insurance has been very obvious, which helps further promote the integration of social insurance and commercial insurance, improves the role of commercial insurance in China's public health system, and gives full play under the guidance of the government to the commercial insurance mechanism to realize the "big country, big insurance" model In fact, during the COVID-19 pandemic, there has already been a prototype of "big country insurance". The prototype refers to the situation whereby the government relies more on commercial insurance to solve social problems and gives full play to its insurance function under the guidance and participation of the government. After the outbreak of COVID-19, Hainan launched the "Comprehensive Insurance for pandemic Prevention and Control and Resumption of Work and Production Enterprises", and Ningbo, Zhejiang launched the "Pandemic Prevention and Resumption Insurance for Small and Micro Enterprises". The former is used to protect company expenditure from product losses, employee wages, and isolation expenses caused by the government's pandemic prevention and control requirements for closure or isolation, with an insurance liability limit of RMB 2 million. The latter is aimed at small and micro enterprises in Ningbo City to compensate the losses incurred by them due to the suspension of production because of legal requirements related to infectious disease control, with an insurance liability limit of RMB 100,000. The commonality of these two products is that the government and the individual jointly bear the cost of insurance premiums. In the former, the government bears 70% of the cost of premiums, and the enterprise bears 30%, while in Ningbo premiums are equally shared by the government and the enterprise. This model is also known as the PPP model (public + private partnership). In this model, the government and the private sector cooperate to encourage private enterprises and private capital to cooperate with the government. This PPP model innovation during the COVID-19 pandemic will promote the expansion and further model innovation and cooperation between the government and the private sector in the insurance field in the future.

14.1.2.4 *Insurance technology*

The impact of the COVID-19 pandemic has provided a good experimental site for the application of new technology development in the insurance industry and has also greatly promoted the development of insurance technology. During this pandemic, insurance companies have acquired customers through online exhibition tools, client App, WeChat, telephone, and internal and external traffic platforms, managed marketers through online morning meetings, online training, and DingTalk's field check-in, and adopted various strategies such as health check-in, emergency notification, and pandemic prevention robots for the middle and back offices. Therefore, the entire insurance industry has received major education in insurance technology, which has also allowed insurance companies to fully realize the impact of insurance technology, and the important impact it will have on the future.

During the pandemic, insurance technology has been widely used in various contexts in insurance companies in China, such as the exhibition industry, employee management, and claims settlement. In the long term, increased investment in insurance technology will be promoted, which will help the incubation and implementation of a large number of new insurance technology applications and innovative insurance products, and further the promotion of the informatization and digital reform of China's insurance industry. While reducing the labor costs of insurance companies, the sales format of the online exhibition industry has also further changed the traditional sales system dominated by insurance agents, which has switched to online sales through the application of internet technology. The huge demand for technology in the insurance industry has also increased the demand for insurance technology-related experts, forcing academia and the industry to strengthen the training of insurance technology professionals, and provide sufficient guarantees by the availability of a pool of skilled professionals needed for the in-depth development of insurance technology and the insurance industry.

14.2 Analysis of Corresponding Measures to Alleviate the Impact of COVID-19

14.2.1 Mechanism and product response

14.2.1.1 *Guaranteed product development*

Considering the role during the SARS pandemic, played in the development of the insurance industry, it is clear that public health incidents have promoted the growth of health insurance premium income by stimulating people's awareness of health prevention. During the effective control of the SARS pandemic from May to August 2003, the monthly premiums of health insurance policies increased as high as 309%, 265%, 158%, and 131% year on year. Later, normal growth rate was gradually restored when the pandemic was controlled. During the pandemic, residents purchased many health protection products, such as masks and disinfectants, proving that public health incidents can greatly stimulate people's awareness of their own health protection, further strengthen their awareness of long-term health risks, and help improve the level of development of health insurance in China. At present, the development of China's health insurance overall is still short of the level of economic development and foreign insurance markets. There is plenty of room for growth.

Differing from those insurance companies who advocated the development of new products during the SARS period, during the COVID-19 pandemic, insurance companies focused on cultivating consumer awareness of protection for long-term health risks. Under the strict supervision of the China Banking and Insurance Regulatory Commission, the use of pandemic marketing has been forbidden, and life insurance companies must not use specific claims as gimmicks. Insurance companies mainly provide incremental risk protection related to COVID-19 in two respects: the expansion of medical insurance liability and the gift of new coronary pneumonia products. According to the *Securities Daily*, as of February 15, 56 insurance companies have extended the product liability of their original products to COVID-19 and opened a green claim channel for patients. In contrast to the development of new fee-based products, expanding existing product responsibilities strengthens the image of insurance products as long-term risk protection in the minds of consumers, and encourages them to provide risk protection for their own long-term health by purchasing commercial health insurance.

14.2.1.2 *Integrate with medical system reform*

The market mechanism is used to allocate medical resources and continue the improvement of the level of medical service supply. The insurance mechanism is an extremely important part of the operation of the market-oriented medical system and it will further develop in the tide of marketization of China's medical system as it has already played an important role in the construction of China's public health system. In terms of basic medical insurance, the number of people participating in it has continued to increase. In 2018, the number of people participating in basic medical insurance was 1,344.59 million, and the participation rate has remained stable at over 95%, basically achieving full coverage. At present, within the scope of the urban employee medical insurance and urban residents' medical insurance policy, the proportion of hospital medical expenses fund payments has reached 81.6% and 65.6%, respectively. The maximum payment of the overall fund has reached 6 times the average annual salary of local employees and the disposable income of residents. Within the scope of the "New Rural Cooperative Medical Care" policy, the hospitalization expense reimbursement ratio exceeds 75% while the actual compensation ratio for outpatient clinics is more than 50%. This ratio is more than 60% in the counties, and in cities it is closer to 80%. The reimbursement policy for medical treatment in places other than the patient's hometown is an important guarantee for the equalization of medical resources. As of the end of 2018, there were 15,000 designated medical institutions across the country for medical treatment in places other than hometowns, and all designated medical institutions with more than 500 inpatients across provinces (regions, cities) are connected to the remote medical settlement platform. County-level administrative regions have basically achieved full coverage. In 2018, 1.32 million people were directly settled across provinces (autonomous regions and municipalities) for medical and hospitalization expenses in places other than their hometown, which was 6.3 times that of 2017. The construction of China's basic medical insurance system involves the happiness and well-being of thousands of households.

As the third pillar of China's multi-level social security system, in the future commercial health insurance will effectively supplement social insurance, and improve residents' medical security. Currently, the population is growing, and China is starting to face the problem of an aging population. The social security system that relies solely on social insurance and corporate subsidies is under increasing pressure. As an important part of the market-oriented reform of the medical system, commercial health insurance increases the medical security of residents while sharing the financial burdens of government and enterprises. Commercial health insurance such as critical illness insurance provides high compensation when residents suffer a major illness and solves economic problems in the treatment of diseases. Meanwhile, vigorously developing a product that combines health services and health insurance improves the accessibility and treatment efficiency of medical services and optimizes the medical service experience of residents.

14.2.1.3 *Accelerating the construction of a catastrophe insurance system*

As a typical "black swan" event, COVID-19 pandemic has brought huge losses to the development of China's macro economy and small and medium-sized enterprises. Local government awareness of the need for the construction of catastrophe insurance systems is expected to increase.

Small and medium-sized enterprises play two major roles as consumers and suppliers in the macro economy. At the same time, as macroeconomic development gradually shifts to innovation-led development, the importance of the role played by small and medium-sized enterprises in China's economy is increasing. However, SMEs are limited by their profitability during the process of technological development and quick recovery is difficult for them after a catastrophe because fixed costs such as rent and labor costs may cause SMEs to go bankrupt. Catastrophe insurance can help small and medium-sized enterprises quickly resume normal business after a disaster. During the pandemic, some local governments have begun to formulate insurance plans to help small and medium-sized enterprises tide over the difficulties. Hainan's "Comprehensive Insurance for the Prevention and Control of pandemics for Resumption of Work and Production Enterprises" and the "pandemic Prevention and Resumption Insurance for Small and Micro Enterprises" launched by Ningbo, Zhejiang Province are good examples.

14.2.2 Risk management in the "Post-pandemic era"

14.2.2.1 *Systematic risk management*

The systemic risk brought about by this outbreak refers to the social suspension of economic activities in a "shock" manner in order to effectively respond to the pandemic. If this suspension is extended because the pandemic cannot be controlled in a short period of time, all walks of life will face risks. In principle, the insurance industry cannot manage such risks, but the core problem exposed by this pandemic is the serious shortage of medical resources. If medical resources are sufficient, pandemics may be more rapidly controlled. In the "post-pandemic era", the insurance industry's full participation in the reform of the medical system will help improve the level of medical supplies. Through the development of its own medical channels and cooperation with medical insurance institutions, insurance companies have three main channels in which to participate in improving the level of supply of medical services.

(1) The insurance industry could strengthen medical insurance cooperation and promote the construction of a multi-level medical system. The insurance industry could actively cooperate with the market-oriented reform of the national medical system, help commercial

insurance and medical insurance be more closely integrated, and help build a multi-tier medical system. The insurance industry could increase the income of primary health care doctors (in China "grass-roots doctors"), and help implement a system for the triaged diagnosis and treatment of disease. For example, commercial insurance providers could cooperate with community general practitioners who are the first point of contact between a patient and the medical system providing diagnosis and treatment when an insured patient is ill, and when diagnosis and/or treatment is beyond the limits of the community GP, a referral is made to a more specialized medical institution, that is to say the next tier. This realizes the implementation of graded (triaged) diagnosis and treatment.

(2) The insurance industry could increase its investment in the medical industry, such as setting up hospitals and investing in medical device companies. According to *the Several Opinions of the State Council on Promoting the Development of the Health Service Industry*, the state encourages and supports insurance companies participating in the integration of the health industry chain. The new "National Ten Articles" of the insurance industry propose to build a modern insurance service with comprehensive guarantees, complete functions, safety and soundness, integrity and norms, strong service capabilities, innovation capabilities, and international competitiveness in 2020 to meet the needs of China's economic and social development. The newly revised *Health Insurance Management Measures* in 2019 also clearly state that insurance companies are also encouraged to combine commercial health insurance and health services to increase the degree of cooperation with health service providers. As an important part of the multi-level medical security system, the insurance industry plays a pivotal role in the integration process of the medical industry. Building their own medical channels not only strengthens the market competitiveness of insurance companies' own health insurance, but also strengthens the supply capacity of macro-medical resources, achieving a win–win situation for the enterprise and the country.

(3) The insurance industry continues to develop insurance products suitable for the medical field, such as accelerating the implementation of medical liability insurance and developing innovative drug R&D failure insurance. The most important and basic function of the insurance industry is the function of risk management with the protection of special risks in the medical industry, an important responsibility for

the insurance industry in China. Medical liability insurance is an important means to the Doctor–Patient relationship, and also an important link for the cooperation between insurance companies and medical institutions. By providing medical liability insurance for medical institutions, insurance companies strengthen the cooperative relationship with the target hospital while providing risk protection, laying a favorable foundation for the development of follow-up health services. Therefore, the insurance industry's deep participation in the market-oriented reform of the medical system, which increases the supply of medical resources through long-term mechanisms, is the fundamental way to reduce the harm of systemic risks.

14.2.2.2 *Risk management of catastrophes*

Catastrophe risk is a second-level risk of this outbreak. In China, it primarily refers to the violent fluctuation of finances due to large-scale disasters, affecting economic development. This outbreak is a long-tail risk, that is, an event with small probability and high loss. The corresponding risk management product is catastrophe insurance, with the main problem faced by catastrophe insurance being insufficient demand because small probability events are easily ignored in long-tail risk events. China is piloting a catastrophe insurance system; local governments in each pilot program generally use fiscal funds to purchase catastrophe insurance for specific disasters from the co-insurance. For example, in 2019, Hubei had already purchased catastrophe insurance for heavy rains and floods, but the catastrophe insurance did not cover infectious diseases. The demand for catastrophe insurance generally increases rapidly after disasters. Local governments should speed up and improve the implementation of catastrophe insurance pilots in the "post-pandemic era", increase financial investment in catastrophe insurance, expand the coverage of catastrophe insurance, and learn from the pilots to further improve the catastrophe insurance system. Considering the still existing uncertainties of this pandemic, it is possible to encourage insurance companies or local governments to consider issuing catastrophe securities for financing.

14.2.2.3 *Conventional risk management*

The third-level conventional risk caused by the outbreak refers to the fact that in the early stage of the pandemic, the residents could not afford the medical expenses, the family income dropped sharply due to the unfortunate death family members who supported the families, and the enterprises were forced to stop working, resulting in a large number of losses. However, such risks could be managed with conventional insurance products. In the "post-pandemic era", the government could use policies such as tax deferral to encourage residents to purchase protected commercial insurance, to make up for the shortcomings of residents' commercial insurance protection as soon as possible, allowing commercial insurance protection to play its role more efficiently. For small and medium-sized enterprises, by using the experience of more developed countries, local governments could require enterprises to purchase corporate property insurance by adopting measures such as using legislation and loan conditions to cover the liability of profit and loss when conditions permit, and strengthening the ability of small and medium-sized enterprises to resist similar catastrophes. Finally, after the end of the pandemic, in the face of a possible wave of unemployment, insurance companies could be encouraged to increase the recruitment of insurance agents. It is conducive to stability to encourage insurance companies to develop savings insurance that meets market needs and provides help for the society.

14.3 Conclusion

As a major public health emergency, COVID-19 has had a huge impact on the society and economy, and has also had a profound impact on the insurance industry. The insurance industry is an important part of China's social risk management system. This chapter summarizes the impact of COVID-19 pandemic on the insurance industry through the analysis of short-term and long-term impacts of the SARS pandemic. Unlike the impact of SARS, the positive and negative impacts of the new corona pandemic on China's insurance industry coexist, but the negative impact is less serious than that during the SARS period. In the short-term, the positive impact of personal insurance on the income side is greater than the negative. The negative impact of property insurance is large but controllable in the short term. The long-term impact of COVID-19 pandemic will lead to a reconstruction of the business logic of the insurance industry which has attached such importance to the "good start", will strengthen the development of the insurance model promoting public–private cooperation, and will lead to greater investment in product innovation and the application of insurance technology.

The history of human development is also the history of human resistance to various risks. It is a long-term task to prevent and reduce the occurrence of major public health emergencies and avoid the negative impact of such incidents on all walks of life. This chapter has discussed the impact of major public health emergencies on the insurance industry by taking the COVID-19 pandemic as an example. This research aims to better learn from history, improve the strength of the insurance industry to further play its role in risk management, and participate in the anti-pandemic work of the whole society. In the future, the insurance industry should combine its business characteristics and capabilities to further explore the inclusion of major public health emergency risks in underwriting responsibilities, promote insurance innovation and management, and play a more active role in major public health emergencies' risk management systems.

https://doi.org/10.1142/9789811252921_0015

Chapter 15

The Impact of COVID-19 Pandemic on the Global Economy and Global Policy Response

Tian Suhua and Li Xiaoyan

School of Economics, Fudan University, Shanghai, China

The Novel Coronavirus (COVID-19) began to spread globally in February 2020. To stop the spread of the pandemic, governments in various countries introduced measures such as city lockdowns and the suspension of classes in schools; the large-scale outbreak of the pandemic will therefore influence both the social progress and the economic development of China and the world. (Zheng Hong, 2020). History has demonstrated the potential dangers posed by global pandemics on the world economy and people's livelihoods; in Spain and Ireland, the Black Death plague interrupted the continuous economic growth process that began in 1270 AD (Kelly, 2001); the H1N1 virus that spread from American military camps to the European continent during World War I ushered in the 1918 influenza pandemic, killing nearly 50 million people. After the outbreak of COVID-19, supply and demand in the world economy have been severely impacted, which has had a detrimental effect on globalization. During public health emergencies, decision-making must be optimized within a limited time frame, and balanced decisions taken for domestic pandemic prevention and economic development. In the meantime, overall coordination on an international scale must also be undertaken.

15.1 The Impact of COVID-19 on the Global Economy

The total volume of global trade in goods declined in January and February of 2020, and the entry of goods and transportation capacity dropped significantly. The barometer for trade in goods released by the World Trade Organization (WTO) on February 17th, 2020, read 95.5, which is 1.1 points lower than the 96.6 in November 2019. Uncertain expectations about the control of COVID-19 pandemic and fear of the pandemic's effect on the global economy triggered drastic fluctuations in the global capital market.

15.1.1 The economic impact on global demand

After the outbreak of COVID-19, the global demand for medical supplies skyrocketed, and there was a serious shortage of masks, disinfectants, and hand sanitizers. The closure of borders imposed by various countries due to the pandemic increased the cost of cross-border movement of people.[1] In the cruise, shipping, and tourism industries worldwide, demand has severely declined, which has led to the bankruptcy of many companies.

(1) The prices of personal protective equipment, such as masks and disinfectants, have skyrocketed. COVID-19 pandemic has resulted in the demand for masks in the United States exceeding supply. On March 3, 2020, the U.S. Senate Health Committee said in a hearing that American medical workers need 3.5 billion masks, but only 35 million masks could be supplied. The spread of the pandemic has accelerated in Asia, Europe, and the United States, and medical protective products such as masks and disinfectants were snatched up. Correspondingly, price surges for personal protective equipment caused a mask of 0.4 euros to rise to 10 euros (approximately RMB 77.3). A box of 20 N95 masks sold for $387 (approximately RMB

[1]As of March 3, 2020, 87 countries and regions have imposed entry controls on South Korea; Turkey, Afghanistan, Pakistan, and Armenia have closed their borders with Iran; the U.S. government has banned entry of foreigners who had traveled to Iran in the previous 14 days, and had raised travel warnings to their highest level for certain areas in South Korea and Italy; Australia has raised its warning level for travel to Japan and South Korea (see *Huanqiu, Guancha Syndicate, People*).

2,682), and 24 bottles of hand sanitizer rose to US$400. In addition to the shortages for non-medical use, the supplies for first-line medical staff of various countries are also in short supply.

On February 26, 2020, South Korean mask sellers were banned from exporting masks. Mask manufacturers were restricted from exporting more than 10% of the daily output. On March 4, 2020, the French government issued a decree requiring the expropriation of FFP2-type (equivalent to domestic N95 type) respiratory protective masks and medical disposable masks held and produced by legal entities and private individuals before May 31. To urgently respond to the shortage of masks, many manufacturing companies switched to producing masks. In China, Guangzhou Automobile, BYD, Chang'an, and many other auto companies announced their production of masks. Japanese electrical appliance manufacturer Sharp Corporation arranged for its display manufacturing plant to produce medical surgical masks, becoming the first non-medical company in Japan to produce these masks.[2]

(2) The cruise industry has suffered heavy losses. As of March 8, 2020, the "Diamond Princess" docked at the Port of Yokohama, Japan, having a total of 696 confirmed cases of COVID-19. Twenty-one people on the "Supreme Princess" laying off San Francisco tested positive for COVID-19. A cruise ship docked on the Nile in Egypt had 45 confirmed cases of COVID-19. The rest should be remained. "The Diamond Princess" and the "Grand Princess" belong to Princess Cruises of the American Carnival Group.[3] As the number of cruise

[2] See *Financial Times* on March 3, 2020, *Nikkei Asian Review* on March 2, 2020, and CCTV on February 26, 2020.

[3] On the evening of March 3, 2020, a German cruise ship was quarantined at the port of Ugesund in the Norwegian Sea because two passengers on board had contact with a confirmed patient the previous week. Later, the test results of these two passengers were negative and the ship continued its journey as originally planned. On February 28, 2020, the Legend a super-large cruise ship of MSC Mediterranean Cruises was refused permission to dock at the three ports of Jamaica, the Cayman Islands and Mexico due to symptoms such as fever and cough in the crew and passengers. Later, it docked at the port after the intervention of the President of Mexico. After checking that the symptoms of the crew and passengers were not related to the new coronavirus, the cruise ship subsequently suspended the continuation of the voyage and returned to its home port of Miami. (See *Wall Street* on March 6, 2020 and *21st Century Business Herald* on March 7, 2020).

ship infections increased, various countries adopted measures to ban the docking of cruise ships. The market's pessimism and panic toward the cruise industry increased. From January 21 to March 4, 2020, the share prices of the three major international cruise companies fell sharply. Carnival, Royal Caribbean, and Norwegian's share prices fell by 39.7%, 41%, and 44%, respectively. Royal Caribbean cancelled 18 Southeast Asian voyages and adjusted several routes, incurring losses of US$136 million. On March 2, 2020, Japan's Kobe Yeguang Cruise Line declared bankruptcy.

(3) Passenger volume in the aviation industry has plummeted. Due to the spread of COVID-19, it has become the norm to impose bans on air travel in countries with infections resulting from the pandemic. On March 5, 2020, the International Air Transport Association (IATA) estimated that major airlines will lose 63–113 billion U.S. dollars in global air passenger traffic in 2020.[4] The data released by IATA is an important indicator of the status of the aviation industry, and the financial market reacted strongly to the downturn. On March 5, 2020, American Airlines' stock fell more than 13%, the lowest ever since the merger with US Airlines in 2013. From February 12 to March 5, American Airlines' stock prices fell by 46.25%, and more than US$6.06 billion of its market value evaporated. In addition to American Airlines, the stock prices of major US airlines such as Delta, United, and Southwest have all fallen sharply. In response to the decline in passenger flow and the downturn in the aviation industry, United Airlines announced on March 4 that from April it will reduce international flights by 20% and domestic flights by 10%. Declining passenger traffic and falling stock prices were the last straw overwhelming those airlines whose funds were already nearing exhaustion. On March 5, 2020, the British regional airline Flybe announced that it has entered the bankruptcy takeover process due to its inability to withstand the plummeting demand for air travel caused by the pandemic.

(4) Travel restrictions have further resulted in the number of global tourists dropping sharply. According to data from the United Nations World Tourism Organization (UNWTO), the overseas consumption of Chinese tourists reached $10 billion in 2000, and this figure increased

---

[4]IATA has 290 member airlines around the world. Passenger traffic on scheduled international flights accounts for 82% of the world's total.

to $277 billion in 2018. Due to the outbreak of COVID-19 in January 2020, Chinese residents voluntarily chose to stay at home and cancelled most of their overseas travel during the Spring Festival. When the pandemic broke out in Italy in late February, the number of tourists to Europe dropped sharply. The Global Tourism Organization estimates that the world's tourism industry will lose at least $22 billion in 2020. The tourism industry in Hokkaido, Japan, was estimated to lose more than JPY 200 billion (approximately RMB 13.1 billion) in the first half of the year. Because of the heavy losses in the tourism industry in Japan, the long-established ryokan Fujimi-so in Gamagori, Aichi Prefecture, closed in mid-February. The Thai government estimates that the decrease in the number of tourists caused Thailand to lose approximately RMB 11 billion. In 2019, the income of inbound tourism accounted for about 13% of Italy's GDP. After the outbreak in northern Italy, the number of tourists visiting Europe from February 24 to February 29, 2020, fell by 25.9% year on year.

15.1.2 The economic impact on world supply

According to Sea Intelligence, from January to February 2020, at least 21 voyages between China and the United States were cancelled, which equates to 198,500 cancelled containers. In the Asia–Europe trade circle, 10 voyages were cancelled, equivalent to 151,500 containers.[5] According to data from the British consulting company, Drewry, in February 2020, the liner company cancelled about 105 voyages from Asia to North America and Europe/Mediterranean.[6] The large number of cancellations of cargo shipping has increased the cost of trade transportation, and many products and raw materials cannot be delivered on time.

(1) Drugs in many countries are in short supply. In 2018, China's APIs were exporting to 187 countries and regions. India, the United States, and Japan were ranked the top three countries of China's API exports. In 2018, China's export of drug precursors to the United States was $4.267 billion. Of the 150 drug products sold in the United States,

[5] *Wall Street Journal* on January 23, 2020.

[6] Reported in the China Water Transport News on February 12, 2020 and the shipping network on March 3, 2020.

about 14% of the key precursors and about 8% of ready-for-consumption drugs were produced in China. The United States not only relies on Chinese APIs, but also the chemical precursors produced by APIs in China. In Hubei alone, 44 pharmaceutical factories approved by the FDA or EU standards provide precursors for Europe and the United States.

After the outbreak, drug production has stagnated, air transportation has decreased, and the global drug supply chain has been disrupted. Nearly 280 medicines were in short supply in Germany, and cardiovascular medicines and painkillers were scarce in many pharmacies in Berlin. The Federation of Indian Industries warned on February 16, 2020 that Indian pharmaceutical companies are "on the verge of exhausting their raw material supply" and are under pressure from the sharply rising prices of raw materials.[7] (See the *21st Century Business Herald* on March 5, 2020, *Chinese API factories actively resume work to ensure supply to the global industrial chain*). The US Food and Drug Administration (FDA) Commissioner Steve Hahn stated on February 25, 2020: "We are closely monitoring the impact of the outbreak on the US medical supplies supply chain.... Critical medical supplies in the United States may be disrupted. There is even a serious shortage."

(2) The supply chain of the automotive industry is broken. The spread of the pandemic and the suspension of production by Chinese companies has resulted in insufficient supply of raw materials and parts for companies in other countries. Since the outbreak, auto part manufacturers in Hubei Province have not been able to carry out or resume normal production. Prolonged suspension of production has caused a break in China's domestic auto parts production. For example, the Sino-Japanese joint venture Dongfeng Honda has postponed the resumption of production at its Wuhan factory on four consecutive occasions, until March 11, 2020. This means that Honda's Wuhan plant has suspended production for a total of one and a half months, with no output throughout February, and it is expected that the output of vehicles will decrease by nearly 100,000. To prevent the shortage of parts, Honda decided to temporarily reduce the output of two plants in Saitama City, Japan. Nissan Motor suspended two

[7] See Sohu.com report on March 3, 2020.

production lines at the Kyushu plant in Japan on February 14, 2020, and another export car production line on February 17.[8] According to a report in *China Business News* published on March 2, 2020, in addition to Nissan Motors, Japan's Toyota Motors said on February 26 that, due to COVID-19, its Japanese factory operations were affected by the global spread of the pandemic and it faced supply chain disruption.

Pandemic prevention and control measures have hindered the transportation and export of auto parts across provinces and cities. After the outbreak, South Korea's five major vehicle manufacturers (Hyundai, Kia, South Korea GM, Ssangyong, and Renault Samsung) all suffered to varying degrees from insufficient supply of upstream parts and plant shutdowns. Hyundai Motor was forced to suspend production at all five factories in Ulsan, South Korea. In January 2020, South Korean car production and exports dropped by 28.99% and 29.23% year on year, respectively. South Korea's Samsung Electronics' smartphone factory in Gumi City and Hyundai Motor which had resumed production have subsequently all been temporarily closed due to workers having been diagnosed with COVID-19.[9] In addition, Fiat Chrysler's (FCA) plant in Serbia has suspended production due to a shortage of parts from China. It became the first car manufacturer in Europe to stop production in response to COVID-19.[10] According to a Reuters report on March 3, 2020, global car sales for Hyundai South Korea in February were 275,000 vehicles, reflecting a 13% decrease from the same period in 2019. It was the lowest volume in the past 10 years. In response to the supply chain crisis, the South Korean government planned to simplify the logistics and customs clearance procedures for imports of Chinese parts to resume supply as soon as possible (see Figure 15.1).

(3) Technology companies adjusted traditional offline office models. The global and domestic spread of the pandemic have affected many US

---

[8] Yonhap News Agency report, February 18, 2020; China Automotive Network report, February 11, 2020.

[9] See NetEase News on March 2, 2020.

[10] See the Observer Network on February 4, 2020; Bloomberg News on February 21, 2020; Outlook Think Tank on February 26, 2020.

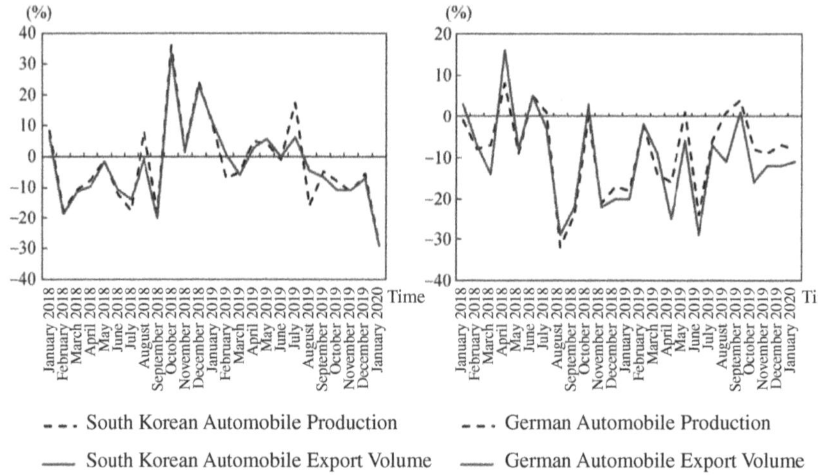

The left figure shows the monthly year-on-year data of South Korean automobile production and export volume in the current month, while the right figure shows the monthly year-on-year data of German automobile production and export volume in the current month.

Figure 15.1: South Korea and Germany's automobile production and export volume.

Source: Wind.

Note: The picture on the left is the month-on-year monthly data of South Korean automobile production and export volume. The picture on the right shows the monthly data of German passenger car production and export volume.

technology companies. Two employees in Microsoft's Seattle work area were diagnosed with COVID-19, so employees in Seattle or San Francisco were allowed to work from home until March 9. Facebook closed its Seattle office until March 9 because an employee in Seattle was infected and workers were encouraged to work from home until the end of March; a Google employee in the Swiss branch was infected with COVID-19; Google's US headquarters stopped all business trips on March 3rd and called on all employees outside the United States to return home as soon as possible. On March 1, two employees of Amazon's Milan branch were infected and on March 3, an employee of Amazon's Seattle headquarters was infected as well. Amazon required all employees to stop non-essential business travel, including domestic travel.[11]

[11] See Sina Finance, March 4 and 5, 2020.

15.1.3 Increasing volatility in global capital markets

The global spread of COVID-19 led to profound pessimism in global capital markets in late February 2020. The yields of 10-year treasury bonds in countries such as the United States continued to decline, and the stock market fluctuated sharply. From February 12 to March 9, 2020, driven by safe-haven funds, the prices of mid-term and long-term Treasury bonds in the United States continued to rise, and the prices of long-term bonds in Europe, especially Germany, hit record highs (see Figure 15.2). On March 6, 2020, the U.S. 10-year Treasury bond yield reached a historical low of 0.768%, showing a drop of 25.1%. The 10-year German government bond yield hit a record low during the session, reaching -0.747%, and the 30-year German bond yield also hit a record low of -0.337%.

Panic caused the global stock market to fluctuate sharply after continued decline (see Figure 15.3). Of them, the U.S. stocks S&P 500 fluctuated most. The European Stoxx index, the UK FTSE 100 index, and the German DAX30 index showed similar trends. On March 6, 2020, the S&P 500 index closed, down 1.7%. The VIX Panic Index, which measures the implied volatility of S&P 500 options, rose by 5.86% to 41.94. The German DAX30 index fell by 3.37%, of which the Technology Index (TecDAX) fell 3.00%, and the Nikkei 225 Index closed, down 2.72%.

Market concerns about COVID-19 pandemic have intensified since March, 2020. Funds flowed from higher-risk assets into safe-haven assets such as gold. On March 6, 2020, the spot gold price rose to $1,676.65. On March 3, iShares Gold Trust achieved the largest inflow since the record price of gold in 2011 of approximately US$215 million.

As the discount on Arabian light crude oil sold to refiners in northwestern Europe was extended to $8 per barrel, the price went as low as $10.25 per barrel. On March 9, 2020 (Monday), the oil price in New York fell by more than 33% in intraday trading, and once dropped to a low of $27.34 per barrel. Brent oil prices fell by more than 30% at one time, with the lowest price of $31.02 per barrel. It was the biggest drop since the United States started the war in Iraq in January 1991. On March 9, Beijing time, the two major international benchmark oil prices in New York and London both fell by more than 21%. Affected by the sharp drop in crude oil prices, on March 9, 2020 (Monday), the Dow Jones Index at opening fell sharply, by more than 1,800 points, or nearly 7%. The Nasdaq Index fell by 6.86%, nearly 600 points; the S&P 500 index fell by nearly 7% at

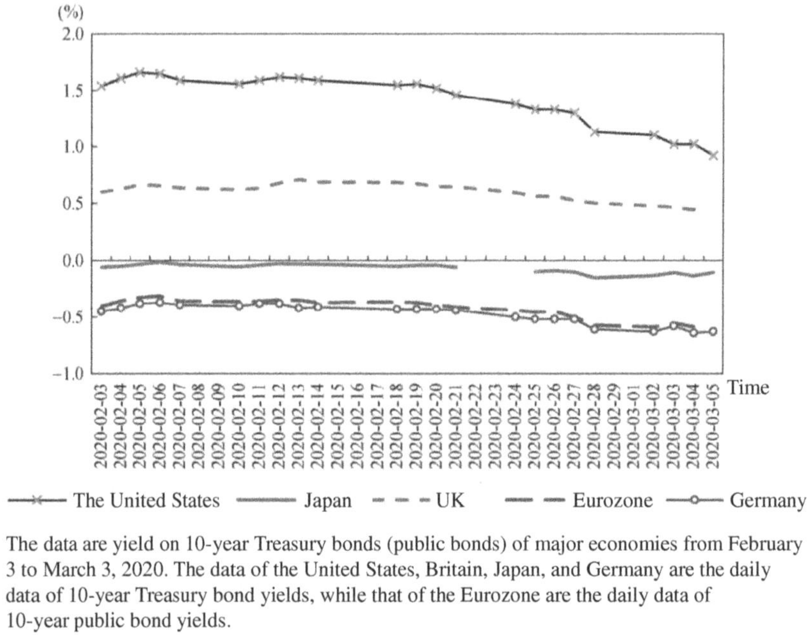

Figure 15.2: Yield on 10-year Treasury bonds (public bonds) of major economies.

Source: Wind.

Note: The data are the 10-year government bond (public bond) yields of major economies from February 3 to March 5, 2020. Daily data on 10-year government bond yields in the United States, Japan, and the United Kingdom are shown. Eurozone data are daily data on 10-year bond yields.

the beginning of the market, triggering the first-layer circuit breaker mechanism. Trade was suspended for 15 minutes, and resumed after the blowout. The S&P 500 index fell to 7.2%, and the Dow Jones index fell more than 2,000 points.

15.2 Corresponding Global Economic Measures to Combat the Impact of COVID-19

To alleviate the economic impact of the pandemic and pessimistic market expectations, countries around the world have adopted unprecedented subsidy fiscal policies and expansionary monetary policies. With the spread of COVID-19 pandemic, central banks of various countries started

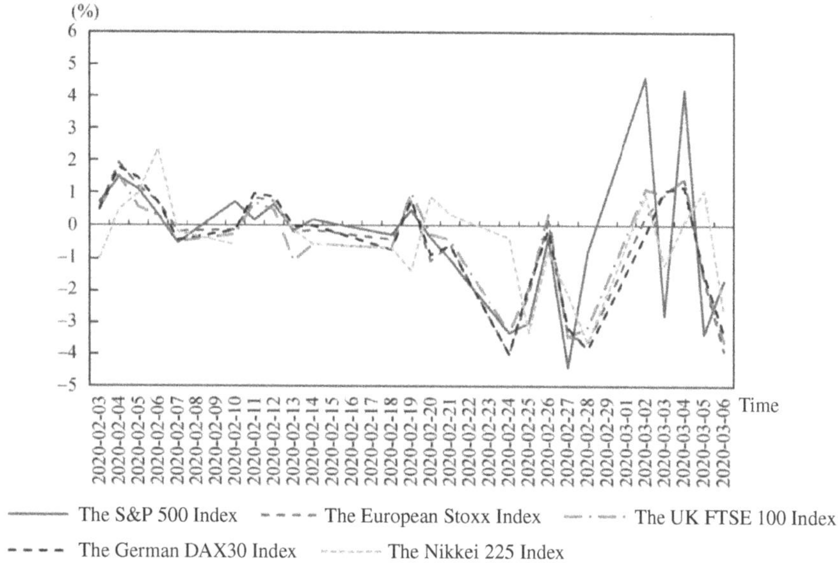

Figure 15.3: The rise and fall of major global stock indexes.

Source: Investing.com.

a new round of expansionary monetary policies at almost the same time to contain financial and economic risks (see Table 15.1). Led by U.S. Treasury Secretary Mnuchin and Federal Reserve Chairman Powell, the Group of Seven (G7) finance ministers and central bank governors held a conference call on March 3, 2020, to discuss measures to deal with the pandemic and its economic impact.

15.2.1 Urgent implementation of expansionary monetary policies

On March 3, 2020, the Bank of Australia announced that it would lower its target interest rate from 0.75% to 0.5%. On the same day, the US Federal Reserve announced that it would lower its benchmark interest rate by 50 basis points to 1.00–1.25%, and would lower the excess reserve interest rate (IOER) by 50 basis points to 1.1%. This was the first time since 2008 that the Federal Reserve has adjusted its monetary policy at a non-interest-rate meeting. After the Fed's emergency rate cut, central

Table 15.1: Expansionary monetary policies implemented by countries in March 2020.

Time	National economic	Monetary policies
2020.03.03	Australia	Cut interest rates by 25 basis points to 0.5%, setting a record for the lowest interest rate in history
2020.03.03	The US	Benchmark interest rate was reduced by 50 basis points to 1.00–1.25%; the interest rate on excess reserves (IOER) was reduced by 50 basis points to 1.1%
2020.03.03	Malaysia	Malaysia's Overnight Policy Rate (OPR) was reduced by 25 basis points to 2.50%
2020.03.03	Saudi Arabia	Saudi Arabia's repo rate and reverse repo rate were both reduced by 50 basis points
2020.03.03	UAE	Cut interest rates by 50 basis points
2020.03.03	Hong Kong, China	Cut base interest rate by 50 basis points to 1.5%
2020.03.03	Macau, China	Cut base interest rate by 50 basis points to 1.5%
2020.03.03	Canadian	Canadian prime lending rate was reduced by 50 basis points to 1.25%

Note: The content of the form only includes policies before March 6, 2020.

banks of other countries simultaneously lowered their interest rates. The Governor of the Bank of Japan issued an emergency statement on March 2, proclaiming: "The Bank of Japan will closely monitor future developments and will strive to provide sufficient liquidity to ensure financial market stability through market operations and asset purchases". Subsequently, the Bank of England stated that it was working with the British government, financial regulators, and international partners to "ensure that all necessary measures are taken to protect financial and currency stability."

15.2.2 Emergency financial appropriation and implementation of subsidy assistance

In addition to implementing expansionary monetary policies, countries have urgently and quickly launched a series of financial allocations and subsidies in response to the new pandemic. On January 31, 2020, the Italian government entered a state of emergency and allocated about EURO 5 million to respond to the coronavirus outbreak. On February 14,

Japan allocated JPY 10.3 billion yen (about RMB 650 million) from the 2019 budget preparation funds to support the increase in mask production and strengthening of border inspections. On February 18, the South Korean government allocated KRW104.1 billion (about RMB 610 million) for the prevention and control of the pandemic. On the same day, Singapore announced an SGD 800 million (approximately RMB 4 billion yuan) medical plan and launched two plans for SGD 5.6 billion (approximately RMB 28 billion). On February 24, the Italian government allocated EUR 200 million (about RMB150 million) to respond to the pandemic. On February 27, the Malaysian government launched a MYR 20 billion (approximately USD 4.73 billion) economic stimulus plan to deal with the possible economic impact of the coronavirus and the global economic slowdown. On March 3, the Japanese cabinet meeting decided to spend JPY 2.2 billion on mask purchases from the preliminary budget of 2020.

15.3 Policy Suggestions

The global spread of COVID-19 pandemic has made huge impacts on health and social activities, and has also affected the world economy, on both the demand and supply side. Medical supplies such as masks and disinfectants have been the target of panic buying and hoarding by residents in various countries. In response to panic and travel bans/restrictions, international travel has decreased, and the cruise, aviation, and travel industries have suffered huge losses. Due to China's suspension of work and production, rising transportation costs, and the global spread of the pandemic, industries with long industrial chains such as the automobile industry have experienced insufficient supply of parts and components. Many auto companies have suspended or reduced production. The spread of the pandemic in countries and regions outside of China has caused pessimistic expectations in the capital market and violent shocks in important global stock markets. To stabilize the financial market and respond to economic downturn risks, central banks of various countries urgently cut interest rates, and the Ministries of Finance of various countries urgently allocated financial and aid subsidies. A new round of expansionary fiscal and monetary policies has been launched globally.

With current super globalization and value chain division of labor resulting in large-scale cross-border movement of people and commodities, the virus easily spreads across geographic boundaries to all parts of the world. Emergent global public health pandemics are difficult to effectively control within specific geographic boundaries in the short term. Hence, it is difficult for individual countries to solve them alone.

China's response to changes in the world economy during the spread of COVID-19 pandemic should consider the following three suggestions:

(1) The timely, orderly, safe, and synchronized resumption of work has to be realized by Chinese and related companies in the global value chain and actively promoted as soon as possible. There is a need to increase confidence in pandemic prevention and control, release information about the latest progress in China's pandemic prevention and control in multiple languages, share pandemic prevention and control experience, and fully reassure the public about global prevention and control of COVID-19 pandemic.
(2) The global economic interconnection mechanism must be utilized to innovate the online and offline hybrid work resumption mode. The Hangzhou Municipal Government and Alibaba have cooperated to track the movement and safety factors of everyone through health check-in and health codes to ensure that workers return to work in a healthy and effective manner. During the pandemic, online teaching, medical care, entertainment, and especially online offices have developed with startlingly rapid progress Online and offline energy efficiency needs to be improved, making full use of cloud technology, big data, network connections, and 5G methods to improve the global value chain's immunity to emergencies. In 2020, China's more than 120 multinational companies could be encouraged to be in the world's top 500 of those exploring global online and offline production and office models, while simultaneously sharing experience in pandemic prevention, and leading and guiding the global value chain on the resumption of work and production. The development of digital and intelligent technologies not only contributes to global economic growth in the short term, but also prevents economic crises caused by the pandemic. It also plays an important role in promoting the long-term growth of the world economy and transforming economic models.
(3) A global long-term pandemic prevention and control system must be established to actively respond to the impact of future public health events in human society. The continuous improvement of human health is the foundation for the stable development of the global

economy and is inseparable from effective international coordination. This COVID-19 pandemic highlights the rationality, necessity, and urgency of a global long-term pandemic prevention and control system and the construction of a community with a shared future for mankind. The key to establishing a global long-term pandemic prevention and control system is to release pandemic and virus information in a timely manner during pandemic outbreak, and coordinate global pandemic prevention and control materials, including temporary organization and adjustments to production. During the pandemic-free period, international organizations such as the WHO should increase the ecological standard testing of trade commodities, coordinate countries to establish and improve disease control systems, and popularize disease prevention and control education.

The WHO is the guiding and coordinating agency for health issues within the United Nations. It aims to promote the prevention and treatment of pandemics and endemic diseases and improve public health. As of 2019, the World Health Organization has 194 member states. However, as the WHO is only a coordinating agency, it can only suggest certain response measures, and cannot force countries to implement them. Due to a certain degree of mistrust between sovereign countries together with their different capabilities for pandemic prevention and control when faced with international public health emergencies, many countries proceed with their own interests and do not make decisions from the perspective of global coordination as recommended by the WHO. Therefore, it is necessary to establish a global pandemic prevention and control system that coordinates both pandemic and economic responses. As the scope of human activities expands, new pandemics will emerge. Human society needs to build a long-term pandemic prevention and control system on a global scale. All countries must take the initiative to coordinate the prevention and control of sudden international public health incidents, maintain the safety of human society, and promote the improvement of global welfare.

https://doi.org/10.1142/9789811252921_0016

Chapter 16

The Impact of the COVID-19 Pandemic on EU Countries and on China–EU Trade Relations and Policy Responses

Ding Chun

School of Economics, Fudan University, Shanghai, China

16.1 The Impact of COVID-19 on European Countries

16.1.1 The spread of COVID-19 in Europe

COVID-19 has been an atypical, unforeseen threat in the era of globalization. It has not only severely affected Wuhan and other parts of China but has also continued to rage in Europe. Its impact on the European economy and China–EU economic and trade relations can be divided into two stages. The lockdown of Wuhan on January 23 marked the first phase, followed by the preventative measures undertaken by various European countries. Due to China's extended Spring Festival holiday and the suspension of production to control the pandemic, European countries experienced supply delays from China, and a decline in import demand from Europe ensued. On March 9, Italy imposed a strict lockdown on many of its cities, which followed the outbreak of the virus in Europe and the second stage of the pandemic. At the same time, China's pandemic was gradually being controlled, with the number of newly diagnosed patients in Wuhan dropping to single digits. On March 12, the National Health Commission announced that the peak of this wave of the pandemic in China had passed.

In contrast, following the diagnosis of the first case in Europe in Bordeaux, France, on January 24, 2020, the pandemic was spreading exponentially. According to the *European Times* website, as of 14:00 on March 16, Paris time, confirmed cases of COVID-19 had appeared in all 27 European Union member states. Of them, Italy and Spain became the hardest-hit areas, and announced the blocking of access in and out the countries. On March 16, the President of the European Commission, Ursula von der Leyen, announced that the EU was considering a 30-day closure of its borders. After fighting COVID-19 pandemic for several months, the situation improved after April, and cities began to reopen. According to the *European Times* statistics, as of 23:00 on August 24, Central European Time (CET), a total of 3,665,960 cases of COVID-19 pandemic had been reported in Europe, and the number of confirmed cases in Spain, the United Kingdom, France, Italy, and Germany exceeded 200,000. The number of COVID-19 infection cases was larger in the West than the East.

16.1.2 Corresponding measures in EU countries

The EU did not pay attention to the pandemic until cases started to skyrocket. At first, they did not realize the significance of the pandemic and delayed adopting preventative measures. However, in March, a severe outbreak in Italy gained attention. EU countries began to take the pandemic seriously and implemented various prevention policies. We can see that Italy responded quickly and immediately took an action that emphasized all inspections should be carried out. The German response was measured and pragmatic, as they responded to the pandemic with different tiers of policies. The focus of pandemic prevention was to respond step by step, to avoid the "over-running" and paralysis of the medical system and exhaustion of medical care staff and resources.

Italy, which was the first of the worst-hit areas, had its first confirmed case on January 30. Since then, the pandemic has spread rapidly, mainly in the northern Lombardy and Veneto regions, which became the epicenter of the second phase. The Italian central government's response to the crisis was fairly positive and on January 22 a response team led by the Ministry of Health was established. Following this, various measures were taken, such as creating relevant websites, monitoring the temperature of passengers flying from Wuhan to Rome, and flight control. After the first patient was diagnosed, direct flights between China and Italy were canceled. The country declared a state of emergency on January 30, 2021, and sent a plane to pick up Italian citizens in Wuhan and other areas. On February 22, a dozen cities and towns in the Lombardy and Veneto regions were closed. On 24, a tent hospital in Italy opened overnight, and on March 4, schools across the country were closed and all teaching activities were suspended. Italy required medical institutions to accelerate the release of intensive care beds and increase medical staff to cope with the pandemic and shortage of staff. Doctors from China and Italy also used video conferences to share experience and exchange information. On March 8, Italian Prime Minister Conte announced that the Lombardy region, including Milan, and many neighboring regions would be officially closed. Italy closely monitored a quarter of the country's population numbering more than 10 million, and closed theaters, museums, and other facilities. On 9, Prime Minister Conte announced that the entire territory of Italy would be under lockdown.

In Germany, the government mainly emphasized an appropriate and orderly response, gradually upgrading response measures, and focusing on hard core issues such as the supply of pandemic prevention and control materials and equipment. At the federal level, a crisis response team comprising the Ministry of Health and the Ministry of the Interior was established. In accordance with the analysis and evaluation by the Robert Koch Institute, the German disease control agency, the risk level of COVID-19 was upgraded to medium, and a number of prevention and control measures were formulated to coordinate with local governments, including prioritizing the procurement of pandemic prevention materials for clinics, hospitals, and federal departments; prohibiting the export of pandemic prevention materials and equipment; strengthening cooperation with states; highlighting the risk of cruise travel; informing Germans abroad to comply with local government quarantine requirements; issuing strict entry declarations; formulating risk assessment guidelines for large-scale events, and giving local governments the authority to decide whether to cancel activities and close schools. At the same time, to cut off the spread of the virus, blocking cities and regions was an option in extreme cases. Chancellor Angela Merkel, speaking at the press conference of the new corona pneumonia pandemic in Germany, warned on March 1 that 60–70% of German citizens may be infected. After that, on March 12,

Chancellor Merkel stated that Germany was in a situation that was more unusual in every sense than that of the financial crisis of 2008–2009.[1] Since then, Germany has controlled its borders with neighboring countries.

In France, while emphasizing the need not to overreact, President Macron announced a decree on February 4 to requisition masks to ensure the needs of medical staff. On February 29, he announced that France had entered the second phase of preventing the spread of the virus. On March 3, all stocks of masks and production units were requisitioned. President Macron made a televised speech on March 12, announcing that all schools in France would be closed the following Monday. He said that COVID-19 was the worst health crisis that France has suffered in nearly a century.[2]

16.1.3 Responses from EU

The health sector still forms part of the sovereignty of each member state, therefore, the EU primarily plays a coordinating role. However, after the breakout of COVID-19, the European Union has paid considerable attention to coordinating pandemic control measures. The Council of the European Union, which represents the interests and sovereignty of member states, held an emergency meeting on February 13, 2020. The health ministers of all member states participated in this emergency meeting to discuss coordination and response, and issued a combined document, urging member states and the European Commission to cooperate, share information, and invest in vaccine research and development. This document required countries to take appropriate prevention and control measures to prevent the spread of the pandemic. It was recommended that entry regulations be standardized and uniform to facilitate understanding the movements of patients for contact tracing, strengthen cooperation with WHO and countries affected by the pandemic, and avoid shortages of medicines and protective equipment during the outbreak. In addition to France and Italy, 20 member states put forward proposals for joint procurement of personal protective equipment. As the pandemic became more serious, the Council of the European Union held its second meeting

---

[1] China News Network, March 13, 2020.

[2] *Ibid.*

of health ministers on March 6, calling for strengthening the coordination of pandemic containment and information exchange. The meeting focused on raising public awareness of the threat of COVID-19, informing the public on transmission, curbing the spread of false news, promoting global and cross-industry collaboration, avoiding possible shortages of protective products and equipment, protecting medical staff, and subsidizing vaccine development costs up to EUR 7 million. France, Germany, the Czech Republic, among others, restricted the export of relevant pandemic control equipment and medicines, but relations among member states were strained. Nevertheless, according to information disclosed after the meeting, the joint bidding process for anti-pandemic drugs and equipment in various countries was in good shape (Ding Chun, 2020). On March 16, leaders from the G7 and the EU took part in a video conference and discussed implementing the EU's temporary "non-essential performance" ban.

As a transnational executor, the European Commission reflects the common interests of all member states. On March 2, the European Center for Disease Control and Prevention (ECDC) raised the risk of COVID-19 in Europe from "low to medium" to "medium to high". European Commission President Ursula von der Leyen set up a team responsible for COVID-19 prevention measures. The team was responsible for unifying and coordinating specific pandemic responses throughout the EU. It was led by five significant European Commissioners in charge of health and food safety, crisis management, immigration and civil affairs, transportation, and macroeconomic affairs. The team cooperated with member states to respond to the pandemic in three fields: medical care, transportation, and the economy. In the medical field, the Directorate-General for Food Safety and Health (Group), in collaboration with the European Centers for Disease Control and Prevention, and the European Medicines Agency (EMA), were responsible for compiling daily pandemic monitoring information in various countries, formulating guidelines for medical technical procedures, cooperating with the WHO and China, strengthening the research and development of anti-virus vaccines. In the field of transportation, the General Department of Transportation (Group) issued transportation and travel recommendations based on the progress of the pandemic, and adjusted internal border measures in the Schengen area. In the economic field, the Directorate General of Macroeconomics (group) conducted in-depth research and evaluation of tourism, transportation, trade, the industrial chain, and macroeconomics and proposed corresponding countermeasures. In addition, the EU's Directorate-General for Crisis Management was responsible for coordinating crisis management actions at the EU level.

16.1.4 Characteristics and effects of pandemic control in EU countries

Certain EU countries have become epicenters of the second phase of COVID-19 pandemic. The effectiveness of COVID-19 pandemic controlling measures have depended on several factors, including the judgement of the relevant authorities, the habits of citizens, social consensus, institutional decentralization, medical care resources, and government execution.

The EU's fight against the pandemic has the following five characteristics: (1) emphasis on personal freedom: valuing personal choice and privacy protection. The government does not make compulsory policies. Instead, the government calls for action. For example, the German Chancellor and the government called for the cancellation of large-scale gatherings and proposed school closures. Mandatory isolation measures cannot be issued. (2) The decision-makers and ordinary people believe the impact of panic is heavier than that of COVID-19 itself. According to expert advice, the prevention and control strategy is to increase the level of prevention and control measures in a step-by-step fashion, depending on the development of the pandemic. The strongest mandatory isolation measure is city closure. (3) Both the people and the government do not advocate over-protection. They were against preventing COVID-19 pandemic by wearing masks. They would rather leave the masks for the use of medical staff. (4) A high degree of trust in experts and medical prevention systems for the country. (5) In the prevention, control, and response to the pandemic, the EU and even the central governments of various countries have been responsible for formulating rules and organizing coordination tasks, while local governments have enjoyed great autonomy. In Italy, many decisions of the central government have been difficult to implement locally. In Germany, the chancellor and the federal government can only call on the states to act. Judging from the implementation effects so far, depending on alliances, national conditions, systems, and governance experience, countries have had different efficiencies, leading to different results. Many countries, including Italy, started to take various measures early but had dissatisfactory results. However, Germany has again showed the world its rigor and pragmatism in achieving outstanding results in pandemic control.

16.2 The Impact of COVID-19 on the EU Economy and China–EU Economic and Trade Relations

In the first stage, the impact of COVID-19 on the economy of the EU was not that apparent or severe. The impact was mainly concentrated in trade and commercial chains. In the second stage, COVID-19 spread globally; it had a more profound and long-term impact on the stock markets, economies, and even the collective economy of European countries, especially EU member states. From the perspective of China–EU economic and trade relations, there are mainly two aspects.

16.2.1 The impact on the EU economy and its member states

16.2.1.1 *Severe turbulence in European stock markets*

The spread of the pandemic on a global scale, especially in Europe and North America, the refugee shock caused by Turkish pressure to open its border to the EU, and Saudi Arabia's cut in oil prices caused shocks that have not been seen in many years on the stock markets in Europe and the world. At the same time, they triggered market concerns about global economic recession, liquidity, and solvency issues.

Stock markets in many European countries have shown huge turbulence. In early March of 2020, many stocks in the European stock market plummeted. The UK's FTSE 100 Index fell about 11% in the first week of March. The German DAX30 index fell 12.5% in the same week, and the French CAC40 index fell nearly 12% as well. The value of European stock markets during that week evaporated by about $1.5 trillion, the worst weekly performance since the 2008 financial crisis. By mid-March, the British, French, German, and Italian stock markets had fallen more than 30% from the beginning of the year. However, the European financial market stabilized and market confidence gradually recovered because the EU took effective economic measures.

16.2.1.2 *Further aggravation of the weak economic recovery of EU countries*

In 2019, the EU economy was affected by several factors, such as global trade protectionism and China–US trade frictions. Therefore, the speed of the EU's economic recovery was slow and economic growth was small with the overall average growth rate being lower than that in 2018, at only 1.5%. The rate in the Eurozone was only 1.2% (see Figure 16.1).

(1) The economies of EU member states such as Germany are export-oriented. Therefore, EU member states have suffered a lot in response to China–US and Europe–US trade frictions. In 2019, the German economy grew by only 0.5%, and with negative growth in the second quarter. Since then, the economy had almost fallen into a technical recession. Since the European debt crisis, Germany's economy, which had been hailed as the economic powerhouse of the European Union and the Eurozone, had clearly stalled.
(2) In France, President Macron had previously taken measures such as tax cuts and activating the labor market, which had achieved a certain success. Moreover, the French economy's external dependence was relatively light, barely reaching 1.2%. However, the "yellow vest"

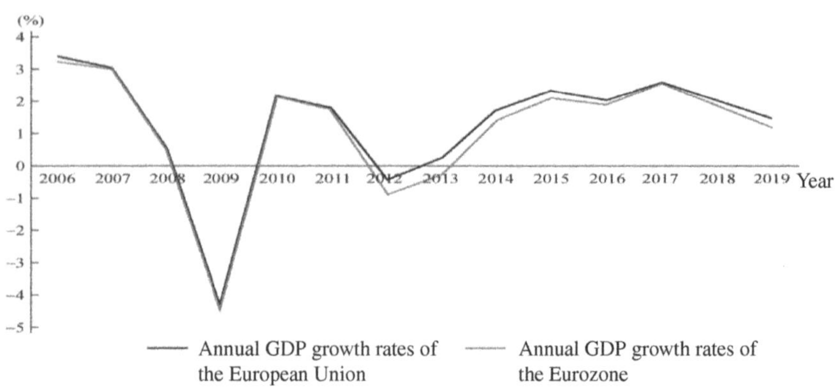

Figure 16.1: Annual GDP growth rates of the European Union and Eurozone from 2006 to 2019.

Source: Eurostat.

protest among other protest waves has had an apparent negative impact on French fiscal and economic growth.

(3) Britain officially left the European Union at the end of January 2020. Although the formal Brexit brought an end to the three-and-a-half-year-long Brexit process, which had a positive stabilizing effect on the British economy, the negotiations on Britain's future economic and trade relations with the EU have not yet reached a result, and the model for cooperation has not yet been settled. There are still great uncertainties about whether the negotiations will be officially concluded by the end of 2020 and whether the UK and Europe will continue to maintain close economic and trade ties.

At the industry and corporate level, the situation is not optimistic. Shipping and logistics industries were the first to bear the brunt of the pandemic. The data show that in many major tourist destinations in the European market, the number of ticket bookings has shown at least a double-digit decline. Reservations from the Asia-Pacific region fell by 114.2% year on year. Reservations from the Americas fell by 68.1%. Bookings from Africa and the Middle East dropped 49.9% year on year. The tourism industry was also hard-hit. For EU member states such as Italy and France, where the tourism industry accounts for a high proportion of the economy, even the loss of tourism income caused by the first phase of the pandemic was enough to bring about a cold winter in the industry, let alone losses in the second wave when the pandemic spread in Europe. In the second wave, Italy, Spain and other countries were forced to close cities, causing huge negative impacts on shipping and logistic industries. Due to the pandemic, exhibitions were postponed, sports events were canceled, restaurants were closed, and leisure activities were curtailed. European countries, especially countries relying on tourism such as Italy, France, and Spain, suffered greatly in the service industry, including tourism, catering, accommodation, and luxury goods.

According to the *British Financial Times*, the situation of the manufacturing industry in 2020, which was the engine of the German economy, was the worst in the past 10 years. Large companies such as Mercedes-Benz also had their worst performance in 10 years. The impact of the pandemic had made the situation worse.[3]

[3] Sina Finance February 10, 2020.

16.2.1.3 *COVID-19 lowers the economic development expectations of the EU and its member states*

The World Bank, the International Monetary Fund, the European Union, and its member states all praised China's decisive measures to restrict the movement of people in response to the pandemic. They were all optimistic about China's economic growth and predicted that the Chinese economy would rebound after the pandemic. However, there were worries about the uncertainty brought about by the pandemic to the European and world economy. IMF President Georgieva said: "The way the pandemic affects the global economy and value chain is still unclear. However, compared with the SARS period in 2003, the Chinese economy is of much greater significance to the world economy today." European Central Bank President Lagarde warned on February 6 that: "The COVID-19 pandemic has replaced the China–US trade friction and has become a major risk for economic growth. It is still difficult to determine its impact on the Chinese economy and the global economy." The EU's Winter 2020 Outlook, released on February 13, stated: "The COVID-19 pandemic may have an impact on foreign trade and supply chains, and German industry is greatly exposed to this risk. The EU's economic growth this year may be slower than last year, especially for Italy. Although Italy is the EU's third largest economy, its economic performance has been poor since the European debt crisis. Italy's GDP growth rate was only 0.2% in 2019, which was far below the overall EU level of 1.2%. Its total GDP has not yet recovered to the level it was before the 2007 crisis. The overall unemployment rate is still as high as 11%. The youth unemployment rate is among the highest in Europe, and public debt is the second highest in the Eurozone. The Lombardy, Emilia-Romagna, and Veneto regions, where the pandemic raged the most, contribute to one-third of the country's gross national product and approximately one-half of the country's exports. The pandemic has undoubtedly made the originally fragile Italian economy even worse."

16.2.1.4 *The pandemic has caused an increase in the fiscal expenditures of the EU and its member states, leaving indebted countries, including Italy, in a worse situation and increasing the risk of triggering debt and financial secondary crises again*

At present, many European Union (euro area) countries are in poor fiscal health. In 2019, Greece, Italy, Portugal, and France, the countries with the highest public debt ratio in the Eurozone, had accumulated public debt exceeding the upper limit of 60% of GDP. The average public debt in the Eurozone had reached 86.1%, far exceeding the 60% GDP debt ceiling (see Table 16.1). That was why the scope for expanding fiscal expenditures in pandemic control and prevention and economic stipulation was limited. It also pushed the European Central Bank to issue a loose monetary policy to deal with emergencies. Since the European Central Bank had implemented a negative interest rate policy and restarted its quantitative easing policy in 2019, the room for active monetary policy implementation was also limited. According to data released by the European Union, in the first quarter of 2020, 24 out of the 27 member states saw a share of their government debt in GDP rise. A heavily indebted country

Table 16.1: Proportion of government debt in GDP of 19 countries in the Eurozone in 2019

	States	**The ratio of government debt in GDP in 2019 (%)**
1	Greece	178.2
2	Italy	137.3
3	Portugal	120.5
4	France	100.5
5	Spain	97.9
6	Cyprus	97.0
7	Belgium	80.1
8	Austria	71.1
9	Slovenia	68.1
10	Ireland	62.6
11	Germany	61.2
12	Finland	59.4
13	Netherlands	49.3
14	Slovakia	48.4
15	Malta	48.1
16	Latvia	36.4
17	Lithuania	35.9
18	Luxembourg	20.2
19	Estonia	9.2
	The average debt ratio of the 19 countries in the Eurozone	86.1

Source: Eurostat.

like Italy may suffer from a debt crisis because the increase in fiscal expenditure for pandemic prevention may increase the public debt ratio. If not handled property, a European debt crisis may occur again, which is what most worries people.

16.2.2 The impact of COVID-19 on China–EU economic and trade relations

16.2.2.1 *The pandemic caused a sharp drop in China–Europea trade in the short term, damaging bilateral economic and trade exchanges*

Since the European debt crisis, the EU has been China's largest foreign trade partner, and overall bilateral total import and export volume has been increasing (see Figure 16.2). In the first stage of COVID-19, due to the pandemic and the ultra-long Spring Festival holiday, China's foreign trade imports and exports from January to February 2020 saw a large-scale decline. According to customs statistics, the import and export of goods in the first two months of 2020 decreased by 9.6% compared with the same period in 2019. The European Union,[4] became the second largest

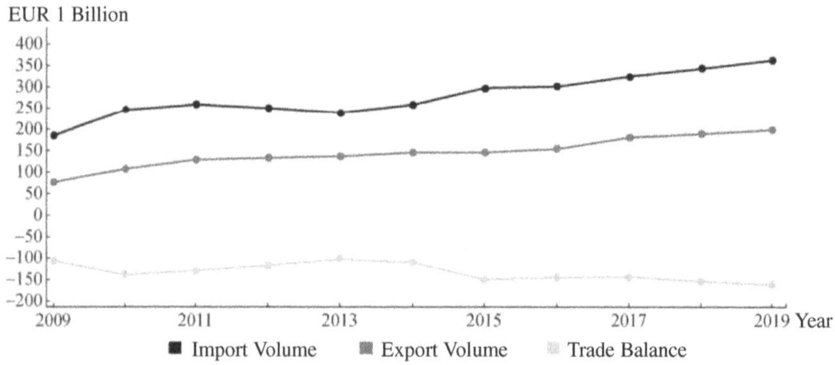

Figure 16.2: 2009–2019 China–EU import and export trade volume and trade balance.

Source: Eurostat.

[4]Except the United Kingdom.

trading partner. The total amount of imports and exports denominating in RMB fell by 14.2%, and the proportion of foreign trade fell to 13.5%. Of these, China's exports and imports to Europe fell by 17.1% and 9.9%, respectively, and China's trade surplus with Europe narrowed by 34.1%.[5] Throughout the first half of the year, China's imports and exports to the EU were RMB 1.99 trillion, showing a decrease of 1.8% over the same period last year.

In the second stage, major EU countries that rank high in economic strength and scale were fighting the pandemic, such as Italy, Germany, France, Spain, and even Britain, which had already left the EU. The pandemic had a negative impact on China–EU economic and trade dealings. Firstly, with the continuous strengthening of physical isolation measures in EU countries, such as entry restrictions and the reduction, suspension, and interruption of flights, the density of personnel exchanges between China and Europe as well as the speed of commodity logistics flow decreased. Secondly, in the short term, isolation measures such as city closures resulted in decreased consumption, except for pandemic prevention materials and equipment. Thus, import demand also slowed down, creating disadvantages for China's exports to Europe. Thirdly, in the medium term, the financial support and deficits of the EU and related countries increased due to the pandemic. The economy suffered and people's income declined. Therefore, consumption demand decreased. It led to a decline in European demand for imports from China. To a certain extent, it was possible that Europe's investment strength in China would also decline.

16.2.2.2 *The pandemic has had a negative impact on the operations of related companies through industry chain channels*

(1) China is currently the largest trading partner of more than 100 countries worldwide and is also the largest source of imports for 65 countries, including the United States. China's manufacturing industry accounts for 25% of world production. It has contributed more than 30% to world economic growth in the past ten years. The pandemic

[5]China's government website, March 7th, 2020.

has caused many countries, including some countries in the European Union, to restrict personnel exchanges with China. Continued suspension of work has affected the circulation and import of commodities. In the short term, it has reduced China's exports, but most importantly the stability of the global industrial chain may be affected as well as the recovery of the world economy. As an intermediate and key link in the global supply chain, manufacturing in China has the characteristics of being complete, systematic, and irreplaceable in the short term. Germany, for example, is China's largest economic and trading partner among EU member states and its manufacturing industry especially accounts for nearly one-third of China's economy and trade. Germany has a huge influence in the entire industrial chain of Europe, especially Central and Eastern Europe. The German industrial chain is closely connected to China's, a major manufacturing country. Hence, China's economic losses due to the pandemic will undoubtedly have a serious impact on the economies of Germany and other EU member states, especially automobile manufacturing and parts supply companies, which are pillar industries. Professor Ferdinand Dudenhoeffer of the University of Essen in Duisburg, known as the"godfather of automobiles"in Germany, said; "The German automobile industry has been highly integrated with China, and the pandemic has also caused severe damage to the German automobile industry." According to the research data of his automobile research institute, the German automobile industry earns EUR150 billion in sales in China each year, which is equivalent to 35% of the single-year sales of the German automobile industry.[6] One of the worst hit areas, Hubei Province, is also one of China's four major automobile production bases. Wuhan, Shiyan, Xiangyang, Suzhou, and other cities have formed a cluster of automobile industrial bases. Foreign brands such as Peugeot Citroen and Renault are also gathered in these clusters. The annual output in 2019 was 2.24 million vehicles, accounting for 8.8% of the country's total (Li Xiaohong, 2020). In addition, to complete the manufacturing of vehicles, many domestic and foreign companies provide support through manufacturing auto parts, including auto parts supply giants such as Bosch, Valeo, and Delphi. As a result, their suspension of production has had a

[6]China News Network, February 24, 2020.

considerable impact on the global automotive industry, especially on European companies.

(2) The European Union and related member states such as Germany have long been China's largest sources of high-tech components, and their position in China's high-tech imports and industrial chains is very important. In terms of commercial chains, many of the mid-to-high-end components of China's products come from upstream EU companies. For example, in the automobile industry some high-end models of SAIC Volkswagen, such as the Phaeton, have parts and accessories from Germany and Italy. If the pandemic has an adverse impact on logistics and affects German and Italian manufacturers and suppliers, or suspends production, Chinese car companies face the risk of a "black light" state. Such a situation is quite common when high-tech spare parts are supplied by outside producers, especially in machinery, electronics, automobile, and other industries.

(3) The pandemic may cause changes and reorganization of the industrial chain in China and Europe. As a result of the pandemic, the United States and Europe have discovered that, except for a small number of highly profitable patented drugs, many generic drugs, APIs, and medical supplies are produced mainly in China and India. This is because American and European producers are profit-driven, leading them to seek out low cost labor and production in far away regions like China, and as a result, when the pandemic hit, their domestic supply was insufficient. Many countries have promulgated export bans and even intercepted foreign pandemic prevention materials; the German confiscation of Swiss masks is a prime example of this. It is possible that after the pandemic, even within the period of pandemic prevention, domestic industrial chains will be rebuilt and to a certain extent production capacity in China will be withdrawn.

16.2.2.3 *The pandemic may have a dual impact on the deepening of China–EU economic and trade relations*

From one perspective, China and the EU have been working together to control the pandemic and avoid an economic recession, which requires bilateral cooperation and coordination. However, the leaders and officials of Europe, including the EU and its member states, have been devoting their energy to fighting the pandemic, with little time left to discuss cooperation with China, especially economic and trade negotiations. The European Trade Commissioner Hogan has said the pandemic has delayed China–EU consultations and it may also cause the postponement of the China–EU Summit and the China Central and Eastern European Conference. This is obviously not conducive to enhancing bilateral coordination and cooperation between China and Europe and supporting free trade and globalization in the context of China–US trade frictions and the tide of anti-globalization.

16.3 Economic Response Measures of the EU and Its Member States and China

16.3.1 Measures taken by EU member states to respond to the economic impact of COVID-19

In the first stage of the outbreak of COVID-19, EU member states had different practices. Some countries, like Italy, quickly grounded civilian flights between China and Italy and evacuated those overseas from Wuhan. Other EU countries like Germany have made it clear that they would not overreact or suspend flights between the two countries while still evacuating their overseas citizens. Leaders of many EU countries, including Germany, France, and Italy, have expressed their understanding and support for the Chinese government's city closure. They have promised to provide support and assistance within their capacity and have donated pandemic prevention and control materials. They have believed that the pandemic will not change the long-term good development of China's economy. They have hoped that China will stop the spread of the pandemic as soon as possible and resume and restore production to pre-pandemic levels. In the second phase of the pandemic, member states of the EU exerted all efforts to prevent the spread of the pandemic and introduce large-scale financial assistance measures to promote economic development so as to avoid recession.

(1) Italy: The Italian central government had to introduce economic measures to alleviate the impact of COVID-19 on the economy while controlling the pandemic and treating patients. By July 2020, Italy had issued an emergency rescue plan of EUR 80 billion, and released

a further EUR 750 billion, providing loan guarantees to companies facing financial hardships. Italy has also issued an export promotion plan to provide funds for the internationalization of enterprises.

(2) Germany: When the pandemic posed an emergent situation, the German government realized that the consequence of the pandemic may be comparable to that of the European debt crisis. Therefore, Germany responded quickly with a German-style rigorous and pragmatic approach, issuing a series of relevant pandemic control measures and policies. It is the strongest economic power in the European Union and among the Eurozone countries, and not only maintains its fiscal balance all year round, but in some years it has also had a surplus. The government always seeks to take measures within its power. After joining the Eurozone, Germany was worried that other countries would not comply with the fiscal deficit and public debt standards set by the EU's *Stability and Growth Pact,* leaving German taxpayers to pay the bill. Thus, out of concern for this moral risk, Germany strengthened fiscal discipline setting itself as the example. During the pandemic period, the German government has agreed to abandon the balanced budget policy it had always adhered to and did not hesitate to use a fiscal stimulus package such as deficit finance to maintain the normal operation of the economy. Germany passed an economic stimulus plan totaling EUR130 billion, in line with the previous EUR 750 billion economic relief package, using a phased response strategy to provide enterprises with unlimited loans. German Economy Minister Altmaier said: "When necessary, the government will consider holding shares in key enterprises of strategic significance and temporarily nationalizing them. It depends on the subsequent development of the economic situation". The Minister of Finance and Deputy Prime Minister Scholz claimed that the government did not set priority selection criteria for companies in need of assistance due to sufficient funds.[7]

(3) France: While preventing the spread of COVID-19 pandemic, the French government has introduced economic policies to help companies in various ways, such as reducing costs, maintaining operations, and overcoming financial difficulties. The French government provided EUR 45 billion of financial assistance to companies and employees affected by the pandemic. Moreover, the French

[7] *Sina News*, March 1, 2020.

government provided EUR 300 billion of state guarantees for corporate bank loans and proposed a rescue plan for the aviation industry of approximately EUR 15 billion. The rescue plan contained exemption measures for late delivery of government procurements. The French Ministry of Finance has determined that the COVID-19 pandemic is a force majeure situation encountered by enterprises and thus excuses relevant companies from contractual penalties for late delivery of government procurement contracts. The French government has also planned to share social and tax burdens with enterprises and allowed some enterprises facing difficulties to defer social security contributions. At the same time, the government has also implemented amended unemployment policies. For example, companies that are temporarily facing economic difficulties may apply for prior authorization from relevant government departments, allowing the enterprise to reduce the working hours of its employees and unemployment benefits would compensate employees for the loss of income caused by the reduction in working hours.[8]

(4) Spain: Spanish Prime Minister Sanchez has launched an unprecedented EUR 200 billion economic assistance plan. Half of the funds will be used to provide credit guarantees for companies to ensure the operation of social public services, and the other half will be used to provide assistance and loans to vulnerable groups.

In addition, Portugal, the Netherlands, Croatia, Sweden, Norway, and other EU member states have also introduced economic relief and stimulus plans of various scales to restore the economy and stimulate growth.

16.3.2 EU's measures to respond to economic challenges during the pandemic

(1) The European Commission has introduced a series of comprehensive economic response measures, including the introduction of a EUR 100 billion SURE mechanism to alleviate the risk of unemployment in Europe, protect small and medium-sized enterprises, protect key EU technologies and assets, introduce emergency guidelines for foreign investment review, and temporarily cancel import duties and

[8] *Xinhua News Agency*, March 12, 2020.

value-added tax on imported medical equipment and protective equipment. Relaxation of EU fiscal rules exemption clauses has also been included, which refers to the European Commission's initiation of the general relaxing of budget rules in the *Pact for Stability and Growth.* At the same time, the European Commission has introduced a recovery plan that has attracted the attention of all parties and was finally adopted after several days of discussions at the EU summit, the "Next Generation EU". The plan includes a total EUR 750 billion of which EUR 390 billion is for free grants and EUR 360 billion is for borrowed money. Most of the free grants will be used for southern European countries that have been severely affected. Frugal countries, such as the Netherlands and Austria, will receive certain refunds for the long-term budget in 2021.

(2) The European Central Bank uses monetary policies such as quantitative easing to stimulate and support the economies of member countries. On March 12, while deciding whether to maintain the three major policy interest rates, the European Central Bank introduced a series of loose monetary policies to stimulate demand and alleviate the economic shock caused by the pandemic.[9] There are mainly three aspects to this:

Liquidity measures: General measures are abandoned, while specific measures are preferred. Temporary implementation of more long-term refinancing operations (LTROs) provides immediate liquidity support for the euro area's financial system. Methods such as targeted long-term refinancing (TLTROs) are used to support banks in providing loans to enterprises severely affected by the pandemic, especially small and medium-sized enterprises.

Enhanced quantitative easing policy: Before the end of 2020, a temporary cap of 120 billion euros for net asset purchases will be increased to ensure the success of the private sector purchase plan. This is an active expansion of the existing asset purchase program, which can provide approximately 12 billion euros as additional funds per month. Together with the existing EUR 20 billion asset purchase program (APP), this will provide more favorable financing conditions for the real economy when the pandemic is severe.

---

[9] *Xinhuanet*, March 13, 2020.

Make more use of expansionary fiscal policy: Countries should be called on to make use of expansionary fiscal policies to more effectively and accurately support the economies of EU member states that have been dragged down by the pandemic. The reason for taking this action instead of cutting interest rates is that interest rates are already negative with limited room for further interest rate cuts. At the same time, member states are allowed to temporarily break the red line of the 3% deficit rate. Member states can use active fiscal stimulus policies to stabilize the economy and promote growth.

16.3.3 The effect of China's response to the pandemic on the economy of China and Europe

16.3.3.1 *China has maintained close communication and has shared information and its experience of dealing with the pandemic*

Since the outbreak of COVID-19, China and the EU have been actively cooperating in many aspects, such as information sharing and pandemic control. President Xi Jinping has held telephone communication with German Chancellor Merkel, French President Macron, British Prime Minister Johnson, and Italian Prime Minister Conte. Premier Li Keqiang and European Commission Chairman von der Leyen have also had a phone conversation. China actively provides information on the pandemic to Europe, assists some EU countries in evacuation activities, and promotes the control and alleviation of the pandemic. China has alleviated the concerns of the international community and provided support for economic recovery. The Chinese envoys to Europe also accepted interviews with television stations and newspapers from various countries, in which the envoys introduced how China has fought COVID-19 pandemic, promoting Europe's understanding of China's pandemic control measures. The envoys also helped overseas Chinese and promoted local economic and social stability.

16.3.3.2 *China summarizes its own experience and helps Europe to fight the pandemic*

The COVID-19 pandemic is a serious challenge to the world. While controlling the spread of the virus step by step, China has overcome difficulties and provided within its capacity European countries with assistance in the fight against the pandemic. China's National Health Commission and the National Center for Disease Control and Prevention, together with the European Commission's Directorate-General for Health, and the European Center for Disease Control and Prevention, have established a joint expert group to respond to the pandemic. They have exchanged information on how COVID-19 has been dealt with in Europe and China, and the latter has shared its experience in preventing the spread of the pandemic. In terms of cooperating with member states, China has also actively carried out medical and health cooperation with Italy. China has sent a medical team to Italy to assist in prevention and control measures and has also agreed to remotely conduct exchanges in the medical field.

16.3.3.3 *China has taken multiple measures to promote the resumption of work and the production of companies, including European companies in China*

Globalization means that the interests of China and Europe are deeply integrated and entangled. In response to the adverse impact of the pandemic on economic production and material supplies, China's central and local governments have taken various measures to support the resumption of work and production of European companies based in China. First, governments at all levels have strengthened financial support, provided return-to-employment guarantees, implemented support for key enterprises, promoted the resumption of work and production of domestic enterprises in China in accordance with the law, and have striven to ensure the restoration of the supply chain. Second, China continues to promote high-level opening-up, and strives to do a good job stabilizing foreign investment and foreign trade, helping foreign-funded companies solve the practical difficulties caused by the pandemic, especially for leading companies. Further, for these companies China has tried its best to ensure the resumption of work and production. For relevant European companies, the Chinese government has actively responded to the difficulties reported by EU companies in China through the Chamber of Commerce and worked hard to facilitate the resumption of work and production of EU companies in China.[10] Meanwhile, China–Europe Express trains have

[10]Chinese Mission to the EU, 2020.

gradually resumed normal operations. To ensure the smooth flow of goods between China and Europe, the General Administration of Customs has especially introduced measures to support the development of China–EU trade.[11] According to data from the National Railway Group Co. Ltd., in the first half of 2020 a total of 5,122 China–Europe Express trains operated, representing a year-on-year increase of 36.5%. According to customs statistics of the same period, China–Europe freight trains transported 5.105 million tons of import and export goods, a year-on-year increase of 30.9%, which has become a highlight of China–EU relations.

[11] *Xinhua News Agency*, March 2, 2020.

https://doi.org/10.1142/9789811252921_0017

Chapter 17

The Impact of the COVID-19 Pandemic on Supply Chains and Policy Response

Luo Changyuan and Fan Haichao

School of Economics, Fudan University, Shanghai, China

China, the "world's factory", is the Asian center of the global value chain. Since the outbreak of the COVID-19 pandemic, some companies have not been able to deliver goods and services on time, and thus, some countries and regions with supply chain relationships with China have been affected. This situation has led to concerns about the safety of China's supply chains, causing a heated discussion among those in academic and industrial circles. Against this background, this chapter presents some thoughts on the matter, and the structure of the chapter is as follows: the first part describes the background of the impact of COVID-19 on supply chains; the second part assesses and judges the impact of the COVID-19 on supply chains; the third part introduces various ways to alleviate the impact of the pandemic on China's supply chains; and the final part suggests how to improve the business environment and the position of China within global supply chains.

17.1 The Background of the Impact of COVID-19 on Supply Chains

Hubei Province, especially Wuhan City, was the hardest hit by COVID-19 in China. Wuhan is a significant city that connects nine provinces, serves as a transportation sector hub, and maintains strong economic connections with other regions. Hubei province, with its center in Wuhan, is a major upstream supply chain for industries like electronic information, intelligent manufacturing, and automobiles. In addition, it is also an important gathering place for the digital, biological, healthcare, new energy/material, and aerospace industries. Until September 2019, Wuhan's annual utilization of foreign capital exceeded USD10 billion, ranking in the forefront of sub-provincial cities. The total number of foreign-funded established enterprises exceeded 7,200, and the number of Fortune 500 companies increased to nearly 300 (*Changjiang Daily*, September 25, 2019).

Due to insufficient production capacity, poor transportation, and delays in resuming work, the impact of the epidemic on the supply chains in Wuhan City, Hubei Province, and the entire mainland has been continuously amplified, spreading the impact from East Asia to the entire world. Foxconn has a production base in Wuhan with more than 20,000 employees, operating as a foundry for HP, Dell, and other computer companies. Foxconn has more than 200,000 employees in each of its factories in Zhengzhou and Shenzhen, and its resumption of work is related to Apple's entire supply chain (Zhou Yuan and Chen Xiaoxiao, 2020). On February 4, due to a shortage of parts which should have been purchased from China, Hyundai Motor suspended production at its domestic plant in South Korea. On February 6, the CEO of Fiat Chrysler stated that if the supply of parts deteriorated further, production at a European assembly plant may have to be suspended at the end of February or early March. According to the data from the German Automotive Research Center, if China delays the restart of production by even one day, the German auto industry loses EUR 72 million a day (Liu Junqing, 2020). Several electronic products being developed by large Silicon Valley tech companies also had to be delayed due to the suspension of work by Chinese suppliers. According to the forecast of TrendForce Consulting, it was predicted that 275 million smartphones were to be produced between January and March 2020. This represented a 12% decrease from the same period in 2019, of which Apple's output would also decrease by 10%.[1]

The pandemic is a disaster serving as a mirror, which reflects the impact of China's manufacturing on the global supply chain. For China, its important manufacturing status is an asset of significance to the world

---

[1]*Source*: https: //www.infoxmation.com/article/9847.

economy has been spotlighted. At the same time, it is also a shortcoming, as it highlights China's contractual manufacturing responsibilities to the world economy. If China wants to continue shouldering this responsibility, it needs to improve its national capabilities, especially in product production, disease prevention and control, and industrial restoration.

17.2 Evaluation and Judgment of the Impact of COVID-19 on Supply Chains

In this section, the latest information has been integrated to make assessments, judgments, and in particular clarifications on the impact of the COVID-19 on supply chains.

17.2.1 Adjustment and transfer of the supply chain happened before the outbreak of the epidemic

The impact of the pandemic on supply chains has once again focused attention on the transnational transfer of industries. However, the transfer of industries did not happen after the outbreak; compared with the impact of the pandemic, the China–US trade friction initiated by the Trump administration was the biggest external shock that caused the relocation of industries. According to recent research by Li Wenlong and Zhang Shiming (2020), supply chain adjustments triggered by trade frictions had already begun to take shape before the advent of the pandemic.

Trade between East Asia and the United States provides an example. In terms of automobiles, South Korea's exports to the United States have grown the fastest and began to partially replace China's market share. However, in terms of mechanical and electrical equipment, China is the most important supplier to the United States, but America has obviously slowed down the pace of imports from China, while the pace of its imports from Malaysia is accelerating. The supply chain of mechanical and electrical equipment shows the trend of a shift to ASEAN member states. In terms of mobile phones and communication equipment, China is the world's largest mobile phone manufacturing base, serving as the most important production base for Apple's mobile phones and is still the most important and stable supplier of mobile phones to the United States. Nevertheless, there may be future changes.

Research by Li Wenlong and Zhang Shiming (2020) shows that since 2019, the growth of the U.S. economy has not led to a simultaneous growth of consumption of Chinese goods, and in fact the U.S's reliance on Chinese goods has decreased. Starting in October 2019, the growth rate of US imports from the world began to improve, but imports from China have yet to improve. Relatively speaking, the United States has formed closer trade relations with Canada, Vietnam, and South Korea.

Faced with the impact of the epidemic on the supply chain, it is understandable that concerns are held about the relocation of industries. However, the bigger exogenous shock has been the trade friction between China and the United States; if the current status quo does not undergo fundamental changes, the trend of supply chain adjustment will continue, and the epidemic is only a catalyst.

17.2.2 The United States has taken advantage of China's plight, intensifying concerns about China's supply chain security

When China was responding to the COVID-19 pandemic, many countries and international organizations offered generous help; however, some disgraceful politicians in America took advantage of China's epidemic, arousing the vigilance of the Chinese people.

On January 15, 2020, the first phase of the China–US trade negotiation agreement was signed. This agreement pressed the pause button on the escalating trade frictions which had been going on since March 2018, and temporarily eased the tense geopolitical relationship between China and the United States.

However, the implementation of the first phase and the start of negotiations for the second phase have not ended trade frictions. The United States has still found multiple excuses to again increase tariffs, which remains the biggest uncertainty for China's foreign trade development in 2020. To a certain extent COVID-19 has eased the US's aggressive attitude toward China, but it has not changed the game pattern between China and the US in the trade field. When China was sparing no efforts to stop the spread of the epidemic, some American politicians and those in the media showed their evil intentions; on January 30, US Secretary of Commerce Wilbur Ross bluntly stated that the epidemic in China was a good thing for the United States, since it would accelerate the return of job opportunities to North America (Bai Ziwen, 2020). On February 3, the *Wall Street Journal*, with the title "China is the real sick man of East Asia", used COVID-19 to launch racist attacks on China (Li Xiaohua, 2020). In early February, during his visit to Eastern Europe and Central Asia, the US Secretary of State attacked China on almost every visit (Yang Jin, 2020). On February 14, the Speaker of the U.S. House of Representatives Nancy Pelosi once again used Huawei to attack China at the Munich Security Conference (Li Yao, 2020). On February 18, the U.S. State Department listed Xinhua News Agency, China Radio International, China International Television, *China Daily*, and *People's Daily*, with all their branches in US, as foreign diplomatic missions, not independent news media (Yang Yifan, 2020).

During the pandemic prevention period, some American politicians and the media did not stop attacking China. It proves that the pandemic has no bearing on the US's suppression of China. Meanwhile, it has been noted that similar thoughts are echoed even in neighboring Asian countries like Singapore, where the Minister of Trade and Industry, Chen Zhensheng, recently claimed that the pandemic reminded Singapore to diversify its supply chain and avoid excessive dependence on China (Lianhe Zaobao, February 17, 2020). The above remarks have intensified concerns about the outflow of industries and the reorganization of supply chains in the context of the pandemic.

17.2.3 Supply chain adjustment and transnational transfer of industries have inherent laws, and are not irreversible

Vigilance regarding the relocation of industries must be maintained, but at the same time this phenomenon must be approached rationally. Over the past 150 years, the transnational transfer of industries has generally conformed to the laws of economics. According to the economic geography theory of constant returns to scale (Findlay, 1995), industries were initially located in places where raw materials were rich, such as Birmingham in the United Kingdom, Detroit in the United States, and the Ruhr in Germany. With the reduction of transportation costs, this division of labor has been reversed. Countries with scarce resources have in turn become the pioneers of industrialization, such as Japan. Based on the economic theory of increasing returns to scale (Krugman, 1991), those countries with initially relatively large industrial scales have become industrially developed central countries, and others peripheral countries. This division of labor will be reversed again due to changes in transportation costs and labor costs. Peripheral countries may also become new industrial bases.

These theories explain why Japan, which has scarce resources, has become a highly developed country, and also explains why China has become a rising star and an industrial powerhouse. However, nothing is set in stone; as these theories show, the pattern of division of labor may be reversed. The reflow of manufacturing to the United States in particular, needs to be rationally analyzed. Although the U.S. manufacturing industry's added value to GDP in the second quarter of 2019 hit a record low of 11% (Associated Press, 2019), according to the data from Quick and Easy, during the first years of the Trump administration in 2016 and 2017 this proportion had been, respectively, 11.12% and 11.15%. The rate of decline in the share of manufacturing had been curbed, reflecting the attractiveness of basic conditions in the United States to the manufacturing industry. Initially, the discovery of shale gas changed the pattern of energy supply and demand in the United States. Energy has become one of the sources of American competition. The second attraction comes from the tax cuts adopted by Trump after he took office. Currently, the average corporate income tax rate in the United States is 21%, and in China it is 25%. The average personal income tax rate in the United States is 37%, and in China it is 45%. Lastly, the United States imposes tariffs on products from China, which to a certain extent also protects the US manufacturing industry.

There are inherent laws in the transnational transfer of industries and the adjustment of supply chains. No country can maintain its dominant position for a long time, and the pattern of the international division of labor can be reversed. This pattern explains the relocation of Chinese industries and the return of US manufacturing industries, which reflect the dynamic changes in the comparative advantages of various countries, thus calling for a rational and cool-headed analysis.

17.2.4 China's supply chain status depends increasingly on its economies of scale and local market effects

The basic status of China's supply chain stems from the "fullness" and "length" of China's industrial chain. China's supply chain has truly demonstrated its power since the initiation of the reform and opening-up policy in 1978. Industrialization and urbanization have allowed surplus labor in the agricultural sector to combine with the industrial chain to increase production capacity and competitiveness, which is fully reflected in the process of globalization through exports. To put it simply, since 1978, especially since China's accession to the WTO in 2001, the logic of China's supply chain development has been: "complete industrial categories + industrialization/urbanization (labor mobility) + globalization = world factories". In this way, China's industrial chain mainly serves production, hence its status as the "world's factory". China's industrial chain serves the international market, especially the US market, through exports.

In 2008, the global financial crisis occurred. After Trump was elected President of the United States and formally provoked trade frictions with China in 2018, this logic became unsustainable. Whether China wants it or not, transformation is a must. The fact that the material basis for this transformation is already in place needs to be realized and the new competitiveness of China's supply chain will gradually be revealed. The logic is therefore "advanced industry category + modernization (demand upgrade) + economies of scale = world factory + world market". At this stage, China's advantage increasingly depends on its own economies of scale, which is the so-called "local market effect" (Krugman, 1980). In 2019, China's per capita GDP exceeded 10,000 U.S. dollars and the economies of scale it produced are difficult to replicate in other countries (*People's Republic of China 2019 National Economic and Social Development Statistic*al Bulletin). This logic implies that China is no longer just the "world's factory", but also the "world's market"; China is on the supply side, but it is also on the demand side. Say's story (theory) of "supply creates demand" is fully demonstrated here (Say, 1998).

During the outbreak of the COVID-19 pandemic, many people worried that foreign companies would leave China. According to the logic, this worry is untenable. More and more foreign companies no longer regard China as a platform for export processing. The main purpose of foreign companies entering China is to directly serve the Chinese market (McKinsey China Report 2019). Suzhou Matsushita Electric is an example of a foreign company mainly serving the Chinese market, with only part of its production capacity serving Japan. If this is the case, an exogenous epidemic will certainly not push foreign companies out. Therefore, there is no reason for China to abandon confidence.

17.3 For Content on Improving the Business Environment and Enhancing China's Supply Chain Status[2]

The COVID-19 pandemic around the world is currently in a stalemate, so China must therefore remain vigilant against a resurgence of outbreaks. Meanwhile, it is now a critical time for traditional enterprises to resume work, and labor mobility has gained momentum. From the overall situation of the country, it is not advisable to focus on one end, but rather take a more varied, balanced approach; the scientific attitude should be to gradually and systematically resume production while strengthening strict epidemic prevention methods. The impact of COVID-19 and corresponding measures have to be considered from the perspective of the business environment.

17.3.1 The impact of COVID-19 on the fundamentals of the economy and measures to alleviate the impact

For a country like China, which is in a stage of quick development, the fundamentals of the economy determine the business environment. If the foundation is not strong, development is not stable. A deep understanding of the impact of the epidemic is needed, as well as the development of strategies to alleviate this impact.

17.3.1.1 *The impact of COVID-19 on the fundamentals of the economy*

The impact of COVID-19 on the fundamentals of the economy covers three aspects (Zhi Yan and Luo Changyuan, 2020). First, the epidemic hit Wuhan, the geographical center of China's economy. As mentioned earlier, Wuhan is a city which connects nine provinces. Wuhan's role as a geographical center is not only reflected in its serving as a transportation hub, but it is also shown in its economic relationships; due to the epidemic in Hubei province, the outflow of labor in neighboring Hunan, Anhui,

[2]Please refer to the article titled *The Impact and Response of the New Crown Epidemic from the Perspective of the Business Environment* published by the author on *The Paper* on February 28, 2020.

Henan, Jiangxi, Zhejiang, and Guangdong have also been affected. This is different from the SARS period, when mainly Guangdong and Beijing were affected.

From the perspective of industry, the epidemic has affected the service industry, the leader of China's industrial development. The outbreak occurred at the end of the Lunar New Year, during the Spring festival. Industries, such as the transportation industry, accommodation, and catering industry, culture, sports, and entertainment industry, as well as the real estate industry have been severely impacted. According to the latest data, the added value of the service industry in 2019 accounted for 53.9% of the entire GDP, while in 2003, when SARS broke out, the service industry accounted for 42.3% (see Figure 17.1). Since the service industry already accounts for more than half of the entire economy, the impact on the service industry is bound to have a greater negative impact on the entire economy.

From an enterprise perspective, the epidemic has impacted the microfoundation of China's economy: small and medium-sized enterprises (Economic Daily News, February 12, 2020). The service industry comprises many small and medium-sized enterprises which have the weakest ability to resist risks and were hardest hit by the epidemic. According to

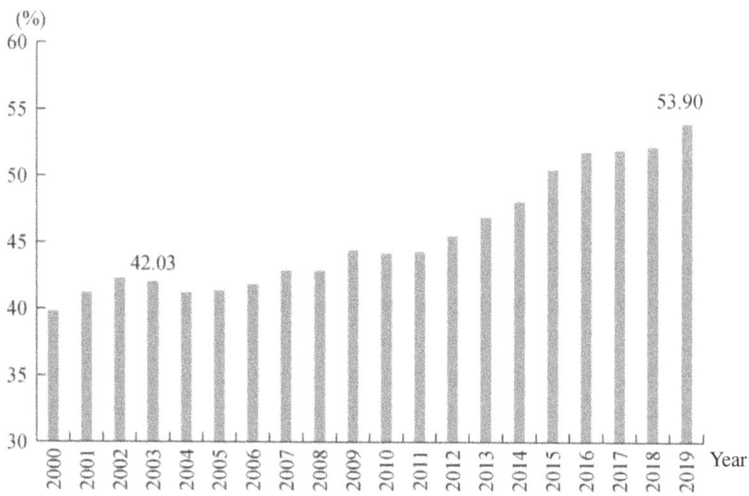

Figure 17.1: The proportion of service industry in GDP (2000–2019).

Source: National Bureau of Statistics

statistics, Chinese SMEs contribute more than 50% of tax revenue, more than 60% of the national GDP, more than 70% of technological innovations, more than 80% of urban labor employment, and account for more than 90% of all enterprises (Tang Wei, 2020). The impact on small and medium-sized enterprises will have a stronger impact on the entire economy.

17.3.1.2 *The fundamentals of the economy and repair of the business environment*

To stabilize China's business environment, repairing economic fundamentals is the priority after the pandemic is completely eradicated. Three policy recommendations are made.

The first is to call on the central government to set 2020 as the year of economic construction as trade frictions with the US have been one trouble, and the pandemic, the other. The year 2020 has various aims. One aim is to achieve double income; poverty alleviation is another. At the same time, 2020 is the last year in the "Thirteenth Five-Year Plan", with heavy pressure for economic development. American politicians such as Pompeo and Ross hoped the epidemic would cause China's economic collapse, leading to a deviation from China's development plan of economic construction. Therefore, setting 2020 as the year for economic construction is a way to be rid of bureaucracy, formalism, and capitalism, and to inspire all localities and departments to actively participate in economic recovery after the epidemic.

That loose macroeconomic policies be implemented is the second recommendation. In this special period, to boost expectations and market confidence, it is necessary to implement a more proactive fiscal policy and loose monetary policies. Of the three carriages for the development of GDP, the bulk of GDP growth is consumption, accounting for nearly 60%. Consumption was also the sector most severely affected by the epidemic (see Figure 17.2). In the short term, it is difficult to recover exports quickly. Under this circumstance, China needs to reduce administrative expenses and unnecessary expenditures as much as possible. It is also necessary to appropriately expand government expenditures and increase investment. Investment should be tilted toward the construction of social infrastructure, including medical care, to further consolidate the foundation for high-quality and sustainable development of China's economy. It is necessary to make plans for the fiscal deficit to exceed 3%. Many

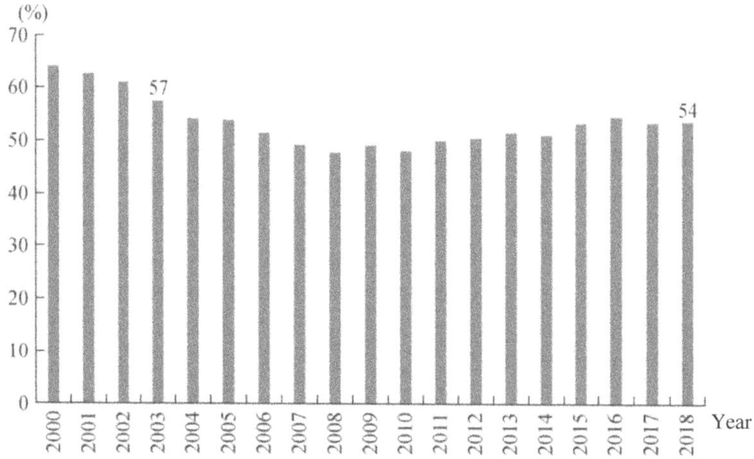

Figure 17.2: The percentage of final consumption expenditure in GDP (2000–2018).
Source: National Bureau of Statistics.

companies, especially small and medium-sized enterprises, lack basic working capital and have large liquidity gaps. Thus, looser monetary policy is a must. Considering the status quo of China–US trade frictions and the China–US interest rate differential, it is a perfect opportunity to implement loose monetary policies.

The third recommendation is the targeted implementation of support for special regions, industries, and enterprises. Compared to universal and moderately loose macroeconomic policies, targeted support should be implemented for Hubei and related regions, service industries, and small and medium-sized enterprises. Targeted support should especially include credit policies and tax policies.

17.3.2 Improve China's status in the global business environment, and create a good external environment for supply chains

17.3.2.1 *Improve the status of Mainland China in the global business environment*

Through the restoration of economic fundamentals and the repair of the relationship between the government and the market, efforts will be made to improve China's business environment and hedge against the economic harm caused by COVID-19. According to the latest business environment report, China now ranks 31st, 15 places higher than its previous ranking, but China still lags behind Singapore (2nd), South Korea (5th), Malaysia (12th), Thailand (21st), and Japan (29th) in the Asian economic circle. China also lags behind the G20 countries, including the United States (6th), the United Kingdom (8th), Australia (14th), Germany (22nd), Canada (23rd), Russia (28th), and Spain (30th). China should use these economies as a reference to make greater progress in administrative management, market access, property rights protection, credit arrangements, and the legal environment.

17.3.2.2 *Continue to reduce fees and taxes to maintain international competitiveness in taxation*

According to statistics from Trading Economics, in terms of corporate income tax, China's (25%) is higher than that of the United States (21%). China's income tax is comparable to that of Asian countries, such as India (25.17%), South Korea (25%), and Indonesia (25%). However, China's income tax is higher than that of Malaysia (24%), Thailand (20%), Vietnam (20%), Singapore (17%), Turkey (22%), and Russia (20%).

The personal income tax of China (45%) is higher than that of the United States (37%). It is also higher than that of many Asian countries, such as South Korea (42%), India (35–88%), the Philippines (35%), Thailand (35%), Vietnam (35%), Indonesia (30%), Malaysia (28%), and Singapore (22%). Moreover, China's income tax is higher than that of Mexico (35%), Turkey (35%), Brazil (27.5%), and Russia (13%).

The sales tax in China is higher than that of many Asian countries, including the Philippines (12%), Indonesia (10%), Malaysia (10%), South Korea (10%), Vietnam (10%), Singapore (7%), and Thailand (7%). In terms of taxation, China still has a lot of room for adjustment using the aforementioned economies as a reference.

17.3.2.3 *Ensure the safety of energy supplies, and reduce the disadvantages of energy costs*

China needs to continue strengthening friendly relations with Russia, accelerate free trade zone negotiations with the GCC, ensure the security of China's energy supply, and reduce its disadvantaged position in energy costs.

17.3.2.4 *Speed up various trade negotiations to create a low-tariff international trade environment for China's supply chains*

China continues to work on the second phase of the China–US trade negotiations. Political relations between China, Japan, and South Korea are getting better. China needs to accelerate the negotiation process of the China, Japan, and South Korea free trade area. In 2020, the Regional Comprehensive Trade Agreement (RCEP) will finally be signed. Through bilateral, multilateral, and regional trade negotiations, we strive to create a low-tariff international trade environment for China's supply chains.

https://doi.org/10.1142/9789811252921_0018

Chapter 18

Challenges Facing the "Post-Pandemic Era" Healthcare System and Policy Responses

Feng Jin

School of Economics, Fudan University, Shanghai, China

The outbreak of COVID-19 posed a severe challenge to the healthcare systems of all countries, many of which were caught by surprise. The problems in China's healthcare system were also exposed, however they were fewer than those that emerged during the SARS outbreak in 2003. Since 2003, the Chinese government has attached great importance to investment and reform in the field of medicine and healthcare; the public financial input in medical and health care has increased substantially, from 77.8 billion yuan in 2003 to 339.4 billion yuan in 2009, and to 1,679.7 billion yuan in 2019, showing an average annual growth rate of 19.8% over 17 years. The proportion of medical and health expenditure of all public financial expenditures has increased from 3.2% in 2003 to 52% in 2009 and 7.0% in 2019. The share of total health expenditure (including government expenditure, healthcare expenditure, and personal spending) in GDP has increased from 4.8% in 2003 to 64% in 2018, showing that the gap is narrowing between China and other industrialized countries like Japan and South Korea.

Since 2003, China's reform of its healthcare system has therefore entered a new stage. In terms of public health emergency response measures, both the central and local governments have stepped up efforts to establish Centers for Disease Control and Prevention (CDC), and have formed a four-level disease control system with 3,500 CDC centers, with 190,000 personnel. In terms of healthcare security, a pilot program of a new rural cooperative healthcare system was launched in 2003, and a medical insurance system for urban residents was launched in 2007. With these two programs, and the reform of the medical insurance system for urban workers which began in 1998, China has basically achieved (full coverage of) universal healthcare insurance. In 2019, more than 1.35 billion people (96% of the total population) were insured. In terms of the implementation of medical reform, on April 6, 2009, Xinhua News Agency was authorized to issue the *Opinions of the CPC Central Committee and the State Council on Deepening the Reform of the Medical and Health System*. The basic roadmap of the reform included realizing universal health insurance, establishing at a preliminary level a national system for provision of essential drugs, improving community-level medical service systems, and promoting equal access to basic public health services, as well as the pilot reform of public hospitals. In May 2010, at the National Working Conference on Deepening the Reform of the Medical and Health System, Premier Li Keqiang pointed out that the focus of medical reform should be "to meet basic medical needs, strengthen grassroots, and build up mechanisms", which by way of explanation, refers to ensuring extensive coverage of medical insurance to guarantee meeting residents' basic medical needs; putting more people and money into grassroots medical institutions; and to establish various mechanisms for the standardized and effective operation of the medical and healthcare system. The Standing Committee of the National People's Congress twice amended the Law of the People's Republic of China on the Prevention and Treatment of Infectious Diseases in 2004 and 2013, which clarified prevention policies, and classified the treatment and management of various types of infectious diseases.

In October 2016, the CPC Central Committee and the State Council issued the *Outline of the Healthy China 2030 Plan,* which proposed the strategic goal to establish a basic medical and healthcare system, with Chinese characteristics, to cover both urban and rural residents, and continue to raise people's awareness of healthcare and improve the health service system, so that everyone has access to basic medical and health services, as well as basic sports and fitness services, forming a comprehensive integrated well-structured health industry by 2030. In effect, China's main health indicators rank high among middle- and high-income countries. Chinese people have seen an increase in life expectancy, with the life expectancy at birth increasing from 71.4 years in 2000 to 77 years in 2018, ranking 53rd in the world according to the World Health Organization.

Despite this, the incidence of chronic diseases in China has been increasing, and health management of these conditions is falling behind. The case rate of hypertension is as high as 44.7%, which almost levels that of 45.5% in the United States. However, the control rate of hypertension in China is only 7.2%, which is much lower than the 43.5% found in the United States. The prevalence of diabetes in China is about 10.9%, similar to the 10.8% in the United States, but only 32% of diabetes patients in China are receiving treatment, while only 1.2% of diabetes patients in the United States are untreated. (Yip *et al*., 2019) It should be noted that the case rate of infectious diseases is also increasing; from 2004 to 2014, a total of 549,84,661 cases of infectious diseases were reported, with an annual incidence of 417.98 per 100,000. The incidence of infectious diseases increased by an average of 5.9% a year, with the growth rate slowing down after 2009.[1]

The COVID-19 outbreak took place at a time when China had begun to increase investment in and promote improved reform of the healthcare industry, especially as compared to the period of the SARS pandemic in 2003. However, the country's health system was still caught unprepared when the COVID 19 virus started to fiercely ravage the country. The first part of this chapter analyzes the impact of the pandemic on the supply and demand of medical resources, community health services, public health, and internet medical care; the second part compares the coping measures during the outbreak of COVID-19 and those during the SARS outbreak, so as to analyze the hidden dangers of China's medical and healthcare system, and put forward ideas on that basis for further reform. Finally, conclusions are formulated based upon our analysis.

18.1 Analysis of the Impact

The COVID-19 pandemic spread rapidly; by March 9, 2020, 80,904 cases had been diagnosed in China, of which 58,684 patients recovered and 3,123 died (Figures 18.1 and 18.2). In the face of the pandemic, the healthcare system has been severely tested.

[1]New data: How high is the incidence of infectious diseases over a 10-year period? *The Physician's Journal*, Apr. 25, 2017, https://www.sohu.com/a/136217101_374890.

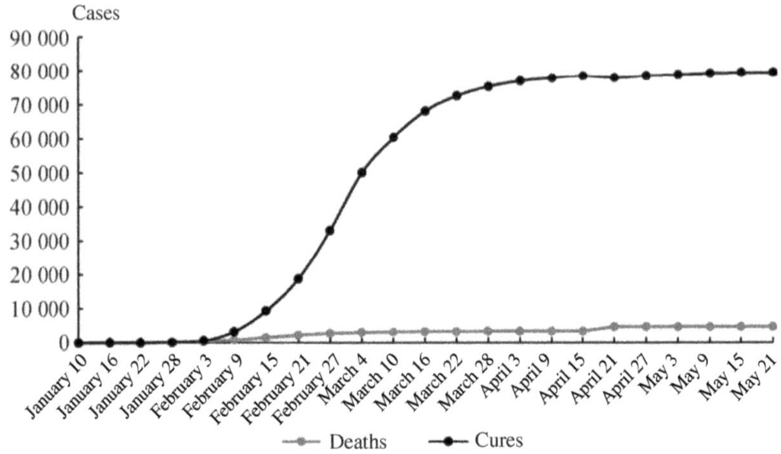

Figure 18.1: Cumulative number of deaths and cures (10 January 2020–21 May 2020).

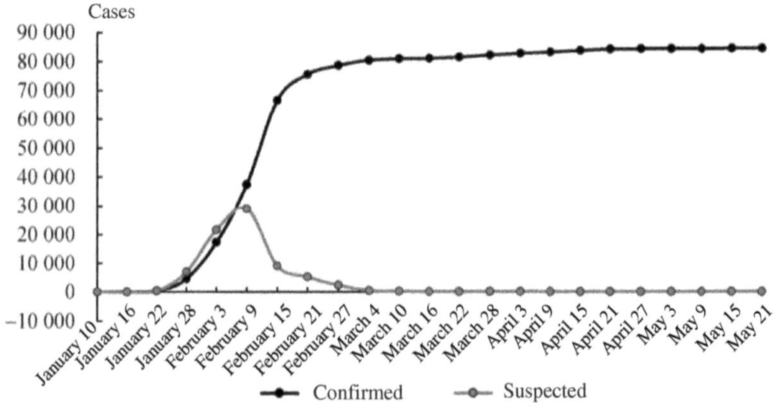

Figure 18.2: Cumulative number of confirmed and suspected (10 January 2020–21 May 2020).

Source: Ali Health.

18.1.1 A run on medical resources

"A run on medical resources" is a new expression used during this outbreak. It means that in a pandemic, people flock to hospitals, causing long queues and panic, similar to a run on a bank during an economic recession. The outbreak which spread rapidly on a large scale has had a huge impact on the healthcare systems of Wuhan and Hubei province. Patients with common colds, fevers, and coughs flocked to hospitals out of fear, while patients infected by COVID-19 were not able to get timely and effective treatment. In effect, patients experienced emotional breakdowns, and doctors and nurses were extremely tired, which further imposed a negative impact on treatment and pandemic prevention.

According to the National Health Commission, at the beginning of the pandemic, more than 90% of fever patients were not infected with COVID-19. Their presence at the hospital caused a multitude of problems; first, during long waiting times, cross-contamination and infection of other patients easily happened, aggravating their condition; second, they consumed the limited available resources, meaning treatment for seriously ill patients was delayed; third, some COVID-19 patients did not go to the doctor at a time when they should have sought diagnosis and treatment because they anticipated "difficulties". Therefore, they were not isolated in time, which effectively made them a source of another possible wave of infection; and fourth, doctors became more susceptible to infections with their immunity weakened because they were overloaded, which is the main reason that some medical workers in Wuhan became infected with COVID-19.

18.1.2 Pressure on primary medical service institutions

For a long time, China's primary health services were not very satisfactory; for example, tertiary hospitals were often overrun by patients, while coping measures, such as forcing residents to have their first diagnosis in the community, have had little effect. Community medical and health institutions face the problems of insufficient medical service capacity, uneven development, inadequate equipment, and the shortage of medical personnel (Shen Shuguang and Zhang Bo, 2016).

The pandemic has put more responsibility on the weak primary healthcare system. According to the *Notice of the General Office of the National Health Commission on the Accurate Classification of Grassroots Medical and Health Institutions in COVID-19 Pandemic Prevention and Control*, community medical and health institutions should strengthen their work responsibilities, make overall plans for tasks including pandemic prevention and control, daily diagnosis and treatment, chronic disease management, and health guidance to ensure that urban and rural residents have ready and timely access to basic health services. On January 27, The National Health Commission proposed that "county-level medical institutions should set up fever clinics to facilitate medical treatment". On February 18 and 19, based on the application of the policy, "Quality Service at the Grassroots Level", conducted by primary medical and health institutions, the Institute of Medical Information of the Chinese Academy of Medical Sciences conducted a survey on the operation and medical services of primary medical and health institutions through a WeChat questionnaire. The survey covered 31 provinces, autonomous regions, and municipalities, and the Xinjiang Production and Construction Corps, involved 3,562 primary medical and health institutions (including 576 community health service centers and 2,986 township health centers) in 335 prefectural cities and 1,698 counties (districts), which accounts for 7.8% of the total (of which the community health service centers accounted for 6.2% and township health centers accounted for 8.2%). According to the survey, 51.0% of all institutions had fever clinics. Many primary medical institutions were not authorized to or were unable to open fever clinics. At the beginning of the pandemic in Wuhan, community health service centers did not have fever clinics, causing many patients to flock to larger hospitals.

Even after a dozen years of exploration and practice, China still did not have a smooth pathway for the triaging and systematization of diagnosis and treatment. However, because of the COVID-19 pandemic, Wuhan in just one month realized how to implement efficient primary diagnosis at the grassroots level, two-way referrals, triaging those in need of urgent or non-urgent treatment, and "upper and lower linkage" ("Wuhan Realizes Hierarchical Diagnosis and Treatment in One Month, This Medical Reform Problem Has Found the Key Due to the pandemic", Sohu, February 7, 2020, https://www.sohu.com/a/376320865_467288). This survey involved 117 primary medical and health institutions in Hubei province, among which 104 institutions, representing 88.9%, provided normal medical services, and 97 institutions, representing 82.9% had opened fever clinics. Community health systems now have better coping mechanisms than they did at the start of the outbreak.

18.1.3 A test of the public health system

In the prevention and control stage of the pandemic, though CDC personnel at all levels did emergency work including epidemiological investigation, disinfection of contaminated areas, virus sampling and sample delivery, and tracing close contacts, their work was still controversial. Some shortcomings have been exposed in the CDC mechanism for major pandemic prevention and control, and its special position has not been fully recognized.[2] In China, the CDC is a social service organization, a public institution, and a department that implements government disease control services. Its efficiency is relatively low in carrying out isolation and coordinating the control of infectious diseases. Meanwhile, the budget and personnel recruitment of China's CDC lag far behind that of the U.S. CDC, and with a major problem being its shortage of professionals at the grassroots level. In addition, regional CDCSs are not only guided by the National CDC, but are also, in different regions, controlled by local health commissions, which has led to problems like inconsistent policies.[3]

18.1.4 The Rise of Internet Medical Care

The development of China's Internet medical services started in 2014, with Internet giants such as Baidu, Alibaba, Tencent, and Xiaomi all getting involved. On April 25, 2018, in the context of "Internet +", the General Office of the State Council issued the *Opinions on Promoting the Development of "Internet + Medical and Health"*, which encourages medical institutions to use the Internet and other information technologies to expand medical services. The number of users in China's mobile healthcare market was 380 million in 2015 and exceeded 400 million in 2018. By the end of 2017, there were a total of 221 investments, mergers, and acquisitions in the Internet medical field in China, compared with 161 in 2018 (Sun Chenmin and Tian Kan, 2019). In August 2019, the National Health Care Security Administration issued the *Guiding Opinions on*

---

[2]"Face to face on pandemic prevention and control: Zhong Nanshan's latest statement delivers a lot of information", *People's Daily* Online, February 9, 2020, http://yuqing.people.com.cn/n1/2020/0229/c209043-31610440.html.

[3]Dialogue with Chen Zhuo: Aaphasia in the Disease Control System, Where Should We Go After the End of the pandemic? "Dingxingyuan" official account, March 9, 2020.

Improving "Internet +" Medical Service Price and Medical Insurance Payment Policies, which officially included Internet medical service projects within the scope of medical insurance payments. In Beijing, 80% of hospitals above Grade II have Internet related services. In Guangzhou, it was required that more than 50% of its Grade A hospitals should have opened online hospitals by 2019. Before the pandemic, however, Internet medical users grew slowly due to insufficient business supply and homogenization, which made it difficult for the existing products and services to attract more users (Yu Baorong *et al*., 2019).

The pandemic has increased the demand for Internet healthcare. Since patients want to have medical treatment in a safe, no contact way, Internet medical treatment stands out for its ability to deliver remote medical consultations. After the outbreak of the pandemic, JD.com and Baidu established a Medical and Health Business Division. Alibaba transformed Ali Health through an acquisition and Tencent released the "COVID-19 pandemic service platform". Several Internet medical companies such as Dingxingyuan, Hao doctor, Chunyu Doctor, and Weiyi all launched platforms to deliver remote medical consultations. By January 31, 2020, in Guangdong, Shandong, Zhejiang, Jiangsu, Shanghai, and other provinces, 166 public hospitals had set up online free diagnosis platforms.[4]

18.2 Analysis of the Response

18.2.1 Emergency response to the outbreak

18.2.1.1 *The response of the healthcare system*

To cope with the extreme shortage of medical resources in Wuhan and other cities in Hubei province, Health Commissions across the country set up medical teams to support Wuhan. By March 8, 2020, there were altogether 346 medical teams numbering 42,600 people who had arrived in Wuhan and other cities of Hubei to work with local medical staff. The five largest supporting medical teams by March 4 were the PLA Medical Team (4,000 personnel), Jiangsu Medical Team (2,757 personnel), Guangdong Medical Team (2,452 personnel), Liaoning Medical Team (2,045 personnel), and Zhejiang Medical Team (1,985 personnel). Medical support on such a scale is unprecedented in China's history.

[4] *Internet medical treatment becomes a pioneer against pandemic*, Qianzhan.com, February 27, 2020, https://www.qianzhan.com/analyst/detail/220/200227-5c8d7f09.html.

In order to ease the shortage of beds for COVID-19 patients, Huoshenshan Hospital (Fire God Mountain Hospital) and Leishenshan Hospital (Thor Mountain Hospital) were built in Wuhan and were modeled on Beijing's Xiaotangshan Hospital built during the SARS period. Located in Caidian District, the two hospitals were built in just 10 days: on January 24, Huoshenshan Hospital was completed and it was put into use on February 2, and on February 3 patients were officially admitted. On January 25, it was decided that Leishenshan Hospital would be built in Huangjiahu, Jiangxia District; on February 8, it was officially put into use, and patients were admitted that night.

Later, according to the characteristics of the population infected by COVID-19, Hubei adopted "mobile cabin hospitals" for a large number of patients showing no severe symptoms. Several sports venues and exhibition centers were gradually transformed into mobile cabin hospitals. In total, 16 mobile cabin hospitals were established, taking in more than 12,000 COVID-19 patients in the 35 days since starting operations on February 5. By March 9, 11 cabins suspended operations because a large number of patients had been discharged from hospitals, and the number of new patients decreased significantly. On March 10, all 16 mobile cabin hospitals suspended operations. Such a response is also unprecedented in China's medical and health history.

18.2.1.2 *The response of the health insurance system*

In response to the pandemic, the National Healthcare Security Administration has introduced support measures to reduce the burden of medical expenses and facilitate long-distance medical treatment and Internet medical treatment (Table 18.1).

Compared with medical insurance policy during the SARS outbreak in 2003, it has undoubtedly made great strides forward, reflecting the "wide coverage" of medical insurance since the SARS pandemic. This time, both confirmed and suspected patients do not have to cover medical expenses, while during the SARS outbreak, only confirmed cases were covered, and moreover, uninsured individuals also had to shoulder the burden of their medical expenses. In addition, the medical insurance policy during the COVID-19 pandemic covers medical treatment of confirmed and suspected cases diagnosed in other places, which is a breakthrough in China's medical insurance reform. Moreover, the central government gave more subsidies and financial aid to local governments.

Table 18.1: Safeguard measures introduced by the National Healthcare Security Administration during the pandemic.

Time	Files	Key contents
2020.01.23	*Notice of the National Healthcare Security Administration and the Ministry of Finance on Improving the Medical Security of Novel Coronavirus Infected Pneumonia.*	(1) For confirmed patients, the medical expenses shall be subsidized by public finance after they pay for the basic medical insurance, serious disease insurance, and medical assistance. (2) For confirmed patients diagnosed in other places, treatment should be given first before settlement. The regulation on the reduction of the proportion of payment for medical treatment transferred from other places shall not be implemented for reimbursement. (3) For confirmed patients, expenses for needed medicines and medical services will be temporarily covered by medical insurance funds. (4) For medical institutions receiving a large number of patients, medical insurance departments can pay in advance for expenses incurred in the treatment of the disease.
2020.01.27	*Supplementary Notice of the Office of the National Healthcare Security Administration, the General Office of the Ministry of Finance, and the General Office of the National Health Commission on the Medical Security Work of Novel Coronavirus Infected Pneumonia.*	(1) For suspected patients with COVID-19 treatment plan, medical expenses shall be subsidized after they pay for basic medical insurance, serious disease insurance, and medical assistance. The local government shall formulate financial subsidy policies, arrange funds, and implement integrated support. The central government shall accordingly provide appropriate subsidies. (2) The expenses paid for by medical insurance in other places shall be prepaid by local medical insurance departments. The information of patients insured in other places should be recorded, accounts of medical expenses kept and liquidated on a unified, national basis after the pandemic. (3) The expenses for treatment and services for suspected patients will be temporarily covered by the medical insurance fund.

Table 18.1: (*Continued*)

Time	Files	Key contents
2020.02.13	*Notice on the prevention and control of novel coronavirus pneumonia pandemic fund security policy.*	For confirmed patients, the medical expenses shall be subsidized by public finance after they pay for basic medical insurance, serious disease insurance, and medical assistance. The expense will be prepaid by the local treasury, which will be subsidized by the central treasury at 60% of actual expenses incurred.
2020.03.02	*Guidance of National Health Insurance Administration, National Health Commission on Promoting "Internet +" Medical Insurance Services during the COVID-19 Pandemic Prevention and Control Period.*	For designated medical institutions approved by the health administration department to set up Internet hospitals or carry out online diagnosis and treatment, the "Internet +" re-consultation service for common diseases and chronic diseases provided is covered by the medical insurance fund based on the principle of voluntariness, after they sign a supplementary agreement with the regional health insurance agencies.

During the COVID-19 pandemic, the medical expenses for confirmed patients were subsidized by public finance after patients paid for basic medical insurance, serious disease insurance, and medical assistance. The expenses were prepaid by local finance departments, which were subsidized by the central treasury at 60% of the actual expenses incurred. During the SARS outbreak, the central government subsidized local governments of poor areas in the central and western regions at 50% of the actual expenses incurred. Lastly, the "Internet +" re-consultation service for common diseases and chronic diseases provided for insured patients was covered by the medical insurance fund.

18.2.1.3 *The response of the public health system*

The CDC at all levels mainly provided technical guidance during this pandemic. The responsibilities changed as the pandemic evolved. *Guidelines on the Novel Coronavirus-Infected Pneumonia Prevention and Control*

(Second Edition) (hereinafter referred to as the *Prevention and Control Plan*), has required disease control institutions at all levels to organize, coordinate, supervise, and evaluate the monitoring work and collect, analyze, report, and give feedback from the monitoring data. They were also required to conduct field investigations, laboratory tests, and specialized technical training, and provide public health education. The *Prevention and Control Plan* (Third Edition) additionally requires the CDC at all levels to provide guidance on personal protection for the public and certain groups, as well as on the disinfection of specific places. The *Prevention and Control Plan* (Sixth Edition) emphasizes that the CDC should strengthen its role of providing technical guidance for the prevention and control of the pandemic. For example, the guidelines on COVID-19 should all be formulated by the CDC, including epidemiological investigation, investigation and management of close contacts, laboratory testing, disinfection of specific places, and the protection of certain groups and individuals.

18.2.2 Thoughts on the new round of reform of the medical and health system

The measures introduced above show that Chinese people are united and determined to fight the pandemic. They certainly played a positive role in treating patients quickly, reducing the burden on medical resources and controlling the further spread of the pandemic. However, it should also be noted that the cost of such measures is quite high, which is not only limited to the expense of medical care, but more importantly, their impact on socio-economic activities; for example, the impact of "city lock-downs" on the flow of materials and personnel, the cost of the lives of committed medical staff, and the logistical costs of transporting supplies to Hubei Province. Therefore, temporary emergency measures exposed some shortcomings in China's medical service system. After the pandemic, to improve the capacity of China's medical and health system to cope with major public health threats and meet basic medical needs, a new round of medical reforms is imperative.

18.2.2.1 *Improve the public health emergency management system*

From SARS in 2003 to the current COVID-19 pandemic, the problems of China's public health system have not been entirely solved. The entire public health system is lagging far behind in personnel, technology, and equipment, which is the fundamental reason why prevention and control of the pandemic was initially not possible (Huang Qifan, 2020).

In fact, China has already taken several measures to solve problems in the public health system. In 2003, the State Council approved the *Plan for the Construction of a Medical Treatment System for Public Health Emergencies*, which starting in 2004 set out to accelerate the development of public health undertakings with a focus on the construction of a national disease prevention and control system and a medical treatment system for public health emergencies. In March 2006, the State Administration for Disease Control and Prevention and the State Administration for Health Supervision were established, which means that a disease prevention and control system and a health supervision system have basically been established at the central, provincial, municipal, and county levels. In 2009, the *Opinions on Deepening the Reform of the Medical and Health System* issued by the CPC Central Committee and the State Council proposed that a four-in-one basic medical and health system should be established that covers both urban and rural residents with a public health service system, medical service system, medical security system, and medicine supply security system. However, in terms of the response to the COVID-19 pandemic, there is still a significant gap between these goals and real practice. Further reform is needed in the following four areas.

(1) To increase input into public health. Since 2003, though the government's spending on healthcare has increased by 19.8% annually, the proportion of public health expenditure in medical and health expenditures has declined in recent years from 14.3% in 2010 to 13% in 2018. Public health investment has been lower than the fiscal expenditure on public hospitals since 2014. This is similar to the case of the treatment of disease receiving more emphasis than prevention, which is reflected in the fiscal expenditure structure (Figure 18.3). The highest proportion of healthcare financial expenditure from the government at all levels is the subsidy to the medical insurance fund. About 70% of the medical insurance expense for urban and rural residents are from fiscal subsidy, which pressures and squeezes funding from other health programs.
(2) Attract higher quality professionals to the public health profession. Public health institutions are public welfare institutions which after

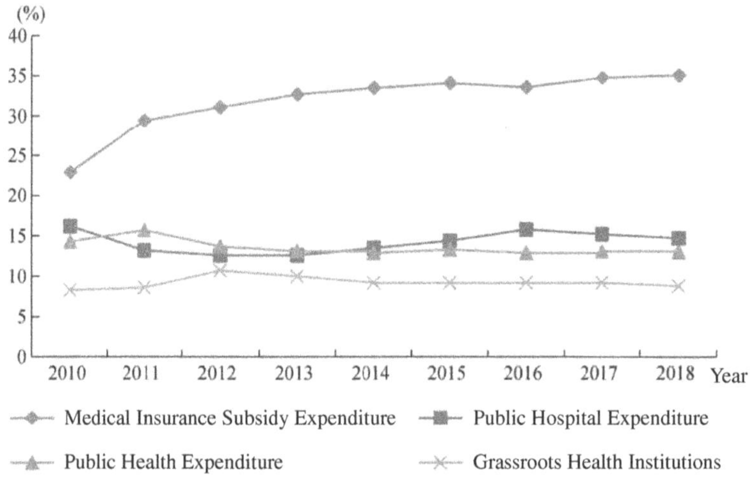

Figure 18.3: The proportion of public health expenditure in government medical and health expenditure.

Source: Report on final accounts of public finance of the Ministry of Finance over the years.

reform saw a general decline in the staff income, resulting in a serious loss of personnel. In the future, the salary of public health professionals needs to be raised to attract more expertise and competence, and more universities should be encouraged to set up Schools of Public Health. Currently, among 3,000 universities in China, only just over 80 have established a School of Public Health.

(3) Informatization should be advanced. In 2003, the *National Health Informatization Development Program from 2003 to 2010* was issued, which provided planning and guidance for public health informatization. Since the outbreak of SARS, direct reporting systems have been established at the local level with 11,157 agencies in 31 provinces, autonomous regions, and municipalities nationwide, together with the initial establishment of a network of public health agencies. However, neither public funds nor professional experts are sufficient for information construction. In the future, more capital investment channels should be introduced to attract health informatization professionals with inter-disciplinary backgrounds such as Medicine, Public Health, and Informatics (Wang Kun *et al.*, 2019).

(4) Administrative empowerment should be enhanced. China's CDC lacks administrative power, making its status far lower than that of its U.S. counterpart which is administered by the White House and reports directly to the President's Health and Security Council. China also needs to establish a complete social emergency organization system (Huang Qifan, 2020).

18.2.2.2 *Balance the allocation of medical resources*

For a long time, Chinese people have been accustomed to going to tertiary hospitals for treatment. As a result, patients with minor complaints have utilized a large proportion of medical resources that are designed to be used for the treatment of specialized diseases. One result of this is tertiary hospitals are overcrowded, leaving patients' needs unsatisfied, while conversely, primary medical institutions are not playing their due role, which aggravates the mismatch of medical resources.

In China, the allocation of medical resources is concentrated in tertiary hospitals.[5] Overall, tertiary hospitals have far more doctors and equipment than primary medical institutions, together with a higher growth rate in terms of the number of people attending the tertiary facilities. Nearly 65% of practicing doctors are in tertiary hospitals, while only 30% are in primary institutions like community health service centers. In 2017, the number of patients attending tertiary hospitals increased by 6.06%, while those attending primary medical institutions only increased by 1.43%. Meanwhile, the average outpatient charge per visit in tertiary hospitals is 1.5 times that of secondary hospitals and twice that of primary

---

[5] Based on their technical level and scale, Chinese medical institutions are divided into three levels: Tertiary hospitals provide specialized medical services, treat serious and difficult diseases, and function as research and teaching centers. Secondary hospitals provide health services to several communities. Primary hospitals are grassroots hospitals that directly provide comprehensive services such as medical treatment, health prevention, rehabilitation, and healthcare. The triaging of diagnosis and treatment, dependent on the severity and urgency of the disease and the difficulty of treatment, aims to treat differing health needs at different levels of the medical system. In China, such a goal is summarized as "primary diagnosis at the grassroots level, two-way referral, separation of urgent and non-urgent treatment, and co-ordination of upper and lower tiers". Despite this, most people prefer to see a doctor in a tertiary hospital, which leaves the goal unfulfilled.

hospitals. Though tertiary hospitals provide better medical treatment than that provided by secondary or primary hospitals, it is not necessary for all patients to go to tertiary hospitals.

Because of the allocation of resources, patients also flock to tertiary hospitals. In 2012, the growth of medical institutions in China slowed, along with the general slowing of the economy and fiscal revenue which occurred almost at the same time. However, for many years the growth rate of visits to tertiary hospitals has been much faster than that in secondary hospitals and primary medical institutions. The proportion of patients visiting tertiary hospitals increased from 29% in 2005 to 52% in 2018 (Figure 18.4). In China's medical system, resource allocation, service supply, and patient selection are all inclined to secondary and tertiary hospitals, forming the "Matthew effect", where the strong get stronger.

There's no doubt that public health emergencies will reoccur in the future, and temporary emergency measures are not sustainable in the long run. Instead, it is imperative to have a division of labor and cooperation within the health system. We should improve the allocation of medical resources through "setting up mechanisms", to incentivize patients to head to local medical centers rather than tertiary hospitals, and resolve

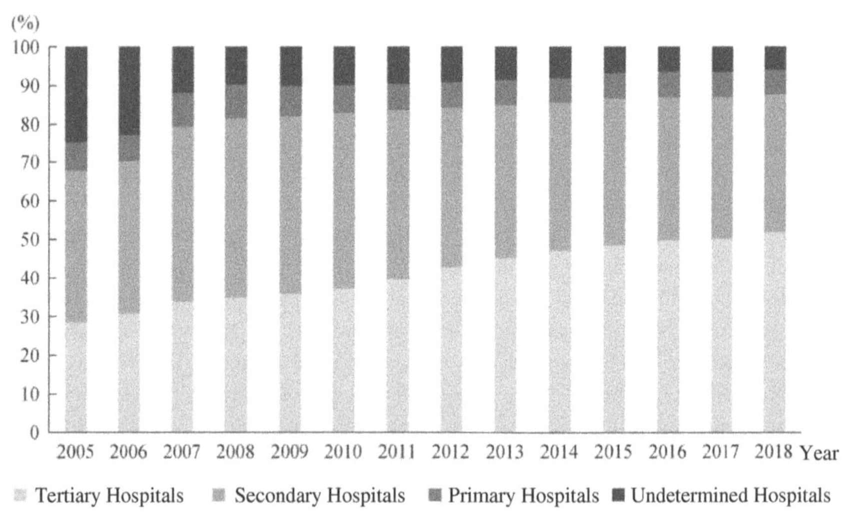

Figure 18.4: Ratio of outpatient visits in medical institutions of all levels.

Source: *China Health Statistical Yearbook, China Health and Family Planning Statistical Yearbook.*

through daily health maintenance the possible harms caused by unpredictable public health emergencies. In 2015, the *Guiding Opinions of the General Office of the State Council on Promoting the Hierarchy Diagnosis and Treatment System* was issued, which first proposed that China should establish a hierarchical diagnosis and treatment mode featuring "primary diagnosis at the grassroots level, two-way referrals, separation of urgent treatments and non-urgent treatments, and co-ordination between upper and lower levels". It shows that the policymakers have realized the necessity of allocating more medical resources to grassroots institutions. Since China has already seen a tremendous gap between secondary and tertiary hospitals and primary medical institutions in terms of medical resources and treatment capability, the models of other countries are not able to be copied to reconfigure medical resources. In China's context where tertiary hospitals play the dominant role in treating patients, current efforts are aimed at trying to build medical treatment combinations based on existing practices. Its advantages and disadvantages are gradually being revealed.

In 2019, in order to implement the *Guiding Opinions of the General Office of the State Council on Promoting the Construction and Development of Medical Treatment Combination* (Guo Ban Fa, 2017, No. 32), the National Health Commission and the National Administration of Traditional Chinese Medicine decided to carry out a pilot on the construction of an urban Medical Treatment Combination (MTC).[6] MTC is established to first strengthen the capacity of community-level medical services, and second, to form divisions of labor and cooperative

[6]MTC refers to the combination formed by the vertical or horizontal integration of medical resources among different levels and categories of medical institutions. At present, there are four modes of MTC: (1) MTC (Medical Treatment Combination), the main mode of urban MTC, in which a tertiary hospital functions as the lead unit, and a number of urban secondary hospitals, rehabilitation hospitals, nursing hospitals, and community health service centers are combined to construct "1+X" MTC; (2) Medical Community (MC), the main model for rural MTC; (3) Specialist Unions, a combination formed by specialized cooperation between medical institutions; (4) Telemedicine Collaborative Networks, which are established in grassroots medical institutions in remote and underdeveloped areas. The biggest problem faced by grassroots institutions is that they lack good doctors and quality medical care, which makes people reluctant to use the service. In the short term, to allocate more medical resources to primary and grassroots hospitals, the Medical Treatment Combination may be a method worth trying.

mechanisms between medical institutions. There are three main ways to achieve these two goals; first, since the grade assigned by administrative evaluation plays an important role on a hospital's reputation, grassroots institutions enjoy the reputation brought about by the association with tertiary hospitals attracting more people; second, since "advanced medical technology" is the main reason patients choose tertiary hospitals, if doctors and experts are sent from tertiary hospitals, the medical quality of primary hospitals can be improved; third, when primary hospitals have a greater market share, the overall operating costs will be reduced.

18.2.2.3 *Establish a system of a "gatekeeper" for national health*

During the pandemic, elderly people with underlying diseases are more likely to contract the virus and develop severe diseases with a high fatality rate after infection. People above the age of 60 accounted for 80% of all COVID-19 fatalities. Most of them had one or more underlying diseases.[7] A study conducted by the Chinese Center for Disease Control and Prevention of more than 70,000 cases of COVID-19 patients in China found an overall mortality rate of 2.3% among COVID-19 deaths, with a significantly higher mortality rate among patients with underlying disease, of 15% for cardiovascular disease, 7.3% for diabetes, and 6% for hypertension.[8] In China, the number of people suffering from chronic and other underlying diseases is increasing. Recent figures show that in China there are 160–170 million people with high blood pressure and 92.4 million with diabetes, most of whom are elderly people. The pandemic is a wake-up call for good health management of the elderly.

The relationship between the healthcare system and citizens' health status in other countries shows that countries adopting the "gatekeeper" system with family doctors see longer life expectancies and lower costs of health services (Dusheiko *et al.*, 2006; Dolton, 2016). Most developed countries attach great importance to primary medical institutions. For example, in 1948, the United Kingdom established the family doctor

---

[7] Why Most Fatal Cases in the Pandemic are of Old People? JD Huyi, March 2, 2020: https://www.cn-healthcare.com/articlewm/20200302/wap-content-1091880.html.

[8] Covid-19 Emergency Response Mechanism Epidemiology Group, Chinese Center for Disease Control and Prevention, 2020.

system whereby initial diagnoses were made by family doctors. Family doctors are general practitioners who deal with health problems of patients at all ages, which greatly promoted overall health. In 1965, the United States began to build the Community Healthcare Service (CHC). By 2008, a total of 8,000 CHCs had been established, mainly serving the elderly and low-income groups. An evaluation of the system showed that in the ten years after the establishment of CHCs, the mortality rate of residents over 50 years of age was reduced by 7 percentage points to 13 percent, and in areas where CHCs were established, the proportion of elderly people having regular checkups increased by 23 percent, and pharmaceutical costs reduced by one-third (Bailey *et al.*, 2015).

With the gradual exploration of this field, China has attached great importance to the construction of a family doctor system[9] in the past two years, Shanghai was one of the first cities in China to pilot the family doctor system. In 2011, it launched a pilot program to sign up family doctors. Since 2015, it has further implemented the "1+1+1" combination of medical institutions based on family doctors, which means in addition to signing up with a family doctor, one can also choose to sign up with a district hospital and a city hospital. If the family doctor is unable to confirm a diagnosis, the contracted residents have priority in making an appointment with a specialist in a tertiary hospital. The reform has achieved some preliminary results: a survey of the contracted services of family doctors in Shanghai's Changning district found first that contracted residents were mostly the elderly and those with chronic diseases, and second, contracted chronic disease patients enjoyed better services than non-contracted patients in terms of community treatment, chronic disease prevention and treatment, and chronic disease cost control (Lu Wei *et al.*, 2016).

Improving the treatment offered by general practitioners, and recruiting competent doctors who are willing to provide services in primary medical institutions has always been a difficulty faced by China's medical reformers. From the experience of the UK, the US, and Japan, such problems are not impossible to solve; general practitioners enjoy high incomes as well as high social status. In these countries, the career pathway to

[9]Which can be seen from the *Notice on Printing and Issuing Guiding Opinions on Promoting Contract Services of Family Doctors* (National Health Care Reform Office [2016] No. 1) and the *Notice on Effectively Conducting Contracting Services for Family Doctors in 2017* (National Health Foundation Letter, 2017, No. 164).

being a general practitioner is basically the same; after passing medical examinations, a doctor works in a hospital for a period before setting up his own clinic. He then treats residents in the community based on his skill and reputation. More than 80% of outpatient and emergency visits in these countries are performed by community clinics. In terms of income, in 2015 the salary of general practitioners in the UK, Canada, and Germany was about 4 times the average salary, while in China the income of a GP was roughly only the same as the average salary. In terms of the number of doctors, China's general practitioners accounted for 6% of the total number of doctors, far lower than that of the United States (12%), the United Kingdom (28%), Germany (42%), and Canada (48%). There is still a long way to go to improve the environment for training general practitioners, which involves the reform of staffing (Zhu Hengpeng, Lin Qiqing, 2015), medical marketization, and of medical insurance payments. Though complicated, it may be the only way to solve the problem of resource mismatch in China's medical system.

18.2.2.4 *Bring the incentive role of medical insurance payment into full play*

During the pandemic, medical insurance provided a safety net for both confirmed and suspected cases in terms of medical expenses, showing strong support in times of crisis. The healthcare department estimated that the pandemic has had a limited impact on the health insurance fund. Though the treatment costs for COVID-19 patients have increased, due to the pandemic the number of visits for other diseases decreased significantly compared with the same period last year. Even if there may be compensatory visits afterwards, the health insurance fund will not be much affected. On February 21, while meeting the press, officials from the National Healthcare Security Administration said that outlays related to the pandemic did not much affect the health insurance fund. Since other patients are less willing to see a doctor during the pandemic, the outpatient and inpatient services of medical institutions decreased significantly compared with the same period last year, with a decrease of about 20%. China's medical insurance system has developed rapidly in the past 20 years and has basically achieved full coverage. At the same time, however, the health insurance fund faces the challenge of striking an effective balance between meeting the needs of the people and maintaining its sustainable operation. Medical insurance funds play a unique role in controlling hospitals and patients' behavior (Feng Jin and Yu Yangyang, 2008). For China's medical reform, it is necessary to have an incentive mechanism for medical insurance to promote hierarchical diagnosis and treatment, improve the quality of basic medical institutions, and limit medical expenses. In June 2017, the General Office of the State Council issued the *Guiding Opinions on Further Deepening the Reform of the Payment Method of Basic Medical Insurance,* which clarifies that the main goal of the reform is to further strengthen the budget management of the medical insurance fund, and comprehensively carry out the compound payment method mainly based on DRGs (Diseases Related to Groups).

(1) Incentivize tertiary hospitals to work together. Changing hospital incentives through the reform of medical insurance payments is worth further exploration. Specifically, non-referral patients in tertiary hospitals have a lower reimbursement rate, or hospitals are paid according to the cost (scheduled fee) of community healthcare institutions. Meanwhile, the payment for primary healthcare services should be limited, or even not covered by medical insurance, so that tertiary hospitals and primary healthcare institutions form a cooperative relationship, rather than a competitive one.
(2) Raise the salaries of outstanding general practitioners through the reform of medical insurance payments. For general practitioners who are responsible for community health services and residents' health management, medical insurance can be provided on a capitation basis, which is also the model adopted in many countries. A capitation payment is the fixed fee payment agreed upon in a capitated contract between a health insurance agency and the designated medical institution. Designated medical institutions define the medical services they undertake to provide according to the number of medical insurance recipients and the reimbursement quota standard for each person. Therefore, medical institutions are incentivized to work on daily health management, and effectively control medical expenses. On this basis, medical institutions adopt the general practitioner contract system. They pay the salary of general practitioners according to the number of signed doctors, and strengthen competition among general practitioners, so that excellent, competent professionals get higher returns.

(3) Reduce medical costs through the reform of medical insurance payments. Traditionally, setting reimbursement rates, minimum and top payment lines were adopted to curb potential excessive consumption of medical insurance. However, due to information asymmetry in the medical service market, hospitals and doctors have more decision-making power in medical expenditure. As a result, since the 1980s, the United States has shifted the focus of medical insurance cost control to guiding the behavior of medical suppliers. Throughout the world the prepaid system including payment based on DRGs, global budgets, and capitation has been widely adopted. Medical insurance institutions are changing incentives for doctors by reforming the way payments are made. Doctors have incentives to reduce medical expenses rather, which to some extent helps control medical costs. In recent years, China has accelerated the reform of medical insurance payments, with the goal of carrying out the compound payment method based on DRGs.

18.3 Conclusion

Over the past 20 years, though China's medical and health system have undergone many reforms, the pandemic has thrust many hidden problems into the limelight. The medical and healthcare sector has seen a decent increase in public financial investment, but medical resources are still under pressure. Primary medical institutions are weak despite the three-level medical system having been established for a long time. A four-level public health management system has been established, but it has encountered a crisis of confidence. Therefore, it is imperative for China to have a new round of medical and health system reforms.

This new round of medical reforms must face the basic and fundamental problems in the medical and health system. Over the years, China's medical reform has always adhered to the guiding principle "to meet basic medical needs, strengthen grassroot delivery of service and build up mechanisms", but little development has been seen at the grassroots level and in the establishment of new mechanisms. Instead, further reforms should be conducted in these respects: to improve the public health emergency management system, balance health resource allocation, set up a system of gatekeepers for health, and bring into full play medical insurance payment incentives so as to form a medical and health system with public health services, medical services, medical security, and drug supplies which are compatible with each other.

By deepening reforms of the medical and health care system, China can promote the healthy growth of its economy. A Government finance transfer from infrastructure to public health and other public facilities should be carried out so as to improve the quality of the supply of public health, and promote the sustainable and high-quality development of China's economy (Huang Qifan, 2020). A sound and sustainable medical and health system will serve as an important driver to promote China's social and economic development.

https://doi.org/10.1142/9789811252921_0019

Chapter 19

Waging a "Green Development" War Against the Pandemic: Challenges and Policy Responses for "Green Growth" During the Pandemic

Li Zhiqing

School of Economics, Fudan University, Shanghai, China

In the context of green development, environmental protection and economic development have been deeply affected by the outbreak of the COVID-19 pandemic. As environmental and economic development are inextricably linked, a challenge is posed to the established ways of building an "ecological civilization", and green development strategies. "Ecological civilization" refers to a social form with the basic purpose of harmonious coexistence, virtuous circle, all-round development, and sustained prosperity between man and nature, man and man, and man and society. In the short term, with pandemic prevention and control being a top priority, green development must adapt to current times, and intensify work in relevant areas; in particular, in the critical period when the economy is affected by the pandemic, green development needs to be conducted in a way that helps mitigate economic impacts, supports the economy, and resolutely stops the spread of an "economic pandemic". In addition, any measures undertaken simply cannot allow the pandemic to affect economic development and environmental protection. In the medium to long term, commitment to the construction of an ecological civilization, to follow the principles of green development, and to continue to fight the "tough battle" against pollution should be maintained. Further, the focus on addressing the imbalance and inadequacy between environmental protection and economic development should continue so as to achieve a balance between the two.

On March 3, the *Guiding Opinions on Building a Modern Environmental Governance System* issued by the General Offices of the CPC Central Committee and the State Council specifically stressed that the concept of green development should be firmly adhered to. It also provided detailed plans and deployments centering on building environmental governance systems of leadership responsibility, corporate responsibility, civil action, supervision and regulation, market planning, credit management and laws, regulations, and policies. It is fair to say that these guidelines have highlighted green development during the prevention and control period of the pandemic and play a positive role in preventing the recurrence of pandemics and other public environmental health events in the medium and long term.

At the regional level, Shanghai, Jiangsu, Zhejiang, and Shandong provinces have also introduced and implemented measures to promote green development. In general, these initiatives have focused on the fundamental needs of pandemic prevention and control, and local governments have taken various green development measures in response to the impact of the pandemic, serving and contributing to stable social and economic development.

19.1 Analysis of the Impact of the COVID-19 Pandemic on Green Development

19.1.1 Inherent relationship between the COVID-19 pandemic and the neglect of green development

The outbreak of COVID-19 has allowed reflection on many aspects of governance and economic development, especially on economic development models, of which the most noticeable is how to coordinate and strike a balance between environmental protection and economic development, that is, green development (in its broadest sense, "sustainable development"). During this outbreak, it has been seen at least from several aspects that the pandemic is related to the neglect of green development.

In addition, the outbreak of the pandemic has shown that the importance of green development has been greatly underestimated.

The first problem is ecological imbalance. Whether wild animals are to blame for COVID-19 has yet to be scientifically proven (According to the medical experts, "a growing body of scientific evidence suggests that the COVID-19 virus originated in bats".[1]). However, a balance must exist, which is also the nature of ecological balance, both between animal species within nature, and between wild animals and human beings. The outbreak of the pandemic, and the fact that disease is spreading on such a large scale, suggests to some extent that this balance has been disrupted. The underlying reason is that, in the process of development, the ecological system (of which wild animals form an integral part) is over-utilized, resulting in a serious decline in biodiversity. Scientific evidence indicates a rapid decline in diversity within species and between species and ecosystems. In the 21 countries in which detailed assessments have been recorded, an average of about 25% species are threatened. The diversity of domesticated plants and animals has declined, and endemic species have lost their diversity and function. The average abundance of native species in land-based habitats has declined by at least 20%, and the number of invasive alien species has increased by about 70%.[2] In this regard, the most stringent wildlife protection laws and regulations currently in place are in fact compensating for the poor protection of wildlife in the past.

The second concerns the deterioration of the environment. Ecology and environmental protection constitute a whole, with the former emphasizing the ecosystem and biological diversity, while the latter focuses on the atmosphere, water, soil, and other natural environments. Due to over-development, many pollutants are emitted in the progress of industrial production and consumption, heavily burdening the natural environment, way beyond its own capacity to shoulder such burdens. As a result, the environment has deteriorated and been degraded with sewage overflow, strong atmospheric haze, and contaminated soil. These seem to have

---

[1]*About COVID-19, 9 answers from the expert group of Chinese Academy of Medical Sciences*, CYOL.com, January 27, 2020: http://news.cyol.com/app/2020-01/27/content_18341684.htm.

[2]"Hou Yanzhen, Zhao Wenwu, Liu Yanxu: *"Unprecedented" Natural Decline and "Accelerated" Species Extinction Rate", Brief Introduction of IPBEs Global Assessment Report, Acta Ecological Sinica*, No.18, 2019.

nothing to do with the pandemic, but in fact they are connected; the deteriorating environment acts a "hotbed" for the spread of viruses. For example, if dust concentration in the air is high, the virus clings to the dust, which facilitates viral spread. Studies have proven that "the increase in the concentration of fine particulate matter in the air will cause more people to catch the flu and aggravate the spread of influenza".[3]

The third problem is climate change, the latest environmental challenge facing mankind. Though greenhouse gases may seem harmless, their ability to induce global warming poses a deadly threat to human beings. According to the United Nations Intergovernmental Panel on Climate Change (IPCC), climate change will increase the likelihood of severe, pervasive, and irreversible impacts on people and ecosystems.[4] Global warming can cause more than a dozen major changes, including rising sea levels and the release of deadly "ancient" pathogens. A recent unconfirmed report of mysterious "blood-like water" underground in Antarctica has been found to contain bacteria relying on sulfur and iron compounds, which could be a threat to humans if released from melting ice and snow. A further example is provided by an incident in 2016, on the Yamal Peninsula in the arctic, a 12-year-old boy died of an anthrax infection, and at least 20 people were hospitalized. Such an anthrax outbreak was caused by a reindeer that died from anthrax infection a few decades ago, its body sealed in the permafrost under the surface. In the summer of 2016, because of the thawing of the permafrost, this reindeer was exposed, and the contagious anthrax was released into nearby water and soil. Anthrax then entered the food supply chain, eventually causing human infections.[5] What's more, studies have shown that global warming will also change the living environment of humans, animals, and plants and accelerate their migration. Under these circumstances, human beings will have more contact with wild animals, which will further facilitate the spread of disease.

Fourth, in addition to these challenges, environmental economists have also made a statistical study of ecological and environmental

---

[3](Wang Lulu, Zhang Juan, *Dynamics Modeling and Analysis of the Influence of Haze on the Spread of Influenza, Journal of Chongqing University of Technology (Natural Science)*, No.4, 2018).

[4]United Nations Intergovernmental Panel on Climate Change (IPCC): IPCC Fifth Assessment Report, November 2, 2014.

[5]BBC Future Report on Unexpected Impact of Arctic Melting, BBC Future, May 4, 2017.

disasters, which shows that with the accelerating development of human society, there exists a heavy-tailed distribution (or fat-tailed distribution) in the occurrence of these disasters.[6] Put simply, the probability of "black swan" events is increasing, and even though the probability of a catastrophe, such as this pandemic, remains low, when it does occur, it imposes a severe blow on an established social and economic order.

In fact, human beings have attached unprecedented importance to green development in recent years. However, despite the sustainable development movement prevailing in the international community, and a green development strategy adopted by China in recent years, public health emergencies like the COVID-19 outbreak have not been brought under control, which shows that the importance and urgency of green development has still been underestimated. To prevent the crisis from reoccurring, a tremendous upfront cost is inevitable, but compared with the price that would be paid should another pandemic reoccur, such early costs are worth it.

19.1.2 The impact of the COVID-19 pandemic, and the challenges it posed to green development

Since the outbreak of COVID-19, most researchers have focused on the analysis of the economic impact of the pandemic, while few have paid attention to fields related to green development, such as ecological environmental protection and resource and energy utilization. In fact, green development has also been greatly affected by the pandemic. Some reasons are directly related to the pandemic, such as the increase of various environmental pollutants like medical waste and wastewater, while others are indirectly related, for example, the pandemic has had an impact on the economic sector, which in turn affects green development. Based on the current situation, it is believed that the COVID-19 pandemic will affect and challenge green development in the areas of ecological environment governance, consumption and production emissions, and energy and resource utilization.[7]

---

[6] Wagner, G., and Weitzman, M. L., *Climate Shock: The Economic Consequences of a Hotter Planet*, Princeton University Press, 2015.

[7] Li Zhiqing, Prevention and control of pandemic disease from the perspective of environmental economy, *China Environment News*, February 17, 2020.

19.1.2.1 *The impact of the pandemic on ecological and environmental governance*

The use of masks, protective clothing, and other medical protective equipment has increased sharply due to pandemic prevention and control measures, which will directly lead to a large amount of medical waste. It is estimated that in 2020, altogether China will see an additional 162,000 tons of discarded masks nationwide.[8] Undoubtedly, this makes environmental protection like waste classification and disposal more difficult. In the short term, particularly in those areas hit most severely by the pandemic, both local environmental protection departments and related industries and units face great pressure in ecological and environmental protection.

For example, according to the notice of the Ministry of Ecology and Environment on the environmental supervision of the treatment and disposal of medical waste and medical waste water nationwide, "by March 3, 2020, the national medical waste disposal capacity was 5,948.5 tons/day, an increase of 1,045.7 tons/day compared with 4,902.8 tons/day before the pandemic, of which, that of Hubei province increased from 180 tons/day before the pandemic to 663.7 tons/day, and that of Wuhan city increased from 50 tons/day to 261.7 tons/day. Since January 20, 123,000 tons of medical waste have been disposed of nationwide".[9] This shows that medical waste and wastewater discharges have increased significantly in a short period of time because of the pandemic, posing a huge challenge to ecological and environmental governance.

Meanwhile, due to the shutdown of most enterprises during the pandemic, the implementation of ecological and environmental protection and management projects was to a certain extent hindered, which affects ecological and environmental management. Projects will be delayed or halted in areas including air improvement, water pollution control, industrial solid waste control, and soil remediation. Though in the short term there will not be problems like business failures or cash flow interruptions of small micro enterprises, environmental companies will be hit most

[8] Jin Yezi, Where are the used face masks? Medical waste disposal market to hit 8.5 billion yuan in two years, *China Business News*, February 28, 2020.

[9] "The Ministry of Ecology and Environment reports the national medical waste, medical waste water disposal and environmental monitoring", Ministry of Ecology and Environment website, March 9, 2020: http://www.mee.gov.cn/xxgk2018/xxgk/xxgk15/202003/t20200306_767526.html.

severely during the pandemic because of project suspension, delayed bidding, limited construction, staffing shortages, overburdened fixed costs, supply chain disruptions, and the resulting credit and debt risks.[10]

19.1.2.2 *The impact of the pandemic on consumption-based emissions*

To prevent and control the COVID-19 pandemic, tertiary industries in China including catering (in-house dining) and entertainment were basically closed in February 2020. These closures not only directly affected economic output, but also changed the consumption pattern of Chinese people with them moving to home consumption, online consumption, and fragmented consumption. These changes have had an impact on the environment because the consumption emissions of communities and households surged, resulting in a rapid growth in domestic sewage discharge, electricity and energy consumption, and household waste, thus creating pressure for environmental disposal.

For example, during the pandemic, sales of all kinds of goods soared due to the impact of the stay-at-home economy. According to the *2020 Spring Festival Stay-at-home Economy Big Data* released by Meituan, the sales of yeast products increased by nearly 40 times. According to Suning's big data report, sales of disinfectant hand sanitizers, hairdresser chairs, and massage chairs soared by 2,315%, 731%, and 436%, respectively. In addition, to promote pandemic prevention and control as well as economic and social development, many shopping centers have launched "safe delivery" services for the catering industry and started online shopping. With all kinds of online sales in full swing, a large quantity of delivery packaging waste has been generated, causing a sharp increase in household waste emissions.

19.1.2.3 *The impact of the pandemic on production emissions*

In the short term, the pandemic has had three affects: first, on the bright side, with the shutdown of some manufacturing enterprises, people have used less transportation, which greatly reduces emissions into the

---

[10]Lin Rongzhen, Impact of the pandemic on China's Environmental Protection Industry and Analysis of Future Industrial Development, Official Account of Internet Industry Research Institute of Tsinghua University, March 3, 2020).

environment. Second, since the pandemic has lasted longer, the emissions of pollutants from protective equipment enterprises who have been working overtime at full capacity to restore and expand production, have increased, placing pressure on the local government to fulfill environmental protection targets. Third, some cities (especially large cities) have developed home-bound economies (including home-based offices, home-based education, and home-based services), which increases solid waste emissions from households and communities. In the long run, if both production investment and consumption see a "recovery" (or even "retaliatory") increase after the pandemic, there will be a "sharp rebound" in emissions, putting more pressure on environmental protection.

Using carbon emissions as an example, an analysis shows that because of measures taken to control the pandemic, production in major industrial sectors has been reduced by 15–40%, which could result in a reduction of CO_2 emissions by 200 million tons, meaning a 6% reduction in total global emissions. Meanwhile, measures taken by countries worldwide to contain the outbreak have had a huge impact on air traffic. It has been pointed out that compared with the week beginning January 20, the capacity of international routes departing from China in the two weeks before March 6 was reduced by 50–90%, and the domestic flight capacity was reduced by 60–70%. Such widespread groundings and cancellations mean that global CO_2 emissions from passenger flights have been reduced by about 11% in those two weeks.[11] In addition, preliminary analysis by the International Energy Agency (IEA) and the Organization of Petroleum Exporting Countries (OPEC) suggests that the impact of the outbreak could reduce global oil demand by 0.5% from January to September 2020, with corresponding reductions in carbon emissions.

19.1.2.4 *The impact of the pandemic on the use of energy resources*

After the outbreak of the pandemic, production and consumption have faced a short pause. Compared with usual consumption, the overall utilization of resources including that of electricity, water, and transportation in the first quarter has been reduced significantly, which is good for conservation efforts.

---

[11] Osaka, S., Coronavirus: The Worst Way to Drive Down Emissions, 20200305: https://www.nationalobserver.com/2020/03/05/news/coronavirus-worst-way-drive-down-emissions.

In the short term, for example, the pandemic has led to a sharp reduction in outdoor activities with cities "locked down", public transport suspended, and travel and parties banned. It has had a significant effect on electricity consumption in industries such as entertainment, catering, retail, and tourism. Industrial electricity consumption has also been affected since enterprises postponed the resumption of work because of the pandemic. Human resource intensive enterprises, such as the textile industry and power & electronics contract manufacturers, have seen a sharp decline in electricity consumption.

According to statistics, the levels of coal consumption by electricity and industrial output (the average level of 14 days) after the Spring Festival holiday in 2020 was far lower than usual levels in previous years. The following provide examples: the coal consumption of power plants fell by 36%, and the operating rate of major steel mills fell by more than 15%. The coal throughput of the largest coal port fell by 29%. The utilization rate of coking plants fell by 23%. The NO_2 level based on satellite observations fell by 37%, and the utilization rate of refining capacity fell by 34%.[12]

However, the pandemic has also had a "side effect" on the utilization of resources; after the pandemic, to boost economic growth, both production and consumption inevitably saw a "recovery" (or even "retaliatory") increase, which has aggravated the contradiction between supply and demand of resources and caused tension in the utilization of energy resources. What should be noted is that the economic difficulties may become operational difficulties for industries and enterprises, thus stimulating the expansion of traditional energy-intensive industries.[13]

19.2 Combating the Pandemic with "green development": A Response to the COVID-19 Pandemic

In the short term, green development should be conducted in the context of pandemic prevention and control. Prevention and control of the pollution should be integrated with that of the pandemic, which means green development should be in line with pandemic prevention and control

[12]The Impact of the pandemic on China's Energy Consumption and Carbon Emissions, "International Energy Data" WeChat Official Account, March 6, 2020.

[13]Zhang Ke, "*A roadmap for building a beautiful China during the 14th Five-Year Plan period: environmental and economic policies will be implemented*", *China Business News*, March 11, 2020.

measures to achieve the balance of "pandemic prevention" and "pollution prevention".

19.2.1 Short-term response of green development

In the short term, green development should be a part of pandemic prevention and control measures and contribute to the fight against the pandemic. At the same time, it has helped improve urban and rural sanitation and restore economic normalcy.

(1) The focus of green development should be shifted to pandemic prevention and control in a timely manner, to prevent the spread of pollution such as medical solid waste and waste water and prevent the effects of the pandemic from "spilling over" to the ecological environment. The garbage classification system should continue to be fully implemented, continue the strict implementation of the scientific classification of medical waste, and carry out a national health campaign to cut off the "production chain" of the pandemic from both the source and the end to resolutely prevent a "second wave of the pandemic".

These measures have been supported by governments at all levels who have issued corresponding policies and formulated relevant laws and regulations:

In terms of the prevention and control of medical solid waste and waste water, a careful plan has been made in the *Guiding Opinions on Coordinating the Prevention and Control of the Pandemic and the Ecological and Environmental Protection for Economic and Social Development* issued by the Ministry of Ecology and Environment, which stated "We will spare no efforts for environmental protection related to pandemic prevention and control with the main goal being to fully cover the environmental supervision and services of all medical institutions and facilities, collecting and transferring medical waste and waste water in a timely and effective manner, and ensuring that pollutants are 100% treated and disposed of". Initially the principle of handling medical waste and wastewater must be strictly enforced as much as possible, which means that by assigning designated medical sites as key areas, the production, collection, transport, storage, treatment, and disposal of medical waste and waste water in various regions should be comprehensively understood. Secondly, with Hubei Province as the focus and Wuhan City as the top priority, efforts should be sped up to overcome the shortcomings exposed in collecting and transporting medical waste and hazardous waste, as well as to solve the problems of treatment and disposal facilities. There should be coordination between regions, between medical waste units and hazardous waste units, between fixed facilities and mobile equipment, and to appropriately deploy effective emergency responses to prevent and control the pandemic as well as protect the environment in Beijing. Medical institutions have been encouraged to collect medical waste by source, disposal companies have been urged to give priority to the collection, transportation, and disposal of medical waste from the pandemic, and to ensure the stable operation of centralized disposal facilities. Third, strengthening the supervision and management of key processes such as the collection, treatment, and disinfection of medical wastewater and urban sewage will be continued, and the discharge of untreated medical wastewater is prohibited.

In terms of wildlife protection legislation, on February 24, the Sixteenth Meeting of the Standing Committee of the 13 National People's Congress approved the *Decision of the Standing Committee of the National People's Congress on Banning the Illegal Wildlife trade, Ending the Habit of Eating Wild Animals and Protecting People's Health and Safety*. Based on the Wildlife Protection Law, the document expands the legal adjustment range and establishes a total ban on the consumption of wild animals. It stipulates a total ban on eating "terrestrial wildlife of important ecological, scientific and social value" and other terrestrial wildlife under state protection, including those artificially bred or raised. Meanwhile, it was also made clear that those who violate the provisions of existing laws shall be given a heavier punishment than existing punishments. Additional violations identified in this Decision shall be punished with reference to the relevant provisions of existing laws, demonstrating stricter management and deterrence through severer punishments.

In terms of medical waste classification, the Ministry of Ecology and Environment issued the *Guidelines on Emergency Management and Technology of Medical Waste Generated by COVID-19 Infection (Trial)* to guide all localities to dispose of medical waste in a timely, orderly, efficient, and safe way and standardize the management and technical requirements for emergency disposal of medical waste generated by COVID-19 patients. Jiangsu province has allocated RMB 200 million to support medical waste disposal in various regions. Shanghai Municipality has formulated and launched a plan for the collection, transportation, and disposal to ensure daily collection and disposal of medical waste in designated hospitals and medical institutions with fever clinics. Shenyang (in Liaoning province) established accounts for its 4,842 medical institutions to identify the possible risks of each link in the process of collection, transportation, and disposal of medical waste, and ensure the whole process is a closed management system. Meanwhile, due to the large number of masks produced, some places have taken scientific and effective prevention and control measures in discarding, collection, transportation, and disposal. The first step was increasing publicity to educate people that used masks should be discarded separately and tightly wrapped in small plastic bags; next, the collection bins for masks were modified. They were locked and fitted with small outlets so that discarded masks cannot be removed easily. This measure effectively prevented pollution caused by scavenging and controlled the spread of the virus carried on masks. Then, discarded masks are transported by special vehicles to avoid cross-contamination with other garbage. Finally, special areas for receiving discarded masks were set up in the incineration plants so that once transported to the incinerator, the masks would immediately be put into the furnace and disposed of innocuously.[14]

On February 23, the national health campaign office issued the *Notice on the In-depth Patriotic Health Campaign and the Prevention and Control of COVID-19 Pandemic*, requiring local governments to consider the local pandemic situation and take further measures to ensure the management of production, livelihood, shopping, transportation, and community after the resumption of work and production. While avoiding crowded activities, full play must be given to the overall management and coordinating role of the national health campaign, and the mobilization of all departments, units, and people to fully participate in the long term.

According to the notice, local governments should launch activities to clean up the environment of enterprises, public institutions, and communities, comprehensively improve the market environment, clean up the environment of other key places and that of households, and publicize popular science. Through these activities, all localities should improve environmental hygiene, implement the biological control and scientific

[14]Zhao Haitao, *Neither Prevention and Control of the Pandemic nor Garbage Sorting Should be Left Behind*, February 14, 2020, https://www.cn-hw.net/news/202002/14/70654.html.

disinfection of disease vectors, and publicize health knowledge based on each area's particular characteristics.

It is also stressed that patriotic health campaign offices in different localities fully play the role of coordination and cooperation with relevant departments and units in health, civil affairs, urban and rural housing development, transportation, agriculture and rural areas, and market supervision. Building upon the patriotic health work network at all levels, they should make continuous efforts to mobilize people so that they will together take the initiative to participate in prevention and control work and fight against the pandemic.

It is fair to say that all these measures, with the aim of green development, have played a positive role in effectively preventing and controlling the pandemic in terms of ecological and environmental health.

(2) The implementation of green development should also consider the production needs of pandemic prevention and control, especially the production and transportation of strategic protective materials. Temporary environmental protection standards and measures should be implemented through a step by step and targeted process. On the premise of ensuring safety and legal environmental standards, certain "environmental exemptions" should be granted to special places, industries, enterprises, and units, which means a flexible environmental management system should be adopted during the fight against the pandemic.

    In terms of industrial development related to pandemic prevention and control, the Ministry of Ecology and Environment has drawn up two positive lists in the *Guiding Opinions on Coordinating Pandemic Prevention and Control and Ecological and Environmental Protection in Economic and Social Development* and has adopted corresponding measures of "environmental exemption".

First, make a positive list for the implementation of EIA approval to facilitate the construction of projects and exempt some projects from EIA procedures. The EIA emergency service guarantee policies are already in place for three types of projects, namely, medical and healthcare, material production, and research; these will be tested to identify which are urgently needed during pandemic prevention and control. Integration with the emission permit system needs to be strengthened. The environmental impact registration form will no longer be required for industries listed in the *Classification and Management Catalog of Environmental Impact*

Assessment of Construction Projects (hereinafter referred to as the Catalog), the *Classified Management List of Discharge Permits of Fixed Pollution Sources (2019 Edition)*, and for projects of social undertakings and service industries which do not involve the 10 categories and 30 sub-categories of industries including storage, logistics, and the distribution of toxic, harmful, and dangerous goods. Meanwhile, the pilot reform of the approval system for the notification and commitment of EIA will be expanded to include employment-intensive industries which have a generally controllable impact on the environment, which have been greatly affected by the pandemic, and are related to people's livelihoods. This includes engineering construction, social undertakings, services, manufacturing, animal husbandry, and transportation, which altogether will involve 17 categories and 44 sub-categories of industries in the Catalog. In addition, the EIA approval service for projects will be strengthened. For the resumption of work and production of key projects, such as large-scale pig breeding projects, the initiative will be taken to provide EIA approval services and charge to an account. The way EIA is managed should also be innovated; basic environmental data should be made public, the management process should be optimized, and approval should be given without the need for "meeting each other".

Second, a positive list of oversight and law enforcement will be formulated and implemented to give full play to the role of incentives and guidance. In terms of specific measures, first, some enterprises will be exempted from on-site law enforcement inspections. No on-site law-enforcement inspections will be carried out on enterprises that are closely related to the production of pandemic prevention and control materials and the protection of people's livelihood, which have small pollution emissions, strong employment capacity, that are involved in major projects and key areas, and have standardized management and high environmental performance. Second, the implementation of off-site supervision will be promoted making full use of technological means such as remote sensing, unmanned aerial vehicle inspection, online monitoring, video monitoring, monitoring of energy consumption and big data analysis, as well as reminding enterprises after resuming work and production to operate pollution control facilities as usual. Third, the "two randoms, one open" supervision will be implemented. (This process involves the random selection of inspection targets, and the random selection of law enforcement inspectors, with the results being made public). Standardized discretion will be exercised in administrative penalties, enforce laws in strict accordance with statutory limits of authority and procedures, and take prudent measures to seal up, detain, restrict, or suspend production. Enterprises directly affected by pandemic prevention and control may not be punished for minor environmental violations if they have quickly corrected the violation and have not caused environmental harm, and further they shall be urged to rectify the problem as soon as possible. If the rectification is not completed on schedule due to the direct impact of pandemic prevention and control, the time for rectification may be extended as appropriate. Moreover, criminal acts violating environment law must be resolutely investigated and punished, such as the secret discharge of pollutants, malicious discharge, falsification of monitoring data, and illegal acts related to the disposal of pandemic medical waste and wastewater, that would threaten people's health, or which are strongly condemned.

Third, resource investment in green development needs to be increased. Both during and after the pandemic prevention and control period, ecological environmental protection is bound to be an important task related to the overall security of society. With the whole society being more aware of environmental sanitation, sanitation products are likely to be in short supply, along with medical supplies. In this regard, it is necessary to plan in advance and encourage more capital and enterprises to join the ecological and environmental protection industry through fiscal, taxation, financial, and technological innovation policies to meet the needs of environmental protection development.

Guidelines on serving the industrial needs of special fields, such as ecological and environmental sanitation, are also included in the above-mentioned *Guiding Opinions of the Ministry of Ecology and Environment.*

To help enterprises solve the problem of pollution treatment, increased technical assistance is needed. The national comprehensive service platform for the transformation of ecological and environmental scientific and technological achievements should be made full use of. Enterprises in need of environmental pollution treatment plans should be connected to technologies and suppliers, and free technical consulting services should be provided for enterprises. Industrial parks and enterprises will be guided and encouraged to promote third-party governance, and service models such as environmental hospitals, environmental stewardesses, and environmental consultants will be promoted. Activities like providing support and assistance in pairing, and providing policies, technologies, and services, will also be conducted.

Cooperation in the implementation of relevant policies will be actively provided to ease the financial difficulties of enterprises. The role of national green development funds will be given full play to encourage local governments, financial institutions, and private capital where conditions permit the setting up of regional green development funds. The management of funds for pollution prevention and control projects will be strengthened, and priority given to areas severely affected by the pandemic, and to the work of pandemic prevention and control. For enterprises severely affected by the pandemic and eligible for pollution treatment, an extension of the payment of environmental protection tax will be approved. Furthermore, we will encourage financial institutions to further implement green credit.

When conducting green development, the need for high-quality economic development should be a focus, which means full consideration should be given to the particularities of the pandemic prevention and control period as well as striving for balanced development between the environment and the economy. Initially, favorable conditions for high-quality economic development should continue to be created and environmental protection work carried out considering local conditions. Next, attention should continue to be paid to the environmental protection appeals of various producers, especially small and medium-sized enterprises, to resume their work and production, and further improve efficiency in environmental protection procedures and supervision so as to reduce the burden on enterprises and serve the urgent needs of enterprise development. Further, in terms of the environmental economy, hard work should be done to the largest extent possible to "reduce burdens" and "increase profits" by lowering the "pricing" level of environmental and economic policy tools, such as environmental taxes and emission rights trading, so as to lower the economic cost of environmental protection. At the same time, support for environmental investment through green finance needs to increase, to stimulate and guide the overall recovery of the economy.

Jiangsu Province provides a very good example as it is committed to pandemic prevention and control work, as well as the green development of the economy and society. On February 26, the video conference held by the Jiangsu Provincial Department of Ecology and Environment stressed that environmental prevention and control measures should provide service guarantees to promote the resumption of work. It should support pandemic prevention and control and at the same time, work on high-quality development of services. In particular, it was pointed out that "different localities should provide targeted step-by-step guidance for different regions, groups of people, industries, and enterprises. It has been necessary to learn more about the needs of enterprises and provide effective services in accordance with the law and regulations so as to promote the resumption of work and production, accelerate the construction of major projects, pay full attention to production safety, and solve the difficulties of enterprises, especially small, medium, and micro enterprises, with targeted goals, countermeasures, and precise implementation."

To this end, the Department of Ecology and Environment of Jiangsu Province "customized" a "green development service package" for the province's enterprises, which is very representative of other initiatives in other regions, including a total of 18 measures which can be divided into six sections.[15]

Open up the green channel for approval: "no meeting" environmental protection approval will be implemented so that all kinds of environmental protection administrative permits can be filed and awarded online with one's cellphone or laptop and delivered by mail. EIA reports (forms) will be accepted online, and there will also be online environmental protection consultation services. For projects that are urgently needed for pandemic prevention, such as medical care, material production, and research, measures for emergency services of the EIA will be implemented. Projects comprising temporary construction, renovation, expansion, or the switching of production lines will be exempted from EIA procedures. Medical diagnostic equipment urgently needed for pandemic prevention is exempted from going through EIA or isotope transfer approval procedures or having radiation safety permits. During the pandemic, where licenses have expired and on-site verification has not been carried out, the expiry date can be automatically extended, or the enterprise may apply to the local government for an emergency response until the pandemic subsides. For newly built medical waste disposal facilities that meet operating conditions have not obtained a license for hazardous waste operations, they may be allowed to carry out emergency disposal before being issued the license under the premise of ensuring environmental safety. Hazardous waste disposal enterprises should be given guidance to

[15] *Jiangsu Provincial Department of Ecology and Environment takes multiple measures to create a "comprehensive service package*" for Jiangsu enterprises, *Xinhua net*, March 10, 2020: http://www.js.xinhuanet.com/2020-02/20/c_1125602080.htm.

gradually and systematically resume production. But those having difficulties in disposing of hazardous wastes then should be given help to find the receiving units to help them based on the nearby principle. For radioactive materials that cannot be safely held in medical institutions, coordinated arrangements shall be made for temporary and standardized storage in the nearest source depot.

Environmental supervision and management are to be improved; enterprises identified by national and local Party committees and governments as related to pandemic prevention and control should be put onto the positive list of environmental regulations, which means they do not have to be often inspected and they enjoy exemptions from suspension of production or production limits to ensure their normal production. A concise manual on environmental protection services will be formulated for enterprises to resume work and production, with relevant information being sent to enterprises online to guide and assist them in identifying potential environmental safety hazards, conducting proper pollution treatments, and ensuring that their emissions meet the standards. Full use will be made of the comprehensive monitoring platform for the battle against pollution as well as the full utilization of the big data platform for ecological environment. Methods such as "off-site" monitoring, "non-contact" law enforcement, and "information-based" supervision will be adopted during the pandemic prevention and control period to improve the standardization and precision of environmental management. If there are no special circumstances, enterprise environmental statistics reports will be submitted online in electronic form, to reduce the burden on grassroot institutions.

The principle of trust and protection will be adhered to: for environmental infrastructure construction projects or environmental treatment projects which have been delayed because of the pandemic, the contract period is allowed to be extended with reference to the relevant statutory exemption clauses of force majeure. As for enterprises that cannot complete the rectification or improve the discharge standards as planned due to the pandemic, a window period shall be set aside to guide enterprises to complete the rectification according to their unique situation. Supervision will be both inclusive and prudent: for enterprises that commit unintentionally a minor violation of the law for the first time and promptly correct the violation, they may be exempted from administrative punishment. Enterprises that lost marks in the environmental protection credit evaluation because of the pandemic shall be exempted from credit punishment depending on the circumstances. The lawful property rights of enterprises shall be protected in accordance with the law, and compulsory measures, such as sealing up, detaining, and freezing, will be taken prudently to protect the lawful interests of enterprises.

Fiscal, taxation, and financial support will be strengthened: tax authorities will be consulted and the first work will be undertaken on approving deferral of environmental tax for qualified enterprises that resume production, which are severely affected by the pandemic and have difficulty in production and operation. Preferential policies will be implemented such as enterprise income tax for special equipment for environmental protection, enterprise income tax for third-party governance, and value-added tax refund for sewage, waste, and sludge treatment as well as recycled aquatic products. Enterprises severely affected by the pandemic that apply for the right to discharge pollutants but have temporary financial difficulties are allowed to withdraw their application and postpone or pay for the use of pollutant discharge rights in installments. Financial institutions will be coordinated with to provide extension or renewal of loans to enterprises severely affected by the pandemic and having difficulties in repaying their "environmental protection loans" when due and offer appropriate reductions in interest on the extension or renewal of loans, instead of simply withdrawing, cutting off, or withholding loans. Overall, the total size and coverage of environmental loans will be increased, as well as providing more support for environmental financing for small and medium-sized enterprises.

The precise allocation of funds of production and resources: provincial environmental protection funds will give priority to areas and enterprises that are severely affected by the pandemic and have shouldered more responsibility for environmental treatment. The total pollutant discharge quota should be adjusted to prioritize the needs of key enterprises conducting major projects, livelihood projects, or pandemic prevention and control tasks. If localities face difficulties in allocating quotas, the provincial government will adjudicate and help solve the problem. The implementation of annual major provincial environmental governance projects will be sped up, as well as environmental protection projects, and more social capital will be channeled into the ecological and environmental sector.

Efforts to provide support services will be undertaken: the plans for "enterprise environmental protection reception day" will be adhered to and the project of "1,000 environmental protection officials help enterprises in pairs" will continue, in which enterprises will be helped to solve pollution problems in a timely manner through methods like telephone interviews, video conference calls, online meetings, and teleservices. The "Jinhuan Dialogue" (finance and environmental protection dialogue) mechanism will be made full use of, as well as environmental governance supply and demand platforms being used to identify in a timely manner the needs of enterprises, provide services accordingly, and promote coordination between the government, banks, and enterprises, as well as in-depth cooperation between suppliers and consumers.

19.2.2 Long-term response to green development

In the long run, more effort needs to be invested in green development and "green finance" and other tools need to be developed to prevent the recurrence of public health events such as the COVID-19 pandemic.

(1) The idea of harmonious development between humans and nature should be adhered to: Scientific studies have shown that the outbreak of this pandemic is largely related to "nature" and "ecology", because humans have always chosen economic development that emphasizes material growth, while ignoring the organic, harmonious, and symbiotic relationship between the economy and the environment, and between humans and nature. This outbreak is thus a wake-up call; after the pandemic, the current development model must be rethought, and the systems, policies, and practices that do not respect nature and neglect ecological and environmental protection must be reformed. It is necessary to conduct a comprehensive and systematic review of existing ecological and environmental protection systems, especially in the field of wildlife protection. The improvement and adjustment of the system in a systematic, rational, scientific, and practical way is needed so that "ecological civilization" development is implemented in all areas of social and economic development, and applied to the existing legal framework.
(2) The "pre-positioning" of major ecological and environmental protection and management measures should be promoted: This pandemic has brought us many painful lessons, one of which is that the coronavirus has "passed through" layers of blockades, which shows the necessity of "pre-positioning" some ecological and environmental

health protection and management policies. In fact, in public affairs such as ecological and environmental health, excessive emphasis on "in-process" or "post-event" protection and management measures is detrimental to the effective prevention of events like pandemics. It has been shown that once a major event, such as a pandemic, occurs and subsides, it causes many "established" social and economic losses that cannot be compensated for by "in-process" or "post-event" control. It is necessary to comprehensively identify "in-process" or "post-event" policy measures in the fields of ecological and environmental health, and adjust in a timely fashion the management process related to public security.

(3) A nationwide stress test on ecological and environmental risks should be undertaken to structure effective mechanisms: There are several factors to reflect on in the economic and financial sector's response to the pandemic. First, these sectors do not have enough risk awareness; not only did they not effectively assist the ecological and environmental health department to give warnings in advance, but they also failed to quickly respond to minimize the economic impact of the pandemic. The main reason is that they lack "rehearsal", that is, risk stress tests in terms of national risk events. Though the outbreak is not of the ecological environment field, if there exists a corresponding risk prevention mechanism in that area, and if economic and financial regulatory departments intervene in the risk management process in advance, then, the risk warning ability of the whole society would be improved so that the disease may be prevented from happening or its impacts reduced. Therefore, it is necessary in the medium and long term to form an effective mechanism to carry out ecological and environmental risk stress tests on a regular basis in the economic and financial fields, and to improve the ecological and environmental risk management capacity of the economic and financial regulatory authorities.

(4) It is necessary to further develop eco-environmental finance (green finance) to promote the mutual encouragement and compatibility between finance and eco-environmental protection and give play to the positive role of finance in the discovery, identification, prevention, supervision, and response to eco-environmental health risks. For example, a mandatory green insurance system will be implemented to promote green insurance and other new types of insurances in agriculture and animal husbandry, so that the dual warning and intervention

is achieved by both the government and the market in major ecological and environmental health incidents. Furthermore, in terms of issues related to ecological and environmental protection, such as the response to climate change, investment in financing construction needs to be actively carried out, and social capital brought in to strengthen them, so as to prevent the occurrence of health pandemics at their source, that is, the ecological environment.

(5) The government should adapt to the "green-oriented" modern governance model as soon as possible. The idea of the "modernization of governance capacity and governance systems" requires "the imbalance of ecological governance" to be fully recognized. As a public organization with the ability to conduct macro-control, the government plays an irreplaceable role in building green production and green life, which is mainly reflected in assessing the achievements of local governments and major leaders, as well as enhancing the assessment of green indicators and management. Enterprises should increase their vitality and creativity, and make continuous efforts in the research and development of green technologies and green products so as to develop green industries. News media outlets should publicize the necessity and importance of a green lifestyle, and disclose more information about green environmental protection, including new policies and regulations, capital investment, environmental protection reports, and green industry development, so that the government can conduct regular self-examination, and correct deficiencies in a timely manner. Ecosystem management should be placed on the priority agenda of government work at the right time.

19.3 Conclusion

Green development should play an important role in the prevention and control of the pandemic. The COVID-19 pandemic will have a profound impact on green development, such as the discharge of waste, the green development of production and consumption, the protection of the ecological environment, and the utilization of resources and energy. On the whole, green development focuses on "benefits" in the short term but faces more pressure in the long term. In addition, the impact of the pandemic on green development brings both "risks" and "opportunities"; the challenges it poses are great, but it may also bring an opportunity to truly change the pattern of economic growth and development.

In the short term, the pandemic will greatly affect the economy, so it is most important to coordinate the prevention and control of the pandemic while providing for social and economic development. When focusing on fighting the pandemic, medical waste must be disposed of well to improve the urban and rural environment. Meanwhile, green development should give full impetus to economic development, and assist the resumption of work and production creating a green channel for ecological and environmental services. To this end, government departments should spare no efforts to serve the ecological environment, resources, and energy services. Taking this as an opportunity to better understand the traditional green development field, the obstacles and deficiencies in the public service field may be overcome, to better realize the transformation of government functions, and reform green development.

In the long term, we should prevent public environmental health events like pandemics from happening again through green development. Updated ideas need to be adopted to achieve harmonious coexistence between humans and nature. Wild animals should be effectively managed, and concepts such as ecological security, resource security, and biological security should be integrated. Also of importance, the current development model needs to be transformed to include green production and consumption. Further, innovation of development tools, especially green financial instruments, is needed. Technologies like big data and blockchains should be combined with green development to build a scientific and technological system for green development and green finance. Finally, an institutional framework for green development needs to be built, which should be an organic system including laws, administrative regulations, economic incentives, publicity, and education.

https://doi.org/10.1142/9789811252921_0020

Chapter 20

Governance of "Post-Pandemic Era" Urban Modernization

Wu Jianfeng[*] and Jing Yijia[†]

[*]*School of Economics, Fudan University, Shanghai, China*

[†]*School of International Relations and Public Affairs, Fudan University, Shanghai, China*

This chapter mainly discusses economic development from the perspective of urban governance in the "post-epidemic era". Undoubtedly, the impact of COVID-19 has gone beyond what is even imaginable for a public safety crisis; its outbreak and spread have shattered many people's confidence in China's public health system, which was well established after the SARS epidemic in 2003. During this pandemic, some shortcomings in the capacity of Chinese cities to modernize governance and their ability to respond to public health emergencies have been highlighted. Faced with the rapid spread of the virus across different regions, China is mobilizing the whole nation to fight against the COVID-19 pandemic and coordinating with the international community to protect more people. In recent years, China has explored the modernization of governance in many areas and put concrete work into this process. Though these efforts have played a role in the prevention and control of the pandemic, at the present stage given the problems that have been exposed, governments at all levels need to further improve their governance capacity and learn more from experience. Increasing transparency and effectiveness in pandemic prevention and control work is important domestically in raising people's sense of security as well as their expectations for the future, and important abroad to strengthen global investors' confidence in China's future development.

In the context of political science, urban governance refers to the integration of resources through a series of inclusive strategies to achieve collective goals. In this chapter, "urban modernization governance" is defined as the process of maximizing the opportunities for economic and social development while minimizing the risks brought about by environmental and social integration. Pandemic prevention and control needs emergency management, but intrinsically it is also about institutional construction, and implementation of urban modernization governance, which will affect not only the main body of urban society, but also institutional construction and the remodeling of the social order. Throughout human history, every time a large-scale epidemic has broken out, it has profoundly and comprehensively affected the progress of human civilization. From this perspective, the impact of the pandemic on urban governance needs analysis, together with how to improve urban modernization governance in the context of China's development and cultural needs.

The chapter includes three parts.

The impacts of the COVID-19 pandemic on urban governance with be discussed in the first section. As a systematic comprehensive system, urban governance includes the administration of public health, urban space, as well as inter-city and urban–rural coordination. In terms of impact, the problems exposed, and the cost incurred by society, the prevention and control of COVID-19 must be a critical case study of urban governance. There is no doubt that it will have a profound impact on China's urban governance, including the public health system, inter-city public health synergy, urban space, urban household registration policy management, and the settlement of mobile populations within cities.

The measures to improve governance capacity will be considered in the second section. In view of the problems exposed by the COVID-19 pandemic, three clear trends have been recognized in the transformation of Chinese cities from traditional governance to modern governance, namely, the urbanization of Chinese society, spatial networking, and smart cities. On this basis, to cope with the "post-epidemic era" modernization of urban governance several measures are put forward, including improving citizens' social capital, promoting the integration of social organizations into community governance, and selecting competent city officials with high governance abilities.

The final section of this chapter is the conclusion.

20.1 Impact

The impact of the COVID-19 pandemic on urban governance is examined from the following four aspects.

20.1.1 The governance capacity of the urban public health system is in urgent need of improvement

The COVID-19 pandemic has shown that China's urban governance has much to improve, and there is still a long way to go for China to build a modern public health system. As for the goals that were set to establish a modern public health system, first was to improve the urban living environment and reduce the occurrence of infectious diseases as far as possible; second, to prevent the spread of infectious diseases and person-to-person transmission by controlling the source of infection and transmission routes as well as focusing on the needs of vulnerable groups and providing medical care. The pandemic has had a bigger impact on human civilization than that of war, revolution, or riot. In 2003, SARS swept through many Chinese cities, which triggered the reform of China's public emergency management system and raised people's awareness of public health. In recent years, China has integrated the modernization of national governance into its economic, political, cultural, and social development, as well as its "ecological civilization construction", which has played an important role in the current prevention and treatment of COVID-19. For example, big data technology and non-governmental organizations (NGO) have solved problems faced by local governments in terms of coordinating relief supplies. Nonetheless, from the long-run perspective, China's public health system still has many shortcomings.

A review of how human beings fight infectious diseases shows that the pandemic has led to progress in defensive methods and medical technology, especially the establishment of public health systems and the research and development of vaccines against different infectious diseases. Many developed countries and regions have made the idea "Prevention is better than cure" a national policy for epidemic prevention and control after having paid a huge price in severe epidemics. The cholera outbreak in London in August of 1854, for example, was directly caused by a contaminated water pump on Broad Street. With rundown infrastructure and high population density of 432 people per acre, and many residents who were from a working-class background, infectious diseases were easily triggered and spread. (Ambrus *et al.*, 2020). After this outbreak, Britain carried out an urban public health revolution, with measures like housing reform, which turned the once overcrowded cities into healthy, livable places, and which greatly increased the life expectancy of its citizens. Drawing on Britain's experience, later many European countries established similar public health systems. A study of economic history shows that public health policy has greatly contributed to Europe's economic development and military expansion, and it was one of the important factors for the increase in the national strength of European powers. America's public health system was built after the devastating toll brought about by the 1918 flu. To take a recent case as an example, China and Hong Kong also established a health system to cope with public health emergencies after the SARS epidemic in 2003. During SARS, the Amoy Garden in Hong Kong in a short period of time became the most concentrated area of SARS infections worldwide, because the virus spread to hundreds of people in the community through the feces of the first infected person due to a blocked sewage system. Having learned the lessons, Hong Kong initiated an emergency response of the public health system at the early stage of the COVID-19 outbreak, which successfully contained the source of the imported infection and prevented it from developing into a huge outbreak like SARS.

20.1.2 The strengthening of the synergistic capacity of inter-city public health governance is urgently needed

Diseases and pandemics have accompanied humankind throughout its history. A world-renowned pathologist once said, "The history of mankind is the history of disease". Compared to the past when epidemics broke out in limited places, the spread of infectious diseases after the 20th century has much to do with the popularization of modern transportation, through which international trade is more frequent, people travel rapidly, and different types of food are transported quickly between different regions. In the context of globalization, it is no longer the physical distance between cities that affects the spread of disease, but the way people travel. Highly connected cities, which in most cases are the entry points for travelers and goods, have also become important hubs for speeding up the spread of disease. By March 11, 2020, 110 countries worldwide had confirmed cases of COVID-19. As more people around the world became infected, the WHO declared the COVID-19 outbreak to have the characteristics of a pandemic. Therefore, in an increasingly globalized and regionally integrated world, every city is part of a global network. It is not enough to improve the governance capacity of one single city, but more importantly, the coordination of public health governance among different cities must be strengthened.

Since the 2000s, other infectious diseases have spread globally following a similar path of transmission, showing the importance of synergistic public health governance among cities. From the outbreak and spread of several pandemics since 2000, including SARS (Severe Acute Respiratory Syndrome), Middle East Respiratory Syndrome (MERS), and currently COVID-19, as well as Ebola which has affected many West African countries in the last two years, it is obvious that if a way to deal with the virus quickly is not found, an infection that starts in one place will easily spread via the flow of people and grow into a pandemic. In the past, however, such transmission would have taken generations to occur in different regions, societies, or peoples.

20.1.3 Urban space governance is in urgent need of change

The outbreak of COVID-19 reveals that China's urban governance is still a traditional management and control system and has not developed into a modern systematic management. To improve the level of urbanization does not only mean a larger urban population, but more importantly, it requires balanced and sustainable development of urban space, including high quality urban space. With population aggregation in cities comes accumulated risks; epidemiological and economic studies reveal that epidemics are closely associated with urbanization. Economists define a city as a highly dense concentration of people and economic activities in a certain geographical space. Cities are important sources of economic growth; for every 10% increase in a city's size, its productivity can be increased by 0.3–0.8% (Rosenthal and Strange, 2004). China's reform and opening-up in the past 40 years also shows that the higher the rate of urbanization in a region, the higher the level of economic development (Wu Jianfeng, 2018). However, the high density of cities and the high mobility of people easily breeds infectious diseases. During earlier epochs of human history, people lived in scattered places, with independent living areas, so the risk of getting and spreading infectious diseases was relatively small. When human beings stepped into the era of urbanization, the population became increasingly concentrated in a limited space, providing a hotbed for various diseases. Researchers found that a high population density and close human contact make cities potential hot spots for the rapid spread of these infectious viruses. High population densities and the expansion of shared spaces increase the risk of people being infected by epidemic diseases such as influenza, measles, and mycobacterium tuberculosis. Medical historians who have examined the plagues in 14th century in Europe believed that cities were hotbeds for diseases. Some literature found that in the urban areas of Karachi, Pakistan, the incidence of tuberculosis was 329 per 100,000 people, much higher than the national average of 171 per 100,000 people (Aliro *et al.*, 2011). In addition, the unique spatial structure of cities enables the easy breeding of certain germs in certain locations, such as public toilets and rooms equipped with air conditioning systems. While the urban public health revolution has led to numerous modern public health infrastructure and management institutions, as well as the realization by people of the importance of public health responsibilities, once a problem occurs, the risk of infectious diseases spreading within cities will increase dramatically.

In terms of urban space governance, the risk of the spread of infectious diseases due to a high urban population density needs to be fully recognized. First, the higher the density of a city, the higher the frequency there is of person-to-person contact, allowing the quicker spread of pathogens. The recent epidemic of Zika virus provides a relevant example; for the past few decades, the Zika virus has been mainly transmitted between animals. Its arrival in cities in the Americas allowed its spread more widely and rapidly via the yellow fever mosquito (*Aedes aegypti*). Second, pathogens persist longer in denser populations. The heavy reliance of urban populations on social interactions make the prevention and control of infectious diseases ineffective, and make it easier for pathogens to spread, which is seen by cluster cases that have appeared in cities during the COVID-19 pandemic. Finally, high population densities in cities may make pathogens more lethal. In most cases, pathogens grow less lethal as they spread. However, when population density is high, the lethality of the pathogen will increase as it spreads. This was true of asymptomatic patients with COVID-19 who carried higher viral loads, which allowed the deadly pathogen to spread through the air or through human contact to infect more people.

Urban space governance not only addresses public health, but also the management of public sanitation facilities, such as water resources and water environment, housing environment, and orderly land development. There is evidence from several research papers that the COVID-19 virus probably came from an animal host. In terms of urban governance, reducing contact with wildlife through effective space governance measures, such as preventing unrestricted urban expansion, is an important way to lower the risk of the breeding and spread of infectious diseases. If the outward spread of urban space is unregulated, human beings are more likely to have close contact with wildlife and contract zoonotic diseases, which can easily lead to outbreaks of infectious diseases with a global impact. Hassell *et al.* (2017) studied the relationship between cities and the formation of diseases. Having reviewed the emergence of new pathogens from wild animals in the city and the drivers of zoonosis, they provided up-to-date scientific evidence on epidemiology: houses on the outskirts of big cities may be the hotbed for zoonoses; exposure to domestic animals and hunting wild animals make it more likely for infectious disease agents to move from animal hosts to humans; in places with fast urbanization, humans have closer contact with bats and even primates due to deforestation and the conversion of agricultural land to urban land, and thus they are more likely to be infected by viruses from these animals. Studies have shown that due to the acceleration of urbanization, human and animal habitats overlap so that the adaptability of many viruses in humans has been enhanced, resulting in mutations, and even the emergence of new infectious diseases. According to statistics, of the newly identified infectious diseases worldwide from 1940 to 2004, more than 60% were zoonoses (Jones *et al.*, 2008).

20.1.4 Urban mobile population and settlement policies are in urgent need of reform

In China, many cities have been relying on the "dividends" brought about by migrants who work within a city, but these same workers cannot obtain a household registration, and thus cannot benefit from local public services. However, the COVID-19 pandemic has caused Chinese cities to pay a huge cost for such a settlement policy. For the prevention and control of the pandemic, most cities in China have implemented controls on population flow, which slows down urbanization. Currently, though the policy is effective in controlling the disease, it will have a far-reaching impact on the national economy and will generate huge social costs. For example, because of the regulation, the availability of material supplies tightens, and the cost of living rises. Many service-oriented small and medium-sized enterprises face a severe employment crisis. In addition, people with other illnesses have trouble seeing a doctor in a timely manner for treatment. If better settlement policies existed in our cities, there would be less pressure on society because the scale of migration between urban and rural areas would be much smaller during the Spring Festival.

Global experience shows that reducing population mobility also helps control the spread of infectious diseases. From one perspective, the mobile population between urban and rural areas may provide space for the spread of viruses from rural areas, which turns an infectious disease confined to rural areas into an urban one, thus causing it to spread more widely and more rapidly. A case in point is in recent years in many South American cities, Schistosomiasis was introduced by people from the countryside. From another perspective, the migration of people from the countryside also contributes to the spread of those diseases which are already present in cities. A recent example is in Kinshasa, the capital of the Democratic Republic of Congo, where displaced people from other parts of the country got infected with African trypanosomiasis resulting in a tenfold increase of reported cases (Alirol *et al*., 2011).

20.2 Response

20.2.1 Urban modernization governance: Three principles

As core content of urban politics study, urban governance refers to the integration of resources through a series of inclusive strategies to achieve collective goals. In the case of urban modernization governance, it may be defined as the process to maximize the opportunities for economic and social development, while minimizing the risks brought about by environmental and social integration. At present, to improve the capacity of urban modernization governance in China, it is necessary to have a sufficient understanding of China's social development trends, including the trends of urbanization, networking, and smart cities.

The trend of developing an urban society exists in China today. At the beginning of the reform and opening-up period, China's urbanization level was less than 20%, while since 2012 it has been over 50%. In 2019, it exceeded 60%, which means that nearly two-thirds of the population were partaking in jobs related to urban sectors. According to the *United Nations Outlook on Globalization and Urbanization*, China will continue to advance its urbanization process, and is expected to reach 75.8% by 2050, realizing complete urbanization. Therefore, China is an urbanized society where cities are not just places for more people to live; it will be more complex than the traditional society. Urban societies are more diverse, with various ethnicities, cultures, and styles of eating and dressing, as well as different lifestyles. The bigger the city, the more diverse it is. Take Shanghai as an example; by simply walking on the street, it is likely for an ordinary person to meet different cultures and cuisines, visit museums of different styles, and enjoy stage plays from different countries. Urban society is also a concentration of technology. People with high education and skills tend to cluster in megacities and engage in creative knowledge-based economic activities because urban society provides a platform to interact and learn and more opportunities to obtain highly skilled jobs, making the city more dynamic. Urban society is more inclusive and serves as a testing ground for a variety of transcendental policies and measures. It has bred a middle class that creates and plays by the rules, whose ability for information identification and autonomous governance helps identify the rationality of urban policies as well as the advancement of cities.

Chinese cities are now highly interconnected, thus establishing the trend of urban networking. In recent years, with the large-scale construction of transportation infrastructure, China has deepened regional integration, which has greatly improved urban connectivity, and formed an urban network characterized by urban agglomeration. Due to the frequent flow of capital and personnel between different cities, and even the spatial flow of people and animals, urban governance has had to adapt to networking. Interconnection between cities also forms a core city with a high node position. Wuhan, for instance, made use of the advantages of human capital accumulation and low factor cost to quickly integrate into the global high-tech industrial chain. With its nodal position in the global city network constantly being improved, it has maintained strong economic and trade ties with major cities around the world. It must be realized that focus in the future should not be to improve the governance capacity of a single city, but to improve that of all cities. Otherwise, a crisis caused by poor governance in one city, whether in terms of the economy or public health, easily spills over to other cities in the network.

Due to the wide use of big data, many Chinese cities have explored smart city construction, which has also become a trend. From telemedicine to smart transportation, from smart logistics to online offices, smart cities have the capacity to be more powerful in dealing with public events. Although it had a late start, China's smart city construction has attracted heavy investment from enterprises because of the support of all levels of government, and has made great progress. Smart cities are mainly characterized by digitalization, networking, informatization, intelligence, and greening. In the era of smart cities, urban governance is more in line with the needs of data and information flow. Even though system and data resources within the city should be integrated, the city needs to cooperate with all levels of management departments, break down barriers to information sharing, focusing on facility interconnection, resource sharing, and system interconnection, so as to realize the mutual integration, interconnection, and cooperative operation on both the vertical and horizontal level.

20.2.2 Urban modernization governance in the "post-pandemic era": Response measures

Controlling the spread of disease and protecting people's health is both the aspiration of society as well as one of the basic responsibilities of government. As far as China is concerned, whether it develops a modern governance system that can respond to public health emergencies at any time bears not only on the health of its own people, or its economic development, but also on international relations. China is now an urbanization-driven society which remains pervious and closely connected to the outside world, playing an important role in the global industrial chain and economy. "City lock-downs", banning travel, and pooling national efforts to prevent and control the virus are effective measures, but they come at a huge cost. To deal with possible emerging infectious diseases, a global vision in urban governance must be adopted, information management must be refined, and crisis management capability with extensive participation implemented. An effective urban modernization governance system needs to focus on three main parts: citizens, communities, and officials.

20.2.2.1 *Enhance the social capital of citizens*

The citizens form the main body of urban governance and are those who obey the rules and commit to the social contract. In traditional Chinese society, trust and mutual assistance tied people together. These qualities were also important signs by which ordinary people judged whether the society was peaceful or not, so without trust, people lost their sense of security. However, in the era of urbanization, especially for a urban society with hundreds of millions of members of the middle class, it is more important to cultivate social contracts within civil society. If the relationship between people is built on contractual cooperation, it not only reduces the cost generated by "face-to-face relationships" of the "acquaintance" society, but also adapts to the maintenance of public order in the mobile-social space. As a principle the social contract based on a spirit of personal responsibility within a structured society lacks a foundation in China. For example, the debates occurring between Chinese netizens on waiting in line in public spaces, offering ones' seat to others on public transportation, and smoking in public places show that Chinese society has not adapted to cooperative relationships based on the social contract. Therefore, for urban modernization governance, contract-based institutional arrangements and abstract procedures need to be combined with traditional Chinese values and at the same time, there must be an awareness of the externality of individual behavior to enhance citizens' social capital power. In terms of public health education, starting to popularize basic expectations is needed, which is to respect people, animals, and the environment, as well as recognize their equality. Based on these principles, citizens are guided to cultivate personal hygiene habits and change those dietary behaviors which do not conform to modern life, including putting an end to eating wild animals. Shanghai residents are often regarded as the most socially, contractually minded in China, and an ethos of public morality prevails. This is largely due to the internationalization of Shanghai, and the relatively high educational level of the population. Since the outbreak of Covid-19, Shanghai has been at the forefront of epidemic prevention and control in China, because of its good emergency response mechanisms, and its citizens having high public health awareness.

China, despite the rapid growth of urbanization, is still a rural–urban society. To enhance the social capital of urban citizens, new settlement policies should be implemented as soon as possible promoting the settlement of the newcomer population. In terms of policy, cities with a population inflow should be encouraged to liberalize or relax the restrictions on population settlement, so that more migrants can integrate into the cities and become members of the local civil society. According to McKinsey, migration from the countryside will be the main source of population growth in many Chinese cities over the next decade (McKinsey Global Institute (MGI), Preparing for China's Urban Billion. Research Report, 2009). This means accumulation of social capital by the migrant population is crucial to the advancement of governance capacity and China's future urban governance. The lagging reform of the household registration system has excluded many migrants from the local public service system and made them vulnerable to unfair treatment and more reliant on the moral values of traditional society, as well as less able to obtain social rewards from abiding by the rules; for example, the behavior of migrant workers who ignore queuing, try to squeeze onto transportation vehicles, and fight for seats on the bus, has been reported by the media, and complained about by some city dwellers. However, this is the result of the long-term exclusion of migrants from the governance of our cities. The slightly disruptive behavior of newcomers results from their instinct for self-protection because there is no opportunity for them to integrate into the city. Therefore, allowing such integration is an important part of improving China's overall social capital. Whether they become rule-abiding citizens with high social capital in accordance with the spirit of the social contract is an important yardstick to measure whether China's urban governance has reached the standard of modernization.

20.2.2.2 *Promote the integration of social organizations into community governance*

In terms of social management, the community is the smallest unit of implementation for national governance, social governance, and urban governance. In urbanized China and in the era of the planned economy, communities have replaced traditional multi-generational families. The degree and capacity of community governance determines the degree of modernization of urban governance.

The COVID-19 outbreak has provided an example: it highlights the lack of bottom-up community governance in Chinese cities. From one perspective, the role of the neighborhood committee is misplaced, in that, as an autonomous organization of residents, it bears too many administrative functions. In contrast, the government replaces the residents as the main body of the community, which deprives the community of its foundation as a social organization. Due to these two dilemmas, China's community governance is disordered; horizontal social coordination and cooperation are underdeveloped; and vertical administrative forces are too strong to form a real institutionalized social organization mechanism. In this pandemic, it was found that when the administrative power of the community was weakened due to concrete measures such as formalism, community residents helped themselves and each other, which in fact demonstrated the essence of community governance, reaching a balance between government and non-governmental autonomous forces, and this played an important role in the prevention and control of the pandemic during later stages.

Therefore, social organizations should be supported and encouraged to integrate with community governance to improve the modernization capacity of urban governance in the "post-epidemic era". If community organization becomes both the structural and functional element of community governance, the two dilemmas mentioned above will be solved and overall community governance capacity will be improved. This means that as a basic element of community governance, the participation of social organizations will better connect members of community organizations and will increase their mutual trust and assistance so as to form a social network of participation. Further it follows that the spillover of individual action will be exerted to the greatest extent, and the accumulation of social capital in communities will be increased. Moreover, once social organizations join the community, there will be a willingness to collectively express demands based on collective interest, which will provide information for the government's decision-making, and form effective supervision of the government by residents. It shows that the integration of social organizations into community governance would reshape the relationship between the state and society through bottom-up organizations and break the "administrative dilemma" of grassroots governance. In addition, the development of social organizations would help generate shared norms as well as social order arising from autonomous community management. It will encourage social organizations, especially those with advocacy and public welfare characteristics, so that the social forces within the community will grow stronger. The common values and norms of conduct of the community will be formed within a certain area so that the community will return to its natural state of "being a community". Since the outbreak of COVID-19 in Wuhan, many volunteers whose efforts must be acknowledged have organized themselves to participate in the prevention and control of the pandemic. For example, after the "lock down" of Wuhan, the Blue Sky Rescue Team from the private sector participated in the transportation of all kinds of emergency supplies and equipment, playing an important role in combating the pandemic.

In the past few years, many city governments have been actively exploring ways of integrating social organizations into community governance. For example, the "Three-Part Co-ordination" model linking communities, social organizations, and social work, and the "Community Collaborative Governance" model, which calls on community residents to play a synergistic role in community public affairs, such as planned gatherings, neighborhood assistance, mediation, and professional services, acting as a supplement to government management. Overall, however, the role of social organizations has to a considerable extent been suppressed due to excessive administrative power. In the "post-epidemic era", the community should be encouraged to develop its strength so that bottom-up governance is established to build and shape resilient urban communities and lay a solid foundation for modern urban governance.

20.2.2.3 *Select city officials with high administrative ability*

Professional officials who administer local governments are another key to improving government modernization and governance capacity. In modern society, public policy, carried out at different levels, closely interacts with businesses, citizens, universities, and NGOs, promoting a "network" model of inter-departmental and multi-channel cooperation. Whether a professional city official works well in such a network management model is the key to enhancing urban governance capacity. Because of their credibility, strategic foresight, and efficient execution of tasks, they are more likely to win market recognition and defuse environmental, public health, and social integration risks caused by urban development.

Within the current system, China's governmental officials are selected through a series of selection mechanisms. Xi *et al.* (2018) believes that these mechanisms strongly demonstrate the characteristics of elite politics. Its advantage lies in that the examination of performance of officials in different positions, those with higher abilities standing out, increases the efficiency of policy-making and avoids the populism of policies. However, it is different when superiors' select local officials. The researchers found, for example, when officials are making decisions, they are likely to be affected by short-term opportunism, which makes them short-sighted in designing local economic development policies and ignoring long-term sustainable development goals. What's more, the selection system leads to simplification, which makes it difficult for creative officials to stand out. After the outbreak of the pandemic, some local officials were exposed as being professionally incapable of responding to public health emergencies, and lacking evidence-based decision-making ability, which is clear proof of the disadvantages of the current selection system. It also shows that the selection system of officials still needs a lot of improvement to realize national governance.

In this pandemic, local officials in Shanghai, Henan, and Zhejiang have been more effective in responding to the public health crises, demonstrating their strong governance capabilities, which shows that, in addition to the ability to take on responsibilities, it is important for urban government officials to be highly educated and professional with an international vision, and have experience at the grassroots level. Therefore, in the "post-epidemic era", when selecting cadres, those departments responsible for hiring should avoid unfairness, such as cronyism and seniority, and establish selection mechanisms for making staff appointments that fully mobilize officials, as well as choosing highly competent officials with a deep understanding of urban development.

20.3 Conclusion

The COVID-19 pandemic will pass eventually. It is a test for China's acceleration of urbanization and globalization. The lessons learned from the pandemic are important to reflect on and improve the modernization level of urban governance. After the outbreak of the pandemic, many places, and people from all walks of life across the country managed to thwart its spread by applying a "sharp brake" to block the transmission of the virus. The next problem is work resumption: whether another wave of the pandemic will be prevented and controlled, and the resumption of work and production carried out systematically depends on whether the city governments learn from experience and turn the "crisis" into an "opportunity". In the process of pandemic prevention and control, local governments at all levels should improve the market, political, and legal environment, and promote the construction of a civil society where the power of community governance at the grassroots level is reshaped, and information management and modernization development coordinated to comprehensively enhance urban governance capacity. The development and application of population data played an important role in the prevention and control of the pandemic. However, when using big data, a balance between information privacy and pandemic prevention needs to be struck to prevent improper disclosure and abuse of personal information on the Internet, which is another requirement of modern urban governance. What's more, with the spread of the coronavirus worldwide, it is imperative for China to strengthen cooperation with other countries on health management and promote joint prevention and control at the regional and global levels to prevent the spread of the pandemic. This is also a new test to improve the capacity of urban governance.

https://doi.org/10.1142/9789811252921_0021

Chapter 21

Reflections and Recommendations on the Governance System and the COVID-19 Pandemic

Li Qingjuan* **and Kong Xue**†

*Fanhai International School of Finance, Fudan University, Shanghai, China

†Huaxia Economic Development Research Institute, Shanghai, China

The global spread of the coronavirus indicates that the fight against the pandemic is no longer confined to a certain region or country, but is a public health emergency for mankind. Underestimating the transmission capacity of the virus would be a manifestation of the government's irresponsibility.

Because of the impact of the pandemic on the economy, the government should perform its function of macro-control, work on the mechanism failure of the market, and promote economic recovery and development. The powerful algorithm optimization system formed by the combination of artificial intelligence (AI) + big data + 5G + blockchain will lead to the revolutionary development of many industries in 2020, and improve the operational efficiency of the whole society. The government should refocus in time to help traditional enterprises transform, and promote the development of emerging industries.

Sun Tzu: The Art of War states, "Therefore, armies don't have a fixed plan, just as water doesn't have a fixed shape. Commanders who win the war by adjusting to the enemy are to be called god", which emphasizes that change is the inevitable state of society, and the trend of industrial development. It is possible to predict that existing online projects like e-commerce, short videos, virtual games, online education, and paying for knowledge online will usher in a new wave of development. High-tech industries like unmanned retail, unmanned catering, and unmanned drone delivery will also be further developed, and the prosperity of online services will be a new driving force for industrial development. Therefore, this chapter focuses on how to optimize and reform economic and social governance. The current model of the national paid leave policy needs to be reevaluated including issues related to preparing for the large-scale movement of people, encouraging flexible telecommuting, and promoting the integrated development of emerging and traditional industries to guide the orderly, healthy, and sustainable development of the country.

21.1 Reflections on the Governance System of the Chinese Government Triggered by the COVID-19 Pandemic

21.1.1 The problem with the governance model

21.1.1.1 *The influence of the governance model in the field of public health*

Given the severity of the COVID-19 outbreak, the government has moved into emergency management mode and established a coordinated command system for prevention and control from the level of the central government to local levels: at the central level, a leading group has been set up to respond to the pandemic with the mechanism for joint prevention and control under the State Council. At the same time, local government have taken precise action. Though disease prevention and control fall under the joint responsibility of the central and local governments, based on the current situation of the COVID-19 pandemic prevention and control, local administrative power has not been extensive enough to meet implementation needs. The government's leading role in the development and supervision of public utilities is seriously lacking, misplaced, and offside, especially in the division of fiscal authority and expenditure responsibility, which is reflected in the following: First, the legal basis for the division of power and responsibilities between the central and local governments is insufficient and unreasonable, and the rule of law and standardization is not developed enough to meet the needs of social governance. Second, administrative efficiency is low in the current governance structure due to the large number of requests for instructions and reports. The local government does not bear the corresponding responsibilities, which results in a gap between decision-makers and information producers, thus affecting the nature of decision-making. Third, the division of financial rights between the central and local governments in the development of public utilities is extremely unclear. The pandemic has negatively affected the proper operation of government finances, especially fiscal revenue in the first quarter of the year, which, in summary includes the increased expenditure on prevention and control, treatment and assistance, as well as the exhaustion of tax sources caused by shutdowns and people staying at home. The impact of such revenue reduction will continue to be assessed.[1]

21.1.1.2 *Inadequate prevention in the public health system*

Compared with the SARS pandemic in 2003, the COVID-19 pandemic has been fiercer with faster transmission. After it was taken seriously by the country, governments at all levels responded quickly and actively. Though the central and local governments were determined and decisive in controlling the pandemic, a weakness in the government's response was the early prevention of the pandemic. In an era filled with risks, risk prevention is the most basic requirement of the public of a governance system and its governance capacity.

Yang Gonghuan, former deputy director of the Chinese Center for Disease Control and Prevention (CDC), said in an interview with the *Economic Observer* that China had spent a lot of money on establishing a surveillance and information system for infectious diseases and public health emergencies after the SARS pandemic in 2003. Unlike that of a step-by-step (hierarchical) reporting system, as soon as a hospital clicks to report a case in the online system, the CDC could immediately receive

[1]Li Jingyou: Three financial strategies for pandemic response, Zhongnan University of Economics and Law website, March 6, 2020, http://www.zuel.edu.cn/2020/0306/c1236a239520/page.htm.

this notification.[2] However, COVID-19 was not included in this online reporting system until January 20, when the State Council classified COVID-19 as a Class B infectious disease under Class A management. Due to the fact that a new virus cannot be reported if it has not been included in the infectious disease directory, the system was not able to play its preventative role, which means that its advanced preventative function could not be realized. In addition, the staff who manage the network system of some medical institutions do not have sufficient professional knowledge, and their professional quality also varies from region to region. In some regions, there are a few medical institutions which even lack staff specializing in infectious disease reporting. Such places where little emphasis is placed on an online reporting system also hinder the prevention of infectious diseases.

In addition, inadequate stockpiles of strategic medical supplies and personal protective equipment are also an important reason for the lack of medical supplies during the current pandemic. To save hospital costs, most hospitals have no more than a month's reserve of protective materials, and some even have zero reserves. Since no large-scale public health incidents occurred in China in recent years, hospitals, the Red Cross, as well as the government have paid little attention to the storage of medical protective equipment.

21.1.2 The dilemma caused by the collective vacation model

China has adopted the collective vacation model for national holidays, which means 1.4 billion people take holidays at the same time. From the statistics of national holiday population flow, the Chinese style of collective shutdowns and vacations has led to the embarrassing moment of "blocked high-speed in holidays". Such a "long-term shutdown, collective vacation" model is also a dilemma for enterprises. In recent years, the State Council has drawn up a new "holiday reform plan", the content of which still does not depart from the collective vacation mode. It is worth noting that large-scale migration has also accelerated the spread of the

[2] Yang Gonghuan, "Why did the direct reporting system for infectious diseases built by the state after SARS not start in time", *Economic Observer*, February 3, 2020, http://m.eeo.com.cn/2020/0203/375484.shtml.

coronavirus, which hit hard the tourism-related hotel industry and passenger transportation industry. Five million people had left Wuhan before the city was shut down on January 23, whose whereabouts and composition have attracted much attention. According to an article in the *Economic Observer* on January 28, about 70% of the people had gone to surrounding cities in Hubei province, followed by neighboring provinces and municipalities including Henan, Hunan, Anhui, Chongqing, and Jiangxi. In terms of personnel composition, the vast majority were migrant workers returning to their hometowns.[3] Therefore, the question remains on how to develop a vacation model to meet the needs of future social development?

The long holiday model was proposed by Premier Zhu Rongji in the 1990s. The purpose of making both National Day and Spring Festival a "seven-day holiday" was to improve people's welfare and provide more opportunities for them to have a longer break. It also increased the proportion of consumption in tourism, the service industry, and other tertiary industries in the GDP. As incomes have risen in China, this kind of holiday means short-term, concentrated, and expensive consumption in travel markets and facilities around the world. Now, with the changed mindset of the public, the primary needs of setting a "golden week" or "mini-break" have also been changed, so the vacation mode should also adjust to the needs of the times.

In addition, during the pandemic, the government has encouraged enterprises to adopt intelligent online offices and conduct democratic consultations with their employees based on the principle of equality and voluntariness to reach agreements on salary adjustment, working hours, job assignments, and vacations. As the intelligent office is replacing the traditional working model, and the "nine-to-five" working model is gradually transforming to that of "completing a certain number of tasks", whether a flexible working model is necessary or will even become the norm will be the focus of future labor relations. If intelligent offices within the Internet economy becomes the norm, it will not only bring about the development of an intelligent economy such as the popularization of video conferencing equipment, the upgrading of office software, and the improvement of terminal data storage, but also bring about a great

[3] Zhang Weiwen: "When the pandemic meets the Spring Festival travel rush: high-quality implementation of 100 million people's hukou is imminent", *The Paper*, February 13, 2020.

change in the field of law. The *Labor Law*, as both a public and private social law, balances the rights and obligations of enterprises and workers. During the current pandemic, the balance of the interests of both sides has been broken. In the face of such a change, what will happen to rights and interests as regulated by law? How should this new type of labor relations adjustment be treated in legislation, to meet the needs of enterprise development and at the same time protect employees' rights and interests, and then regulate the new trend of intelligent offices?

21.1.3 A healthy lifestyle has not yet come into being

21.1.3.1 *Sanitation of public facilities*

Public facilities in crowded places, such as shopping malls, hotels, cinemas, museums, waiting rooms, and office buildings, often contain a large number of health and safety hazards, especially the inanimate object where the COVID-19 virus has been found to survive. The information collated about the pandemic confirmed that most people got infected in public places, so it has become necessary to regularly disinfect the vectors in places with high densities of bacteria. On January 30, 2020, the State Council issued the *Guidelines for the Health Protection of Novel Coronavirus Infected Pneumonia in Public Places* for the Joint Prevention and Control Mechanism of Novel Coronavirus Pneumonia Infection. The Guidelines, including operational hygiene guidelines and personal protection guidelines, are applicable to the health and safety of public places like hotels, shopping malls, cinemas, swimming pools, museums, waiting rooms, and office buildings where people often gather.

In the current *Animal pandemic Prevention Law*, government veterinary authorities are mainly responsible for pandemic prevention, which leaves out other processes, such as breeding, transportation, slaughtering, processing, and management. In fact, the spread of the coronavirus is connected with cold chain processing.

21.1.3.2 *People are not used to individual servings at the table*

The catering industry has been greatly affected by the pandemic. The longer the outbreak lasts, the more likely it is that the catering industry will reconfigure. After the pandemic, people's dining habits will have changed, and consumers will focus more on food safety and protection. Individual dining will be a new direction for the catering industry to develop in the future. If individual plating is not adopted, Helicobacter pylori, infectious pathogens, and respiratory diseases are more likely to spread. Each year, liver cancer, stomach cancer, and other diseases caused by oral bacterial infections have no less impact than COVID-19. Though individual dining is more common in Western countries, such as Europe and the United States, it is not an imported method. According to present archaeological excavations, shi'an (Chinese tray) first appeared in the Warring States Period, and Copper tray was found in the Warring States Tomb in Lijiashan, Jiangchuan, Yunnan Province. In the frescoes of the Han Dynasty, as shown in *the Picture of Banquet, the Picture of a Couple Feasting, and the Picture of the Historical Records of Xiang Yu*, people had their meals in individual servings.[4] It was not until the Tang Dynasty that shared dish dining began to appear, and individual plates were gradually replaced because of the evolution of tableware, rich ingredients, and diversification of cooking. This was later influenced by Western civilizations and pandemics, to the point where even "public chopsticks" were not encouraged at times. However, this has not been implemented in China because it would lead to estrangement and affect family harmony. Although, many people have accepted the idea of individual plated dining, they have only given it up because they feel embarrassed proposing it or insisting on it at dinner parties. The consensus on individual plates became popular after SARS, but has not been integrated into normal practice. This pandemic should become a driver for the reform of China's catering industry. The opportunity for the comprehensive implementation of individual plating of food has come.

21.1.4 The impact of the pandemic on the economy

21.1.4.1 *New economic industries represented by artificial intelligence*

(1) Smart economy: For industries, adopting artificial intelligence has become a common trend. The intelligent economy has mostly been seen in the fields of service robots, AI recognition, unmanned retail,

[4]Gao Kejia: The Evolution of Chinese Food System, *Art and Technology*, No. 7, 2018.

UAV, and big data. The pandemic has accelerated the development of artificial intelligence. Start-up intelligent enterprises often face problems like insufficient cash reserves, high operating costs, and excessive reliance on financing. In order to alleviate the economic pressure brought about by the pandemic, local governments have successively introduced policies and a series of measures, such as reducing taxes and rents, most of which are aimed at relieving the pressure to survive experienced by enterprises. The difficulties encountered in the development of artificial intelligence in China are as follows: lack of innovation, singularity in the layout of research and development systems, the shortage of cutting-edge personnel, and the lack of policies, regulations, and standard systems.

(2) Service industry: The service industry is represented by the new retail industry and modern logistics industry. In the new retail industry, the transformation of online sales has brought new dividends to the sales industry. However, due to strict traffic control caused by the pandemic, except for products necessary for daily life, other products were not delivered on time due to disruption of the logistics and distribution chain. Meanwhile, the zero-contact lifestyle has gained more attention, especially unmanned deliveries in the logistics industry, which played an important role during the pandemic. The effect of these factors has been that operating costs continue to rise, and the cash flow of enterprises will continue to be interrupted to varying degrees, thus making it difficult for small and medium-sized enterprises to survive. Just as transfusions are not as helpful as hematopoiesis (the capacity of the body to produce blood), current measures are more like the transfusion of blood to enterprises, which can be effective in the short term, but there is still a need for further hematopoietic mechanisms that require the transformation and upgrade of enterprises.

(3) Health industry: The health industry in the United States is divided into four major parts: family and community health services (50%), hospital medical services (19%), medical commodities (14%), and health risk management (11%). In general, the United States is relatively mature in healthcare and services, while China's health industry is mainly traditional, and composed of traditional medical products. Therefore, China's health industry is far from mature, and still needs to be improved upon. After the pandemic, people will focus more on

personal health, so the expansion of the Chinese health industry market is inevitable.

21.1.4.2 *The development of the film and television industry*

Xu Zheng (a Chinese film director) signed a contract with Bytedance to upload unreleased films online after the Spring Festival movie season was canceled, which generated profits for both the producer and the App operator. It demonstrated the new concept of "online cinema", and the pandemic has further expanded it and helped it mature. The disadvantage of a single source of income in the film and television industry is more pronounced during this pandemic. In particular, more than 90% of the income from Chinese films comes from the cinema, which is detrimental to the diversified development of the industry. Although in recent years, China has paid more attention to copyright, pirated movies and TV series have from time to time been circulated. In addition, the gap between online and offline film distribution makes it even more difficult for cinemas to profit offline. At present, the network film and television industry has formed a multi-profit model of "Subscription Video on Demand (SVOD) + advertising revenue + member payment + e-commerce". With an enhanced distribution capacity of network cinemas, the simultaneous release of offline cinemas and online cinemas may become a trend for the film and television industry.

With the development of the intelligent economy utilizing the joint loading of 4K, HD, and 5G, the watching of movies in cinemas faces new challenges that can only be overcome by adapting to current trends. This pandemic has also sounded the alarm for the transformation and upgrading of offline cinemas: comprehensive improvement is needed to upgrade the viewing experience of the audience. As a new business model, influenced by market competition, the online release of films is still in its infancy and needs timely guidance.

21.1.4.3 *The development of online education*

As early as 2010, the outline of proposed educational reform in China put forward requirements and expectations for the development of networking and informatization of education. On January 29, 2020, the Ministry of Education postponed the opening of the school year to prevent and control the spread of COVID-19. Meanwhile, local education departments took measures like online video teaching so that primary and secondary school students were still able to learn, despite the closing of the schools. Such large-scale online teaching is not only a challenge to traditional education, but also a development opportunity. It is better than the traditional education model in terms of cost and efficiency, private benefits, and social benefits, and even solves the problem of unfair distribution of education resources, so problems faced by distance education, such as financial subsidies and financial aid systems, need to be solved. Since 2018 in the field of "paying for knowledge online", several apps have seen a great increase in the number of playbacks, reward amounts, and number of fans. Enterprises with such skills and knowledge are embracing new development opportunities. At present, the field does not need much macroeconomic regulation and control, because benign competition in the market is the fertile soil for the development of enterprises.

21.1.4.4 *The development of intelligent telemedicine*

The first medical service of COVID-19 in the United States used intelligent robots to provide a diagnosis and treatment. Telemedicine is an important application of 5G technology. Based on 5G communication, telemedicine integrates wireless communication technology, small devices, high-speed mobile communication technology, and traditional medical treatments. It realizes remote surgical operation, wireless remote consultation, patient monitoring, and real-time follow-ups, emergency rescue command and decisions. With telemedicine becoming increasingly intelligent, virtual medicine will be more likely to achieve equity in the medical field. In 2019, the scale of China's construction of the smart medical industry exceeded RMB 88 billion, and it is expected that this figure will exceed RMB 100 billion in 2020.

Telemedicine, a new model of medical treatment, has been supported by the State Council; in terms of hardware technology, high-speed broadband networks to cover urban and rural medical institutions are approved, and special Internet lines are being established to guarantee the needs of telemedicine as well as receiving more subsidy funds. However, in practice, the lack of medical personnel restricts the universal development of telemedicine services and prevents it from developing at the community level. Various problems, such as the lack of awareness of telemedicine, and the absence of systematic telemedicine supervision, have not been properly solved.

21.2 Suggestions for Strengthening Macro-Governance and Policy Support

21.2.1 Improving the governance model

21.2.1.1 *The governance model*

The functional reform of governments at all levels in China is urgently needed. The requirement to have law-based and standardized social governance forces the massive upgrading of government functions. First, in the context of ruling according to law, the division of administrative power and financial responsibility legislation between the central and local governments needs to be promoted. The exercise of central fiscal authority should be appropriately regulated so as not to damage the activity of local governments. Basic public services that are closely related to residents should be subject to local fiscal authority, and the division of fiscal authority and responsibility between the central and local governments should be formed within a legal framework. The local government should exercise financial authority correctly, streamline the reporting process, abandon "dogmatism" in the application of law, and improve the administrative efficiency of the government. Second, the gap between decision-makers and information needs to be bridged. The pandemic has exposed some problems, which are in essence caused by the inefficient exercise of power such as the lack of timely information disclosure, the gap in the governance capacity of local governments at all levels, government inaction, and the lack of transparency and inefficiency of social organizations represented by the Red Cross. To enhance the public nature of power, the generation and operation of power must be guaranteed as being consistent with the rule of law and the constitutional system and properly exerted through democratic mechanisms, supervision mechanisms, and third-party institutions. Further, the good structure of government input and expenditure can ensure the sound operation of the fiscal system, and it should be specified when conducted in the health sectors. The old-fashioned thinking model regarding the use of government funds should be changed, and appropriate budgets for the upcoming New Year should be implemented to ensure they meet people's needs. When the central government allocates funds to local governments to support them and provide them with incentives, it is necessary to pay attention to transparency and openness in the use of fiscal resources. The responsibility of the public in supervision should be given play, and form a joint force in supervision.

21.2.1.2 *Preventive principles in the public healthcare system*

Prevention of public health emergencies should be carried out before occurrence. Such advanced preparation tests the government's ability to detect and respond to health events and puts forward higher requirements for governance capacity. Precaution makes all the difference, and prevention in advance is no exception. The specific treatment, prevention, and control work appears to be only "professional" and "technical" work, but it requires the leadership, organization, coordination, and operational strength of all levels of the political system. The traditional mode of risk elimination after the event must be replaced by the risk prevention before the event. "Risk prevention" is a basic principle put forward by the international community on environmental issues. The prevention and control of hazards and the prevention of risks (potential damage) will become the focus of public health safety system debugging. The *National Emergency Plan for Public Health Emergencies* emphasizes that making prevention a priority requires always being on alert, and various preparations should be made in advance to deal with public health emergencies. In particular, the direct pandemic reporting system of the CDC needs to be amended, where COVID-19 cases should have been reported despite it being a new virus. For unknown viruses, risk prevention should also be carried out to thwart its spread from the very beginning. Meanwhile, it is particularly important to popularize the knowledge of infectious diseases among CDC staff, because only with trained professionals is early detection, early isolation, and early elimination of a pandemic possible.

The life of law lies in its enforcement. After this pandemic, the government should strongly rectify the shortcomings of management institutions of public health emergencies, and improve the emergency response capacity of professional technical teams. It is necessary to comprehensively train CDC staff on identifying infectious diseases and balance the professional teams in different regions. Scientific and timely warnings should be provided for possible emergencies to control the spread of a pandemic by reducing the risk in the early stage of transmission.

21.2.1.3 *Improve emergency management mechanisms*

The mechanism for handling emergencies which threaten urban public security is an indispensable part of modern urban governance. It was not until 2018 that China established the Ministry of Emergency Management and set up specialized emergency management agencies to respond to public safety, natural disasters, and other emergencies. On the contrary, in 1933, after the Great Depression, the federal government of the United States established the Federal Emergency Relief Agency (FEMA) to manage urban risk events. Since the emergency management mechanism involves multiple departments, levels, and processes, to give full play to its role, it is necessary to set unified goals, ensure the implementation of responsibilities, control emergency risk events through prevention, early warnings, and decision-making, to ensure the normal operation of urban functions.

The pandemic has also highlighted the lack of information about emergency supplies reserves, and shortcomings in the comprehensive management of emergency supplies in the face of public health emergencies, and inadequate planning was also obvious when stockpiling and deploying emergency supplies. Therefore, the government should provide administrative guidance to help build up the information base of emergency material reserves, and that of the comprehensive management of emergency resources and equipment. Medical supplies should be stored in accordance with a scientific emergency supplies inventory, and the reserve quota should be updated according to the turnover period of the supplies, to guarantee supplies and equipment for a better response to public health emergencies.

As part of public procurement, at present, procurement of emergency supplies is excluded from the legal regulations of *Government Procurement Law* and the *Tendering and Bidding Law*, which means that it is not subject to strict procurement approval procedures, not that the government does not have the authority to unilaterally procure and deploy them. It is worth noting that during special periods when the government is endowed with more administrative power, civil power should be better protected. Therefore, China's emergency materials procurement management system should be improved in terms of procurement basis, procurement mode, procurement path, supplier database, response speed, and market price.

(1) Procurement basis. As the fundamental law of China, the *Constitution of the People's Republic of China* stipulates that the state may, in the public interest, requisition for its use in accordance with the law, so the procurement of emergency supplies is not illegal. However, in specific procurement cases, there is no specific legal guidance, so the relevant laws applicable to a state of emergency are the only reference. After this pandemic ends, if necessary, the government should formulate an emergency materials procurement law.
(2) Procurement mode. In the era of big data, intelligent procurement greatly improves the efficiency of procurement and meets the demand for "fast speed". Through the mode of "Internet + supply chain", online and offline supply chains can be fully mastered. Meanwhile, both domestic and foreign procurement may be carried out simultaneously; fragmented resources are integrated, and channels for receiving foreign materials are opened.
(3) Supplier database. Suppliers cannot be effectively used and managed without the establishment of a supplier database. Through the management methods of selection, use, cultivation, and retention, quality suppliers are screened in advance of emergencies, to build a timely response mechanism. Meanwhile, the effectiveness of the supplier database is ensured through periodic and regular centralized evaluation.
(4) Response speed. Procurement of emergency supplies can be distributed to large online shopping platforms in the form of service outsourcing because with efficient and advanced data service systems, these platforms are capable of achieving extensive global direct procurement.
(5) Market price. The procurement of emergency materials shall be negotiated in the form of a contract, to protect the legitimate rights and interests of the administrative counterpart. If there is no time for negotiation, the government should set a price after the compulsory purchase, balancing the cost and profit reflected in the market, and reserve the right of the counterpart to object to the administrative action.

21.2.2 Reform the model of taking public holidays

Britain and the United States have similar vacation systems, with fewer public holidays and more paid holidays. Take the UK for example, where there are only seven public holidays with the Christmas holiday being only two days long. Employees are generally entitled to around 25 days of paid annual leave, which can be taken at any time of the year after the company has authorized the leave. Summer and Christmas are the peak seasons for holidays. Most Europeans take a two-week holiday around Christmas to spend time with their families, while non-Christians who do not celebrate Christmas tend to stick to their jobs during this time and use their annual leave for other times of the year. Many small businesses close from Christmas to New Year, taking the working days of 27–30 December as annual leave.

Japan is similar to China regarding public holidays, but it adopts the "switch to work" mode, which provides three days of rest.[5] Three-day holidays are adopted when holidays and weekends coincide, and research results have shown that three-day holidays are more beneficial to the economic development of tourism.

To avoid collective leave which may cause pressure on tourism, it is suggested that the government learn from other countries' holiday systems and after the pandemic introduce new legislation to reform China's holiday arrangements. The vacation reform should incorporate people's needs: the number of vacation days should be increased based on the overall trend of China's economic development, and the implementation of the vacation system should be guaranteed by the government.

First, the power of mandating holidays could be delegated to local governments. On the basis of not changing the overall number of existing holidays, local governments could mandate holidays according to local traditions and customs, so as to be innovative in policies which could be used to showcase local characteristics and at the same time promote tourism. Secondly, the mandatory consecutive two-week leave could be retained, but the specific dates are negotiated by workers and enterprises provided that it will not affect the operation of the enterprise. Thirdly, more three-day vacations could be arranged and a new working and attitudinal model would be introduced. Compared with two-day vacations,

---

[5]Dong, Junran, Zhang, Feng. Research on the Optimization of China's Legal Holiday System. *Overseas English*, 2015, 21.

three-day vacations better enable workers to go out and enjoy their holiday time, which will develop leisure tourism and stimulate the consumer economy. Finally, after changing the public holidays, they must be enforced to be taken, to protect laborers' right to rest. It should be strictly regulated to avoid situations where the enterprise pays allowances to buy out the employees' leave, or the employees voluntarily give up the leave. For the enterprises that violate the provisions for vacations, necessary legal relief measures such as complaint and arbitration systems should be instituted to protect workers' legitimate rights and interests.

In addition, the intelligent office should protect workers' legitimate rights and interests from being infringed upon. If the situation changes, the government should introduce relevant policies to regulate this work model. While the government encourages intelligent office, intelligent office service companies and intelligent furniture product companies may also be supported to promote the research and development of intelligent technology as well as intelligent industry.

21.2.3 Major measures to restore prosperity after the pandemic

With the COVID-19 pandemic gradually being brought under control, the government, within the framework of the rule of law, has increased financial support such as fiscal and taxation, credit, finance guarantees, and loan interest discounts, and provided policy support such as reduction of corporate rent, reduction of insurance premium rates for employees, and refunds of already paid unemployment insurance premiums. The government has helped enterprises to prevent and control the pandemic and achieve a steady and orderly resumption of production and work. The prosperity of the online service industry has become a trend in economic development. To enhance economic vitality, it is suggested that the government pay attention to the following factors.

21.2.3.1 *Measures for the development of new economic industries represented by artificial intelligence*

(1) Innovation is a national strategy. The following phrases, "improving innovation capacity", "building an innovative country" and "innovation-driven" encapsulate policies which have supported the

development of enterprises. Innovation is the life blood of research and development (R&D). Mature, systematic, and efficient R&D management plans are currently the most widely used management model in American innovative enterprises. On the public platform, the government outputs its systematic management model research and development for science and technology enterprises and has built an enterprise exchange and sharing platform to avoid the homogenization of the artificial intelligence industry, and to realize the innovative development of the intelligent economy. In terms of support for innovative projects, the government has made policy adjustments such as tilted funds through investment, subsidies, and tax cuts, for enterprises engaged in new science and technology research and development, and has realized communication between enterprises and the government in terms of smart government projects.

(2) Artificial intelligence: High-achieving professional experts in artificial intelligence are still in short supply. Since all walks of life continue to ask for more communication infrastructure, technology application services that can improve the efficiency of the industry, such as artificial intelligence, big data, and cloud computing, are paid more attention and have a promising future (Guan Xiqing, "Analysis of the Impact of COVID-19 on the Economic Development of Shanghai Development Zone", Reisen Park Think Tank, March 3, 2020). The government should guide industries and organizations to set up a global academic alliance on artificial intelligence with first-class international and domestic universities so that through the strengthening of technical exchanges, the pace of Chinese intelligent products going out and moving toward the goal of "selling to the world" can also be sped up. Intelligent enterprises should be encouraged to provide more professional internship positions for college students to simultaneously develop production, education, and research. Based on enhancing the practical ability of college students, the teaching direction should be adjusted regularly and high achievers should be continuously trained to be better adapted to the new problems they may face.

(3) Participate in formulating industry standards and connect with international standards. For intelligent products to compete in the international market, international policy coordination must be carried out, especially for reaching agreement on industry standards, so that domestic intelligent products will only be minimally affected by

international trade barriers. As President Xi Jinping has pointed out, "Rules should be made by the international community, rather than by those who have more power. Pragmatism and double standards which define the legitimacy of the rules based on the country's own interest should not be adopted." Whether for international responsibility or national interest, our government should make efforts to participate in making international industry standards.

(4) Guide the development of the health industry. Based on China's traditional health management system and the model of "Internet + health management", the focus of medical development is to launch a health industry that "combines medical care with old-age care". With the development of the health industry, new technologies and new forms of business have also received more industry support, such as the new service model of health management driven by cloud computing and big data. Health management data resources will also form national health data resources, which will promote the development of data analysis. At present, as the health industry is still in the early stage of development, the government should standardize the health management service industry as soon as possible, and set up standardized, institutionalized, procedural, and scientific access rules to ensure its development. Meanwhile, preferential industrial policies should be optimized in terms of taxation, land, and finance, to promote the development of the health management service industry.

21.2.3.2 *Coping measures for the development of the film and television industry*

First, the development of the film and television industry needs strong support from the government. It is important to strengthen the legislative construction of laws and regulations and clarify the government's responsibilities for creating a good institutional environment. Especially when the industry is experiencing changes, it is essential to give full play to the rule of law regulating the business behavior of film and television and adjust the legal relationships involved in the development of online cinemas. Second, the industry should be motivated to be self-disciplined, to construct a good environment for market competition, safeguard the legitimate interests of all parties, and promote the healthy development of the industry to create both economic and social benefits. Based on the concepts of streamlining administration and delegating power, government functions should be streamlined to realize its regulatory responsibilities, with the aid of industry associations. Third, the cinema industry should be assisted to establish an anti-pandemic fund to support individuals and enterprises in difficulties and better implement national policies. Assistance should be provided to cinemas hard hit by the pandemic through interest-free loans or funding for new products, and support and shared responsibility in the areas of policy, management, and marketing to contribute to the sustainable development of the industry. Fourth, the industrial chain should be guided and aggregated to integrate the whole process from the creation to the publicity and screening. Innovation in the digital age should be encouraged and this online launch is seen as an opportunity to integrate the fragmented film industry. In addition to the incentive policies for the industry, more guidance for online film and television should be provided. Small, medium, and micro film and television companies should be supported, so that the market can be prosperous. Fifth, quality films and television series should be provided platforms to output their products. In the context of cultural exchange promoted by the "Belt and Road" project, the government provides support in the upstream of the film industry chain by purchasing services to develop the film industry.

21.2.3.3 *Measures to promote online education*

First, the role of government subsidies in promoting online education should be strengthened. Fine subsidy policies for online education should be formulated and managed to promote the development of online education in a targeted way and give priority to realizing equity in elementary education. As for adult education, online education including skill acquisition should be set at a reasonable level based on the government subsidy policy. Second, the government should ensure the standardized management and implementation of the government subsidy fund application, review, issuance, use, and verification, and improve the quality and efficiency of government subsidies to realize the value of online education. The online education subsidy policy should provide support in quality rather than quantity, so it should increase the subsidy for high-quality courses and expand supply to promote the stable development of education. Third, the advancement of online education requires not only financial support, but also a national online education platform supported by the government so that public resources and high-quality teaching resources are shared. Education certification could be realized through a national network platform, so that education services are innovated with the effect of co-construction and sharing mechanisms of digital education resources. Fourth, 5G technology should be integrated into educational resources and educational equipment. By conducting research, a new understanding may be gained and promote the stable development of education.[6]

21.2.3.4 *Measures to promote telemedicine*

Talent cultivation is the foundation of telemedicine. Increasing the training of targeted medical and health personnel is the cornerstone of promoting telemedicine, so the government should establish the system of training medical and health personnel. Meanwhile, to popularize telemedicine in the community the government should make policies to encourage medical and health professionals to work at the grassroots level. For example, highly competent staff should be motivated to work at grassroots medical and health institutions by providing housing subsidies, increasing salaries, and optimizing living conditions, so as to optimize the allocation of medical resources and attract more experts for the better development of telemedicine services.[7] Second, health departments should strengthen publicity about the availability of telemedicine services by focusing on their advantages, so that most medical staff will embrace this new medical model. Meanwhile, since patients in primary health hospital have not yet established enough trust in the efficacy of telemedicine, and the cooperation of doctors in local hospitals is needed to apply for telemedicine services, making the application process complicated, it is more important for them to understand the role and advantages of telemedicine so that patients are more willing to accept it. Finally, but of equal importance, in view of the universality and freedom of telemedicine, the existing medical law system must be adjusted. Policies relevant to telemedicine should be adjusted and regulated in a timely manner, and

---

[6] Wang Xiaochen, Application of 5G Technology in Online Education, *Electronic Technology and Software Engineering*, No. 24, 2019.

[7] Mu Jianbo, Zhai Yunkai, Cai Yao, *et al*. Discussion on the Continuous Operation Mode of China's Telemedicine System, *Chinese Health Service Management*, 2014, (12).

regulations for telemedicine should be established, which should include clear provisions on the legal qualifications, legal service scope, privacy protections, informed consent, and standardized operational processes for remote practicing doctors and medical institutions. An e-health innovation partnership project should be established based on government open resources to promote the sustainable development of telemedicine.

21.3 Conclusions

The prevention and control of the pandemic is a test of the governance system and capacity of the Chinese government. Reforms should be carried out in the political system, economic system, and social governance to make national governance institutionalized, proceduralized, standardized, and law based. Full play should be given to institutional advantages, and the national governance system and capacity should be improved. Social governance needs to be strengthened and become innovative to fight the pandemic and at the same time develop the economy and society. Accurate analyses of the pandemic, as well as economic and social development, needs to made, our ability to respond to major public health emergencies needs to be improved, the legal guarantee of economic development strengthened, a scientific and rational vacation model promoted, and healthy living habits advocated for. Based on the development of smart industries, such as information technology and digitization, the digital and intelligent upgrading of industries and governance need to supported, so as to establish a social governance system which is controlled by the government, assisted by the whole society, participated in by the public, guaranteed by the rule of law, and supported by science and technology.

https://doi.org/10.1142/9789811252921_0022

Chapter 22

Turning a Crisis into an Opportunity for the Future: A Path for Strategic Development of Enterprises in the "Post-Pandemic Era"

Huang Ming

School of Economics, Fudan University, Shanghai, China

Since the outbreak of the COVID-19 pandemic, provinces, autonomous regions, and municipalities have launched a first-level response to a major public health emergency, which has rapidly and greatly affected national economic growth.

To reduce the negative impact of the pandemic on Chinese enterprises, national and local governments have introduced a series of supportive measures to solve the operational difficulties they have faced. The pandemic has caused great changes to the development of enterprises in terms of the space, time, mechanisms, scope, and boundaries. It is of strategic significance to objectively evaluate the impact of the pandemic and propose and suggest measures for the sustainable development of Chinese enterprises from the perspective of global competition and strategic development. From this perspective, this chapter will reveal the impact of the COVID-19 pandemic on Chinese enterprises in both the long term and the short term. The effect of current policies will be analyzed, and suggestions will be proposed from the perspective of the government and enterprises so as to improve the adaptability of Chinese enterprises to cope with major environmental changes, and grasp the opportunities found in the "post-pandemic era" to integrate traditional Chinese enterprises with sustainable development.

22.1 Analysis of the Impact of the COVID-19 Pandemic on Enterprises

As a public health emergency, the COVID-19 pandemic has been highly destructive, has had wide influence, and been of long duration. It not only has significantly affected the production and operation of enterprises in the short term but will also continue to influence their development and strategic positioning in the long term. It will impact the resource reserve and the competitive edge of enterprises, and systematically change their habitats, the global industrial chain, as well as the macro environment.

22.1.1 The challenges and opportunities faced by enterprises in the short term

22.1.1.1 *The challenges faced by enterprises in the short term*

(1) In terms of different industries:

How and to what extent the COVID-19 pandemic has affected different enterprises differ from enterprise to enterprise. Key enterprises related to the national economy and people's livelihood have operated continuously, such as those of energy, water supply, and heating, large-scale production bases for daily necessities, and designated supply supermarkets. With large market demand and guaranteed product delivery, they have been less affected by pandemic prevention and control measures. However, offline service enterprises that expect customers to walk into stores have been greatly affected, especially offline retail, catering, tourism, and transportation enterprises, whose operating income has been significantly reduced. As a result, their upstream and downstream industries have also encountered problems, such as reduced orders and scant demand, which results in excessive inventory and a decline in revenue. Even though sales are low, enterprises in these industries will face rigid expenses such as rent, labor costs, and the cost of capital which cannot be reduced, and some of these expenses may even increase substantially. According to the survey of SMEs conducted by the China Association of Small and Medium-sized

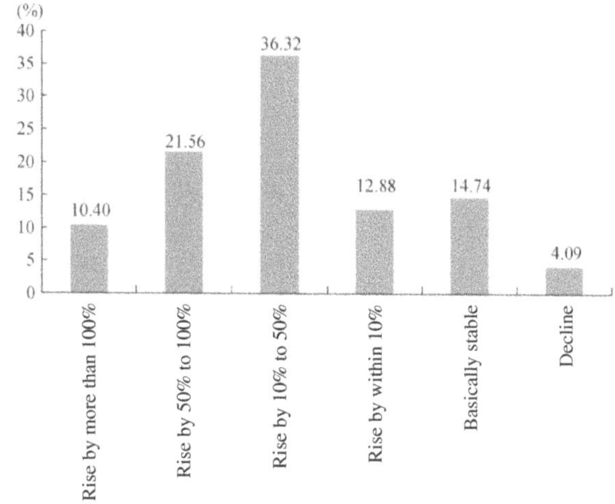

Figure 22.1: The impact of the pandemic on the cost of the enterprises.
Source: China Association of Small and Medium-sized Business Enterprises.

Business Enterprises and Baidu in February 2020, 68.28% of enterprises said that their costs would rise by more than 10% after the outbreak of the pandemic, of which 31.96% said that their costs would rise by more than 50% (Figure 22.1). The "high cost of prevention and control of the pandemic" and "rising human resource costs" are the main reasons for increasing costs. It is estimated that 75.92% of enterprises expected the pandemic to cause losses of more than 30%, and 43.26% believed that number could be more than 50% (Figure 22.2). For those losses, "staff costs" and "vacant rental costs" are the main causes.[1]

In general, the COVID-19 pandemic makes these enterprises less able to generate profits and pay their debts. Some of them will face severe challenges in terms of cash flow, and those with weak qualifications will be cleared up by the market and face bankruptcy in a short time.

(2) To analyze the challenges faced by enterprises in the short term according to their own characteristics:

[1]China Association of Small and Medium-sized Business Enterprises: *To Understand the Situation of Small and Medium-sized Business under the Pandemic Through the Results of 7290 Surveys*, China Association of Small and Medium-sized Business Enterprises website, February 22, 2020.

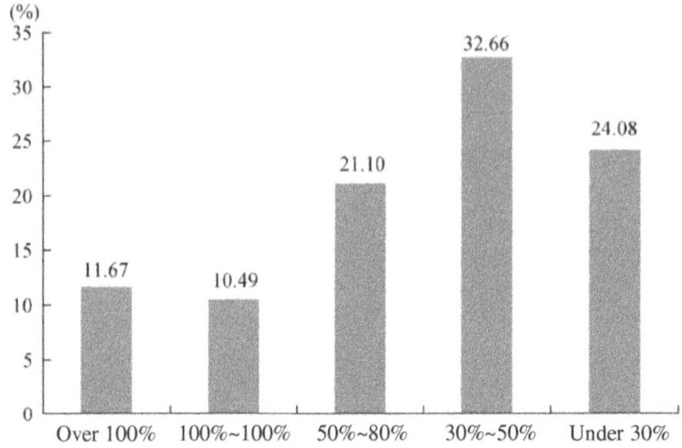

Figure 22.2: Estimated losses of the enterprises due to the pandemic (based on 2019 revenue).

Source: China Association of Small and Medium-sized Business Enterprises.

During the pandemic, enterprises from different industries and of different scales were all faced with a crisis, however, those with certain characteristics demonstrated stronger adaptability.

First of all, in terms of scale, leading enterprises with advantage in scale have stronger resistance in the event of a crisis: their high credit rating enables them to obtain collateral for bank loans, and obtain lower interest rates during the period of the pandemic; they have stronger bargaining power when collaborating with upstream and downstream partners, so they have the capacity to delay payments during procurement, and to deliver sold inventory on time; and appeals issued by such leading enterprises are easily paid attention to.

Second, in terms of the integrity of the industry chain, enterprises with integrated industrial chains are better able to resist risks. Though the pandemic will weaken enterprises of different types in terms of generating profits and paying debts, those with a complete industrial chain have shown a stronger ability to resist risks. For example, e-commerce giants such as Alibaba, Pinduoduo, and JD.com have been hit hard by the overall economic downturn due to the pandemic. However, it has been shown that the revenue of JD in the first half of the year is RMB 201.05 billion, up 33.8%, and the net profit attributable to common shareholders reaches RMB 5.9 billion, up 66.1% from a year earlier. One key factor to JD's rapid growth is its own logistics, which is characterized by a low transaction cost, high control over each segment, high investment, and high staff cost. During the COVID-19 pandemic, JD Logistics asked its employees to continue serving customers. In contrast, major courier companies like Shentong Express, Yuantong Express, Zhongtong Express, and Yunda Express have all faced the problem of workers stopping work, which resulted in service inefficiency.[2] Therefore, during the COVID-19 pandemic, JD's integrated business model of industrial chains demonstrated greater ability to provide services and resist risks than the market transaction model.

Third, in terms of financial models, enterprises which are financially sound are more resilient to risks than those which are financially aggressive. For the former enterprises, the overall level of financial leverage is low and book funds are abundant, so they are more resilient in the face of the pandemic. For example, Jinjiang International, the leading enterprise in the hotel industry, holds abundant monetary fund's so it maintains strong solvency even during the pandemic. However, in the short-term private enterprises with less profits and less cash reserves face greater pressure when covering debt repayments. Meanwhile, these companies have a large volume of restricted assets and external guarantees, which further decreases their solvency and exposes them to more credit risks.

In terms of business models, when facing risks, enterprises which are innovation-driven are weaker than traditional offline enterprises which focus on cash flow. For example, some popular tea brand catering enterprises, characterized by innovation in business models, have been weaker in risk resistance in the face of the pandemic compared with traditional offline catering enterprises, because their development depends on constant equity financing in the primary market. The traditional offline catering industry has better cash flow that sustains its operations in the short or medium term, even if it is hit by the pandemic. However, if those popular tea brands cannot obtain new financing, in the absence of any operating income, they will instantly face problems in their operation.

---

[2]According to the State Post Bureau, most of China's courier companies did not start work until after Feb 8. For example, the resumption of work of Zhongtong, Shentong, and Yunda was postponed to February 10th. Further, most couriers in those companies had to be quarantined for up to 14 days before they could officially return to work. Under this circumstance, Jingdong with its own logistics, showed a far greater ability to resist pressure than the other companies.

Finally, in terms of how enterprises respond to the market, companies that are more responsive to the market will be less impacted: some quickly adopt ways like intelligent office, telecommuting and automated production to resume production, and others set out to explore new markets and develop new business models, showing a strong ability to respond to the market. For example, during the pandemic, offline education institutions quickly organized staff to design and record online courses, which helped them successfully cope with the crisis.

(3) To analyze the challenges faced by enterprises in the short term according to different regions. During the pandemic, to a large extent the governance capacity of different local governments also affects business operations:

First, challenges brought about by control measures during the pandemic to enterprises' short-term operation.

In the early stage of the pandemic, some regions, having little professional knowledge or scientific understanding, unable to predict the spread and import of the virus, were not fully prepared for prevention, and reacted slowly to "joint prevention and control". In contrast, in some regions, pandemic prevention and control measures were carried out beyond the required standard, in an excessive, static, and rigid way, which severely affected local enterprises. While some regions demonstrated a higher governance capacity: some government departments took emergency measures to maintain the normal production and operation of enterprises on the premise of ensuring the effectiveness of pandemic prevention and control. For example, tax authorities canceled the deadline for handling tax rebates, and customs opened a green channel for agricultural products' clearance. Some government departments adopted innovative prevention and control measures to alleviate the impact of the pandemic on enterprises by, for example, mobilizing grassroots communities to carry out joint prevention and control, and using big data to make an accurate analysis of the pandemic and realize intelligent and efficient prevention and control.

Second, the impact of different measures taken by the government in the later stages of the pandemic on enterprises' short-term operation.

Some local governments, to realize the prevention and control of the pandemic, simply set up approval standards and raised the threshold for work resumption, which seriously delayed the resumption of work, while others tried to make the policies and measures more scientifically based, by formulating and improving differentiated strategies based on the actual situation of different regions. When the situation improved, they coordinated finding a balance between pandemic prevention and resumption of work by introducing policies that encouraged people to return to work so as to help enterprises resume production and operations as soon as possible.

22.1.1.2 *Opportunities brought to enterprises in the short term*

It is obvious that the pandemic has brought new market opportunities to medical assistance enterprises and created a huge demand for Internet companies. Since the prevention and control of the pandemic, activities related to people's daily life, education, government affairs, business, and office activities all relied heavily on the internet, and enterprises such as Internet platforms, e-commerce, and office software witnessed huge demand. According to Baidu statistics, the Baidu index of online education, online medical care, online entertainment, and e-commerce on fresh products all increased by more than 100% a month before March 6, 2020 (Figure 22.3).[3]

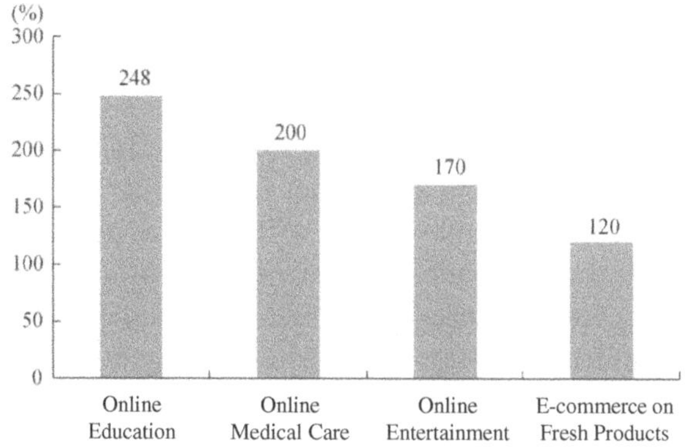

Figure 22.3: The Baidu search index of different industries.

Source: Sina Finance.

[3]TMTPost, "Insight on Searching for big data under the pandemic: which industries will boost?", Sina Finance, March 9, 2020.

For example, the e-commerce of fresh products during the pandemic, where fresh delivery platforms including freshhema, Meituan Maicai, Daily Youfresh, and Jingdong Home increased significantly in terms of transaction scale. The average daily order increased by a factor of 2–3. Even JD Home, which provides delivery services to supermarkets, saw explosive growth during the pandemic, with turnover increasing by more than 374% compared with the previous year.[4]

22.1.2 The impact of the pandemic on the long-term development of enterprises

22.1.2.1 *Changes in people's opinions and consumption habits will bring new business opportunities*

(1) "Non-contact consumption" has resulted in great development. Because of the pandemic, several consumption activities have been conducted online, which will last for three to five months. As a result, the public have cultivated a new consumption habit with "non-contact" as its core, which has brought more development opportunities to consumer industries. Traditional industries such as department store retailing, advertising, printing, labor export, and offline training will likely see a shrink in demand, while enterprises focusing on unmanned retailing, unmanned restaurants, unmanned drone deliveries, online medical care, online education, and e-commerce on fresh products will embrace a huge market opportunity, which will in turn speed up the development of internet enterprises.

(2) Products promoting healthy living will be more popular among consumers. After the pandemic, consumers will constantly focus on products that prevent diseases and meet nutritional needs, including medical supplies for disinfection, lower density households with better ventilation, and healthy food that enhances human immunity. In addition, refrigerated/frozen pre-packaged chicken may form the mainstream of poultry consumption in the future. Since live poultry markets will continue to be closed in the post-pandemic era, markets

[4]Quan Xiaojing, "Under the pandemic, a dramatically-changing $5 billion market," Quanjing Finance, February 10, 2020.

selling frozen pre-packaged food, which are clean and hygienic, are expected to be the primary suppliers of poultry meat in the future.

22.1.2.2 *The state's emphasis on health and pandemic prevention will boost the development of related enterprises*

In the future, the country will expand investment in public health facilities, improve the quality of supply, and establish a sound national public health emergency management system. This will stimulate a large demand for enterprises in healthcare infrastructure construction, medical informatization, and the internet (such as the establishment of electronic medical record systems, surgical anesthesia management systems, ICU information systems, and remote diagnosis and treatment systems), medical and health supplies production, medical personnel training, and consulting services for the medical and health system, so that those enterprises will grow rapidly.

22.1.2.3 *The following changes in business philosophy are expected to be seen*

(1) Prudent management will be valued. The pandemic has conducted the ultimate stress test on the risk resistance ability of Chinese enterprises: enterprises with high leverage and insufficient cash flow encountered a crisis of survival and have lost the opportunities of merger and acquisition after the end of the pandemic. Therefore, prudent management will be regarded as an important business philosophy in the future.
(2) The need for the ability to cope with uncertain risks. The suddenness of the pandemic has once again proved that uncertainties prevail when enterprises develop, and systemic risks cannot be transferred by an act of human will. The key to the sustainable development of an enterprise is to strengthen its strategic management in an environment of uncertainty and extreme events, rationally reserve resources, and improve an enterprise's ability to deal with uncertain risks.
(3) Business models featuring industrial chain integration are expected to replace intermediate organizational measures like strategic alliances.

In the face of high uncertainty, the availability of raw materials and delivery capacity of products to customers are primary considerations, rather than transaction costs. During the pandemic, because of the previous integration of the industrial chain, the supply of raw materials and the export of products were better guaranteed. Therefore, models that control supply chains from upstream and logistics to downstream are expected to be the mainstream in the future, while other models like strategic alliance and equity cooperation will be weakened.

(4) There is increased awareness of the business ethics and social responsibility of enterprises. During the pandemic, many companies have actively undertaken their social responsibilities and demonstrated business ethics. Therefore, the public and other stakeholders now regard business ethics and social responsibility a basic requirements of an excellent and compliant enterprise. In the future, enterprises that embody social equity and social responsibility will obtain high status conducive to increased resources including ability, morality, and recognition, and will be more readily accepted and supported by the society, thus gaining organizational legitimacy (Meyer and Rowan, 1997), and which in turn alleviates external pressure so that they survive and develop.

22.2 Analysis of the Strategies to Cope with the COVID-19 Pandemic

22.2.1 Current economic policies to "fight the pandemic" and the improvement of such policies

Since the outbreak of the COVID-19, national ministries and local governments have introduced a series of economic policies to reduce its impact on enterprises.

One group of policies aim to reduce enterprise costs: first, enterprises are provided with various tax exemptions, including those of VAT, income tax and donations, fee reduction, extension of the maximum period for loss carryover, and financial interest discounts on loans. Second, operating costs of enterprises are reduced. Policies have been released to reduce the enterprises' social security premium rate and postpone the social security payments; support has been given to places like entrepreneurship parks to reduce or exempt rents for small and medium-sized enterprises;[5] central government-owned enterprises have implemented rent reduction policies for tenants; capacity (demand) electricity charges have been reduced;[6] and national toll roads are free of vehicle tolls.

The second group relates to policies aiming to stabilize the supply of the factors of production. In terms of human resources, subsidies have been provided for job stability, employment, and training; social security subsidies and job subsidies have been temporarily extended; industries have been encouraged to create more jobs;[7] and it has been ensured that unemployment insurance is paid, personal income taxes reduced, and loans guaranteed for individual entrepreneurship. In addition, financial support has been provided: institutions like the People's Bank of China, and the National Development and Reform Commission have issued documents to increase credit support for those fields related to pandemic prevention and control. Differentiated and preferential financial services have been provided for regions, industries, and enterprises that have been severely affected by the pandemic. Development and policy banks have been encouraged to increase their credit support for key sectors, such as manufacturing, small and micro businesses, and private enterprises, and meet the needs on bond financing of those affected areas and enterprises taking part in pandemic prevention and control.

In general, economic policies during the "anti-pandemic" fight have mitigated the impact of the pandemic on enterprises, but they still need to be optimized: first, the support to enterprises should be more targeted and

---

[5]For example, Shandong province has provided operational subsidies for up to 3 months and a 30% reduction on rent, with a maximum of RMB500,000 to provincial business incubation demonstration bases, demonstration parks, and provincial human resource service industrial parks which have offered rent remission to small and medium-sized enterprises during the pandemic.

[6]*Notice of the General Office of the National Development and Reform Commission on Adopting a Supportive Two-part Electricity Price Policy to Reduce Electricity Costs for Enterprises during the Pandemic Prevention and Control* (Development and Reform Office, No. 110 (2020).

[7]For example, Shandong province has encouraged enterprises to recruit people who have difficulty finding jobs and unemployed graduates. Enterprises which have been affected by the pandemic but keep all employees and pay salaries on a regular basis can enjoy social insurance subsidies and post-pandemic subsidies. If the term expires after February 4, it shall be extended to June 30, 2020.

focused. A classification system should be established to support enterprises, provide precise solutions, and prevent relief resources from being misallocated or distributed inefficiently. Second, more research on policies in the post-pandemic era should be further conducted. Since the pandemic is now gradually being controlled, policies should be made with the focus on achieving the strategic transformation of enterprises, restructuring industrial chains, and establishing social risk prevention systems.

22.2.2 Suggestions on policies to support sustainable development of enterprises in the "post-pandemic era"

The government should give "forward-looking directives" and play a leading role; governments at all levels need to organize professional staff to conduct more research on the probability of new emergency events, their impact on micro-economic organizations, and the measures to cope with these contingencies. Generally speaking, emergencies are divided based on their impacts into natural disasters, accidents, public health events, and social security events. In the "post-pandemic era", Chinese enterprises may face more major environmental changes. At present, the country still has shortcomings in dealing with emerging emergencies and their impact on micro-economic organizations. Therefore, together with professional staff, the government response to emergencies should be more comprehensive and further research on and responses to emerging major emergencies (such as economic and trade conflicts between countries and competition for high technology) should be conducted. In addition, attention should be paid to the impact of major emergencies on micro-economic organizations, as well as the role of hedging economic policies and emerging technologies in dealing with emergencies.

A network system should be established with the aim of helping enterprises guard against major environmental changes by carrying out division of labor and promoting coordination. From the dimension of enterprise species and enterprise community, it is suggested that industry associations and local governments take industrial clusters and industrial chains as the starting point, and conduct in-depth studies on their sensitivity, impact, and prevention measures for major emergencies, and make risk prevention measures more targeted, economical, and effective. In addition, it is recommended that the division of responsibilities in the case of specific events between local governments, enterprises, industry associations, and non-governmental organizations be clearly defined, and that all sectors dedicate resources to actively improve the adaptability of enterprises to cope with emergencies.

Public risk awareness should be raised so that enterprises better cope with major environmental changes. Over the years, with its people living in peace and stability, China's economy has rapidly grown, and its overall national strength has steadily improved, but many economic entities have ignored potential risks. The COVID-19 pandemic has been another wake-up call after the trade frictions between China and the United States. Therefore, to better deal with major emergencies from its root, Chinese enterprises should work on publicity and education for the public to promote a sense of potential crises, a practical and steady style of work, and cultivate risk awareness so that officials, entrepreneurs, and the public all take part in risk prevention.

The construction of ecological civilization, that is the harmonious and sophisticated evolution, development, and refinement of humans and nature, should be sped up, through the passing of relevant legislation. Engels once warned: "We should not be too intoxicated with human victory over nature because for each such victory, nature takes revenge on us.".[8] The outbreak of COVID-19 has shown the utmost importance and urgency of accelerating the building of an ecological civilization. In the "post-pandemic era", China needs to speed up education on ecological civilization values, further protect natural ecosystems and the environment, improve relevant legislation, and promote harmonious development between humans and nature.

The construction and improvement of the legal system to respond to public emergencies should be sped up. As an important feature of modern society, the rule of law is also the cornerstone of social governance. Both the government and the corporate sphere need to function within and according to a legal framework. The legal environment itself also constitutes an important part of the living environment of enterprises. Therefore, speeding up the construction and improvement of the legal system for dealing with public emergencies is also an important measure to realize the rule of law.

---

[8] *Selected Works of Marx and Engels* (Vol. 3), People's Publishing House, 2012, p. 998.

22.2.3 Strategies to develop enterprises' adaptability in the "post-pandemic era"

(1) Entrepreneurs should have more respect for, be sensitive to, and able to foresee major changes in their operating environment. An entrepreneur functions as the brain of a business. According to Schumpeter, the spirit of adventure is what lies beneath entrepreneurship, while Drucker and Simon believe that since entrepreneurs are risk-takers, they should make efforts to reduce risks. While working hard to make progress, entrepreneurs should fully respect environmental uncertainty. They should stay calm when investing, and take "risks" in a scientific way, which means knowing what kind of risk is worth taking and try to avoid destructive risks. In the "post-pandemic era", Chinese entrepreneurs should have a comprehensive understanding of what is meant by "The world is undergoing profound changes unseen in a century", so as to fully respect, be sensitive to, and foresee major changes that may occur in today's world. They should make plans for the enterprises' organizational strategy, structure, resources, and capabilities in advance in terms of politics, economics, society, and culture.

(2) The strategic adaptability of enterprises should be enhanced in multiple respects. In the "post-pandemic era", enterprises should carry out contingency planning to enhance strategic adaptability. In the face of "profound changes unseen in the world in a century", enterprises should develop models of different extreme scenarios, in which major environmental variables undergo profound changes, and at the same time formulate countermeasures, so that when major changes do occur, they can quickly adjust their strategies and "shift gears". In addition, companies also must make changes in the speed of their responses, diversification, and supply chains. In terms of diversification, business distribution, regional layout, and stakeholders should be diversified so that enterprises are less dependent on specific businesses, geographical regions, and stakeholders. In terms of supply chains, information technology and alliances can be used to make enterprises more adaptive and adjustable to other members of the supply chain in terms of the category, price, and quantity of products.

(3) The financial flexibility of enterprises should be established rationally. In the "post-pandemic era", when facing "unprecedented

changes in the world in a century", as well as the new normal of China's economy and supply-side reform, Chinese enterprises should analyze several costs. The following should be subject to careful consideration, the cost of holding cash, the cost of external financing when seizing growth opportunities, and the difficulty of adjusting the asset–liability ratio based on the analysis of the potential growth opportunities of the industry. Further, the extent to which enterprises can grasp opportunities and the profit which may be generated needs to be analyzed. All these questions are aimed at allowing enterprises to strike a balance and reasonably set the financial flexibility.

(4) The flexibility of human resources should be enhanced. From one perspective, this refers to the flexibility of employees' skills, that is, during recruitment or training, the focus should be on whether employees have diversified skills and adaptability for multi-tasking, with flexible arrangements for those with different skills according to requirements. From another perspective, the practice of human resources should be more flexible, that is, it should adapt to different situations faster and to a greater extent, including the number of employees, staff management, working hours, salaries, and working models.

(5) The adaptability of the production system should be improved. First, the organizational design of the production system should be optimized to promote modularized product design and manufacturing. Second, the industrial internet should be further applied in the manufacturing industry to connect all the elements of the industrial chain. Through the real-time synchronization of supply, production, market, and other information, the switching speed of the production line between different standard products is accelerated, so that enterprises realize optimal capacity allocation and intelligent optimal production scheduling.

It is true that when faced with major changes in the operating environment, how and to what extent different enterprises are affected will differ because how they grow to cope with changes differs. For example, manufacturing companies need to better adapt to production systems than do service companies; while large enterprises need to be more sensitive to and able to foresee major environmental changes due to their multiple management levels even while entrepreneurs tend to be far away from the market. Therefore, each enterprise should cultivate its own adaptations to cope with major changes based on the characteristics of the industry, enterprise resources, as well as its specific capability.

22.2.4 Strategies for enterprises to grasp the opportunities of the great change in the "post-pandemic era"

The first strategy is to grasp the opportunity of strategic transformation. Such transformation is initially seen in new technologies: entrepreneurs should take this crisis as an opportunity to help companies enter a new stage of development through product innovation, the market development, and management reform brought about by new technologies such as cloud computing, 5G, big data, the Internet of Things, mobile internet, artificial intelligence, and blockchain. Further, transformation is moving toward ecological development: responsible entrepreneurs should consider consumer interest, ecological civilization, and human progress when setting the mission and purpose of enterprise development. Therefore, the enterprise will be transformed by ecological development and will strive to practice and demonstrate the values of ecological civilization. Finally, management will be transformed to ethical management: enterprises committed to sustainable development will gain consumer recognition and trust for the quality of their products, their civic behavior, and brand image, thus shaping a good public image.

Making full use of the value chain reformation caused by the COVID-19 pandemic is the second strategy, including the business opportunity generated by the "non-contact business model" as well as the increased demand for health products and the development opportunity derived from the medical and health industry chain. After the outbreak of the COVID-19 pandemic, industries related to national health security (such as medical supplies, antibiotics, and genetic drugs) have been regarded as strategic industries, which will be more likely to implement import substitution. It will bring great opportunities to industries related to medical and health infrastructure, medical informatization, as well as medical supplies.

The third and final strategy relates to grasping industrial development opportunities like "new infrastructure construction" which will exert a far-reaching impact. To mitigate the negative impact of COVID-19 on the economy, the country is expected to introduce consumption incentives for industries such as new energy vehicles and the mobile phone industry chain, and vigorously promote "new infrastructure construction", which, compared with general economic stimulus policies, is a long-term industrial development opportunity and will have a more profound impact on enterprises. In addition to making full use of the "new infrastructure construction", by further analyzing its impact on the value chain, enterprises also need to seek out new opportunities for conducting low-cost and differentiated businesses, to gain new competitive advantages.

22.3 Conclusions

The sudden outbreak of the COVID-19 pandemic highlights the so-called butterfly effect; it not only has had a short-term impact on the production and operation of enterprises but has also profoundly changed the environment in which they operate, providing an opportunity for enterprises to transform and develop. Since the pandemic is still not over, the government should grasp this "opportunity" to build China in the new era and optimize policies in the "post-pandemic era" to promote the sustainable development of Chinese enterprises. Those enterprises, on the other hand, should cultivate the ability to adapt to all kinds of environments, and seize the strategic opportunities brought about by current great changes to grow into top world enterprises in the near future.

https://doi.org/10.1142/9789811252921_0023

Chapter 23

The Impact of the COVID-19 Pandemic on Public Services and Policy Responses

Liu Hanbin

Shanghai Development and Reform Commission, Shanghai, China

Since the outbreak of the COVID-19 pandemic, several cities across China have faced a scarcity of medical resources. To cut off the source of infection in time, local authorities took the measure of "city lock-downs", which directly halted transportation, schools, and manufacturing. Residents were "grounded"; face masks and disinfectants were sold out; vegetables, meat, and eggs in supermarkets were initially in short supply and panic spread nationwide. The sudden outbreak of the pandemic has had a strong impact on urban public services, forcing the rethinking of questions about dealing with major disasters, and maintaining social order and giving full play to public services. Based on the impact of COVID-19 on urban public services, this chapter analyzes the lessons learned through theoretical explanations and case analysis, summarizes the scientific and efficient responses after reviewing a series of national and provincial responses, then looks to the future improvement of urban public services.

23.1 What are "Urban Public Services"

Urban public service systems consist of four parts: urban facilities construction services, comprehensive services for the development of enterprises and institutions, comprehensive services for residential life, and universal services for science and cultural education. On this basis, to better serve vulnerable groups in urban areas, and help people cope with public disasters, services directed at urban vulnerable groups and public disaster prevention services were added. Specifically, they cover schools, hospitals, sports facilities, social welfare, and security facilities, commercial facilities, and services, residential public facilities, and services, among others (road traffic, drainage, communication, radio and television, gas, firefighting, and sanitation).

In 2018, the Institute of Marxism within the Chinese Academy of Social Sciences released the *Evaluation of the Basic Public Service Capacity of Chinese Cities (2017)*, which comprehensively evaluated and studied the basic public service capacity of 38 major cities in China. It found that in recent years public transportation, healthcare, and public housing are the issues people most care about. Public services form the basis of maintaining general social fairness, and usually act as a "buffer" for social conflicts. Therefore, strengthening public services is conducive to alleviating prominent conflicts faced today through economic development, and to coping with the major challenges in the process of urbanization.

23.2 The Difficulty of Urban Public Services Coping with "Public Crisis"

According to Dutch scholar Uriel Rosenthal, crises are "a serious threat to the basic structures or the fundamental values and norms of a social system, which — under time, pressure, and highly uncertain circumstances — necessitates making critical decisions." In response to crises, Robert Heath proposed crisis management, that is, the management of the whole process of crisis events, which is embodied in readiness, response, and recovery. Managers' analysis of the types and effects of crises is conducive to a better handling of crises when they occur. Xue Lan *et al.* were early domestic scholars who systematically proposed the theory of public crisis management. Based on a summary of foreign studies, they believed that for a crisis to develop and evolve, it would mainly go through four stages, namely precursor, emergency, endurance, and solution. Therefore, the government needs to make timely adjustments according to the different stages to reduce or even avoid damage. During the pandemic, with the implementation of prevention measures such as the closure of residential areas, public area control, and emergency traffic control, people's demand for normal daily life surged. Their living needs were not being supplied by the limited urban services, which further expanded the pandemic into an "urban public crisis".

23.3 The Impact of the Pandemic on Urban Public Services

23.3.1 The impact on living supplies

Living supplies include daily necessities such as grains and agricultural supplies (vegetables and grains), which had to be guaranteed by the market during the pandemic prevention and control period. People in most cases had believed in a coming "shortage" of goods, which would lead to panic buying and a further short-term surge in demand. In terms of medical supplies, due to the shutdown of factories during the Spring Festival, masks and disinfectants were in short supply and major pharmacies were out of stock because of "panic buying". In areas most stricken by the pandemic where local governments did not have enough reserves to meet people's daily consumption, unscrupulous business owners hoarded large quantities of pandemic prevention materials, illegally raised the prices of masks, and even sold fake masks. In particular, the high-grade N95 masks and personal protective equipment that were needed by medical staff every day were usually only effective for "one to two days" and surgical masks for residents were even harder to get. Because of the pandemic, medicines to prevent colds and fevers were also hoarded. The goods and supplies in cities depended on allocations within communities and villages, to be balanced.

In one respect, the government has not built an effective "wartime" system to deal with emergencies due to its insufficient reserves of emergency supplies and inadequate capacity for short-term balancing. In addition, timely media publicity and information transparency were not adequate. In effect, many people were not able to keep up with the latest situation, highlighting the need to set up an emergency media team.

23.3.2 The impact on medical and health services

In terms of the provision of emergency medical services, hospitals for infectious diseases lack comprehensive medical services; for example, they do not have departments with multiple comprehensive functions, such as surgery, obstetrics, pediatrics, and disease prevention. As a result, their medical personnel are usually not able to conduct clinical diagnosis and comprehensive treatment for complex diseases that are multi-symptomatic and affect all sectors of the population. This is mainly due to China's existing medical training system, which focuses more on cultivating specialists rather than general practitioners.

In the face of severe infectious diseases, a hierarchical system of medical institutions has not been launched in time for the pandemic, resulting in the difficulty of isolating confirmed and suspected cases, as well as mild and severe cases. The example of Wuhan shows that with a registered population and permanent resident population of 14 million, it only has two specialized infectious disease hospitals, namely the Jinyintan Hospital and the Pulmonology Hospital, with a total of little more than 900 beds, that is 0.64 beds per 10,000 people, which is far lower than China's set standard of 1.2–1.5 beds per 10,000 in an urban, non-agricultural population.

In terms of the technical measures taken in response to emergencies, problems have been exposed in the detection and isolation of the virus. Though medical technology could develop virus detection kits in a short time in the event of an outbreak, how to initiate emergency procedures and transfer testing authority to qualified medical institutions as quickly as possible while ensuring test quality and biosafety has become one of the key issues of pandemic prevention and control.

To solve the problems, further increased investment in medical and health services is needed. Since the SARS outbreak in 2003, the proportion of allocated public health expenditure has increased from 3.2% in 2003 to 7.1% in 2018. This increase, however, has slowed down, as the growth rate of government fiscal revenue has gradually slowed down since 2014. In terms of expenditure structure, according to the statistics of the National Health Commission, the proportion of government, social, and personal health expenditure of total health expenditure in China in 2018 accounted for 27.7%, 43.7%, and 28.6%, respectively. Compared with developed countries in China, the proportion of personal health expenditure of total health expenditure is relatively high. According to WHO, US government spending accounted for 51.3% of total health spending in 2017, while the figures for social spending and private spending were 41.6% and 7.1%, respectively. In the UK, the figures are 80.7%, 10.7%, and 8.6%, respectively; in Japan, 54.8%, 37%, and 8.2%; and in Singapore, 45.6%, 36.2%, and 18.2%. Therefore, Huang Qifan, vice chairman of the China Center for International Economic Exchange, has suggested an increase of RMB 200 billion to 300 billion in the 14th Five-Year Plan period to make up for weaknesses in China's public health system.

23.3.3 The impact on transportation

To control the pandemic, local governments to varying degrees have controlled the movement of people. In general, they all followed the principle of "no travel unless necessary, and drive if necessary". In terms of passenger transport, the 2020 Spring Festival travel rush was "smaller in the scale of return and longer in the cycle of return[1] with a lower peak value than previous years". It is reported that with the worsening of the pandemic, especially since "person to person transmission" was confirmed on January 20th, people who had previously decided to return to their hometown or travel near the Spring Festival canceled their travel plans, resulting in a decrease in the number of tourists returning to their hometowns. From the data released by the Ministry of Transport, the commercial passenger volume in the first 22 days of the 2020 Spring Festival travel rush (from Jan. 10 to Jan. 31) dropped by 20.6% compared with the same period last year. In particular, the passenger volume from Jan. 28 to Jan. 31 (the fourth to the seventh day of the first lunar month) witnessed a year-on-year decline of 82.9%. By contrast, the passenger volume in the first six days of the Spring Festival travel rush (from Jan. 10 to Jan. 15) rose 2.7% year on year. Moreover, freight traffic on the country's highways from Jan. 21 to Jan. 30 witnessed a month-on-month decrease of about 80%.

[1]Spring Festival is the most important festival in China. On this day, all Chinese people will return to their hometown for the New Year. Due to the COVID-19, quite a lot of people didn't go back to their hometowns in 2020.

23.3.4 The impact on electricity, water, and gas supplies

After the outbreak of the pandemic, to maintain the normal operation of cities, it had to be ensured that people's basic needs such as the need for water, electricity, and gas can always be met. To this end, several policy documents have been issued on "ensuring people's livelihood".

In terms of water supply security, the Ministry of Ecology and Environment issued the *Notice on the Supervision and Control of Medical Wastewater and Urban Wastewater from Novel Coronavirus Infected Pneumonia Pandemic* in February and the *Technical Plan for Emergency Treatment of Medical Wastewater Contaminated by Novel Coronavirus (Trial)* guiding local governments to monitor designated hospitals, urban sewage treatment plants that were receiving sewage from designated hospitals, and centralized quarantine sites. The sewage treatment facilities operation and the terminal disinfection measures were monitored, with viral residue serving as a core indicator.

In terms of electricity security, because of the pandemic most people turned to indoor activities. Therefore, household electricity consumption increased, whereas electricity consumption for industries such as public transportation, entertainment, catering, retail, and tourism declined. After the pandemic, workers may have been required to work extra hours to speed up production, so electricity consumption was likely to rebound after the second quarter. Regionally, the growth rate of electricity consumption in central and eastern China, most severely stricken by the pandemic, had declined sharply. Annual electricity consumption was predicted to grow by around 4.5%. For its 2.4 million residential electricity customers, Hubei Electric Power Co., Ltd. decided that electricity would not be cut off if the bill was overdue. The company also launched a first-level response at the earliest time and ensured the power supply of "Huoshenshan (Fire God Mountain) Hospital" for five days; "Leishenshan (Thunder God Mountain) Hospital" for 3 days; and "mobile cabin hospitals" for three hours.

In terms of urban energy resources, the National Development and Reform Commission further coordinated the monitoring of coal, electricity, oil, and gas. First, the *Notice on the Establishment of a Coal Storage Monitoring Mechanism in Key Power Plants* was issued to establish a daily monitoring system. Provincial economic operation departments were required to report the coal storage of key power plants daily to ensure a stable supply during the pandemic prevention and control period.

For power plants with thermal coal stocks of less than ten days, special personnel were assigned to coordinate with enterprises to work on resources and distribution, to ensure that their inventories could be raised to a reasonable level. Second, the coal mines which had stopped production were encouraged to resume. Key coal mines resumed their work systematically on the premise of taking strict pandemic prevention measures. Furthermore, communication with provinces with low rates of resumption of work of coal mines was strengthened to steadily increase the return rate. Third, the road transport of coal was coordinated and guaranteed.

23.4 Analysis of the Coping Strategies of Urban Public Services

23.4.1 Quick launch of "mobile cabin hospitals" in view of insufficient public medical resources

Due to the surge of critically ill patients that exceeded hospital bed capacity, and the requirements for the diagnosis and treatment of infectious diseases, the "mobile cabin hospital" previously typically used during wartime was utilized. This is a medical platform that can be deployed rapidly, and is generally composed of a medical function unit, ward unit, and technical support unit. The "mobile cabin hospital" performs various functions, such as emergency treatment, surgical treatment, and clinical examination. Because of its several advantages such as good mobility, rapid deployment, and strong environmental adaptability, it adapts to sudden emergencies, and medical rescue missions. Though by the end of 2018 China's health institutions had exceeded the one million mark, with 32,000 hospitals and about 10 million beds in medical and health institutions nationwide, the hierarchical diagnosis and treatment capacities for severe infectious diseases were still insufficient. The establishment of "mobile cabin hospitals" has alleviated the problem of beds during an emergency. In February 2020, the National Health Commission and related departments established Huoshenshan Hospital, Leishenshan Hospital, and 13 "mobile cabin hospitals" in Wuhan. In particular, the establishment of "mobile cabin hospitals" reversed the passive situation of "people waiting for beds", enhanced patient confidence, and curbed the trend of mild cases turning into severe cases in Wuhan.

Figure 23.1: Online shopping model.

23.4.2 The launch of "online reservation + community delivery" system targeted at people's living necessities

To meet the daily needs of residents trapped at home, community services adopted a group purchase mode using "e-commerce", "WeChat business", "group bargaining" and the "acquaintance economy" to collect orders, contact designated supermarkets and food markets, distribute products, and deliver them to the community. See Figure 23.1 for details.

To avoid person-to-person contact, all communities adopted the "contact-free distribution of daily necessities" protocol: the goods were placed at a designated location, such as outside the gate or the door. The exact place and time had been communicated through WeChat so that buyers and delivery staff avoided face-to-face contact. The same methodology was adopted in home delivery services. Meanwhile, for special groups such as the empty-nesters, pregnant women, the disabled, and patients with chronic diseases, each community official and cadre had his/her own share of responsibility and door-to-door service was provided to take good care of these special groups.

23.4.3 Promoting the resumption of work and production according to the demand for masks and disinfectants

The National Development and Reform Commission has made every effort to coordinate and promote the enterprise resumption of work and production to produce urgently needed medical supplies. Through pairing with local governments and enterprises, the Commission had a detailed understanding of those enterprises manufacturing medical protective clothing and coordinated with them to resume work and production as soon as possible. These companies may have had to work overtime to meet production capacity. Meanwhile, exports were shifted to serve the domestic market, manufacturing enterprises equipped to deal with large supply contracts reconfigured to the manufacture of domestic emergency medical supplies, and enterprises capable of so doing were encouraged to produce N95 surgical masks and national standard protective clothing. At the end of February 2020, the National Development and Reform Commission had paired with key provinces and enterprises to help 13 enterprises expand to increase capacity, with a total capacity expansion of 50,000 pieces per day. In order to ensure raw materials for the production of medical supplies, the Commission coordinated with seven different provinces and cities, namely Jiangsu, Zhejiang, Guangdong, Shandong, Henan, Tianjin, and Anhui to investigate the production of and existing problems for enterprises manufacturing raw materials needed for protective clothing, such as composite film non-woven fabric and composite breathable film, and at the same time continued to focus on the resumption of production in large enterprises. Meanwhile, they worked on the labor shortage and financial difficulties: learning of the difficulties faced by enterprises in recruiting workers, they found that 14 manufacturing enterprises needed 1,200 workers, and hence worked with relevant departments to solve this problem. The collaboration with local governments and enterprises continued, and a total of more than RMB 25 billion needed by seven groups of enterprises was provided in a short amount of time.

23.4.4 In view of the resumption of work and production, the joint prevention and control model was constructed

After the pandemic, with the resumption of work and production, people started to get together. Local public services faced many difficulties such as how to implement local pandemic prevention and control measures, and how to reasonably coordinate these measures with economic and social development. To solve these problems, the "health QR code" has been adopted to manage and track the health of the population. Relying on the mobile terminal "Suishenban (government online–offline Shanghai)", the Shanghai "unified online government service" launched "Shanghai QR Code" for its citizens, serving as a service code, aiming to

Red	The red code means the holder has not been relieved of medical management measures, has not been discharged from hospital after diagnosis, or is suspected to have not been excluded. Quarantine is suggested.
Yellow	The yellow code means the holder is from key areas and has been in Shanghai for less than 14 days. Observation is suggested.
Green	The green code means that no abnormality has been seen or the holder has been relieved of medical management measures and is thus allowed to pass.

Figure 23.2: Classification of the health assessment of Shanghai QR Code.

meet people's various needs in terms of work, life, and travel. Meanwhile, open to various platforms like WeChat, Alipay, and DingTalk, it adopts the three-color dynamic management, namely "green code, yellow code, and red code", relying on the data of national and municipal public administration institutions which were gathered by the Shanghai big data resource platform. Through data modeling, analysis, and evaluation, three risk states, namely red, yellow, and green, are calculated for reference in different situations. See Figure 23.2 for details.

23.4.5 Flexibly adopt urban traffic management plans in view of public transport crowds

After the Spring Festival holiday, according to the State Council Pandemic Prevention and Control Headquarters, medium and low risk areas were allowed to resume work and production in an orderly manner, ensuring safe travel has become an integral part of every region. The summarized coping strategies based on the urban traffic operation management regulations issued by Beijing, Shanghai, and other megacities are shown in Table 23.1.

23.4.6 Develop "cloud government services"

In terms of government services, "contact-free services" have been promoted. Local governments with the aid of major cloud service platforms like Ali Cloud, Tencent Cloud, and UCloud have set up information management systems, sharing a system of public security data and a mask reservation system. Thanks to technologies like cloud computing, big

Table 23.1: Strategies on public transport management during the pandemic.

Number	Strategic steps	Specific measures
1	Set safety standards in vehicles	1. Cooperate with public health departments to study the safe distance between passengers on public transport vehicles in consideration of the disease transmission risk and mask protection and set measures to conduct ventilation and disinfection of carriages.
2	Regulate demand through the promotion of staggered work start times	Encourage enterprises and public institutions to work from home through telecommuting or video conferencing, or adopt flexible working hours, such as a staggered rush hour plan, to reduce the pressure on bus passenger flow during peak commuting hours.
3	Control the density of passengers in vehicles	Limit passenger crowding at the station hall floor according to the number of disembarking passengers and the type of subway, as well as its composition. Control the passenger flow onto the platform and the safety passenger flow density of each carriage as well as the number of passengers on regular buses.
4	Increase the transport capacity of public transport during peak hours	Increase the number of buses allocated during rush hours and raise the frequency of subway service. Maintain the basic capacity allocation of buses and subways while reducing the number of passengers per car.
5	Make travel appointments	Further promote the reservation of travel on the Internet. For passengers with relatively fixed travel times and travel routes, more customized buses should be put into commuter channels and bus routes where needed.
6	Enhance publicity of pandemic prevention on public transportation	Increase publicity of pandemic prevention and safety measures for passengers taking public transportation through various means, so that understanding, and cooperation can be fostered.

data, and artificial intelligence, the pandemic has been effectively prevented and controlled, and everyday problems faced by businesses and citizens have been able to be solved online. See Figure 23.3 for specific cases.

Since January 23, the Qingdao Municipal Government has been relying on the "government service cloud" ("government big data and cloud computing center") to guarantee information processing for pandemic prevention and control. Therefore, the "government service cloud" has served as the information processing center. In ten districts and towns in Qingdao, 2,294 servers of 524 systems in 56 municipal institutions have been "connected to the cloud", effectively breaking down technical barriers, such as network disconnection and difficulty in exchanging information between departments. The Human Resources and Social Security Department of Qingdao took the lead in establishing the "Qingdao Model" of big data authentication for qualifications of retirement benefits, relying on the government service cloud. Through the comprehensive analysis of medical insurance, transportation, banking, public security, and other information about the retirees, the eligibility for the retirement benefits was determined. This resulted in 92.6% of the elderly not having to "run errands" at service desks so the silent certification featuring "no meeting and no disturbance" has been realized. Relying on the government service cloud, civil affairs departments have shared government service information so that the accuracy of social assistance and the effectiveness of relief funds have been enhanced and real estate registration departments have realized "comprehensive acceptance and one-stop-service", with the processing length being reduced from 40–50 minutes to 10–20 minutes.

Figure 23.3: "Cloud government service" in Qingdao.

23.5 Reflections on Urban Modernization Governance in the "post-pandemic era"

Urban modernization governance in the "post-pandemic era" needs to focus on the theme of "resilient cities" with "emergency services and rapid recovery". Therefore, "stress tests" should be adopted in various areas such as urban planning and when public service facilities are being constructed. In other words, "back-estimates" should be done on whether existing infrastructure has the capacity to bear the pressure from the most extreme situations, and then the scale and layout of the services should be decided considering factors like material storage, emergency shelters, and medical places based on evaluation results.

23.5.1 On the construction of "low density city" and "resilient city"

During the pandemic, gatherings of people have become the biggest challenge for compact cities. After the end of the pandemic, adhering to the construction of a compact city, preparations and plans should be made at all levels to conduct evacuations in case of large gatherings. In the future, in terms of improving the living environment, the density of people in each community should be reduced as much as possible, so that there will be enough living space for dwellers. During this outbreak, residents were unable leave their buildings, and the cramped living conditions made their life particularly depressing. If residents can enjoy soothing scenery without leaving the community, they will feel relieved emotionally. The problems of urban governance exposed by the COVID-19 outbreak have provided an opportunity for urban administrators, planners, designers, and builders as well as participants to shift from a thinking model of risk to one of resilience, establishing a platform for urban disaster scenario construction and prediction, thus improving emergency preparedness.

23.5.2 How to strengthen the construction of the public health and medical system?

To promote the construction of public health and medical systems, the regional distribution of public health and medical resources should be optimized, and national and regional medical centers established for the treatment of infectious diseases. Investment in infectious disease hospitals should be increased to improve diagnosis and treatment conditions, enhance comprehensive capacity, and improve the diagnosis and treatment capacity of difficult and severe infectious diseases. Furthermore, highly competent and qualified professionals should be educated and trained in various disciplines, the construction of infectious diseases departments in general hospitals should be upgraded, the ability to diagnose and treat should be enhanced, and the treatment of medical staff related to infectious diseases should be improved. Work should be undertaken to build emergency medical services, improve network layout, improve the allocation of emergency vehicles (including negative pressure ambulances), and improve the effective coordination mechanism of scientific research, disease control, and clinical treatment.

To further strengthen the system of hierarchical diagnosis and treatment, the grid layout construction of urban medical groups and county medical communities should be accelerated, the implementation of "total payment, surplus retention, and reasonable overspending sharing" should be promoted within the Medical Association, a smooth referral mechanism to promote the efficient coordination and seamless connection between public health services and medical services should be generated, an improved treatment mechanism of infectious diseases and other major infectious diseases with classification, stratification, and diversion should be established.

To optimize the operation mechanism of primary medical and health institutions and improve the basic medical care and health service system, especially that of the public health service, the infrastructure, material allocation, and grassroots medical and health teams should be further developed to meet the requirements of pandemic prevention and control. Grassroots medical and health institutions should gradually establish a new operational mechanism to play a greater role in providing basic medical services.

To reserve emergency space during city planning, when dealing with the impact of the pandemic, emergency medical space should be considered, to be able to isolate patients and classify diagnosis and treatment. For example, in this pandemic, large stadiums, exhibition buildings, industrial warehouses, and school dormitories were quickly transformed into "mobile cabin hospitals", which solved to a large extent the problem of insufficient medical resources.

23.5.3 On community's construction of "smart governance"

A good layout of urban community units should be planned where facilities to meet people's basic needs of education, recreation, medical treatment, shopping, fitness, and elderly care can be integrated to ensure a normal and orderly operation of the community during an emergency. The integration of existing information facilities can be strengthened from the following four aspects.

With the help of "big data + cloud computing", the urban medical resource allocation system of the "community unit" can be established rapidly. Professional logistics enterprises can be relied on to collect and analyze the data on the use and demand for hospital materials, realize intelligent material allocation, and predict the material demand through big data analysis, to prevent the occurrence of a material scarcity emergency.

Systems for reporting pandemic data including patients should be established as soon as possible. Big data are collected to allow the analyzing of the number of patients in a city and their treatment status. In addition, according to the number of beds, kits, and other medical resources of the hospital, patients can be assigned "intelligently", so that the admission procedure can be simplified, and the use of medical resources maximized to reduce unnecessary investment.

In terms of public transportation, local government departments, together with civil aviation, railway, and communications, have built a system of tracking pandemic-related personnel to achieve maximum collaboration among departments, optimize information collection, promote the integration and sharing of resources, and quickly locate suspected cases or close contacts.

A platform to release grassroots service information and establish a convenient service system should be implemented. The purchase of masks, disinfectants, and other urgently needed products can be arranged according to the information collected through residents' online reporting. Meanwhile, grassroots service platforms can be used to release timely information on the pandemic situation, such as food prices and health and safety information, to sooth people's minds.

https://doi.org/10.1142/9789811252921_bmatter

References

Acemoglu, D. and Autor, D. (2011). Skills, tasks and technologies: Implications for employment and earnings. In Ashenfelter, O. and Card, D. (Eds.), *Handbook of Labor Economics* (Vol. 4B, pp. 1043–1171). Amsterdam: North Holland.

Alirol, E., Getaz, L., Stoll, B. *et al.* (2011). Urbanization and infectious diseases in a globalized world. *The Lancet*, **11**(2): 131–141.

Allard, J. and Blavy, R. (2011). *Market Phoenixes and Banking Ducks: Are Recoveries Faster in Market-Based Financial Systems?* IMF Working Paper No. 11(213): 1–25.

Allen, F., Gu, X. and Kowalewski, O. (2012). Financial crisis, structure and reform. *Journal of Banking & Finance*, **36**(11): 2960–2973.

Allen, F., Qian, J., Shan, C. Y. *et al.* (2018). *Dissecting the Long-term Performance of the Chinese Stock Market*. Fanhai International School of Finance, Fudan University.

Ambrus, A., Field, E. and Gonzalez, R. (2020). Loss in the time of cholera: Long run impact of a disease epidemic on the urban landscape. *American Economic Review*, **110**(2): 475–525.

Analysis of the impact of COVID-19 on transportation industry and counter measures. *China Communication News Net*. 2020.2.11, http://www.zgjtb.com/2020/02/11/content235077.htm.

Analysis of the impact of the COVID-19 on the transportation industry. *China Research Network*. February 19, 2020, http://www.chinairn.com/hyzx/20200219/163714275.shtml.

Asimoglu, D. and Robinson, J. A. (2015). *Why the Country Fails*. Translated by Li Zenggang. Changsha: Hunan Technical Science Press.

Bai, Ziwen. (2020). US Secretary of Commerce Ross said that "the epidemic will help work return to the United States". *Observer.com*. January 31, 2020.

Bailey, M. J. and Goodman-Bacon, A. (2015). The war on poverty's experiment in public medicine: Community health centers and the mortality of older Americans. *American Economic Review*, **105**(3): 1067–1104.

Baker, S. R., Bloom, N. and Davis, S. J. (2016). Measuring economic policy uncertainty. *Quarterly Journal of Economics*, **131**(4): 1593–1636.

Bloom, N., Shleifer, A. and Vishny, R. (1998). A model of investor sentiment. *Journal of Financial Economics*, **49**(3): 307–343.

Bloom, N. (2009). The impact of uncertainty shocks. *Econometrica*, **77**(3): 623–685.

Cao, Huimin. (2020). Study on the risk management of urban public safety from the perspective of governance modernization. *Journal of Hubei University (Philosophy and Social Science)*, **47**(1): 146–157.

Chen, Chunhua. (2020). Influence of pandemic situation on economy and countermeasures and suggestions of enterprises. Chunnaunhuakai. WeChat Official Account, February 1, 2020.

Chen, Shangying. (2015). Routine congestion calls for the reform of holiday system. *China Business Times*. October 9, 2015.

Chen, Zhensheng. (2020). To prepare for the end of the epidemic, companies should ensure diversified resource supply. *Lianhe Zaobao*. February 17, 2020.

Chen, Haiqiang *et al*. More Precise Support for Small, Medium Enterprises. Economic Daily. 7th February, 2020.

Cheng, Shi. (2020). The long-term impact of the pandemic: The acceleration of digital economy's evolution and the sinking of its focus. *China Business News*. February 25, 2020.

China Association of Small and Medium Commercial Enterprise. (2020). Research on small and medium enterprises under COVID-19 with 7290 set survey data. *China Daily*. 2020.2.21, http://cn.chinadaily.com.cn/a/202002/21/WS5e4f6c2da3107bb6b57a1572.html.

China Association of Small and Medium Enterprises. (2020). *Research Report on the Impact of the Novel Coronavirus Pandemic on Small and Medium Enterprises and Suggestions for Countermeasures*. February 15, 2020.

China Cooking Association released a report on the impact of the COVID-19 on the catering industry: Over 90% of catering companies said that the rate of take-out platforms has not dropped. *Phoenix Net Finance*. February 12, 2020, https://finance.ifeng.com/c/7u0eidc4XYe.

China Hotel Association. (2020). By China Hotel Association and Uni Huasheng: The analysis of impact of COVID-19 on global hotel market. *Sohu*. February 17, 2020, http://www.sohu.com/a/373662531_236448.

China Investment Industry Research Institute. (2020). The impact of the pandemic on the mask industry. February 16, 2020.

China Merchants Bank Enterprise Research Joint Group. (2020). *China Merchants Bank Small and Micro Enterprises Research Report*. February 28, 2020.

China Merchants Securities. (2020). Macro report-eurozone: European Central Bank stimulus plan to respond to the new crown pneumonia pandemic. *Sina Finance*. March 13, 2020.

Confirmed cases in France rose to 2,876 and Macron announced the closure of all schools in France. *China News Network*. March 13, 2020.

Cruise Business Department of China Merchants Shekou. (2020). *Research on the Impact of COVID-19 on Chinese Cruise Market*. Cruise Industry News, 2020 China Market Report, 2020. Cruise Lines International Association, 2018 Asia Ocean Source Market Report, 2019.

Dewatripont, M. and Maskin, E. (1995). Credit and efficiency in centralized and decentralized economies. *Review of Economic Studies*, **62**(4): 541–555.

Ding, C. (2020). *EU-China-US Trilateral Relations, in the Evolving Relationship between China, the EU and the USA*. Abingdon: Routledge.

Ding, Chun. (2020). Global pandemic observation by Nancai quick review: How effective is the pandemic prevention in Europe? A re-examination of COVID19. *21st Century Business Herald*. March 9, 2020.

Ding, Lei, Cai, Wei, Ding, Jianqing *et al*. (2020). An interim review of lessons from the novel coronavirus (SARS-CoV-2) outbreak in China (in Chinese). *Scientia Sinica Vitae*, **50**: 247–257. 10.1360/SSV-2020-0044.

Ding, Xueliang. (2020). Prevalence and subjugation of pandemics in human civilization history. *The Paper*. 2020.2.21, https://www.thepaper.cn/newsDetail_forward_5705378.

Dolton, P. and Pathania, V. (2016). Can increased primary care access reduce demand for emergency care? Evidence from England's 7day GP opening. *Journal of Health Economics*, **49**: 193–208.

Dong, Junran and Zhang, Feng. (2015). Optimization research of Chinese legal holiday system. *Overseas English*, **21**: 179–181.

Dusheiko, M., Gravelle, H., Jacobs, R. *et al*. (2006). The effect of financial incentives on gatekeeping doctors: Evidence from a natural experiment. *Journal of Health Economics*, **25**(3): 449–478.

Ebon Dynamics Research Institute. (2020). Online retail research bulletin during the 2020 spring festival pandemic. February 23, 2020, http://www.199it.com/archives/1011807.html.

Epidemiology Working Group for NCIP Epidemic Response, Chinese Center for Disease Control and Prevention. (2020). The epidemiological characteristics of an outbreak of 2019 novel coronavirus diseases (COVID-19) in China. *Zhonghua Liu Xing Bing Xue Za Zhi*, **41**, 145–151.

Fang, H., Wang, Y. and Wu, X. (2020) The collateral channel of monetary policy: Evidence from China, No. w26792. National Bureau of Economic Research.

Federal Reserve. (2020). The Federal Open Market Committee statement. 2020-03-03, https://www.federalreserve.gov/newsevents/pressreleases/monetary20200303a1.htm.

Feng, Jin and Yu, Yangyang. (2008). Health system reform: Marketization, incentive mechanism and the role of government. *World Economic Papers*, (01).

Feng, Xujie, Wang, Yang, Liu, Shuhao *et al.* (2020). Impacts of COVID-19 on urban rail transit operation. *Transportation Research*, **6**(1): 45–49.

Financial observation: Multiple financial measures in Europe responding to the impact of the pandemic. *Xinhua News Agency*. March 12, 2020.

Findlay, R. (1995). *Factor Proportions, Trade, and Growth*. Cambridge, Mass.: MIT Press.

Gao, Hong and Yang, Xiuyong. (2018). Theory, practice and path for the integration of social organization into social governance. *Expanding Horizons*, (01): 77–83.

Gao, Kejia. (2018). Evolution of Chinese meal system. *Art Science and Technology*, (7): 21–22.

Geanakoplos, J. (2010). The leverage cycle. *NBER Macroeconomics Annual*, **24**(1): 166.

Geissinger, A., Laurell, C. and Sandstrm, C. (2018). Digital disruption beyond Uber and Airbnb — Tracking the long tail of the sharing economy. *Technological Forecasting and Social Change*. 2018-6-12, https://doi.org/10.1016/j.techfore.

German manufacturing's worst performance in ten years: Warnings from the president of the European Central Bank. *Sina Finance*. February 10, 2020.

Germany under the pandemic: Economy, what measures has the German government taken? *Sina News*. March 14, 2020.

Goldfarb, A. and Tucker, C. (2019). Digital economics. *Journal of Economic Literature*, **57**(1): 343.

Goeure, B. (2014). Monetary Policy Transmission and Bank Deleveraging, Speech at *The Future of Banking Summit Paris*, 13 March 2014.

Grjebine, T., Szczerbowicz, U. and Tripier, F. (2018). Corporate debt structure and economic recoveries. *European Economic Review*, **101**: 77–100.

Guan, Xiqing. (2020). Analysis of the influence of COVID-19 pandemic on the economic development of Shanghai development zone. *Industrial Innovation*, (2): 58–61.

Guo, Juan, and Cui, Guiyou. (2019). Defense against public health risks and promoting measures of the system of serving spoons and chopsticks. *Journal of Nanning Polytechnic*, (3): 16–19.

Harold, S. D. and Jean, W. K. (2008). *Risk Management and Insurance: Perspectives in a Global Economy*. Hoboken: Blackwell Publishing.

Hassell, J. M., Michael, B., Melissa, J. W. *et al.* (2017). Urbanization and disease emergence: Dynamics at the Wildlife-livestock-human interface. *Trends in Ecology & Evolution*, **32**(1): 55–67.

How serious if the impact of the epidemic on China's economy? *Economic Daily*. February 12, 2020.

Huang, Qifan. (2020). Chinese public health system will spend two to three hundred billion yuan to make up the shortage. *Sina Finance*. 2020.2.21, https://finance.sina.com.cn/wm/2020-02-18/doc-iimxyqvz3955605.shtml.

Huang, Qifan. (2020). Suggestions on the reform of public health and pandemic prevention system in China. *Sina Finance*. 2020.2.11, http://finance.sina.com.cn/review/jcgc/2020-02-11/doc-iimxxstf0635530.shtml.

Huang, Sheng and Sun, Hong. (2010). A preliminary study on the effectiveness of public health measures taken at ports of countries around the world at the early stage of the 2009 H1N1 influenza pandemic. *Chinese Journal of Frontier Health and Quarantine*, Issue 4: 283–287.

Italian government spends 25 billion euros to bail out. *European Times*. March 12, 2020.

Jean Baptiste Say. (1998). *Introduction to Political Economy*. Translated by Chen Fusheng and Chen Zhenhua. Beijing: The Commercial Press.

Jones, K. E., Patel, N. G., Levy, M. A. *et al*. (2008). Global trends in emerging infectious diseases. *Nature*, **451**: 990–993.

Kelly, M. (2001). *A History of the Black Death in Ireland*. Stroud: Tempus.

Krugman, P. (1980). Scale economies, product differentiation, and the pattern of trade. *America Economic Review*, **70**(5): 950959.

Krugman, P. (1991). *Geography and Trade*. Cambridge, Mass.: MIT Press.

Kuhn, P. and Mansour, H. (2014). Is internet job search still ineffective? *The Economic Journal*, **124**(581): 12131233.

Li, Cangshu and Shen, Yan. (2019). Identification, measurement, prevention and control of new financial industry's risks in the era of the digital economy. *Management World*, 12th issue.

Li, Huiwen, Jin, Quan and Li, Wei. (2020). Small and medium-sized private enterprises under the impact of the pandemic: Dilemmas, countermeasures and hope. *Surf News*. February 19, 2020.

Li, Shaoming. (2020). Analysis of China's consumer market trends and countermeasures of commercial enterprises under the impact of the pandemic. *Yangtze River Industry and Economic Think Tank Public Account*. February 27, 2020.

Li, Wenlong and Zhang, Shiming. (2020). How will China's foreign trade and supply chain be affected by China-US economic and trade frictions and the COVID-19. *China Business News*. February 17, 2020.

Li, Xiaohong. (2020). Hubei auto companies under the pandemic: Shock at both ends of production and demand and the time to resume work is not yet determined. *China Automobile News*. February 2020.

Li, Xiaohua. (2020). Accused as the "sick man in Asia", is China overreacting? *China Daily*. February 26, 2020.

Li, Yao. (2020). Pelosi must have never expected that she would meet this Chinese iron lady in Munich. *World Wide Web*. February 15, 2020.

Liang, Ji, Chen, Shaobo and Feng, Lanqi. (2020). Thoughts and suggestions on China's future tax reform: Based on the comparative perspective with the EU. *Fiscal Science*, No. 1: 25–38.

Liu, Gongrun. (2020). The digital economy is a "Preferred Item" for economic development in the post-pandemic period. *China Business News*. March 2, 2020.

Liu, Junfeng, Zhai, Xiaohui, Xiang, Zhun *et al.* (2020). Discussion on the cabin hospital construction management of COVID-19 pandemic situation. *Chinese Hospital Management*, No. 3: 12–14.

Liu, Junqing. (2020). The world without China's industry chain. *Outlook Think Tank*. February 15.

Liu, Quan. (2020). Smart community classification and integrated development from the perspective of product application. *Urban Planning International*, (01): 71–78.

Logic, countermeasures and new trends of urban transportation during the COVID-19. *The Paper*. 2020.2.28, https://www.thepaper.cn/newsDetail forward6217561.

Lu, Wei, Zhang, Yimin, Liang, Hong *et al.* (2016). The performance evaluation based on the demand side of the family doctor contract service: A focus on chronic diseases. *Chinese Journal of Health Policy*, (08): 23–30.

Lu, Yang and Xia, Jiechang. (2020). Impact of COVID-19 on service industry and relevant countermeasure. *China Economic Times*. March 2, 2020.

Luo, Changyuan. (2020). The impact and response of the COVID-19 from the perspective of business environment. *The Paper*. February 28, 2020.

Luo, Zhi and Sheng, Hanzhi. (2020). *Analysis Report of Hubei Enterprise Management in Pandemic*. Economics and Management School of Wuhan University. February 29, 2020, http://ems.whu.edu.cn/info/1587/16075.htm.

Ma, Xiaowei. (2013). *Report of the State Council on the Management of the Physician Team and the Implementation of Practicing Physicians*. April 21, 2019.

Mari, T., Ding, C. and Zhang, X. (2018). *Deepening the EU-China Partnership*. Abingdon: Routledge. Weber, M. (1997). *Economy and Society*. Beijing: The Commercial Press.

Mayers, D. and Smith, C. W., Jr. (1982). Executive compensation in the life insurance industry. *Journal of Business*, (55): 281–296.

McKinsey Global Institute. (2020). *McKinsey China Report 2019*. January 6, 2020.

Merkel said the pandemic situation is more special than the financial crisis. *China News Network*. March 13, 2020.

Meyer, J. W. and Rowan, B. (1997). Institutionalized organizations: Formal structure as myth and ceremony. *American Journal of Sociology*, (83): 340–363.

Hannan, M. T. (2014). *Organizational Ecology*. Translated by Peng Biyu, Li Xi. Beijing: Science Press.

Mu Jian-bo *et al.* (2004). Discussing the sustainable operation mode of telemedicine system in China. *Chinese Health Service Management*, (12):887–889+913.

National Bureau of Statistics. (2020). *Statistical Bulletin of the People's Republic of China on National Economic and Social Development in 2019*. February 28, 2020.

National Bureau of Statistics. (2020). *Statistical Communiqué of the People's Republic of China on National Economic and Social Development in 2019*. February 28, 2020.

Notice on further strengthening financial support for the prevention and control of the novel coronavirus pneumonia. http://www.pbc.gov.cn/goutongjiaoliu/113456/113469/3965911/index.html. January 31, 2020.

Online expert round table: COVID-19 is a big test for urban infrastructure construction. *Beijing News*. 2020.2.17, https://www.bjnews.com.cn/feature/2020/02/17/690618.html.

Overall sales in January fell by 20%. The short-term impact of the pandemic on the auto industry is greater than that of SARS. *China News Weekly*. March 9, 2020, http://auto.163.com/20/0309/08/F78UD9RI000884MM.html.

Pang, Jian and Zhu, Xinmin. (2013). The development trend of foreign digital economy and the national development strategy of digital economy. *Science & Technology Progress and Policy*, **30**(8): 124–128.

Pei, Changhong, Ni, Jiangfei and Li, Yue. (2018). Approach digital economy from the perspective of political economics. *Finance & Trade Economics*, **39**(9): 5–22.

Petersen, M. A. and Rajan, G. R. (1995). The effect of credit market competition on lending relationships. *The Quarterly Journal of Economics*, **110**(2): 407–443.

Powell, W. W. and DiMaggio, P. J. (2008). *The New Institutionalism in Organizational Analysis*. Translated by Yao Wei. Shanghai: Shanghai People's Publishing House.

Quan, Xiaojing. (2020): A major change in a market of 5 trillion yuan under COVID-19. *Panorama Finance*. 2020.2.10, http://www.p5w.net/weyt/202002/t20200211_2376915.htm.

Rejda, G. and McNamara, M. (2019). *Principles of Risk Management and Insurance*. London: Pearson Education.

Report on the Implementation of China's Monetary Policy in the Fourth Quarter of 2019. http://www.pbc.gov.cn/zhengcehuobisi/125207/125227/125957/3830536/3974306/index.html. February 19, 2020.

Research Group of the Fanhai International School of Finance, Fudan University. (2020). *Should the A-Share Market Postpone Opening Amid the Unexpected Pandemic Outbreak?*

Research Group of the Fanhai International School of Finance, Fudan University. (2020). *Impact of the COVID-19 Pandemic on the Chinese Economy and Coping Strategies*.

Research Group of the Fanhai International School of Finance, Fudan University. (2020). *Shanghai's Economic and Financial Development During the Pandemic and Countermeasure Analysis*.

Research Group of the Fanhai International School of Finance, Fudan University. (2020). *Sustainable Development of the Financial Industry and the Advancement of the Shanghai International Finance Center Under the Pandemic*.

Robert, H. (2001). *Crisis Management for Managers and Executives*. Translated by Wang Cheng, Song Binghui, Jin Ying. Beijing: CITIC Publishing House.

Roderick, D. (2011). *The Paradox of Globalization*. Translated by Liao Lihua. Beijing: Renmin University of China Press.

Rosenthal, S. S. and Strange, W. C. (2004). Evidence on the nature and sources of agglomeration economies. In Henderson, J. V. and Thisse, J.-F. (Eds.), *Handbook of Urban and Regional Economics*. Amsterdam: Elsevier.

Rosenthal, U., Charles, M. T. and Hart, P. T. (2014). *Coping with Crises: The Management of Disasters, Riots and Terrorism*. Translated by Zhao Fengping. Zhengzhou: Henan People Publishing House.

Rui, Mingjie and Wang, Xiaosha. (2019). *2018 Annual Analysis Report on China's Industrial Development-The Perspective of Multilateral Trade*. Shanghai: Shanghai University of Finance and Economics Press.

Rui, Mingjie. (2016). *Industrial Economics* (3rd ed.). Shanghai: Shanghai University of Finance and Economics Press.

Rui, Mingjie. (2020). The pandemic is a "black swan", four things companies need to do. *The Paper*. February 7, 2020, https://www.thepaper.cn/newsDetail_forward_5839642.

Rui, Mingjie. (2020). What is the impact of the pandemic on the economy? Stabilizing the service industry is the key to the stability of the growth. *The Paper*. February 5, 2020, https://www.thepaper.cn/newsDetail_forward_5799968.

Shang, Xiaopeng, Xu, Xiaoping, Ye, Chiyu *et al.* (2018). Discussion on public health role evaluation index system in secondary and above general hospitals. *Chinese Hospitals*, **22**(4): 29–33.

Shao, Min and Wu, Peng. (2019). Export trade, human capital and employment stability of migrant workers — With a discussion on the upgrading of China's industry and trade. *Management World*, **35**(3): 99–113.

Shen, Shuguang and Zhang, Bo. (2016). Hierarchical diagnosis and treatment, primary diagnosis and construction of primary medical and health institutions. *Academia Bimestrie*, (02): 48–57.

Shi, Manjiang and Cao, Qi. (2019). Research progress and improvement measures of resilience theory based on perspective of urban and rural planning. *Journal of Human Settlements in West China*, **34**(6): 32–41.
Spain takes a package plan to block 4 cities and towns to deal with the pandemic. *People's Daily Overseas Network*. March 13, 2020.
Stiglitz, J. E. and Weiss, A. (1981). Credit rationing in markets with imperfect information. *American Economic Review*, **71**(3): 393–410.
Sun, Chenmin and Tian, Kan. (2019). Research on the status quo of mobile medical development under the background of "Internet +". *Health Economics Research*, **36**(8): 42–44.
Sun, Qiru. (2020). Pandemic prevention with science and technology by Beijing E-commerce giant to guarantee people livelihood and promote a return to work. *Xinhua Net*. 2020.3.4, http://www.xinhuanet.com/tech/2020-03/04/c_1125659880.htm.
Tang, Wei. (2020). To fight the epidemic together, we should have more empathy. *Guangming Daily*. March 5, 2020.
The European Central Bank takes a package of measures to deal with the impact of the pandemic. *Xinhuanet*. March 13, 2020.
The European Union plans to set up a 25 billion euro fund to respond to the pandemic. *News Network*. March 12, 2020.
The General Administration of Customs: Introduced 10 measures to support the development of China-Europe railway express to ensure its normal and orderly operation. *Xinhua News Agency*. March 2, 2020.
The General Administration of Customs' interpretation of China's foreign trade in the first two months. *China Government Network*. March 7, 2020.
The impact of the epidemic on the global electronics industry. *Zhang Gongzhi*. February 20, 2020.
The Mission of the People's Republic of China to the European Union. (2020). Ambassador Zhang Ming listens to the key concerns of the entrepreneur representatives of the European Union Chamber of Commerce in China under the current pandemic. *Ministry of Foreign Affairs Website*. March 4, 2020.
The number of the world's top 500 companies that have settled in Wuhan has reached 294 and this year it is expected to exceed 300. *Changjiang Daily*. September 25, 2019.
The pandemic overseas: The "Godfather of Automobiles" in Germany viewed the pandemic only a "throttle" for China's auto industry and the Chinese economy. *China News*. February 24, 2020.
The share of US manufacturing in GDP has fallen to a 72-year low. *The Financial Associated Press*. October 30, 2019.
The total number of tourist receptions nationwide during the 2019 Spring Festival holiday is 415 million. *Xinhuanet*. February 10, 2019, http://www.xinhuanet.com/2019-02/10/c_1124096886.htm.

The tourism industry is one of the industries affected by the pandemic with the largest revenue reduction. *China News Network*. March 1, 2020, https://travel.163.com/20/0301/08/F6KBQQ0F00068AIR.html.

Tian Xin *et al*. (2020). Logistics and transportation industry under COVID-19 pandemic: Impact, countermeasures and long-term development. *Economic Daily*. 19th February, 2020.

TMT Post. (2020). Which industries will start to explode with insight to big data under COVID-19. *Sina Tech*. 2020.3.9, https://tech.sina.com.cn/roll/2020-03-09/doc-iimxxstf7500560.shtml.

Tobin, J. (1969). A general equilibrium approach to monetary theory. *Journal of Money, Credit and Banking*, **1969**(1): 15–29.

Tongxin. (2020). Pandemic prevention and control are a major test of China's governance system and capacity. *Qiu Shi*, (5).

Wang, Fanghua and Xi, Youmin. (2020). *Breaking the Encirclement: Advice from 56 Management Scientists*. Beijing: Renmin University Press of China.

Wang, Guojin. (2020). COVID-19 affects global asset pricing, Chinese commercial banks should take the initiative. *China Banking and Insurance News*. February 13, 2020.

Wang, Kun, Mao, Ayan and Meng, Yueli. (2019). Development history, current situation, problems and strategies of public health system construction in China. *Chinese Journal of Public Health*, (07).

Wang, Wei. (2016). Preliminary study on the construction of government's ability to prevent and control the public crisis of animal pandemic. *Contemporary Animal Husbandry*, (21): 80–82.

Wang, Weiling and Wang, Jing. (2019). Research on the development trend and promotion policy of China's digital economy. *Economic Review Journal*, (1): 69–75.

Wang, Xiaochen. (2019). Application of 5G technology in network education. *Electronic Technology & Software Engineering*, (24):12–13.

Wang, Yong., Liu, Mengchu and Wang, Linlu. (2020). *Research Report on the Impact of the Covid-19 Pandemic on Large and Medium-sized Enterprises in China*. China Center for Enterprise Development and M&A and Restructuring Research, School of Economics and Management, Tsinghua University. February 2020.

Watanabe, C., Naveed, K., Tou, Y. *et al*. (2018). Measuring GDP in the digital economy: Increasing dependence on uncaptured GDP. *Technological Forecasting and Social Change*, (137): 226–240.

Watanabe, C., Tou, Y. and Neittaanmäki, P. (2018). A new paradox of the digital economy — Structural sources of the limitation of GDP statistics. *Technology in Society*, (55): 923.

Wei, Zelong. (2019). Business model design and firm performance: The moderating effect of strategic flexibility. *Management Review*, **31**(11): 171–182.

Wei, S. J. and Qian, J. (2020). *Impact of COVID-19 on the Global Economy and Financial System and China's Response Strategies.*

Wei, S. J. (2020). Will the coronavirus cause a major growth slowdown in China?. *Project Syndicate.* 2020-01-27.

Wuhan University, China New Private Economy Research Center, Wuhan City Federation of Industry and Commerce. (2020). *Analysis Report on Business Operations of Hubei Enterprises in the Wake of the Pandemic.* Wuhan University, School of Economics and Management. February 29, 2020.

Wu, Jianfeng. (2019). *Growth, Agglomeration and Imbalance in the 40 Years of Chinese Urbanization, a Great Transformation: The Past, Present and Prospects of China's Reform.* In Zhang, Jun and Wang, Yongqin (Eds.). Shanghai: Truth and Wisdom Press.

Xi, T., Yao, Y. and Zhang, M. (2018). Capability and opportunism: Evidence from city officials in China. *Journal of Comparative Economics*, **46**(4): 1046–1061.

Xue, Lan. (2012). Global public governance: An important issue in China's public management research in the next 30 years. *Journal of Public Administration*, **5**(1): 16–19.

Yang, Canming. (2017). Tax cut and fees reduction: Achievement, problems and the reform path. *Finance and Trade Economy*, **38**(9): 5–17.

Yang, Dong. (2018). Regulatory technology: The regulatory challenges and dimension construction of financial technology. *Social Sciences in China Press*, (5): 69–91, 205–206.

Yang, Gonghuan. (2020). The state pay attention to how to operate the infectious disease network direct reporting system and its application in this pandemic after SARS. *The Economic Observer*. January 30, 2020.

Yang, Jin. (2020). Alert! The United States is cultivating specialized anti-China NGOs in our neighboring countries. *Global Times*. March 7, 2020.

Yang, Peiqing. (2020). The value, development focus and policy supply of the digital economy. *Journal of Xi'an Jiaotong University (Social Sciences)*, (3).

Yang, Yifan. (2020). Trump attacks China again! Being recognized as a "diplomatic mission", what treatment will these five Chinese media receive? *Xinmin Evening News*. February 20, 2020.

Yi, Xingjian and Zhou, Li. (2018). Does digital financial inclusion significantly influence household consumption? Evidence from household survey data in China. *Journal of Financial Research*, No. 11: 47–67.

Yin, Limei. (2020). The role of digital economy in the prevention and control of the pandemic becomes increasingly prominent. *Posts & Telecom Press*. February 26, 2020.

Yin, Z., Gong, X., Guo, P. *et al.* (2019). What drives entrepreneurship in digital economy? Evidence from China. *Economic Modelling*, (82): 66–73.

Yip, W., Fu, H., Chen, A. *et al.* (2019). 10 years of health-care reform in China: Progress and gaps in universal health coverage. *The Lancet*, (394): 1192–1204.

Yu, Baorong., Yang, Jin., Gong, Xifei *et al.* (2019). Development process, business modes and macrocally influencing factors for Internet-based health service in China. *Journal of Shandong University (Health Sciences)*, **57**(8): 39–52.

Zhai, Zhenwu, Chen, Jiaju and Li, Long. (2017). Future trends of China's population and aging: 2015 ~ 2100. *Population Research*, **41**(4): 60–71.

Zhang, Hui and Shi, Lin. (2019). Digital economy: New driving force in the new era. *Journal of Beijing Jiaotong University (Social Sciences Edition)*, **18**(2): 10–22.

Zhang, Jun. (2020). Geometric impact of the pandemic on China's economy. *China Business Times*. February 25, 2020.

Zhang, Weiwen. (2020) Pandemic meets Spring Festival travel rush: It's extremely urgent to realize the settlement of 100 million people with high quality. *The Paper*. February 13, 2020, http://www.thepaper.cn/newsDetail_forward_5934978.

Zhang, Wenchun. (2019). Analysis of global corporate income tax rate characteristics in 2018. *China State Finance*, (12): 72–73.

Zhang, Xiangxian, Chen, Feng and Meng, Xiangteng. (2003). The impact of SARS on the insurance industry and countermeasures. *Insurance Research*, (6): 36–38.

Zhang, Xiaobo, Dai, Ruochen and Hu, Junpeng. (2020). The survival of small and medium-sized enterprises under the novel coronavirus pandemic — Survey on enterprise innovation and entrepreneurship in China (ESIEC). *Public Knowledge*. February 24, 2020.

Zhang, Xiaobo, Dai, Ruochen and Hu, Junpeng. (2020). The survival of small, medium and micro enterprises under the Covid-19 pandemic: A survey on enterprise innovation and entrepreneurship in China (ESIEC). *The Intellectual*. February 24, 2020.

Zhang, Xun, Wan, Guanghua, Zhang, Jiajia *et al.* (2019). Digital economy, financial inclusion, and inclusive growth. *Economic Research Journal*, **54**(8): 71–86.

Zhang, Yuan, Li, Quan and Huang, Lulu. (2019). The theoretical basis of Xi Jin-ping's thought of targeted poverty alleviation[J]. *Studies on Mao Zedong and Deng Xiaoping Theories*, 2019(2): 20–27.

Zhang, Yuan, Li, Quan and Shen Ke. (2019). Empirical bases of household-targeting anti-poverty thoughts[J]. *Issues in Agricultural Economy*, 2019(4): 60–70.

Zhao, Jianwu and Zheng, Guozhong. (2020). Analysis on the changes of macroeconomic situation at home and abroad during the Spring Festival of 2020. Bozhanzhiku. *WeChat Official Account*. February 2, 2020.

Zheng, Hong. (2020). The fight against pandemic in Chinese history. *Seeking Truth*, (4): 48.

Zheng, Wei and Sun, Qixiang. (2003). "Cool" thinking on SARS insurance. *China Insurance*, (7): 8–11.

Zheng, Xiyu. (2019). Research on China's digital economy development strategy in the Internet age — Revelation based on the development experience of the United States and the European Union. *Southwest Finance*, (12): 53–60.

Zhiyan and Luo Changyuan. (2020). The impact of the COVID-19 on China's economy and relevant thoughts. *Study & Exploration*, (3): 99–105.

Zhong, Jun and Liu, Zhichang. (2017). *Blue Book of Public Service: Evaluation of Chinese Cities' Basic Public Service Capability 2017*. Beijing, China: Social Sciences Academic Press.

Zhou, Guangyou, Luo, Sumei and Lian, Shuting. (2020). Research on Fintech innovation, interest rate decision of network lending and financing of small and micro enterprises — Also discusses the management of "Macmillan Gap". (3): 76–86.

Zhou, Yuan and Chen, Xiaoxiao. (2020). The epidemic has brought about 6 major impacts. China's chip and consumer electronics industries are actively helping themselves. *Caijing*, (4).

Zhu, Hengpeng and Lin, Qiqing. (2015). Reform of personnel salary system to establish an effective hierarchical diagnosis and treatment system. *China State Finance*, (08): 69–71.

Zhu, Kunfu, Wang, Shouyang *et al.* (2020). The COVID-19 shock on global production chains and risk of accelerated China's industrial chains outflow. *Journal of the Chinese Academy of Sciences*, **35**(3): 283–288.

Zhu, Min. (2020). The total impact of the January-February pandemic on consumption is expected to be 1.3 trillion yuan. Much effort should be taken to promote an economic rebound. Netease Research Bureau. February 24, 2020, https://t.qianzhan.com/daka/detail/200224-955463e9.html.

Zhu, Zongqian, Li, Jun and Di, Haipeng. (2019). Analysis and countermeasures of sustainability of unmanned economy in China. *Future and Development*, (12): 43–49.

https://doi.org/10.1142/9789811252921_bmatter

Postscript

The Chinese Version of *Waging Economic War on the Pandemic: Policy Measures Against the Economic Impact of the COVID-19 Pandemic* (《经济战"疫"：新冠肺炎疫情对经济的影响与对策) was published by Fudan University press in 2020. The English Version involved four steps: initial translation, first revision by Chinese revisers, second revision by native English-speaking proofreaders and final revision by the sponsor.

Thanks are sincerely expressed to the translators Wu Biyu, Shen Cheng, Kong Jiaqi, and Li Jiawei from East China University of Science and Technology, and to Hu Lingling. Gratitude is extended to the proofreaders Qu Ying, Zhao Jingjie and Wu Yifei from East China University of Science and Technology. Thanks are also due to the revisers: Karl Stefan and Emre Yorgancioglu, both from the USA, and Debra Ann Anthony from Australia.

Thanks should be given to Wang Jianguo from University of International Business and Economics and Sun Hui from Shanghai Technical Institute of Electronics & Information, and editors from Fudan University Press for proofreading the book in its entirety.

Wu Biyu
May 20, 2022

Lightning Source UK Ltd.
Milton Keynes UK
UKHW022358210722
406220UK00003B/191

9 789811 252914